KEELE
UNIVERSITY

LIBRARY

Please return by the last date or time shown

D1426787

5 127 676 3

Literature in the Marketplace is a wide-ranging and innovative collection of essays which addresses important issues in cultural studies and the history of the book. Drawing on speech-act, reader-response, and gender theory in addition to various historical, narratological, materialist, and bibliographical perspectives, the contributors consider different aspects of the production, circulation, and consumption of printed texts throughout the nineteenth century. Topics studied include market trends, modes of publication, the use of pseudonyms by women writers, readerships and reading ideologies, periodical literature, copyright law, and colonial distribution. The volume examines a wide range of printed materials, from valentines, advertisements, illustrations and fashionable annuals, to the more traditional literary genres of poetry, fiction, and periodical essays. The authors examined include Wordsworth, Dickens, the Brontës, George Eliot, Meredith, and Walter Pater.

CAMBRIDGE STUDIES IN NINETEENTH-CENTURY
LITERATURE AND CULTURE 5

LITERATURE IN THE MARKETPLACE

CAMBRIDGE STUDIES IN NINETEENTH-CENTURY LITERATURE AND CULTURE

General editors
Gillian Beer, *Girton College, Cambridge*
Catherine Gallagher, *University of California, Berkeley*

Editorial board
Isobel Armstrong, *Birkbeck College, London*
Terry Eagleton, *St Catherine's College, Oxford*
Leonore Davidoff, *University of Essex*
D. A. Miller, *Harvard University*
J. Hillis Miller, *University of California, Irvine*
Mary Poovey, *The Johns Hopkins University*
Elaine Showalter, *Princeton University*

Nineteenth-century British literature and culture have been a rich field for interdisciplinary studies. Since the turn of the twentieth century, scholars and critics have tracked the intersections between Victorian literature and the visual arts, politics, social organizations, economic life, technical innovations, scientific thought – in short, culture in its broadest sense. In recent years, theoretical challenges and historiographical shifts have unsettled the assumptions of previous scholarly syntheses and called into question the terms of older debates. Whereas the tendency in much past literary critical interpretation was to use the metaphor of culture as "background", feminist, Foucauldian, and other analyses have employed more dynamic models that raise questions of power and of circulation. Such developments have re-animated the field.

This series aims to accommodate and promote the most interesting work being undertaken on the frontiers of the field of nineteenth-century literary studies: work which intersects fruitfully with other fields of study such as history, or literary theory, or the history of science. Comparative as well as interdisciplinary approaches are welcomed.

Titles published

LITERATURE IN THE MARKETPLACE

Nineteenth-century British publishing and reading practices

EDITED BY

JOHN O. JORDAN

*Associate Professor of English Literature,
University of California, Santa Cruz*

AND

ROBERT L. PATTEN

Professor of English, Rice University

CAMBRIDGE
UNIVERSITY PRESS

Published by the Press Syndicate of the University of Cambridge
The Pitt Building, Trumpington Street, Cambridge CB2 1RP
40 West 20th Street, New York, NY 10011-4211, USA
10 Stamford Road, Oakleigh, Melbourne 3166, Australia

First published 1995
Reprinted 1996, 1998

Printed in the United Kingdom at the
University Press, Cambridge

A catalogue record for this book is available from the British Library

Library of Congress cataloguing in publication data

Literature in the marketplace: nineteenth-century British publishing
and reading practices edited by John O. Jordan and Robert L. Patten.
p.   cm.
Includes index.
ISBN 0 521 45247 3 (hardback)
1. Publishers and publishing – Great Britain – History –
19th century. 2. Books and reading – Great Britain – History –
19th century. 3. Literature publishing – Great Britain – History –
19th century. 4. English literature – 19th century – History and
criticism. I. Jordan. John O. II. Patten, Robert L.
Z325.L58   1995   94–27284 CIP

ISBN 0 521 45247 3 hardback

Contents

Illustrations

FIGURES AND PLATES

TABLES

Contributors

LAUREL BRAKE is Lecturer in Literature at Birkbeck College, the University of London. She writes on Victorian periodicals and publishing, literary criticism/theory, Walter Pater, biography, and bibliography. *Subjugated Knowledges: Gender, Journalism and Literature* (Macmillan, 1994) appeared recently.

GERARD CURTIS is a Ph.D. candidate at the University of Essex and lectures in Art History at Sir Wilfred Grenfell College (Memorial University), Newfoundland. He is currently researching the relationship of word to image in Victorian England.

SIMON ELIOT is Senior Lecturer and Staff Tutor in Literature at the Open University and Director of its Book History Research Group. He is vice-president of the Society for the History of Authorship, Reading, and Publishing (SHARP) and coeditor (with Michael Turner) of the journal *Publishing History* and a monograph series *History of the Book – On Demand Series* (HOBODS). He is coeditor (with David McKitterick) of the volume covering 1830–1914 in Cambridge University Press's *History of the Book in Britain*. His publications include a *Comprehensive Microform Edition of the Publishers' Circular and English Catalogue 1837–1900*, *Some Patterns and Trends in British Publishing 1800–1919*, a forthcoming book on Sir Walter Besant and the professionalization of authorship, and various articles in learned journals.

STEPHEN GILL is Reader in English Literature at Oxford University and Fellow and Tutor in English at Lincoln College. He has edited Wordsworth for the Oxford Authors series and published *William Wordsworth: A Life*.

LINDA K. HUGHES, Professor of English at Texas Christian University, is author of *The Manyfaced Glass: Tennyson's Dramatic Monologues* (1987) and coauthor (with Michael Lund) of *The Victorian Serial* (1991). She is guest-editor of the Spring 1995 issue of *Victorian Poetry* on Victorian women poets and is completing a book on fin-de-siècle poet "Graham R. Tomson" (Rosamund Marriott Watson).

MAURA IVES is Assistant Professor of English at Texas A & M University. Her research is in bibliography, textual criticism, and the history of the book in the nineteenth and twentieth centuries. She has presented several papers on these topics and is currently completing a critical edition of George Meredith's publications in the *New Quarterly Magazine*.

JOHN O. JORDAN is Associate Professor of Literature and Director of the Dickens Project at the University of California, Santa Cruz. He has written essays on Swinburne, Dickens, Charlotte Brontë, Thackeray, and Picasso. He is coeditor (with Carol Christ) of *Victorian Literature and the Victorian Visual Imagination*.

CATHERINE JUDD is Assistant Professor at the University of Miami, where she teaches women's studies and nineteenth-century British fiction. She is completing a study of the cult of Florence Nightingale and the image of the nurse in the Victorian novel.

MICHAEL LUND is Professor of English at Longwood College in Virginia. A specialist in serial literature, his publications include *Reading Thackeray* (1988), and *America's Continuing Story: An Introduction to Serial Fiction, 1850–1900* (1993). With Linda K. Hughes he is coauthor of *The Victorian Serial* (1991).

PETER J. MANNING is Professor of English at the University of Southern California. He is the author of *Byron and His Fictions*, *Reading Romantics*, and several essays on the English Romantic poets.

KELLY MAYS received her Ph.D. from Stanford University in 1994. Her current research focuses on the cross-class analysis of reading practices in nineteenth-century Britain.

J. HILLIS MILLER is Distinguished Professor of English and Comparative Literature at the University of California at Irvine. His most recent books include *Ariadne's Thread*, *Versions of Pygmalion*, *Illustration*, and *Topographies*.

ELIZABETH MORRISON is Research Officer to the Academy Editions of Australian Literature project sponsored by The Australian Academy of the Humanities. Formerly a research fellow in Australian Studies at Monash University, her research interests are in the field of nineteenth-century publishing history, focusing on the cultural role of the newspaper press.

ROBERT L. PATTEN is Professor of English, editor of *Studies in English Literature*, and Master of the Graduate House at Rice University. In addition to *Charles Dickens and His Publishers* (1978; reprint, The Dickens Project, 1991), he has written articles on serial publication, publishers' accounts, professional authorship, Thackeray's rivalry with Dickens, the circulation of graphic satires, illustrations, and a two-volume life of George Cruikshank.

JONATHAN ROSE is Associate Professor of History at Drew University and President of the Society for the History of Authorship, Reading and Publishing. His most recent book is *The Revised Orwell* (1991). Currently he is writing an intellectual history of the British working class.

Acknowledgments

For their support at different stages in the production of this volume, we are grateful to Linda Hooper and Lark Letchworth of the University of California Dickens Project, and to Barbara Lee and Betsy Wootten of Kresge College at the University of California at Santa Cruz. Special thanks go to Murray Baumgarten and to our copy editor, Bud Bynack, whose intelligence, good humor, and tact not only improved the manuscript but made him the most congenial of collaborators.

CHAPTER I

Introduction: publishing history as hypertext

John O. Jordan and Robert L. Patten

> One difficulty, said Stephen, in esthetic discussion is to know whether words are being used according to the literary tradition or according to the tradition of the marketplace.
>
> James Joyce, *A Portrait of the Artist as a Young Man*

A few years ago David Simpson called for a "Return to 'History'" in the practice of literary criticism. Specifically, he professed a need for scholars to address "the small and intransigent details that are least susceptible to hermeneutic instability": such matters as costs and formats, size of imprints, and relations among authors, editors, and printers.[1] However comforting it might be to find a bedrock of "fact" on which to construct not only a new literary criticism but also a new history of the manufacture, transmission, and reception of books, that foundation will not be located easily. At every point along the continuum from manuscript through printing and binding to circulation, the "small and intransigent details" differ according to the nature of the story or argument being constructed, exist in varying relationships with other parts of the production process, and in many cases simply are absent as records or as foci of academic concern.

Moreover, our theories of book production range widely and are at many points contradictory. Authorial agency, publishers' incentives, technological developments, cultural and legal formations, and marketplace incentives all figure in various ways depending on the era, country, and text: and hence no comprehensive paradigm of a print culture has yet been promulgated. Indeed, publishing history, "literary sociology," the history of the book, or the "sociology of texts," as the field is variously denominated, "lacks binding theoretical coherence," to quote John Sutherland, and is characterized by what Robert Darnton calls "interdisciplinarity run riot."[2]

In wrestling with the multiplicity of approaches to writing about nineteenth-century British book publication, the papers printed here testify to a subject still in its formative phase, rich with local insights and potential for further investigation but inconsistent even in conceiving of the subject itself, much less in agreeing on appropriate methods for treating its cooperating parts.

Histories of the British book trade have of course been written many times. In the past half century, the field has been conceived in at least five ways – ways that are to some extent chronological in development but that overlap and interpenetrate at every phase. Some of the earliest studies of publishing and readership in this period aimed at providing a conspectus of the conditions under which a print culture flourishes. Thus, Marjorie Plant (1939) provided a still-valuable economic history of publishing; Q. D. Leavis (1932), Amy Cruse (1935), and Margaret Dalziel (1957) addressed the issue of readership and its impact on texts; and Richard Altick (1957) gathered together data on modes of publication, costs, circulation, and other aspects of text reception and the sociology of the common reader that documented "the growth of the mass reading public in England." A specialized but influential study of a particular decade was provided by Kathleen Tillotson (1954) in her introductory chapter to *Novels of the Eighteen-Forties*.[3]

Roughly simultaneously, scholars in the field of bibliography embarked on an intensive effort to codify the principles by which books were to be described and copytexts determined. The meticulous examination of the material aspects of manuscripts and books and the inferences that can be drawn from those physical objects about the integrity and authenticity of the text owe much to the labors of Ronald B. McKerrow (1927, 1929), W. W. Greg (1942, 1950, 1956), and Fredson Bowers (1949, 1964) – who established their editorial principles largely on the basis of Renaissance dramatic texts – and to their successors and revisers, Philip Gaskell (1972, 1978), G. Thomas Tanselle (1987, 1989, 1990), Jerome McGann (1983, 1985), and Peter Shillingsburg (1986, 1992).[4]

Authorized histories of publishing houses have contributed to our knowledge of editorial practices, finance, and marketing. Arthur Waugh (1930) composed an avuncular history of Chapman and Hall; Emily Symonds (1932) wrote admiringly about the John Murrays; Frank Mumby (1934) traced the history of Routledge;

Charles Morgan (1944) honored Macmillans; Simon Nowell-Smith (1958) provided a sound and learned history of Cassell; Royal Gettmann (1960) made provisional sense of the Bentley archives; Asa Briggs (1974) edited a collection of essays commemorating the house of Longman; and Peter Sutcliffe (1978) published during its quincentenary an "informal history" of Oxford University Press. Though some of these studies were little more than lists of the distinguished authors whose works passed through the press, most printed original correspondence and records and thus provided scholars with some of the "intransigent details" of publishing. Nevertheless, as Gaye Tuchman complains, official house biographies "make one think that publishing concerned simply art," and that to consider publishing as a culture industry, with all that such a perspective implies about its commercial motives, would depreciate the publishers' products into mere commodities.[5] Under the editorship of Michael L. Turner, the journal *Publishing History* has initiated exploration of "the social, economic, organizational and literary history of book, newspaper and magazine publishing." Ancillary studies have clarified the nature of women's romances (Dorothy Blakey, 1939), the rise of fiction bureaus (Frank Singleton, 1950; Michael L. Turner, 1975), the legal dimensions of copyright and trade (Simon Nowell-Smith, 1968; Mark Rose, 1993), the disputes over copyright and pricing (James J. Barnes, 1964, 1974), the influence of literary agents (James Hepburn, 1968), the power of circulating libraries (Guinevere L. Griest, 1970), and the modern context of manufacturing and selling (Robin Myers, 1973; F. A. Mumby and Ian Norrie, 1982). One subset of publishing history has been the study of nineteenth-century periodicals, which were much more closely involved in the publication and dissemination of literature and reading practices than their usual separation from such studies has indicated. Miriam Thrall (1934) has written a standard history of *Fraser's*; Spencer Eddy (1970) surveyed the *Cornhill*; Walter Houghton (1966–89) and his associates have provided us with essential information about thirty-five nineteenth-century periodicals; and scholarly quarterlies constitute a forum for articles on newspapers and magazines.[6]

Authors' dealings with printers, publishers, and booksellers were an inevitable part of their careers. In the transition between full-blown New Criticism and the current proliferation of cultural studies, authors' commercial relationships received their own

specialized attention. John Gross (1969) composed an influential (and gender-specific) account of the rise and fall of the
nineteenth-century man of letters, including prose writers, journalists, and reviewers. In some cases (William Wordsworth,
Robert and Elizabeth Barrett Browning, Wilkie Collins, George
Eliot, Anthony Trollope, Mary Ward, Margaret Oliphant, George
Meredith, George Gissing, Thomas Hardy, Walter Besant, Arnold
Bennett), information about a writer's contractual, financial,
textual, and social interaction with publishers emerged in notes
to editions of correspondence or in passages within a more
comprehensive biography; in others, whole books were devoted
to one writer (Patten on Dickens, 1978; Hagen on Tennyson,
1979). What such studies have in common is the conviction that
the author's career was importantly shaped by the marketplace in
all its dimensions and that "genius" alone cannot account for the
production or content of an oeuvre. What they lack is a complete
sense of reciprocity: technology, ideology, politics, commerce, and
various cultural forces may have been greatly responsible for the
shape of texts and the nature of receptions. Nigel Cross's recent
investigation of Grub Street documents the exacting circumstances
under which writers often labored, the marginality of authorship,
and its susceptibility to outside forces.[7]

Contemporary scholars have added to these predecessors a sense
of the complexity of the issues, coupled with inventiveness and
originality in reconceiving and reworking older disciplines. The
relationship of illustrations to texts, neglected (except for Blake)
before John Harvey's pioneering work (1971), has now been
extensively studied in books and articles on particular authors
and artists and in monographs on book design, print and image
technology, and the cross-fertilization of visual, theatrical, and print
modes on one another (Ruari McLean, 1963; Percy Muir, 1971;
Martin Meisel, 1983; Richard Altick, 1985).[8] Cultural studies have
in manifold ways demonstrated that topics and ways of seeing were
shared alike by journalist, novelist, poet, and reader (Richard Stein,
1987; Rowland McMaster, 1990; Richard Altick, 1991).[9] Literary critics have discerned wide-ranging and extremely complex
intertextual commentary circulating among nineteenth-century
writers and scientists as well as novelists (Gillian Beer, 1983;
Jerome Meckier, 1987).[10] The variety of ways in which market
forces operate have been outlined by John Sutherland (1976),

revised from a more Marxist perspective by N. N. Feltes (1986), reconceived in terms of textual implications by Peter Shillingsburg (1992) and of social history and historical sociology by Peter Keating (1989), and analyzed for its differential effects on male and female authors by Gaye Tuchman (1989).[11] Gender and class issues have been explored by Louis James (1963), Vineta Colby (1970), Martha Vicinus (1974), Elaine Showalter (1977), Janice Radway (1984), Mary Poovey (1984), and Regenia Gagnier (1986).[12] Even textual bibliography has undergone extensive revision as the very notion of a stable or an urtext has been challenged. The object on which bibliographers practice their craft – that is, the book – and the goal of "textual criticism," which is "to determine the text of what we are to read," have been questioned.[13] Was not the manuscript more than a mere stage preparatory to print; was it not also separately conceived and executed object with its own integrity and authenticity, and was not the first printed issue, whether in serial part or magazine, at least as important a document as the "definitive" book edition? Does textual bibliography have as its only domain the production of a text, or might its modes of analysis yield other kinds of cultural information?[14]

Simon Eliot opens this book with a survey of the broad patterns of production in the nineteenth century. He documents the general increase in number of titles, the growing secularization of subjects, and the steady reduction in unit cost. He identifies a "plateau" in the 1860s when book production stabilized after an expansion caused by revolutions in manufacture and distribution (1830–55) and preceding a second surge in output (1875–1914) fueled by mechanical improvements, enlarged markets, increased professional opportunities, and mass-circulation publications. He thus suggests that whatever paradigms we might propose for treating the century as a whole need to be adjusted to at least three periods when different combinations of physical, legal, and human conditions differently affected the marketplace.

Even within one author's career, changing markets provided opportunities and constraints for a writer's new and previously issued works. Wordsworth offers an instructive example. In "Wordsworth in the *Keepsake*, 1829," Peter Manning studies the clash between the "dignity of literature" and entrepreneurial opportunism, and explores the surprising complicity between Romantic idealism and the commercial world to which those ideals were

apparently opposed. Manning analyzes the broader cultural significance of that curious, early nineteenth-century form of commodity
publication, the fashionable literary annual. Despite objections to
the florid style, effeminized audience, and crass commercialism of
these flossy compilations, Wordsworth and his contemporaries were
induced by handsome contributors' fees to offer previously issued
and new works to these seasonal "coffee-table" books. Such outlets
redefined the nature of literary production and by their success
encouraged rival publishers and editors to bid high for "names"
with which to promote luxury consumer objects for predominantly
female buyers. Wordsworth's language of men speaking to men
became, through the medium of the *Keepsake*, regendered.

Stephen Gill asks a related question in the expanded context of Wordsworth's production throughout the century: which
Wordsworth was being promoted and read? Drawing extensively
upon previously unpublished manuscripts, Gill focuses on efforts
by the poet's sons and publishers to maintain copyright control
in the decades after 1850, when gradually the corpus entered the
public domain. Rival firms and anthologists eager to print material
out of copyright and to skew it to a particular topographical, religious, or other theme appropriated the Wordsworth canon. Others
seeking access to unpublished material posed an insoluble problem
for the poet's heirs: did they authorize competing publications,
thereby exercising some control over the material and reaping
some financial reward, or did they refuse such requests, thereby
contributing to the proliferation of incomplete, corrupt, and partial
representations of their father's work? The textual complexities that
resulted from the progressive lapsing of copyright, and the versions
of Wordsworth's writings that were issued, insured that readers of
different editions got radically different impressions of the poet's
philosophy and achievement. Paradoxically, in Wordsworth's case
the improved provisions of the 1842 copyright act contributed
to deterioration of textual authenticity and to multiplication of
unrepresentative and misleading editions.

Pickwick Papers has often been identified as the work that ushered
in the Victorian era. Dickens's partly accidental exploitation of
the advantages of the serialized commodity set an example that
other novelists and publishers were quick to emulate. Playfully but
profoundly meditating on "Sam Weller's valentine," Hillis Miller
explores the relationship between the performative or efficacious

in writing and commodifications of language and graphic art in seasonal products like valentines. Using the modifications of speech act theory developed by such critics as Jacques Derrida and Paul de Man, Miller asks how "promises" and avowals of love might be said to function in commercial products, in verbal marriage proposals, in legal evidence, and in serial parts. He provides a capsule history of valentines from the Middle Ages through to the early Victorian period, including their involvement in authenticating gestures (signatures, patents, copyright, delivery) and the difficulties in controlling a response. He concludes by demonstrating the self-conscious, ironic, and performative nature of Dickensian language which critiques the early Victorian ideology and conventions of love and marriage, the subject of bourgeois fiction.

What Dickens promised to the readers of his serial parts has usually been described as suspense and topicality: consumers were guaranteed a continuing, exciting story that at many points made overt or covert allusion to their own times. Robert L. Patten reverses that thesis, arguing in "Serialized retrospection in *The Pickwick Papers*" that *Pickwick* gains forward momentum through retrospection. Each part looks backward to an earlier era, the prior month, and previous fiction; the novel's trajectory goes from death to death and toward the stasis of familiar romantic endings, and is propelled by the reiterated disruptions of those traditional closures. Readers consumed these serial parts, he suggests, because they became familiar with and simultaneously remembered a rhythm of appetency and satiation that dominates the text and their own cycle of desires.

Linda K. Hughes and Michael Lund, in "Textual/sexual pleasure and serial publication," press this thesis even further. Adopting a gendered approach based on recent work in feminist narratology, they posit two rhythms in serial reading: a goal-oriented "male" narrative structure characterized by rising tension, climax, and release, and a "female" pattern marked by anticipation, delay, periodicity, and the issuing forth of new life and relationships at the culmination of the process. Periodical fiction thus appealed to both sexes, diversifying an audience that in other publications was often directed either to male or to female readers.

The chapters on Wordsworth and Dickens conceptualize in different ways relationships between production and consumption. Kelly Mays, in her discussion of "The disease of reading and

Victorian periodicals," attempts to situate some of the key issues that underlie debates about reading practices in the second half of the nineteenth century. Mays is concerned with the politics of reading, with the ways in which readers are constructed and used in social and cultural projects. From the French Revolution forward, she maintains (following Thomas Laqueur), readers were enjoined to pursue "rational recreation" so that they might be fit to seize the opportunities of an industrial society. Readers were also involved in the project of constructing an English polity, a national integrity. Reading practices came to be divided between the exercise of the mind and the stimulation of the body and sensations, with the consequence, much deplored by Victorian reviewers, that lower-class, popular, and female literature stimulated a hunger for more, for indiscriminate sensation, and for perpetual snacking, that is, desultory and interruptible reading. She therefore addresses questions of praxis also raised by Miller, Patten, and by Hughes and Lund. In attending to the disciplinary pedagogics inculcated by the journals, Mays foregrounds another important medium through which "readers" were constructed and instructed.

Not all readers were amenable to instruction, at least of the kinds the quarterlies advocated. Two contributors examine other kinds of resistance and susceptibility to print and images. Jonathan Rose, in "How historians study reader response" maintains that readers' responses to publications should be evaluated not only in quantifiable terms such as circulation and sales but also by the ways they – especially the lower working classes – incorporated fictional prototypes in their own self-representations and self-authorized scenarios of progress. He turns to empirical data for his evidence – library records, reader surveys, and working-class autobiographies – to show how Dickens (preeminently) provided working people with the examples, inspiration, and conventions to narratize their own lives. Gerard Curtis, looking at "Dickens in the visual market," studies the exchange between the visual and the literary within the formats Victorian publishers employed. He instances migrations of visual materials into texts and vice versa, and suggests how intricately the commodities hawked in serial advertisements interpenetrate the processes of seeing, being seen, and being represented articulated by Dickens's works.[15] Curtis concludes with a close examination of the *Nickleby* portrait of the author, which acts as guarantor of the text in ways complementary to signatures on valentines and books and to the canonization of middle-class reading habits that Mays uncovers. Rose and Curtis demonstrate noncanonical kinds of reading that substantiate the hierarchization and heterogeneity of Victorian practice.

But what about female readers and writers? Were their opportunities for self-construction and self-expression, their ways of reading and their subjects of interest different from, and more constricted and subverted than, those for males? (Both Manning and Mays address these issues.) Are not the many instances of female writers adopting male pseudonyms clear evidence that the marketplace was more open to men, especially, as Gaye Tuchman points out, in the later decades of the century, when "high art" became a male preserve? Virginia Woolf maintained in *A Room of One's Own* that "Currer Bell, George Eliot, George Sand . . . sought ineffectively to veil themselves by using the name of a man."[16] In "Male pseudonyms and female authority in Victorian England," Catherine Judd proposes revisions of that assumption. Rather than considering female writers' adoption of male pseudonyms as a strategy of concealment or disguise, Judd argues that "Currer Bell" and "George Eliot" enabled a complex process of gender differentiation wherein Charlotte Brontë and George Eliot could preserve a space for the female self empowered by the Romantic ideal of creative privacy while projecting a male persona that could be both culturally valorized and ironized. Coupled with the "feminization" of serial reading proposed by Hughes and Lund and the "feminization" of audience that Manning shows was achieved by the *Keepsake*s and other annuals, Judd's study of the advantages to female writers of cross-dressed pseudonymity requires rethinking the simplistic paradigms of gendered texts and audiences that earlier generations of Victorianists promulgated.

The effects of format have been a topic considered from various vantage points throughout these chapters. Does format affect readership? Are the ideologies informing the mode of production necessarily replicated by the texts so presented? Does a different format change the nature of the text, its character, style, and substance, or does it determine a different audience? We think of generic conventions as governing the look, feel, structures, and rhetorical strategies of texts: novels appear in volumes, for instance. What changes when a three-decker is serialized in a newspaper or magazine for a foreign market, or when a long poem, such as *In*

Memoriam, is excerpted and rearranged for anthologies such as Palgrave's *Golden Treasury*?

The three remaining chapters approach these questions in different ways. Maura Ives interrogates the assumptions that have governed standard bibliographical practice. Using George Meredith as an example, she instances significant but unobserved variants between the earliest published versions of his texts, often in evanescent serializations, and their "official" publication in volumes carefully described according to professional conventions. Fully notating the context in which these writings first appeared, she argues, might bring out much more than variant readings: it could lead to revaluations of the "voice," audience, and authority Meredith achieved, and alter our assessments of his significance and impact.

A complementary case is made by Laurel Brake for the periodical versions of Walter Pater's *Renaissance*, a set of essays profoundly shaped by the economic and ideological agendas of the two very different magazines in which the chapters were first published. The editorial policies, aesthetic program, and political biases of the *Westminster Review* during the 1860s partly determined the nature of the more radical and subversive essays that Pater published anonymously there, two of them in the guise of (unpaid) reviews of other books. The *Fortnightly Review* commissioned and paid for signed articles; the four that Pater contributed to it were more discreet and conventional analyses of Renaissance artists. When the pieces were recirculated in book form, the disparities between the two kinds of journalism were blurred if never entirely erased. What was fundamentally unsettling and unattributable in the "wicked" *Westminster* became more scholarly and acceptable when combined with the *Fortnightly* articles in a signed, respectable volume.

Elizabeth Morrison presents yet another perspective on the complex relationship between book and serial publication. In the final chapter, she opens up the horizon to the antipodes, studying the Australian newspaper press as publisher of both indigenous (colonial) and imported (British and American) fiction. In a survey complementary to Simon Eliot's, she demonstrates the unslaked appetite of the colonial market for stories from home and abroad. Australian newspapers usually serialized texts from American and British publishers before the first home volume edition; the resulting publicity contributed to the "hype" of best-sellers and the growth of fiction bureaus, notably Tillotson's. If in Australia the availability of works by overseas writers damped the demand for local products, it also helped to forge a more diversified and more intertextually and interculturally literate colonial audience than we have hitherto predicated.

Fissures, then, confront us at every point, fissures that relate to the different directions in which new historicists, Marxists, deconstructionists, poststructuralists, and feminists have been traveling. One such gap opened in August 1991 at the University of California, Santa Cruz when the Society for the History of Authorship, Reading and Publishing (SHARP) was formally founded. Objections were raised to defining the project's orientation by the word "history," for it seemed to some that "history" so announced was tantamount to particular theories of history, the *annales* school, Robert Escarpit's "sociology of authorship," or studies in the connections between printing and the dissemination of ideas to which Roger Chartier and Robert Darnton have made distinguished contributions.[17] "History," desirable for its place in a catchy acronym, might be thought to preclude theories of authorship prominent in gender studies and in deconstruction, theories of reader reception, and whatever might emerge in the near future from thinking about publishing as a more than commercial, or even as a commercial, enterprise.[18] Some wanted to concentrate on gathering statistics, data, those "small and intransigent details least susceptible to hermeneutic instability," at least until basic histories of the book, such as that for Britain announced by Cambridge University Press, are completed. Others believed that any such effort, already acting out of unvoiced theoretical and conceptual presuppositions, precluded thinking about the nature of the subject, about marketplaces, authorship, publishing, literacy, and reading. To entertain such contraries and to foster exploration of their points of divergence and intersection, as this book does, also seemed to SHARP the best course to pursue at present.[19]

What will be needed in the future is not more of the linear paradigms of production that commence with the writer's idea and proceed straightforwardly through composition to publication and reception, but conceptions of the activity of producing and consuming books that decenter the principal elements and make them interactive and interdependent; publishing history, in other words, as hypertext.[20] Readers ignore, support, modify, and imprison authors; publishers serve as producers, gatekeepers, flood dams, censors, merchants, and onlie begetters.[21] Applying to the production of books M. H. Abrams's influential taxonomy of the four principal aesthetic orientations, we can see that viewed as a manufacturing process literary production both participates in and goes beyond those aesthetic principles. Nineteenth-century publishing practices do not privilege imitation, although realism and reproduction of the natural or unique through mechanical means were important constituents of the arts of the period. Audiences are not publishers' only target, although rising literacy, segmenting readership, the constructions of reading practices, and the vast economic, political, and educational projects put reading matter of all kinds, consumed in manifold ways, near the center of Victorian life. Cultivation of expressive rhetorics was often condemned, although feeling, sentiment, genius, inspiration, interiority, and energy, both natural and supernatural, were frequently the expressed motives for producing and the canonical qualities for evaluating imaginative works. Nor did Victorian writers, publishers, printers, reviewers, and readers necessarily conceive texts to be internally coherent and self-constituted objects.

Four other principles, these chapters imply, are likely to figure in any new paradigm of publishing history. First, the principle of mediation. Increasingly through the century, the direct connections between author and publisher, publisher and printing house, and press and audience were moderated by the interposition of other agencies: literary agents, fiction bureaus, and the Society of Authors between author and publisher; technologies between publisher and printing house; distribution and evaluation systems between press and audience. How these mediating agencies altered the nature, pace, and results of publishing will be part of any comprehensive history.

Second, publishing history, however much it starts with physical products, will in the end have to incorporate intangibles: ideological and social formations that privileged print culture, events that lent themselves to verbal formulation and dissemination (news, legislation, gossip, controversy), and particular conjunctions of time, place, and person that stimulated print production, conjunctions such as Kathleen Tillotson, Carl Dawson, and Richard Stein evoke.[22]

Third, future historians will have to cope with the ambiguities of a print culture – the ways in which it supersedes without erasing oral and visual cultures and spawns its own imitations, rejections, and assimilations. Technological progress and commoditization must be complexly understood to accommodate, for example, the Kelmscott Press's printed manuscripts, the Brontës' juvenilia designed to be and not to be handmade/machine-manufactured books, and the "vanity press" first publications of Tennyson and Browning.

Fourth, no history of publishing can hope to be comprehensive if it does not recognize the impossibility of composing a single metanarrative. Print culture generated countless unsuccessful measures to control itself, from taxes on light and paper to copyright laws, censorship acts, regulation of reading, and monetary and honorific rewards for the "right thing." But texts, like copyright laws and valentines, cannot prescribe their effects with any precision; no history is likely to comprehend the whole range of paradoxical and messy consequences of unleashing the power of the press.

Future theorists of textual production may have to start by recognizing the physicality of the product and work from there outward to all the factors impinging on its creation, tracking the multiplicity of forces, tangible and intangible, personal and systemic, that enter into the production process. Even that, however, would be insufficient, for they must also recognize how texts themselves shape their being and bring into being other texts, how their existence or absence affects their time and posterity, and how present values direct the ways in which we invent a past. Moreover, such theorists must address the costs as well as advantages of conceptualizing their subject in physical and commercial terms: what is lost, what is gained, by eschewing older notions of the "history of ideas," the power of genius to transform an age, and the agency of genres, quality, and aesthetic pleasure?

It has been customary recently, in collections of essays about the "new cultural history," to celebrate the diversity of approaches, from close examination of particular cases to manifold, partial, even deconstructing, theories that characterize the state of scholarly discourse.[23] Analogous diversity may be found in this book, and in the range of projects that might be encompassed by "the history of the book." The resistance of "small and intransigent details" to transhistorical theorizing, on the one hand, and the difficulty of accommodating any portmanteau paradigm to the multiplicity of instances any publishing study can document, on the other, leave us with an ongoing and probably perpetually deferred goal: to know more about how books were produced and consumed, and to understand how that knowledge directs as well as contributes to our interpretations of culture and history. This book aspires to engage in a dialogue already underway, and to contribute to that vigorous and innovative revaluation of cultural history that is one trademark of the age.

NOTES

1 David Simpson, "Literary Criticism and the Return to 'History'," *Critical Inquiry* 14, 4 (Summer 1988), 721–47, 742.
2 John Sutherland, "Publishing History: A Hole at the Centre of Literary Sociology," *Critical Inquiry* 14, 3 (Spring 1988), 574–89, 576; Robert Darnton, "What is the History of Books?" *Daedalus* 111, 3 (Summer 1982), 65–83, 67. For a brief, informative survey of the topic, consult D. F. McKenzie, "History of the Book," in *The Book Encompassed: Studies in Twentieth-Century Bibliography*, ed. Peter Davison (Cambridge: Cambridge University Press, 1992), 290–301.
3 Marjorie Plant, *The English Book Trade: An Economic History of the Making and Sale of Books* (New York: R. R. Bowker, 1939). Q. D. Leavis, *Fiction and the Reading Public* (London: Chatto & Windus, 1932). Amy Cruse, *The Victorians and Their Books* (London: George Allen & Unwin, 1935). Margaret Dalziel, *Popular Fiction 100 Years Ago: An Unexplored Tract of Literary History* (London: Cohen & West, 1957). Richard D. Altick, *The English Common Reader: A Social History of the Mass Reading Public, 1800–1900* (Chicago: University of Chicago Press, 1957). Kathleen Tillotson, *Novels of the Eighteen-Forties* (Oxford: Clarendon, 1954). For a survey of developments since Altick's "old book history," see Jonathan Rose, "Rereading the English Common Reader: A Preface to a History of Audiences," *Journal of the History of Ideas* 53, 1 (January to March 1992), 47–70. The resources of the Library of Congress, which houses British as well as US materials, are described in Alice D. Schreyer, *The History of Books* (Washington, D.C.: The Center for the Book, Library of Congress, 1987).
4 Ronald B. McKerrow, *An Introduction to Bibliography for Literary Students* (Oxford: Clarendon, 1927); and *Prolegomena for the Oxford Shakespeare: A Study in Editorial Method* (Oxford: Clarendon, 1939). W. W. Greg, *The Editorial Problem in Shakespeare: A Survey of the Foundations of the Text* (Oxford: Clarendon, 1942); "The Rationale of Copy-Text" (1950), in *Collected Papers*, ed. J. C. Maxwell (Oxford: Clarendon, 1966); and *Some Aspects and Problems of London Publishing Between 1550 and*

1650 (Oxford: Clarendon, 1956). Fredson Bowers, *Principles of Bibliographical Description* (Princeton: Princeton University Press, 1949); and *Bibliography and Textual Criticism*, the 1959 Lyell Lectures (Oxford: Clarendon, 1964). Philip Gaskell, *A New Introduction to Bibliography* (New York: Oxford University Press, 1972); and *From Writer to Reader: Studies in Editorial Method* (Oxford: Clarendon, 1978). G. Thomas Tanselle, *Textual Criticism Since Greg: A Chronicle, 1950–1955* (Charlottesville: University Press of Virginia for the Bibliographical Society of the University of Virginia, 1987); *A Rationale of Textual Criticism* (Philadelphia: University of Pennsylvania Press, 1989); and *Textual Criticism and Scholarly Editing* (Charlottesville: University Press of Virginia for the Bibliographical Society of the University of Virginia, 1990). Jerome McGann, *A Critique of Modern Textual Criticism* (Chicago: University of Chicago Press, 1983); and *The Beauty of Inflections: Literary Investigations in Historical Method and Theory* (Oxford: Clarendon, 1985). Peter Shillingsburg, *Scholarly Editing in the Computer Age* (Athens: University of Georgia Press, 1986); and *Pegasus in Harness: Victorian Publishing and W. M. Thackeray* (Charlottesville: University Press of Virginia, 1992).

5 Arthur Waugh, *A Hundred Years of Publishing: Being the Story of Chapman & Hall, Ltd.* (London: Chapman & Hall, 1930). George Paston (pseudonym of Emily Symonds), *At John Murray's: Records of a Literary Circle, 1843–1892* (London: John Murray, 1932). F. A. Mumby, *The House of Routledge* (London: Routledge, 1934). Charles Morgan, *The House of Macmillan (1843–1943)* (New York: Macmillan, 1944). Simon Nowell-Smith, *The House of Cassell, 1848–1958* (London: Cassell, 1958). Royal A. Gettmann, *A Victorian Publisher: A Study of the Bentley Papers* (Cambridge: Cambridge University Press, 1960). Asa Briggs (ed.), *Essays in the History of Publishing in Celebration of the 250th Anniversary of the House of Longman, 1724–1974* (London: Longman, 1974). Peter Sutcliffe, *The Oxford University Press: An Informal History* (Oxford: Clarendon, 1978). Gaye Tuchman with Nina E. Fortin, *Edging Women Out: Victorian Novelists, Publishers, and Social Change* (New Haven: Yale University Press, 1989), 24.

6 Dorothy Blakey, *The Minerva Press, 1790–1820* (London: London Bibliographic Society, 1939). Frank Singleton, *Tillotsons, 1850–1950* (Bolton: Tillotson & Son, 1950). Michael Turner, "Tillotson's Fiction Bureau: Agreements with Authors," in *Studies in the Book Trade in Honour of Graham Pollard*, ed. R. W. Hunt, I. G. Philip, and R. J. Roberts (Oxford: Oxford Bibliographical Society, 1975). Simon Nowell-Smith, *International Copyright Law and the Publisher in the Reign of Queen Victoria* (Oxford: Clarendon, 1968). Mark Rose, *Authors and Owners: The Invention of Copyright* (Cambridge, Mass.: Harvard University Press, 1993). James J. Barnes, *Free Trade in Books: A Study of the London Book Trade since 1800* (Oxford: Clarendon, 1964);

and *Authors, Publishers, and Politicians: The Quest for an Anglo-American Copyright Agreement, 1815–1854* (Columbus: Ohio State University Press, 1974). James Hepburn, *The Author's Empty Purse and the Rise of the Literary Agent* (London: Oxford University Press, 1968). Guinevere L. Griest, *Mudie's Circulating Library and the Victorian Novel* (Bloomington: Indiana University Press, 1970). Robin Myers, *The British Book Trade, from Caxton to the Present Day* (London: Andre Deutsch, 1973). F. A. Mumby and Ian Norrie, *Mumby's Publishing and Bookselling in the Twentieth Century* (London: Bell & Hyman, 1982). Miriam Thrall, *Rebellious Fraser's: Nol Yorke's Magazine in the Days of Maginn, Thackeray, and Carlyle* (New York: Columbia University Press, 1934). Spencer L. Eddy, Jr., *The Founding of the Cornhill Magazine* (Muncie, Ind.: Ball State University Press, 1970). Walter E. Houghton *et al.* (eds.), *The Wellesley Index to Victorian Periodicals, 1824–1900* (5 vols.; Toronto: University of Toronto Press, 1966–89). Two important scholarly quarterlies are *Victorian Periodicals Review* (formerly *Victorian Periodicals Newsletter*) and the *Journal of Newspaper and Periodical History*. See also *Investigating Victorian Journalism*, ed. Laurel Brake, Aled Jones, and Lionel Madden (Basingstoke: Macmillan, 1990).

7 John Gross, *The Rise and Fall of the Man of Letters: Aspects of English Literary Life since 1800* (London: Weidenfeld & Nicolson, 1969). Robert L. Patten, *Charles Dickens and His Publishers* (Oxford: Clarendon, 1978). June Steffensen Hagen, *Tennyson and His Publishers* (University Park: Pennsylvania State University Press, 1979). Nigel Cross, *The Common Writer: Life in Nineteenth-Century Grub Street* (Cambridge: Cambridge University Press, 1985). For a general study of professional authors, consult Victor Bonham-Carter, *Authors by Profession* (2 vols.; London: Society of Authors; Los Altos, Calif.: W. Kaufman, 1978).

8 John Harvey, *Victorian Novelists and Their Illustrators* (New York: New York University Press, 1971). Ruari McLean, *Victorian Book Design and Colour Printing* (London: Faber & Faber, 1963). Percy Muir, *Victorian Illustrated Books* (London: B. T. Batsford, 1971). Martin Meisel, *Realizations: Narrative, Pictorial, and Theatrical Arts in Nineteenth-Century England* (Princeton: Princeton University Press, 1983). Richard Altick, *Paintings from Books: Art and Literature in Britain, 1760–1900* (Columbus: Ohio State University Press, 1985).

9 Richard L. Stein, *Victoria's Year: English Literature and Culture, 1837–1838* (New York: Oxford University Press, 1987). Rowland McMaster, *Thackeray's Cultural Frame of Reference: Allusion in "The Newcomes"* (London: Macmillan; Montreal: McGill-Queen's University Press, 1990). Richard D. Altick, *The Presence of the Present: Topics of the Day in the Victorian Novel* (Columbus: Ohio State University Press, 1991).

10 Gillian Beer, *Darwin's Plots: Evolutionary Narrative in Darwin, George Eliot, and Nineteenth-Century Fiction* (London: Routledge & Kegan

Paul, 1983). Jerome Meckier, *Hidden Rivalries in Victorian Fiction: Dickens, Realism, and Revaluation* (Lexington: University Press of Kentucky, 1987).

11 John Sutherland, *Victorian Novelists and Publishers* (London: Athlone Press; Chicago: University of Chicago Press, 1976). Norman N. Feltes, *Modes of Production of Victorian Novels* (Chicago: University of Chicago Press, 1986). Shillingsburg, *Pegasus in Harness.* Peter Keating, *The Haunted Study: A Social History of the English Novel, 1875–1914* (London: Secker & Warburg, 1989). Tuchman, *Edging Women Out.*

12 Louis James, *Fiction for the Working Man, 1830–1850* (London: Oxford University Press, 1963). Vineta Colby, *The Singular Anomaly: Women Novelists of the Nineteenth Century* (New York: New York University Press; London: University of London Press, 1970). Martha Vicinus, *The Industrial Muse: A Study of Nineteenth-Century British Working-Class Literature* (New York: Barnes & Noble, 1974). Elaine Showalter, *A Literature of Their Own* (Princeton: Princeton University Press, 1977). Janice Radway, *Reading the Romance: Women, Patriarchy, and Popular Literature* (Chapel Hill: University of North Carolina Press, 1984). Mary Poovey, *The Proper Lady and the Woman Writer: Ideology as Style in the Works of Mary Wollstonecraft, Mary Shelley, and Jane Austen* (Chicago: University of Chicago Press, 1984). Regenia Gagnier, *Idylls of the Marketplace: Oscar Wilde and the Victorian Public* (Stanford, Calif.: Stanford University Press, 1986).

13 For a critique of traditional textual criticism as codified in the quoted instance by James Thorpe in *Principles of Textual Criticism* (San Marino, Calif.: Huntington Library, 1972), vii, see Jerome J. McGann, "The Monks and the Giants," in *Textual Criticism and Literary Interpretation*, ed. Jerome J. McGann (Chicago: University of Chicago Press, 1985), 180–99, as well as *The Beauty of Inflections*, and Allan C. Dooley, *Author and Printer in Victorian England* (Charlottesville: University Press of Virginia, 1992).

14 Donald F. McKenzie, *Bibliography and the Sociology of Texts* (London: British Library, 1986), and "Typography and Meaning: The Case of William Congreve," in *Wolfenbütteler Schriften zur Geschichte des Buchwesens* 4 (Hamburg: Dr. Ernst Hauswedell & Co., 1981), 81–125, quoted in Sutherland, "Publishing History," 586.

15 An analogous argument about George Eliot's fiction was made by Leland Mond, "Commodity/Culture: Selling *Middlemarch*," at the conference Textual Technologies: Text, Image, and History sponsored by the Interdisciplinary Group for Historical Literary Study and the Department of English at Texas A & M University, 26 to 29 March 1992. Some of the concluding remarks in this preface derive in part from the papers presented at that conference.

16 Virginia Woolf, *A Room of One's Own* (1928; Harmondsworth: Penguin, 1945), 52.

17 See also Morris Eaves, "What Is the 'History of Publishing'?" *Publishing History* 2 (1977), 57–77.

18 For a critique of "Marxist literary and cultural historiography in Britain" and an attempt to focus attention on capitalist consumption, see Terry Lovell, *Consuming Fiction* (London: Verso, 1987).

19 For an important study of the development of mass literacy in Britain, see David Vincent, *Literacy and Popular Culture: England, 1750–1914*, Cambridge Studies in Oral and Literate Culture 19 (Cambridge: Cambridge University Press, 1989). Jonathan Rose, "An Introduction to the Society for the History of Authorship, Reading and Publishing," *Publishing History* 31 (1992), 73–74.

20 Roger Chartier offers two pairs of contrasting and interactive terms as "models for making sense of texts, books, and their readers": discipline and invention on the one hand and distinction and divulgation on the other. "Texts, Printing, Readings," in *The New Cultural History*, ed. Lynn Hunt (Berkeley: University of California Press, 1989), 154–75. A less binary, more processive and circular model of the "life cycle" of books, a "communications circuit" that runs from author to reader and back to author, is given by Darnton in "What Is the History of Books?" reprinted in his *The Kiss of Laumourette: Reflections in Cultural History* (New York: W. W. Norton, 1990), 107–35; see chart on 112. For a poststructuralist, posthermeneutic examination from the outside of the inscriptive systems of Romanticism and modernism, with observations on the mediality, the technology, of those systems, consult Friedrich A. Kittler, *Discourse Networks 1800/1900*, trans. Michael Metteer with Chris Cullens, foreword by David E. Wellbery (1985; Stanford, Calif.: Stanford University Press, 1990).

21 Lewis A. Coser, Charles Kadushin, and Walter W. Powell, *Books: The Culture and Commerce of Publishing* (Chicago: University of Chicago Press, 1985).

22 Tillotson, *Novels of the Eighteen-Forties*; Carl Dawson, *Victorian Noon: English Literature in 1850* (Baltimore: Johns Hopkins University Press, 1979); Stein, *Victoria's Year*.

23 For example, Lynn Hunt's introduction to *The New Cultural History*, 1–22.

CHAPTER 2

Some trends in British book production, 1800–1919

Simon Eliot

In Dickens's *Hard Times* the hero, Stephen Blackpool, is keeping a half-waking, half-sleeping vigil by the bedside of his drunken, sleeping wife when he suffers a form of hallucination. He dreams of a shining light that "broke from one line in the table of commandments at the altar, and illuminated the building with the words. They were sounded through the church, too, as if there were voices in the fiery letters . . . the very chimneys of the mills assumed that shape, and round them was the printed word."[1]

The fiery letters within the church are translated into the secular and industrial world and become the printed word that surrounds it. But print products didn't just surround the nineteenth century, they penetrated and pervaded it, became so ubiquitous and so commonplace as to be taken for granted. Something that one period takes for granted is always in danger of becoming invisible to historians from another age. It is not the individual book or the occasional best-seller that is in danger of disappearing, but the broad mass of published and printed material that provided the context in which Victorian texts circulated to Victorian readers.

In order to make the printed context of the nineteenth century more historically visible we need two new sorts of study: first, a broad statistical survey of print production in the nineteenth century in order to have some idea of its patterns and trends, the way in which it grew and varied as the century progressed; and second, a series of case studies of the production records of specific printers and publishers to see how the trends identified by the broad survey expressed themselves in the actual output of printed matter.

Before either sort of study is possible we need to be able to identify and assess the value of the statistical sources available for the period. This chapter will look briefly at some of the major sources and, in its second half, give a few examples of how these

19

sources illustrate the changes in various forms of nineteenth-century and early twentieth-century print production. The study on which it is based[2] is divided into six main sections: the annual pattern of publishing, the monthly pattern of publishing, subject publishing, the price structure of books, periodical publishing, and the printed context. This chapter will describe a few of the sources available and some of the problems raised by their use. It will then summarize something of what can be known of the quantitative side of nineteenth-century publishing, despite the many limitations of the evidence.

SOME MANUSCRIPT SOURCES

Stationers' Company entry books

The entry books are held at Stationers' Hall, London. They consist of a series of volumes in folio in which details of a given publication are recorded across two leaves (that is, verso and recto). The number of works recorded seems to have varied in direct relation to copyright legislation; for instance, between the acts of 1801 (41 Geo. 3, c. 107) and 1814 (54 Geo. 3, c. 156), numbers of titles recorded were small due to the obligation to deposit eleven copies of each title, a strong deterrent to cost-conscious publishers pondering the limited value of a mention in the stationers' records. After 1814 the numbers increased, partly because most deposit copies now had to be provided only on demand. The latter act reaffirmed the role of the warehousekeeper at Stationers' Hall, particularly his obligation to send a list of titles received to the other copyright deposit libraries. (This is the origin of the "Deposited at Stationers' Hall" lists to be found in the Bodleian and Cambridge University Library: being, on the whole, secondary lists these tend to be less comprehensive and less reliable than the original.)

The entry books list entries in accession order: individual items are not numbered, nor is there a regular number of titles per page. In order to collect publication data it is therefore necessary to count each individual item. However, because each of the entries is dated, it is possible to group them into separate months, thus providing information on monthly as well as annual patterns of publication.

Stationers' Company registry books

After the 1842 Copyright Act (5 & 6 Vic., c. 45) entry books were called "registry books". They are currently deposited at the Public Record Office at Kew, Richmond. Each registry book has between 300 and 303 leaves and, as with the entry books, each entry is spread across two leaves. Between 1842 and 1883 (COPY 3/1–29) all deposits are recorded in one sequence of books; between 1883 and 1912 materials are catalogued separately under the headings "Literary" (COPY 3/30–62) and "Commercial" (COPY 3/63–80). Except for deposit from North American and Australian publishers, the record peters out after the Copyright Act of 1911 (1 & 2 Geo. V., c. 46).

The distinction between literary and commercial was not always a clear one: literary could include printed blank diaries, examination papers, and, for instance, an official program for Ascot races in 1906. Nevertheless, this is the only major source that, by classifying at least some of its material as commercial, at least hints at the huge, almost wholly submerged volume of job and general printing that underlies the much more visible figures for book publishing.

One of the many problems confronting the researcher using these sources is the fact that the monthly figures are occasionally distorted by a single publisher depositing a large number of titles at one time. For instance, John Gibson Lockhart registered 46 works by Scott on 13 February 1850; Bulwer Lytton registered a number of his earlier works in December 1853; Bentley registered 75 titles on 23 May 1855; William P. Nimmo, Edinburgh, 151 titles on 3 June 1870 and a further 122 titles on 14 April 1875; in April 1880 Chapman & Hall registered 89 titles, and so on.

From 1900 onwards the registry books record a growing number of US copyright holders registering their titles. By 1903 some US depositors were so frequent that special rubber stamps were made to save the clerks having repeatedly to write the company's name (for example, the International Textbook Co. of Scranton, Pennsylvania or the music publisher John Church Co. of Cincinnati, Ohio). Most publications listed in the registry books after June 1912 were from the United States or Australia. Between COPY 3/1 and COPY 3/29 the entries are in the same irregular pattern as those in the entry books before 1842 (for example, some pages have only three entries, other pages as many as eleven), and thus if numerical work is to be done, the researcher has to count the entries individually. From COPY 3/30 (literary) and COPY 3/63 (commercial), both starting on 3 July 1883, the registry books' double-page spread is divided into ten equal sections by a series of red rules. It thus becomes possible for the researcher to calculate monthly and yearly totals by counting pages rather than individual titles. From COPY 3/36 (literary, starts 5 May 1890) and COPY 3/66 (commercial, starts 30 October 1889), each title is numbered so it is possible merely to record the starting number and the concluding number of each month. By this time each registry book contained a standard 3,000 register places (for example, COPY 3/37 runs from 3,001 to 6,000).

British Museum copyright receipt books

Copyright receipt books are a series of large folio volumes consisting originally of tear-off receipt slips with attached flimsies. The top copy of the receipt would normally have been given to the depositor, leaving the flimsy as a record. Each printed item was given a separate deposit number so that, for instance, a three-decker novel would be given three numbers in sequence, one for each volume. The surviving sequence of volumes begins in 1851. Between 1851 and 1857 numbering was restarted on or around 26 December. After 1858 numbering was begun anew on the first day of January each year. Volumes for 1853 and 1857 are missing. The researcher can record the last number attached to the last receipt of the year, which thus indicates the number of printed items deposited in that year. Although the 1842 Copyright Act had affirmed a publisher's obligation to deposit copies with the British Museum Library, it was only when Antonio Panizzi, as principal librarian, insisted on enforcing this legal obligation from the early 1850s onward that the receipt books came into their own.[3]

Given that each printed item received a number, figures from the receipt books are inevitably much larger than those from any other source. In other ways, also, they are far more useful than figures derived even from the most recently available and most sophisticated sources (such as the *British Library General Catalogue of Printed Books* on CD-ROM – *BLGC*). It is quite clear from even the briefest perusal of the receipt books that, inevitably, the library received more via copyright deposit than it actually cared to, or could, catalogue. As with any copyright deposit library, filtering had to take place. In the British Museum Library's case that must have occurred somewhere between the copyright receipt books and the general catalogue. The receipt books, therefore, more accurately sample the production of British presses than do the volumes of the general catalogue for the simple reason that at the point of filling in the receipts there was no well-intentioned, discriminating librarian to determine which printed item deserved immortality and which did not.

SOME PRIMARY PRINTED SOURCES

Annual Reports of the British Museum – Copyright (Parts)

The *Annual Reports of the British Museum* were printed, beginning in 1811–12, in Parliamentary Papers. They list only gross annual totals and do not differentiate deposits by month. The early years lack detail, so for the purposes of this study the sequence was recorded beginning in 1850. Beginning in 1852 the reporting year spans two calendar years (for example, the 1852 report is labeled 1852/53).

What was actually included under the title *Copyright (Parts)* is a matter of some uncertainty. The report for 1866 defines "parts" as "separate numbers of periodical publications, and of serial works in progress." However, things are less simple than this straightforward definition would seem to suggest. Between 1850 and 1866, music, maps, atlases and newspapers were included in the count; after that they appear not to have been. Given these uncertainties of categorization, figures derived from this source, and those included in the *British Museum Annual Reports – Copyright (Volumes)*, are best used for corroborating trends (particularly those derived from the copyright receipt books) rather than suggesting them.

Annual Reports of the British Museum – Copyright (Volumes)

As with *Copyright (Parts)*, the early years lack detail, so for the purposes of the current study the sequence was recorded beginning in 1850. In a similar way to *Parts*, beginning in 1852 the reporting year spans two calendar years (the 1852 report is labeled 1852/53, for example). *Volumes* are usually defined by these reports as "complete books and pamphlets." However, this was a very uncertain category and varied considerably over the years recorded. For instance, between 1850 and 1863 the figures included music, maps, and newspapers; between 1864 and 1866 they included music, atlases, and newspapers; between 1867 and 1886 they included music and newspapers; between 1887 and 1891 they included music; between 1892 and 1907 they included music and atlases; and between 1908 and 1919 they did not include music, maps, atlases, or newspapers.

"Bent's Monthly Literary Advertiser"

There are very few complete runs of this journal extant; the best is probably that in the Bodleian, which includes issues before 1805. The numerical data itself is listed under two headings in each issue: the "New Publications" list and the "Catalogue of New Books . . . Published in Great Britain."

During its life the journal was published under a number of different titles: *A List of New Publications* (July 1802 to January 1803), *A Monthly List of New Publications* (February to October 1803), *The Monthly List of New Publications* (November 1803 to January 1805), *The Monthly Literary Advertiser* (10 May 1805 to 10 December 1828), and finally *Bent's Monthly Literary Advertiser* (10 February 1829 to June 1860). The last issue was dated 16 June 1860, after which the title was incorporated in the *Bookseller*.

In the early years most of the listings were, like those in the first years of the *Publishers' Circular* discussed below, advertisements rather than editorial lists. However, beginning in 1805 the journal printed an "Index to the New Publications" at the end of each year. In 1826 *Bent's* introduced, in addition to the index, a "Supplement for 1826" that listed about twice as many titles (900 as opposed to 425). In 1827 the supplement was renamed the "Alphabetical List of New Works" and a third list, "Books Entered at Stationers' Hall," was added. This three-list format was repeated in 1828 and 1829. In 1830 the alphabetical list returned to its original name of "Supplement," and the Stationers' Hall listing was dropped; in 1831 the index was dropped. Between 1831 and 1839 the supplement alone was printed. In 1840 this was renamed "Bent's

New Books Published in London in 1840." Beginning in March 1823 the journal began a monthly list. On the whole, the annual lists recorded new titles only, whereas the monthly lists also detailed some of the new editions and impressions.

There are certain gaps in the printed record: in particular, November 1825, November and December 1826, October 1829, December 1830, December 1831, and December 1836.

"Bibliotheca Londinensis"

The full title of this source is *Bibliotheca Londinensis: A Classified Index to the Literature of Great Britain During Thirty Years Arranged from and Serving as a Key to the London Catalogue of Books 1814–46*, compiled by Thomas Hodgson (London, 1848). It lists some 36,000 titles recorded by the *London Catalogue* between 1814 and 1846. Although the sample is a relatively modest one, and the titles are not listed by year (so no year-by-year dynamic study can be undertaken), the *Bibliotheca Londinensis* can provide us with a snapshot of how things were in terms of subject publishing in the first half of the nineteenth century.

As with all nineteenth-century sources of information about subject publishing, the *Bibliotheca Londinensis* has its own picturesque and arbitrary classification system, a system that makes comparisons with other sources particularly difficult. The main subject headings used in the *Bibliotheca Londinensis* were: "Antiquities," "Biography," "Divinity," "Domestic Economy, Sport," "Drama and Poetry," "Education and Learning," "Fiction, etc.," "Fine Arts, Illustrated Works," "Geography, History, Voyages, Travels, etc.," "Juvenile Works, Moral Tales, etc.," "Languages, Ancient and Modern," "Law and Jurisprudence," "Logic, Moral and Mental Philosophy," "Mathematics," "Medical Sciences," "Natural and Experimental Philosophy," "Natural Sciences," "Naval and Military," "Political Economy, Parliamentary, Statistics, etc.," "School and College Books, Educational," "Trade and Commerce," and "Miscellaneous Books."

"The Publishers' Circular"

As no one library had a complete run of the journal and its supplements, copies from the British Library, the Bodleian, and the St. Bride Printing Library were all used for the study under discussion. The data were derived from the recurrent feature "Books Published in the Last Fortnight." For material up to 1900, it is now easier to use the comprehensive *Microform Edition of the Publishers' Circular 1837–1900*, edited by Simon Eliot and John Sutherland (Cambridge: Chadwyck-Healey, 1988).

The figures for 1840 to 1842 are less reliable than those that follow because the *Publishers' Circular* did not begin clearly numbering its entries until 1843. Figures for the years 1840 to 1842 were derived from an article in *The Publishers' Circular*, 5 December 1853. This article gave figures that were higher than those gained by adding the fortnightly lists, that is (with list figures in brackets): 1840: 2,912 [2,528]; 1841: 2,752 [2,366]; 1842: 2,877 [2,536]. In all cases it is probably wiser to prefer the higher annual figure.

The year 1842 was a particularly uncertain period as the *Publishers' Circular* did not organize the lists in a clear, unambiguous order. This year's figures must be treated with particular caution. The annual and monthly figures for the period from 1843 to 1869 can be derived from the fortnightly listings of new publications, which were numbered sequentially. There were occasional failures or jumps in the numbering sequence: for example, on 15 December 1848, when numbering jumps from 4,099 to 5,000; or on 1 May 1851, when sequence jumps from 2,199 to 3,000. From 1870 it is easier to take the figures from the "Analytical Table of Books Published," which was usually printed in the last issue of the year or in one of the first two issues of the subsequent year.

Data for subject analysis can be derived from the *Circular*'s "Analytical Tables." Originally these tables used fourteen categories, but these were reduced to thirteen in 1896 with the conflation of "Novels and Other Works of Fiction" and "Juvenile Works and Tales." The categories were: "Theology, Sermons, Biblical, etc.," "Educational and Classical," "Juvenile Works and Tales," "Novels and other Works of Fiction," "Law, Jurisprudence, etc.," "Political and Social Economy, Trade and Commerce," "Arts, Science, and Finely Illustrated Works," "Travel and Geographical Research," "History and Biography," "Poetry and Drama," "Year Books and Bound Volumes of Serials," "Medicine and Surgery," "Belles Lettres, Essays, Monographs, etc.," and "Miscellaneous, including Pamphlets, not Sermons."

In 1911 the classification system was brought into line with the scheme adopted by the International Congress of Librarians in Brussels in 1910, which offered twenty-three classes: "Philosophy," "Religion," "Sociology," "Law," "Education," "Philology," "Science," "Technology," "Medicine, Public Health, etc.," "Agriculture, Gardening," "Domestic Arts," "Business," "Fine Arts," "Music (Works about)," "Games, etc.," "Literature (General)," "Poetry and Drama," "Fiction," "Juvenile," "History," "Geography and Travel," "Biography," and "General Works." For 1914 the system was further enlarged by the addition of two new categories: "Description and Travel" and "Military and Naval."

The "Bookseller"

There were usually two sources of publication information in each monthly issue of the *Bookseller*: "Publications of the Month" and "Alphabetical List of the Principal English Publications for the Month." Although the latter is easier to count (because each entry took up just one line, it would be possible to calculate the average number of entries per page and multiply that number by the number of pages), it was not as comprehensive as the former (since it dealt only with the "principal" publications). From 1911 onward the *Bookseller* published a "Classified Table of Publications" that performed the same function as the *Publishers' Circular*'s "Analytical Table." The number of categories used by the *Bookseller* varied considerably over the period 1858–1919: in 1858 there were 18 categories; by 1867 this number had increased to 20; by 1877 it was up to 31, and by 1887 to 46. By 1912 the journal was using 65 separate categories.

Although a useful source for information on subjects published, the *Bookseller* is not without its problems. The classification is rough and sometimes unreliable. For instance, in September 1905 some of Shakespeare's works are classified in "Poetry and the Drama" and some in "Albums, Textbooks and Booklets." Literary volumes in Everyman's Library were sometimes classified under "Collected Works and Ana." The occasional publication from the USA, France, and other countries is indiscriminately mixed with UK publications. Sometimes a number of discrete publications are listed in one entry (for example, music, maps, reading books, textbooks, and their associated answer books). The class "Essays and Belles-Lettres" commonly includes a number of works which

might properly be classified elsewhere (for example, under literature or sociology).

For some unestablished reason the listed titles were not classified
into subjects in the October 1859 issue. In 1860, and between 1864
and 1866, the figures for November and December were conflated.
The ways in which these gaps and anomalies were dealt with are
fully explained in one of the appendices to *Some Patterns and Trends
in British Publishing 1800–1919*.

ANNUAL PATTERN (NUMBERS)

What can we say of the general trends between 1800 and 1919
that are darkly visible through the sources discussed above (and
others)? The pattern revealed is not one that Whiggishly-inclined
historians would immediately recognize: there is no simple climb
from the lowlands of preindustrial printing to the sunny uplands
of powered mass production. It is true that by the end of the
nineteenth century the number of titles being published and the
number of tons of paper being produced were substantially greater
than at the beginning, but this was not achieved by production
rising on a smooth curve. For the first sixty to seventy years of the
nineteenth century there was a pattern that, although the overall
trend was upward, contained within it sudden surges and equally
sudden collapses, dramatic peaks followed by featureless plateaus.

The first quarter of the century was characterized by a gentle
gradient interrupted by the occasional year or two-year period in
which production, often in response to a particular political or
social issue, suddenly rose (1803, 1812, and 1815). In this context
the much-vaunted book trade crisis of 1826 can be seen as no more
than a little, local difficulty, a slightly exaggerated version of the
"dip" that almost always followed a year of exceptionally high
production. The early 1830s continued this upward trend with
a minor dip in 1831 and a considerable rise in 1832 (almost
certainly associated with the Great Reform Bill and its surrounding
controversies). The late 1830s (particularly 1836 and 1838) may
have seen a slight downturn, but the decade concluded on a strong
upward trend.[4]

The 1840s seem to have marked a transition point. The early
1840s showed a continuity with the late 1830s, but the rate of
publication of titles seems to have steepened after 1845. By 1849

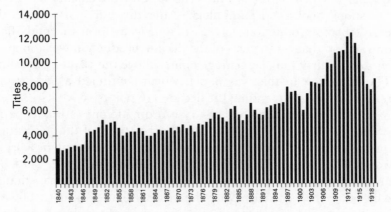

Figure 2.1 *Publishers' Circular*: titles per year, 1840–1919

production was probably between sixteen and thirty percentage points above an 1840–44 baseline. This rapidly increasing volume of production continued into the 1850s and peaked somewhere between 1851 and 1853 at around sixty-seven percentage points above an 1840–44 baseline. There are likely to have been a number of reasons for this dramatic increase: the economic and political disturbances of the mid-1840s (culminating in the revolutions of 1848) must certainly have stimulated production, the debates over the Oxford Movement, the Great Exhibition (and the associated debate over the Crystal Palace), and the death of Wellington all contributed to the upwelling of print in the early 1850s visible in figure 2.1. Curiously enough, however, it was none of these factors that, to a knowledgeable contemporary observer in the form of the editor of the *Publishers' Circular*, explained the flurry of publishing activity around 1850.[5]

In 1850 the Catholic diocesan hierarchy had been reestablished in England. This was viewed by many of the more radical Protestants as a direct provocation, made worse by the shadow cast by the defections to Rome during the heyday of the Oxford Movement. What, to us, is a small footnote in ecclesiastical history was to contemporaries the call to do battle in print on an almost unprecedented scale. Books, essays, and above all pamphlets issued from the British press in their scores and hundreds during the height of the campaign. So great was the melee that the *Publishers'*

Circular devoted a page to advertisers' announcements of "Papal Question" books and pamphlets.[6] After this flurry of print in the early 1850s, production decreased somewhat from the mid-1850s onward, so that by the end of the decade production was, on average, only thirty-four percentage points above the 1840–44 baseline. The exception to this was paper, which continued a very strong upward movement, ending the decade 116 points above its 1840–44 baseline. Between 1850 and 1859, according to one estimate, paper production rose fifty-five percent.[7] Calculations of the percentage increase of paper production over individual decades can be a useful exercise because, with the exception of the 1860s, paper statistics always ended a decade at a significantly higher level than that at which they had started. Only the period 1800–1809 had shown a larger percentage gap between the first year of the decade and the last (64 percent): this was due to the exceptional circumstances of starting from a low base; and, perhaps, to being the decade that saw the introduction of mechanization into the manufacture of paper in the shape of the Fourdrinier machine. Smaller percentage gaps appeared in 1810–19 (15 percent), 1820–29 (35 percent), 1830–39 (42 percent) and 1840–49 (36 percent). After the interlude of the 1860s, it was the 1870s that fully realized the trend in paper production suggested by the 1850s. The section on price structure below includes evidence that there was a significant alteration in the pricing of books in the late 1840s and 1850s, with "cheap books" (those with a cover price of 3s 6d or under) becoming a dominant feature of the market. Cheap books imply longer or at least more frequent print runs and thus would naturally demand more paper. The final abolition of the newspaper duty in 1855 would also have made a major contribution to an increased demand for paper. The 1860s seem to have been characterized by a plateau in production that extended the rates of the later 1850s right through to the late 1860s or early 1870s. Even paper production, although it did rise, did so much more modestly than in the 1850s, and with a number of fluctuations. Indeed, the increase in paper production between 1860 and 1869 was only 16 percent. In some sense this plateau is the creation of the bulge in production of the early 1850s. Without the early 1850s, the 1860s could have been regarded as an extension of the very slow, slightly fluctuating growth pattern of the 1840s. However, in comparison with the 1850s the subsequent decade looks flat and slightly depressed. Odd and difficult to

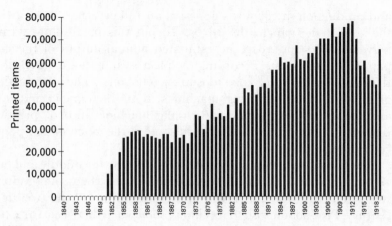

Figure 2.2 British Museum Library: printed items deposited, 1851–1919

explain as it is, this plateauing is visible in most UK sources, including the British Museum copyright receipt books (see figure 2.2). Figures from the new electronic version, the *BLGC*, confirm the impression that output of UK titles did stagnate in the 1860s, but also suggest that this pattern was not visible in books bearing imprints other than those of major UK publishers: in other words, the 1860s plateau seems to be a distinctly British phenomenon.[8]

The early 1870s saw the last of the steady state that had characterized book production since the late 1850s. There seems to have been at least two years during this decade that saw substantial increases in the rates of production (1872/3, and 1877), and by 1879 the rate was probably about thirty-five percentage points above a 1855–59 baseline. Paper, however, as one might expect, was experiencing a much faster rate of increase, being, by 1879, some 193 points above its 1855–59 baseline. Indeed, the 1870s marked the period in which the estimated UK paper production moved ahead more quickly than at any other time. Statistics on paper production had always shown a tendency to increase faster than the other statistics (on average, perhaps, about twenty percentage points more above any given baseline than the other sets of statistics); now, in the 1870s, the difference was multiplied, with a gap of no less than 140 percent between paper and the next nearest production figures.[9] The gap between production in 1870 and production in 1879 was no less than 108 percent, almost twice the size of the gap in the 1850s. To put this in absolute terms, between 1870 and 1879 the estimated annual output of the UK paper industry seems, according to Spicer's estimates, to have more than doubled (from 120,000 tons to 250,000 tons). The introduction of web-fed rotary printing machines in the newspaper industry and the use of Wharfedale and similar machines in book printing (common by this time) will explain some of the much higher paper consumption implied by these figures.

The 1880s continued the trend established by the middle and late 1870s, albeit at a slightly modified rate. In the 1890s the gradient steepened once more, as it did in the first decade of the twentieth century. Production rose to its climax somewhere between 1912 and 1914 at around 284 percentage points above its 1855–59 baseline. As one might expect, production declined during the First World War to, at it lowest point, about 181 points above its 1855–59 baseline. In other words, by 1918 production had been reduced to about 63.5 percent of its prewar volume.

Recovery, however, seems to have been rapid, at least as far as can be judged from one year's figures. By 1919 production had recovered to, on average, about 235 percentage points above its 1855–59 baseline, or 83 percent of its immediately prewar size. However, one should treat these recovery figures with extreme caution. They represent one year's total, which might well have been swollen by titles held up by the war; as we do not have paper production figures for these years, it may well be that the print runs represented by these titles were smaller than their prewar equivalents. Nevertheless, despite the caveats, the figures make clear the fact that in the book industry, as in so many other areas of manufacturing, the first decade or so of the twentieth century was a rehearsal for what was to come, and that, at worst, the First World War represented no more than a temporary disturbance of an accelerating trend visible from the 1870s onward.

MONTHLY PATTERN

The first three decades of the nineteenth century were characterized by a monthly pattern that almost certainly had its origins in the book production customs of earlier centuries: it consisted of a substantial spring season spanning March to May and occasionally taking in June; commonly there was a dip in April. After June, numbers declined through July and August, frequently reaching their minimum in September. Numbers would then increase in October and November, commonly peaking in December; the October–December season was, however, clearly subordinate to the March–May one, and sometimes little more than a recovery after the August–September trough. This pattern can be seen in the first histogram in figure 2.3, which illustrates *Bent's* listings for 1824–29.

During the 1830s a shift in the patterns derived from the stationers' records and from *Bent's* is observable. The spring season remained important but the October–December period grew in significance to a point where, by the late 1830s, it was probably on a par, in terms of numbers of titles published, with the spring. This trend was amplified in the 1840s (by which time we have an additional and more reliable source of figures in the shape of the *Publishers' Circular*). It is quite apparent that by the end of the 1840s the October–December season was larger than the spring one, not by much, but by enough to indicate the arrival of that most important book publication season in the industrial world – Christmas.

Social and cultural historians have, for some time, been pointing

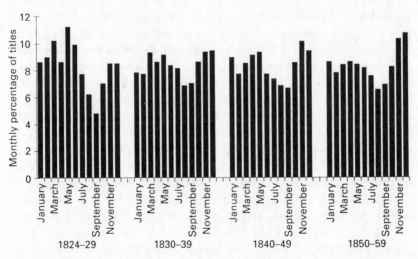

Figure 2.3 The emergence of Christmas: *Bent's* listings, 1824–1859

out the emergence of the modern idea of Christmas as a phenomenon of the 1840s. The Christmas tree and other German traditions
imported into Britain by Prince Albert took root in the 1840s; the
first Christmas card was sent by Henry Cole to his friends in 1843;
and most significant of all, given Dickens's acute sense of the market
for fiction, his celebration of Christmas (rehearsed in 1836/37 in
Pickwick Papers) came into full play with his sequence of Christmas
books which began with *A Christmas Carol* in 1843. The development
of the Christmas season can best be seen in a sequence of four
histograms illustrating the percentage distribution of titles listed
in *Bent's* between 1824 and 1859 (figure 2.3). The new pattern,
with the Christmas season as the most important and the spring
season as a subsidiary one, was to remain essentially unchanged
for the rest of the period.

Once established, the size and importance of the Christmas
season (October–December) grew dramatically in the period from
1850 to 1890. Although all three months witnessed increases
in numbers of titles listed, the largest numbers tended to be
recorded from late November to early December. During the
mid-century period it was common for there to be a large number
of books recorded in January. This was probably the consequence
of publishers overshooting the Christmas market. By the later
nineteenth century the January totals were falling as publishers
targeted their books more accurately on the Christmas season.
In order to avoid the overshoot phenomenon, publishers began
to anticipate the season by a couple of months: by the 1890s
the largest number of titles was issued in October rather than
November or December. Now, instead of rising steadily through
October and November to a peak in December, publication figures were high in September and peaked in October with a
steady decline in November and December. The three-month
Christmas season, so long regarded as the bane of the late
twentieth century, was in fact evident in the publishing industry
of the late nineteenth century. Figure 2.4 illustrates this shift
in publication pattern with data from the *Publishers' Circular* in
the 1880s and 1890s. This new pattern, with October as the
month of most issues, seems to have continued until at least
the outbreak of the First World War. The restrictions on production brought about by the Great War seem to have imposed
a little more uniformity on the monthly pattern, reducing the

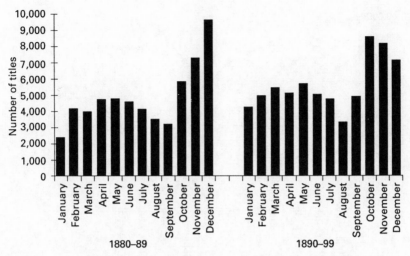

Figure 2.4 *Publishers' Circular*: total monthly listings

size of the Christmas season and leveling the earlier months of the year.

As befits a rather conservative source, the shape of the "Literary" deposits recorded by the Stationers' Company registry books for the period 1884–1909 had a monthly pattern that was less extreme than that produced by the data from other sources (see figure 2.5). Although Christmas was undoubtedly the largest season, it was not so by very much. The rise in spring is visible, as is the trough in the summer months, but in a rather muted form. The upper graph line in figure 2.5, despite the fact that it records late-nineteenth-century publishing output, is more reminiscent of the pattern visible during the emergence of the Christmas season in the 1840s and 1850s. The monthly pattern of "Commercial" listings, however, is more reminiscent of a monthly publication pattern of the pre-1830s in having a generally flatter, less differentiated graph line with a modest spring season and a very minor rise in the October–December period. The sort of jobbing printing illustrated by these "Commercial" entries almost certainly represented a means by which minor printers earned their living, and more major printing works ensured a steady flow of work despite the ups and downs of demand implied by the post-1830 monthly book publication pattern.

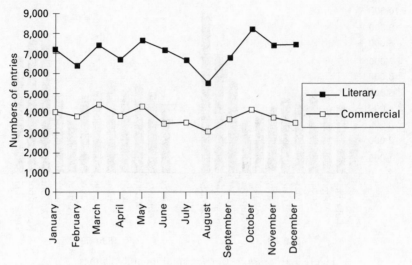

Figure 2.5 Stationers' Hall: Literary/Commercial entries, 1884–1909

SUBJECT PUBLISHING

If one looks at the second column in table 2.1 (the figures in which were derived from the 36,000 entries of the *Bibliotheca Londinensis* covering the period 1814–46) one will see a pattern that, at first glance, those familiar with analyses of eighteenth-century book production will not find too surprising. Religion is the predominant subject, with 20.3 percent of the titles, followed by works on geography, travel, history, and biography with 17.3 percent; and then by fiction and juvenile works with 16.2 per cent. However, in this classification poetry and drama are in a separate category with 7.6 percent of the titles. By adding the two literary categories together it can be shown that literature accounted for just under 24 percent of the titles listed by the *Bibliotheca Londinensis*. In other words, literature was already larger, though not by much, than religion in terms of titles published. It is most likely that the earlier part of the nineteenth century witnessed the transition from a publishing system dominated by religion as a subject to a system that put much more emphasis on secular titles (although one must remember that this is exclusively in terms of number of titles; in terms of print runs it is highly likely that the production of, for instance, Bibles, New Testaments, prayer books, and psalmbooks far outstripped most secular titles).[10]

The most striking feature revealed by subject statistics from the second half of the nineteenth century and the first decade of the twentieth century is the shift from the publishing of religious titles to the publishing of more secular subjects, particularly literature, and within literature, prose fiction. Although the shift was likely to have been a slow, almost imperceptible process during the first half of the century, it certainly gathered speed in the 1850s and 1860s. By the 1870s, at least according to the *Publishers' Circular*, "Literature (General)" titles were being produced in significantly larger quantities than "Religion" titles. From the 20 percent share it commanded in the *Bibliotheca Londinensis*, "Religion" dropped to 15 percent by the 1880s and was to drop to under 9 percent by the first decade of the twentieth century. The progressive diminution of the percentage share of "Religion" was mirrored by a very rapid increase in the share of the total market for "Literature," so that

Table 2.1 *Subjects by percentage*, 1814–1846, 1900–1909, and 1910–1919

	Bibliotheca Londinensis 1814–1846	*Publishers' Circular* 1900–1909	*Publishers' Circular* 1910–1919
Religion	20.3	9	8.5
Geography, travel, history, biography	17.3	12.1	14.2
Fiction, juvenile	16.2	30.1	24.3
Education	11.8	8.4	6.2
Arts, science, maths, illustrated works	8.8	8	14.9
Poetry, drama	7.6	5.1	6
Medicine	5.7	3.3	3.8
Law	4.4	1.9	2.4
Politics, sociology, economics, military, naval	4	7.7	10.8
Logic, philosophy, belles lettres	0.7	3.5	5.6
Miscellaneous	3.2	10.9	3.3

between 1890 and 1910 the latter subject was commanding over 30
percent of the *Circular*'s listings. The preeminent position gained by
fiction during this period goes some way to explain the many and
vociferous complaints from librarians and educators in the 1880s
and 1890s on the subject of fiction and the threat it seemed to pose
to the "more serious" sorts of writing and reading.

The decade 1910–1919 (see column 4 of table 2.1) seems to
have witnessed a minor contraction in "Literature" (particularly
in fiction and juvenile literature) that may have been a consequence
of the 1914–1918 war; "Religion" showed no sign of a compensating
rise during this period and continued its gentle decline in the
Circular's figures, although the *Bookseller* did indicate a marginal
rise between 1914 and 1916.

The percentage share of "Education" seems to have declined
after 1900 (see columns 3 and 4 of table 2.1). This is rather
puzzling, but may well be due to the inverse relationship between
"Education" on the one hand; and "Arts, science, mathematics,
and illustrated works", and "Politics, sociology, economics, military, and naval" on the other. During the period from 1870 to 1899,
"Education" maintained an average of 11.1 percent, while "Arts,
science, etc." commanded 5.5 percent and "Politics, sociology,
etc." 3.6 percent. In the two decades spanning 1900 to 1919 the
average percentage share of "Education" dropped to 7.3 percent
while "Arts, science, etc.," went up to 11.4 percent, and "Politics,
sociology, etc.," climbed to 9.2 percent. Clearly, one could not
depend too much on figures that were derived in part from
these atypical years; nevertheless, it might be argued that the
educational changes ushered in by the early twentieth century
required texts that were not so readily identifiable as traditionally
"educational" and that the increasing stress on technical and
scientific subjects (at the expense of, for example, the classics)
meant that many educational texts tended to be classified under
other headings.

It is noticeable that over the period surveyed whenever the
category "Fiction, juvenile" increased its percentage share, "Geography, travel, history, biography" decreased, and vice versa. It may
well be that these two broad categories satisfied similar needs in
readers (certainly there was a long tradition of travel writing being
fictional or semifictional), and thus one had to give ground as the
other advanced.[11]

PRICE STRUCTURE

In order to avoid overcomplication, book prices were crudely divided into three categories: low (up to 3*s* 6*d*), medium (between 3*s* 7*d* and 10*s*), and high (over 10*s*). Using this categorization, we can see in figure 2.6 that the price structures of 1811, 1815, and 1825 revealed a traditional form in which the high price group took the largest percentage, the medium price group accounted for the second largest, and the low price group the smallest percentage share. In part this profile for the early nineteenth century may be due to the source of information being *Bent's Monthly Literary Advertiser*, which tended to list higher-priced texts of interest to the respectable trade. (In other words, it hardly ever acknowledged the existence of printed materials at 6*d* or under.) Even with the limitation of the source, however, it is quite apparent that the pattern visible in 1811 was not so visible in the figures for 1815 or 1825. Between 1811 and 1825 there was clearly a steady growth in the number of books listed in the high price category (in part, this would be the result of serious price inflation consequent on the disturbances of the Napoleonic period).

By 1835, however, a marked change occurred: high-priced books diminished and medium-priced books became the largest single group. By 1855, according to *Bent's*, the price structure typical of

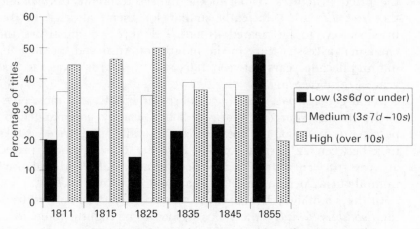

Figure 2.6 *Bent's* price structure, 1811–1855

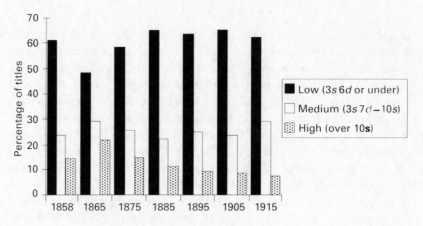

Figure 2.7 *Bookseller* price structures, 1858–1915

the early nineteenth century had been reversed: low-priced books now accounted for the largest percentage share, medium-price books came second, and high-priced books dropped to their lowest percentage ever recorded. The *Publishers' Circular* price figures (not shown here), which start in 1845, suggest that this dramatic change was already under way in the 1840s, so it is probably best to conclude that the price reversal process took place somewhere in the period between 1840 and 1855. Beginning in the late 1850s the price structures visible in the figures from the *Circular* and the *Bookseller* are sufficiently similar for them, at least in this brief survey, to be treated as one.[12] Figure 2.7 illustrates the changing price structure in the months of April and October for the mid-decade years between 1865 and 1915 (1858 was the first year of the *Bookseller*).

What general patterns can we observe? Firstly, and most obviously, in this source low-priced books usually commanded 60 percent or more of the total titles. Secondly, mid-priced books took between 22 percent and 29 percent. Thirdly, books priced at over 10s went into a steady decline after 1865 and collapsed from about 22 percent in 1865 to around 8 percent by 1915.

In this set of figures (and in the corresponding one derived from the *Publishers' Circular*) the 1860s seemed to be slightly anomalous, marking a hiatus, and possibly even a slight retrogression: the relationship between the three price ranges remained the same, but the percentage of low-priced books decreased and the percentage of high-price titles increased in comparison with the 1855 figures. This anomaly in pricing would tie in quite closely with the other anomalies that have already been observed in the data for the 1860s.

Certain subject categories seem to have been characterized by distinctive price structures. "Religion" as a subject category always tended to have a price structure that leaned toward the cheap book. However, many of these publications were heavily subsidized and so are untrustworthy as market indicators. "Literature" also had a characteristic price profile, although that did not fully emerge until the 1875 figures. In the 1858 and 1865 figures "Literature" exhibited a rather conservative pricing policy. The period from 1870 to 1890 witnessed the emergence of the cheap book listed under literature in the trade journals, while the end of the century marked a distinct change in the disposition of some of the bands in the medium and low price groupings. For example, books priced between 5s 1d and 7s 6d accounted for 8.6 percent of all "Literature" titles in 1885; by 1905 this had gone up to 25.4 percent. Books priced between 1d and 6d accounted for 6.4 percent of all "Literature" titles in 1885; by 1905 this had gone up to 16.4 percent. These changes were almost certainly connected with the collapse of the three-decker novel, the development of the "net book" system, and the extensive republication of both copyright and noncopyright fiction in extremely cheap formats (often printed in double columns, bound in paper covers, and selling at 6d or less).[13] In 1915 war production constraints had an impact on all categories, but on Literature somewhat less than any other subject.

BOOK PUBLISHING IN CONTEXT: A SALUTARY CONCLUSION

Standing back from the specific trends in print production in the nineteenth and early twentieth century, and for one moment viewing text production as a purely economic activity, what can be said of the relative value of its different aspects by the end of the period? We are lucky in having the *Census of Production* for the years 1907 and 1924, for these provide a refreshingly new and somewhat unexpected view of the subject.[14]

If one assesses the various parts of the printing industry in terms of their percentage share of the net value of total output, then two parts stand out. The net value of jobbing and general printing accounted for 41.7 percent in 1907 and 32.7 percent in 1924 of the total value. The production of newspapers and periodicals accounted for something over 28.2 percent in 1907,[15] and no less than 45.2 percent of the total net output of the printing industries in 1924. Printed and manuscript books and binding, on the other hand, generated 17.1 percent of total net value in 1907, a total that fell to just 12.7 percent in the *Census of Production* in 1924. By this time books were worth between one-quarter and one-third the net value of periodical publications.[16]

The twentieth century, at least viewed in terms of the economics of printing and publishing, was not going to be the century of the book, but rather the century of the government form and the circular, of the specialized magazine and the tabloid newspaper.

NOTES

1 Charles Dickens, *Hard Times* (Oxford: Oxford University Press, 1989), 113–15.
2 Simon Eliot, *Some Patterns and Trends in British Publishing, 1800–1919* (London: Bibliographical Society Occasional Papers, 1993).
3 See Edward Miller, *The Prince of Librarians: The Life and Times of Antonio Panizzi of the British Museum* (London: Andre Deutsch, 1967), 201–7.
4 Eliot, 15–20.
5 *Publishers' Circular*, 5 December 1853, [478].
6 *Ibid.*, 2 December 1850, [396].
7 A. D. Spicer, *The Paper Trade* (London: Methuen & Co., 1907); see Eliot, table A6, 113.
8 Eliot, 21–22.
9 See *Annual Reports of the British Museum – Copyright (Volumes)*.
10 For instance, between 1837 and 1847 the Queen's Printer in England produced in total 6,900,323 copies of these works; Cambridge University Press produced 3,001,300 copies; and Oxford University Press no fewer than 8,908,900 copies. The Queen's Printers in Scotland produced a total of 5,844,800, not including prayer books. *Ibid.*, tables C10–C13, 132–34.
11 *Ibid.*, 52–53.
12 *Ibid.*, 63–68.
13 *Ibid.*, 72–74.
14 *Ibid.*, 99–101.

15 Due to the way the numbers were calculated in 1907 this is a minimum figure and may well in reality have been higher.

16 "Net value," of course, treats all printed text as though it is an ordinary industrial product coming out of the factory gates; it does not take into account the added value produced by the marketing and distribution of printed matter by publishers and booksellers.

CHAPTER 3

Wordsworth in the Keepsake, 1829

Peter J. Manning

The increase of Wordsworth's reputation in the 1820s brought recurrent invitations to publish in the annuals; those handsomely produced gatherings of verse, prose, and engraved plates that had been the fashion since Rudolph Ackermann had introduced the *Forget Me Not, a Christmas and New Year's Present for 1823*. By 1825 nine rivals had bid for buyers' attention, increasing to an astonishing sixty-two by 1831. The sales justified this repetition of a formula. The *Literary Souvenir*, begun by Alaric Watts whose "dazzling and superb accomplishments" in the genre earned him the title of Father of the Annuals,[1] sold 6,000 copies in two weeks on its appearance in 1825: the following year's edition reached 10,000, and at its peak, despite the competition, the *Literary Souvenir* attained a circulation of 15,000 copies.[2]

In February 1827 William Harrison Ainsworth wrote to a friend:

Heath the engraver and I are going to produce in September the most magnificent Annual ever dreamed about. It is to cost a guinea, and contain twenty plates; the literary matter will be first rate. Amongst other things which will please you, are some lively sketches, in the best *Indicator* style, by Leigh Hunt. The name is execrable – Heath baptizes it *The Keepsake*, which to my thinking savours of a gift from Tunbridge Wells. Can you not supply me with something better? . . . give me something relating to Fashion, for I intend to enrol all the *littérateurs* of the *Beau Monde* under my banner.[3]

This exuberant announcement captures the snobbery and concern with fashion that were the hallmarks of the annual. As the preface to the first *Keepsake* would declare: "Our desire has been, that its pervading characteristic should be an elegant lightness" (vii).

Charles Heath, "the first graphic artist of the day" as the *Gentleman's Magazine* called him,[4] figured on the title page of the

Keepsake as "The Proprietor"; for notwithstanding the language of the gift that surrounded the annuals, they were frankly commercial projects. Appearing just in advance of the Christmas season, annuals were intended to supply the need for presents at once intimate and proper, but saying that ignores the degree to which they were widely publicized to create the very need they claimed to answer. Here is Wordsworth's friend and neighbor John Wilson, writing as Christopher North in *Blackwood's* in January 1825:

Do you wish to give a small earnest graceful gift to some dearly-beloved one, then thank us for the happy hint, and with a kiss, or, if that be not permissible, at least with a smile of severest suavity . . . lay the *Literary Souvenir* upon her tender lap, with a few words, which it would be impertinent in us to particularize; only be sure, "you breathe them not far from her delicate auricle;" and with a low, a deep, and a pleading tone, like the Knight who won the bright and beauteous Genevieve. It is a hundred to one that you are a married man in six weeks or two months; nay, if it be a "large paper copy," one flesh will ye be before the new moon.[5]

Earnest and graceful, erotic and mercantile: the desires ironically but effectually set in motion by the annuals generated an industry that thrived for more than a decade.

The *Keepsake* for 1828 boasted three innovations. The first made clear the function of the annual as a status gift rather than a book to read: an engraved presentation plate at the head of the volume in which the donor might inscribe his sentiments to the fortunate recipient (see plate 3.1). The second was an increase from its predecessors' pocketbook size, and a concomitant boost in price from the twelve-shilling norm of the other annuals to a guinea. The advertisement for the 1829 volume proclaimed: "The Work will be printed by T. Davison, in small 8vo. and delivered, bound in crimson silk, price 1£ 1s. A few Copies will be printed in royal 8vo. with India proofs of the Plates, price 2£ 12s. 6d."[6] Heath correctly gambled that the market would bear the charge if the production justified it; to that end the crimson silk was crucial. When the author of the introductory essay, "Pocket-Books and Keepsakes," expressed the hope that the "genius of binding, we trust, will put forth all its powers on thousands of Keepsakes" (13), he evoked a genre in which appearance was all.[7]

Nor, estimated solely by reference to quantity of contents, was

Plate 3.1 Presentation plate, 1829 *Keepsake*

the price excessive. The *Monthly Review* greeted the first *Keepsake* by emphasizing "the exquisite series of embellishments" that one's guinea bought: "the portrait of Selina alone, not to mention the seventeen other plates contained in the book, would have been valued a year or two ago at the sum for which itself and the whole of its companions may now be purchased."[8] How bluntly the reviewers calculated the cost/benefit ratio may be seen in the comment of the *Monthly Magazine* that

the speculation originally was a well imagined one; and its very popularity has given it means of bidding for popularity which no other position could have afforded. Nothing short of the immense extent of the editions sold could enable the publishers to bring out the books at their present price. A volume, for instance, which costs 700£ (to use the phraseology of the trade) to 'get up,' is sold for twelve shillings! For this sum we have four hundred close pages of letter-press; exquisitely printed, upon the finest paper and in the finest possible type; independent of twelve engravings, of which impressions, purchased separately, would cost considerably more money than the price paid for the entire work.[9]

This analysis articulates the conception of publishing on which the annuals were based: a heavy investment – in artists, writers, and production – loudly trumpeted, to be recouped by volume of sales. Or, in the words of a clever parody in "Pocket-Books and Keepsakes" of the opening soliloquy of Marlowe's *Jew of Malta*: "Infinite profit in a little book" (3–4). Behind this policy lay the steel plate, which from its arrival in 1823 made possible not only a new delicacy of engraving but also a vastly enlarged number of impressions. With the novel fixed in its three-decker format at 31*s*. 6*d*, the *Keepsake* at a guinea was a cheap luxury for those who could afford it. "The proprietors" of the annuals, the *Monthly Repository* judged, "are entitled to our commendation for the fair prices at which these elegant volumes are offered to the public; and this, united with other and higher charms to the patronage of the literary world, will cause them, we doubt not, to be presented to many a young glistening eye and tender hand on the approaching merry days of Christmas and the New Year."[10] Rarely can profit, art, and sentiment have seemed so harmoniously joined.

The third innovation of the first *Keepsake* was the anonymity of its literary contributions, although Heath soon realized the value of celebrity. He replaced Ainsworth with Frederick Mansel Reynolds, and in January 1828 the pair embarked on a northern tour to solicit stronger contributions. In Edinburgh they offered Sir Walter Scott £800 to edit the *Keepsake* and £400 to contribute 70 to 100 pages of text. Scott had no wish to incur a *déclassé* obligation: "Now to become a stipendiary Editor of a Newsyear gift book is not to be thought of, nor could I agree to work for any quantity of supply to such a publication." But he was too canny to reject the overture completely: instead he proposed to sell Heath and Reynolds an article for the "round price" of £500, at which they did not balk. "Received letters from the youth who is to conduct the *Keepsake* with blarney an[d] a £200 Bank note," Scott recorded in his journal a month later: "No blarney in that. I must do something for these worthies." What he did was to reconfigure a story that his publishers had already rejected: "Amused myself by converting the Tale of the Mysterious Mirror into 'Aunt Margaret's Mirror,' designed for Heath's What dye call it. Heath will not like this but I cannot afford to have my goods thrown back upon my hands."[11] Representing the artist as just another commodity producer, and flourishing his artistic resilience and entrepreneurial success, Scott straightforwardly embodies the conditions of the market.

With Scott lined up, the partners journeyed to the Lake District, where Robert Southey had promised Ainsworth "something for your next volume."[12] The poet laureate was sadly aware of his shrinking readership. The midsummer accountings from his publishers were to confirm his fears: "my last year's proceeds were, per John Murray, *nil*; and for all the rest of my works in Longman's hands, about £26."[13] To another correspondent he lamented that "the sale of my Poems is reduced almost to nothing . . . *Roderick* is the only one for which there is any thing approaching to what booksellers could call a demand, & of this 138 sold." But *Roderick, The Last of The Goths*, first published in 1814, had not yet cleared its expenses and so was not turning a profit for its author.[14] Southey thought he knew the cause: "The Annuals are now the only book bought for presents to young ladies, in which way poems formerly had their chief vent" (*LCS*, 5:336).

Hence Southey's readiness to enter what he perceived as the

dominating medium for poetry. "Charles Heath proceeded expeditiously to business," he recounted:

presented me with a *Keepsake* from his pocket, said that he had been into Scotland for the express purpose of securing Sir Walter's aid, that he had succeeded, that he now came to ask for mine, and should be happy to give me fifty guineas for anything which I would supply him. Money, – money you know, makes the mare go, – and what is Pegasus, but a piece of horse-flesh? I sold him at that price a pig in a poke. (*LCS*, 5:322)

Heath shrewdly brandished each notable recruit to make the *Keepsake* more respectable and the enrollment of the next easier. The article of exchange is the name itself, not a work: Heath asks for "anything" that might bear Southey's signature. No sooner had Southey committed his ballad poem to Heath than Allan Cunningham invited a contribution for his annual, the *Anniversary*, or, as Southey cheerfully précised: "he wants a pig also."[15] Cunningham was a friend, but Southey regretfully told him: "First come, first served, is a necessary rule in life" (*LCS*, 5:322). The conservative author fully understood how to transact his affairs within the world of consumption he ceaselessly denounced, but he wondered nonetheless: "Will you believe that of this *Keepsake*, which is bought merely for presents, or for the sake of the engravings, [Heath] has sold fifteen thousand copies! And for binding the next volume he has bespoken four thousand yards of red silk!" (*NLS*, 2:324). At "3*s*. a yard" (*SLS*, 4:99), he added to his daughter: in this commodity relationship literature had become its cover.

Scott and Southey were men of letters whose careers are unthinkable apart from the characteristic mechanisms of nineteenth-century literary production. Wordsworth was haughtier. "I have . . . had applications, I believe, from nearly every Editor," Wordsworth told Allan Cunningham at the end of February 1828, declining his request to contribute to the *Anniversary*, but "had never been engaged in any periodical nor meant to be"; now, however, he accepted a proposal from Reynolds and Heath.[16] The proposition of a hundred guineas for twelve pages of verse proved irresistible. "Father," wrote his daughter Dora to Maria Jane Jewsbury, "could not feel himself justified in refusing so advantageous an offer – degrading enough I confess but necessity has no law, and galling enough but we must pocket our pride sometimes and it is good for us."[17] Dora's condescension points to the cultural import of Wordsworth's decision.[18]

Though Wordsworth was obliged to Reynolds for a remedy for his eye trouble and the *Keepsake* offer came at a moment when the poet faced "formidable" expenses arising from his son John's career (*LY*, 1:489, 1:589–90), the source of his acquiescence lies in the disappointing returns of his recent publications. Though his reputation had risen, his receipts had not. Under his arrangements with Longman, the publisher assumed all costs and divided the profits after they had been met. Wordsworth steadily complained of the advertising costs charged to his accounts, yet even with this publicity his small editions of five hundred sold slowly. The four-volume *Miscellaneous Poems* of 1820, despite the modesty of the title a major enterprise of revision and canon formation, had sold only 485 copies and earned less than £156 by 1826; the second, octavo edition of the *Excursion*, published the same year, sold out by 1824, but brought in less than half as much; *Memorials of a Tour on the Continent* (1822) produced less than £10 in the next three years, and the *Ecclesiastical Sketches*, also of that year, failed to recover costs.[19] Unsurprisingly, when in early 1825 Wordsworth began to consider a new collected edition, he also cast about for a new publisher.

Wordsworth approached John Murray, who took advice from John Lockhart. Weighing the credit to be gained by publishing "a classic Poet of England" against the losses Murray had incurred by overestimating the appeal of a collected edition of Crabbe, Lockhart concluded: "Everything . . . depends upon the terms proposed by the great Laker, whose vanity, be it whispered, is nearly as remarkable as his genius."[20] To Murray, Wordsworth proposed a six-volume edition of 750 copies, the poet to incur two-thirds of the expense in exchange for two-thirds of the profits (*LY*, 1:376); of Longman, who had visited Rydal Mount in September in the hope of retaining the poet, he asked £300 for an edition of a thousand copies (*LY*, 1:383). This the firm declined, nor did Murray step forward with alacrity. In the meantime Wordsworth pursued the suggestion of Maria Jane Jewsbury that he try Hurst and Robinson, her publisher and that of Alaric Watts's *Literary Souvenir*. Wordsworth's account of his slight profits left Watts "astonished beyond all reason," and he offered to serve as intermediary with his publishers (*LY*, 1:390 n.1). Despite this confidence, their first offer was nonetheless "so illiberal" that Watts communicated it

only reluctantly to Wordsworth (LY 1:383 n. 1), and by the time
more satisfactory terms were obtained the crash of Constable in
1826 brought down Hurst and Robinson, his London agents, and
the proceedings came to naught. Thus after almost two years
of "dancing attendance" (*LY*, 1:443) Wordsworth returned to
Longman, gaining at the end of December 1826 the terms he
had ventured to Murray: a five-volume edition of 750 copies, plus
250 extra of the *Excursion*, he to bear two-thirds of the expense in
exchange for two-thirds of the profits. The *Poetical Works* at last
appeared in 1827; the May 1828 accounts show a sale of 254 sets
and 108 of the *Excursion*. Though the edition sold out by 1832
and Wordsworth eventually cleared over £400, these, after all the
aggravation, were scarcely large figures.[21]

Reynolds's offer of 100 guineas for a mere twelve pages of verse
in the *Keepsake*, especially as compared to his income from the
accumulated productions of a career, is an emblem of the force
of the market to which Wordsworth was responding. Although he
loftily maintained that he published chiefly because "as long as
any portion of the Public seems inclined to call for my Poems,
it is my duty to gratify that inclination" (*LY*, 1:327), if the
rules privileged the capital of the name over the labor of the
work, he knew how to play by them. Disappointed at having
been anticipated with Wordsworth as with Southey by Reynolds
and Heath, Cunningham, who managed the workshop of Francis
Chantrey, casts of whose bust of the poet Wordsworth had been
bestowing on his friends, thought to entice a contribution by
volunteering a bronze copy that Wordsworth had lamented was
"above my price" (*LY*, 1:584). This effort to relocate the area of
exchange from commercial transaction at set fee to personal favor
Wordsworth speedily repudiated: "Much as I should value the
bronze Bust it is a mode of remuneration too indefinite for my
present engagements . . . I acknowledge that a wish to gratify you,
and I feel it very strongly, comes and must come second upon an
occasion like this. It is a matter of trade" (*LY*, 1:592–93). In this
economic situation, where writers whose actual works drew little
reward commanded nontrivial sums by their name, the gauge
of value was ruthless. Despite his initial posture of superiority,
Wordsworth endeavored to find a place in the *Keepsake* for Maria
Jane Jewsbury, but Reynolds "replied to my recommendation
that their object was Authors of prime celebrity – and persons

distinguished by rank or fashion, or station or anything else that might have as little to do with good writing" (*LY*, 2:27).

Coleridge possessed the recognition that Jewsbury lacked, and Reynolds and Heath left the Lakes with their way to him smoothed by Wordsworth. Coleridge's narrative demonstrates the gathering momentum by which luminaries were acquired:

Mr. Fred Reynolds called on me with a letter of introduction from Wordsworth, in which Wordsworth informed me that he had been induced, as likewise Southey and Sir Walter Scott, to furnish some poems to a work undertaken by Mr. Heath with Mr. R. as his Editor – that the unusually handsome terms would scarcely have overcome his reluctance, had he not entertained the hope that I might be persuaded to give my name . . . In short, he hoped that I would write.[22]

Reynolds offered Coleridge £50 for eleven pages of contributions to the 1829 *Keepsake*, further stipulating that he would appear in no other annual for that year except the *Literary Souvenir*, with which Coleridge had made a prior agreement, and the same terms for 1830 (*STCL*, 6:749 n.1). The stipulation was common, since monopoly increased value. Heath and Reynolds refused Wordsworth permission to send Watts a contribution in acknowledgment of his help because "they said it was the exclusive possession of my name, which tempted them to offer me so considerable a sum for a few pages" (*LY*, 2:27). Coleridge described his £50 as "more than all, *I* ever made by all my Publications, my week's salary of 5£ as Writer of the Leading Articles in the *Morning Post* during the Peace of Amiens excepted" (*STCL*, 6:752).

This snowballing effect confirms the astuteness of Southey's counsel to Cunningham on the management of an annual: "To me it seems the best policy that you should have many contributors, because every one would, from self-love, wish to promote the sale of the volume" (*LCS*, 5:339). Wordsworth also "endeavour[ed] to induce" Samuel Rogers to contribute (*LY*, 2:13), and, shedding his initial diffidence, he circulated prospectuses at Lowther Castle and "frequently mentioned the Keepsake among [his] friends and acquaintance recommending it so far as to say that if high prices could procure good writing it could be found there." If he could not forbear sometimes adding that the "result was by no means sure," an editor such as Reynolds knew there is no such thing as bad publicity (*LY*, 1:693). Charles Lamb, perusing the notices blazoning the annuals forthcoming in 1829, scoffed: "Wordsworth

I see has a good many pieces announced in one of em, not our *Gem.* W. Scott has distributed himself like a bribe haunch among 'em."[23] A pig in a poke, a bribe haunch: the flagrant commodity quality of the annuals seems to have made such meaty images unavoidable, yet Lamb's mockery is self-inclusive. He too published in them, in "our *Gem.*" The uncertain tone marks the authors' uncertainty in confronting the shifting market.

When the new *Keepsake* (plate 3.2) appeared in November 1828 it flaunted the carefully cultivated aura that led Christopher North to salute the next year's volume as "the most Patrician of Annuals in the whole republic of letters" ("Soliloquy," 959). The contributors included Sir Walter Scott, Sir James Mackintosh, Lord Normanby, Lord Morpeth, Lord Porchester, Lord Holland, Lord F. L. Gower, and Lord Nugent: the habitual roll-call of titles, North pretended, "makes a poor Plebeian like us tremble in our shoes" ("Soliloquy," 959). Beyond these came the compelling list of nineteen plates: drawings by artists including Sir Thomas Lawrence, Thomas Stothard, Alfred Chalon, Richard Westall, J. M. W. Turner, and Edwin Landseer, engraved by Heath, Finden, and other eminent craftsmen.

In 1802 Wordsworth had publicly defined the poet as "a man speaking to men" and privately lectured none other than John Wilson that "gentlemen, persons of fortune, professional men, ladies persons who can afford to buy or can easily procure books of half a guinea price, hot-pressed, and printed upon superfine paper" were corrupt judges of "human nature" and hence of poetry.[24] Now he was appearing in a still more lavish and expensive production primarily aimed at women. In the preface Reynolds and Heath baldly proclaimed the spirit that shaped the *Keepsake*: "on the various departments of the Keepsake, the enormous sum of *eleven thousand guineas* has been expended. 'Necesse est facere sumptum, qui quaerit lucrum'" (iii).

The capacity of "a speculation so extensive" (iii) blandly to assimilate figures associated with opposing political perspectives is a remarkable aspect of the *Keepsake*. To a reader who remembers the violent antagonisms of previous decades, the presence in a single volume of Wordsworth, Coleridge, and Southey with Thomas Moore, Shelley, and Mary Shelley is striking.[25] Only Byron would appear to be missing, but a feuilleton, "An Attempt at a Tour, By the Author of *The Roué*" [Samuel Beazley], begins by quoting

Plate 3.2 Title page, 1829 *Keepsake*

Don Juan (143;13,44). In one of those juxtapositions that establish
the all-incorporating market character of the venture (and so
simultaneously establish the character of the market), *Don Juan* and
The Roué immediately precede Wordsworth's sonnet "*Miserrimus!*,"
an exercise in elegiac pathos concluding: "To save the contrite,
Jesus bled" (156). But the project was not only of the market:
the conjunctions suggest how the seemingly neutral notion of taste
the *Keepsake* promoted subsumed divisive distinctions – radical and
conservative, libertine and pious – into serene solidarity. Masking
issues of class as matters of taste, literature and art function as the
agents of a universality that the price of the *Keepsake* exposes as
specious; the threatening others that the image of consensus the
annuals elaborated was designed to ward off peer through a notice
by Christopher North: "no more clumsy battalion-men be admitted
into the *corps d'élites* . . . Of course, all Cockneys are excluded."[26]

For Mary Shelley, writing for the *Keepsake* valuably supplemented
her £100 annuity from Sir Timothy Shelley, and its *pudeur* suited her
campaign to sanitize the posthumous reputation of her husband. In
addition to two of her stories Mary gave Reynolds three previously
unpublished poems by Shelley and the essay "On Love," to which
The Athenaeum responded as she must have hoped:

Reader! if thou hast ever expressed with your lips, or entertained in your
heart, one hard thought of PERCY BYSSHE SHELLEY, – if thou hast ever
fancied, that . . . he was not one of the most earnest, affectionate,
truth-seeking, humble, and self-denying men that ever lived on this
earth . . . if thou hast ever rashly proclaimed that the gates of mercy
were closed upon one in whom all the fruits of a true heart-faith were
so brightly and beautifully manifested, – read the fragment on Love.[27]

In a paradigm of the two masters to which the *Keepsake* was bound,
the commercial imperative to fill the blank remainder of the page
led Reynolds to follow Shelleyan rapture with his own knowing
epigram:[28]

> That e'er my visits will become
>   Too frequent, much I doubt;
> For though I've found you oft at home,
>   Too oft I've *found you out!*   (49)

To the larger project that the *Keepsake* represents both high
sentiment and its opposite, brittle wit, were germane, for the
annuals were a vade mecum of approved social values to their largely

middle-class purchasers. Hence the attraction of their aristocratic contributors and, increasingly, editors. Aimed at women, the annuals were often directed by titled women: in 1835 Reynolds was succeeded by the Hon. Caroline Norton, briefly by Lady Emmeline S. Wortley, and then by Lady Blessington, who edited the *Keepsake* from the volume for 1841 to that of 1850; from 1834 to 1849, the year of her death, she also edited Heath's *Book of Beauty*. With rank, as in the case of Lady Blessington, or without, as in the case of Mary Shelley, Letitia Landon, and Felicia Hemans (who both contributed to the 1829 *Keepsake*), the gender-demarcated annuals provided a vehicle and support for the woman writer that neatly exposes some of the tensions in the enterprise. Perhaps even more strongly than her *demi-mondaine* past, Lady Blessington's resourceful editorial drudging year after year challenged the notion upon which the annuals were built, that women were domestic, incapable beings.

The ideological cluster that linked gender, conduct, aesthetics, and profit includes nationalism. The fiction of the *Keepsake* is replete with mysterious Italian clairvoyants, French invaders, Spanish exoticism, ghostly lovers, nuns, bigamous marriages, duels, and banditti, but the exotic other is flirted with only to be contained by English decorum. Lord Morpeth's "Scraps of Italy," which immediately precedes Wordsworth's "The Triad" in the 1829 *Keepsake*, models the desired attitudes:

> My steps are turn'd to England – and oh shame
> To son of hers who thrills not at that name!
> Call'd by the inspiring sound, before my eyes
> My home's loved scenes, my country's glories rise;
> The free and mighty land that gave me birth,
> Her moral beauty, and her public worth;
> All that can make the patriot bosom swell –
> Yet one more sigh – bright Italy, farewell!   (72)

In this context even Coleridge's harmless poem "The Garden of Boccaccio" could raise eyebrows: the *Monthly Review* thought it "a charming performance" though connected with "one of the most impure and mischievous books that could find its way into the hands of an innocent female."[29]

Reviewing a half-dozen annuals, North exclaims: "The *Souvenir* shews, in many a shape of loveliness and majesty, what female beauty may be when Britain-born" ("Soliloquy," 955). One key to the success of the annuals was the plates of fashionable women whose dress and attitudes held up to the audience the model of taste, as in that of Mrs. Peel, the prominent frontispiece of the 1829 *Keepsake* (plate 3.3). In such specular acts the beholder beheld herself as she wished to be. The *Monthly Review* explicitly constructed the mirror of emulation:

The fair inhabitant of the loneliest hamlet receives from them an idea of the power which can give form and multiplied existence to gentle thoughts and images; and the gay population of provincial towns are gradually taught that art has a diviner power than that exhibited either by their drawing masters or their milliners. It is next to impossible that any one should have looked at the engravings of these volumes, and endure anything either common or vulgar for the remainder of the year. . . . The inhabitants of the provinces will have something to console them for the want of exhibitions and rare collections, and the daughters of tradesmen and manufacturers, who visit neither London nor Italy, will not want the means of forming a good taste, the best and most valuable adornment, next to the moral ones, of woman.[30]

This passage remarkably absorbs Byronic Romanticism into commercial commonplace. The "power which can give form and multiplied existence to gentle thoughts and images" conflates two memorable moments in Byron's portrait of himself as the suffering, titanic outcast in canto 3 of *Childe Harold's Pilgrimage*: the credo of stanza 6,

> 'Tis to create, and in creating live
> A being more intense, that we endow
> With form our fancy, gaining as we give
> The life we image,

and Byron's darker simile for his creativity in stanza 33,

> Even as a broken mirror, which the glass
> In every fragment multiplies; and makes
> A thousand images of one that was.

The Romantic artist's force, his power infinitely to reproduce his unique self, is paralleled by the market process, which through its power to disseminate the fashionable ideal through the medium of the annuals conforms the backward province to the up-to-date metropolis, and by the spread of taste thus makes a "thousand images of one that was."[31] Capital was of the essence: it was "extensive speculation," as the preface to the 1829 *Keepsake* avowed,

Plate 3.3 Frontispiece, 1829 *Keepsake*

that drove improved presses and the high-capacity steel plate to expanding circulation, the replication of the original in the print run reproduced in the replication of fashion it set in motion. British art fostered British beauty which fostered British manufacture, from dresses to books, a causal chain that might equally be run in reverse: British manufacture required the notion of British beauty to sell its goods, a notion reflected in British art. In propagating its image of femininity, the industry provided employment for some women but profits for the "proprietors" all along the chain of consumption.

The endless self-reproduction of the world of the annuals is especially obvious in the reviews. I have quoted the notices at length to show how thoroughly ostensible evaluation of the annuals is permeated by their discourse. Since the quarterlies, monthlies, and weeklies yearly devoted column after column to the annuals, describing their contents plate by plate and printing extracts, they served less as arbiters of praise or blame than as allies in publicity. The *Monthly Repository* illustrates the pattern of criticism as mimicry:

There they are, the pretty things! Criticise them? We might as well think of criticising the colours of a bed of tulips in full bloom. . . . A critique of them should only be written in a lady's boudoir; by her own taper and jewelled fingers; with finest crow-quill, the gilt and silver tassels hanging from its top, and quivering at every movement of its jetty plumage; in a delicate Italian hand; and on such embossed and perfumed paper as has never, but once, been subjected to the soil of printer's fingers. No, they were never meant nor made for criticism! Enjoy them, or let them alone.

If it was "impossible to write solemnly and austerely" about the annuals, what then was the critic's task? To offer "guidance" for purchase.[32] In the language of the *Monthly Repository* the entire circuit, from the annual, to its purchaser and woman reader, to the reviewer who makes a facsimile of it, is placed beyond criticism. Thus naturalized ("a bed of tulips"), the trifling annuals could accomplish their substantial effects.

When the *Keepsake* reached Rydal Mount at the end of January 1829 Wordsworth tactfully, if somewhat comically, sidestepped Reynolds's curiosity about his opinion by pleading "a fall upon my head" from his horse. Furthermore, he continued: "I deem such judgement of ["the *absolute* merit of works of this kind"] of little Value. What you have to consider is the fitness of the Articles for the Market, everything else is comparatively insignificant" (*LY*, 2:13–14).

This plain dealing determined Wordsworth's eventual rupture with the *Keepsake*. To fulfill his agreement Wordsworth had supplied "The Country Girl" (later called "The Gleaner"), "The Triad," "The Wishing-Gate," and six sonnets. Reynolds had previously informed him that his contributions "only filled eleven pages and a half," and Wordsworth had "readily agreed to make up the deficiency," but when he discovered that Reynolds had caused the shortfall by deciding to print only two of the six sonnets he made a stand: "I certainly don't expect that a claim for more should be grounded upon rejection, for you clearly see, if this principle be admitted – I might write on for ever, before my part of the Contract were fulfilled" (*LY*, 2:14–15).[33] "What think you," Dora wrote to Maria Jane Jewsbury, "Mr Heath says he 'has a right to distribute [the] one hundred guinea contribution over twenty years if he pleases'!"[34] Wordsworth regarded Heath and Reynolds as having "broken the contract" by their actions; he demanded the return of his manuscripts and never again appeared in the *Keepsake* (*DWL*, 53).

This contractual disagreement, not distaste for the publication, led to Wordsworth's quitting the *Keepsake*. In 1826 Wordsworth lamented the "poor account . . . of my progress in Composition" and confessed that he "could not get over the idea which long ago haunted" him, that he had written too much (*LY*, 1:473). In the comparative barrenness of these years the *Keepsake* was invigorating. "The Triad," for example, which Wordsworth thought contained "some of the happiest verses" that he had ever written, "had been promised several years . . . before a fancy fit for the performance struck me – it was then thrown off rapidly – and afterwards revised with care" (*LY*, 1:689). The "fancy" came in spring 1828, after the visit of Reynolds and Heath, the *Keepsake* its impetus and destination. So, too, with "The Wishing-Gate," a memorializing of a cherished spot in Grasmere Vale consonant with the conventions of the annual; and so, too, with "The Country Girl," written specifically to accompany an engraving of a picture by the miniaturist James Holmes.

His obligation fulfilled (as he thought), Wordsworth fell silent. He confided to Quillinan in November 1828: "I have not written a verse these 9 months past – my vein I fear is run out" (*LY*, 1:656).

Yet by mid December, before the arrival at Rydal Mount of the 1829 *Keepsake* and the break it occasioned, he told Reynolds:

Depend upon it one year with another you shall have no right to complain – And this year the account shall be set straight. I am rather rich, having produced 730 verses during the last month – after a long fallow – In the list are two stories – and three incidents – so that your wish may be gratified, by some one or more of these Pieces. (*LY*, 1:692)

As the opening sentence indicates, Wordsworth looked forward to continuing his relationship with the *Keepsake*. If it would be crass to reduce Wordsworth's declaration "I am rather rich" to the satisfaction in foreseeing another hundred guineas, it is equally misleading to posit visitings of imagination wholly independent of financial incentive. Still more important than the payment the *Keepsake* offered was the stimulus of renewed exchange with an audience, fresh starts rather than reworked collected editions. A view that idealizes Wordsworth's creativity and regards his involvement with the *Keepsake* as an unfortunate mistake cannot capture the more complex but less dramatic dynamics of the situation, that of a professional writer responding to circumstance. His engagement represents less apostasy from an earlier purity than a manifestation of an investment in the literary market present from the beginning of his career.

The verse written in the unexpectedly productive month exemplifies Wordsworth's exploration of new genres. The most successful was "The Egyptian Maid," described by the poet as "a kind of romance with as much magic in it as would serve for half a Dozen" (*LY*, 1:663). A beautiful princess, a boat carved with the sacred emblem of the lotus, a shipwreck in the Scilly Islands engineered by a capricious Merlin, the revival of the maid by the purity of Galahad: this invented Arthurian fable remains unique in his canon, but would have been quite at home in the *Keepsake*. Wordsworth had evidently studied the style, and quickly matched it. The poem "rose from my brain, without let or hindrance, like a vapour," he continued, not scrupling to recall for this show of artisanship the sublime revelation of book 6 of the *Prelude*:

> Imagination – here the Power so called
> Through sad incompetence of human speech,
> That awful Power rose from the mind's abyss
> Like an unfathered vapour.   (1850, 592–95)[35]

Wordsworth read the "wizard and fairy" poem to James Spedding, a friend of Tennyson whose "Lady of Shalott" he anticipated by four years. Spedding commented: "I should not have expected anything so good from him which was so much out of his beat."[36] "Beat" is doubly accurate, because for "The Egyptian Maid" Wordsworth improvised an unusual six-line stanza he employed nowhere else; two other erotic narratives from this period equally adapted for the *Keepsake*, "The Russian Fugitive" and "The Armenian Lady's Love," are also written in unique stanza forms.

Because of the disagreement over terms, these works did not appear in the *Keepsake*. Nonetheless, the formal virtuosity and the range of subjects (chivalric, Russian, medieval – Wordsworth also projected an Oriental tale [*LY*, 1:695–96] – far removed from the native English landscapes and earnest tones of his characteristic work) demonstrate how the *Keepsake* rejuvenated Wordsworth, diversifying and lightening his repertory. After a career-long suspicion of popular narrative, the almost sixty-year-old poet was learning new tricks. The poems did appear in *Yarrow Revisited* and helped to make that 1835 volume Wordsworth's most successful in many years.

Wordsworth's accommodation to his audience is conspicuous in the poems Reynolds chose to print, and so, too, therefore are the contradictory signals the *Keepsake* emits. Consider "The Triad." In rejecting the "Naiad," "Dryad," and "Sea-nymph" of classical mythology (ll.8–11) and summoning instead from the "chaster coverts of a British hill" (l.14) the three maids of the title – Edith May Southey, Dora Wordsworth, and Sara Coleridge, under pseudonyms – Wordsworth carries out the concern of the annuals with British beauty. "The Triad" is virtually an epitome of the annual poem, turning the three actual girls of the Wordsworth circle into a duplicate of the three graces at the foot of the volume's presentation plate. In composing a narrative of three beautiful women assembled for a comparative judgment, a replaying of the Judgment of Paris that is finally no judgment at all but a collective compliment, Wordsworth placed within the *Keepsake* a microcosm of the terms in which the annuals themselves were received. North in 1826 welcomes the rival annuals in an extended conceit comparing the "four virgin volumes" to four beautiful girls entering his room, and concludes: "Now, we know not how we could better have expressed our satisfaction on beholding the entrée into our Sanctum Sanctorum of these Four Blooming Perennials. They are all jewels – delights – perfect loves."[37] With "The Triad" Wordsworth distilled the essence of the annual: under the guise of variety and discrimination, the construction of a single image of the feminine.[38]

The dissonant if muted resonances that image sets off sound in "The Country Girl" (plate 3.4). Though Wordsworth said he had in mind "a sweet Creature" who "lives near the Blue Bell, Tillington," the poem was ordered for Holmes's picture. The author who condemned the tyranny of the eye and who in 1846 blasted such popular novelties as the *Illustrated London News*, subordinated his art to the pictorial aesthetics fostered by the steel plate. Only the conclusion sounds a Wordsworthian note; had the girl been carrying "idle flowers" (l.21), the speaker professes, he would have remained captive to the "sweet illusion" (l.25) of "bliss that grows without a care" (l.8), but he has been freed by a sign of labor:[39]

> Thanks to this tell-tale sheaf of corn
> That touchingly bespeaks thee born
> Life's daily tasks with them to share
> Who, whether from their lowly bed
> They rise, or rest the weary head,
> Ponder the blessing they entreat
> From Heaven, and *feel* what they repeat,
> While they give utterance to the prayer
> That asks for daily bread.   (50–51; *PW*, 415)

In the 1828 *Keepsake* there is an engraving of "The Peasant Girl"; as the symmetry suggests, Wordsworth was practicing a formula, but his distinctive chastening of "Arcadian" dreams (l.5) nicely corrects the too-pat conclusion of the anonymous poem accompanying the 1828 plate: "Peasant Girl! I envy thee" (107). As he did with "The Triad" (79), Reynolds completed the page with a *jeu d'esprit* of his own, "On Two Sisters," in the antithetical manner Wordsworth detested:

> Young Dora's gentle, pure, and kind,
> With lofty, clear, and polish'd mind:
> But Dora, rich in mental grace,
> Alas! is somewhat poor in face;
> Pity her noble soul don't warm
> Grecian statue's perfect form!
>
> But, Anne, in thee all charms combine;
> Each gift of beauty, sweet, is thine!
> Thy form surpasses e'en desire;
> Thine eyes are rolling orbs of fire!
> Enchanting, perfect is the whole –
> Pity the statue wants a soul!   (51)

Plate 3.4 James Holmes, *The Country Girl*

Wordsworth, who expended particular attention to the way in which poems in his collections shaded into each other, let this juxtaposition pass without protest.[40]

The opposition in Reynolds's dreadful poem between one sister of "noble soul" and the other whose "form surpasses e'en desire" and whose "eyes are rolling orbs of fire" discloses an anxiety that the *Keepsake* cannot wholly tame. Despite the idealizing rhetoric with which the annual depicts women, the mechanical symmetry of Reynolds's text insists upon "warm" bodily "form." The ample figure, *décolletage*, and coy sidewise posture of Holmes's country girl betray the same eroticism, repeated in Wordsworth's celebration of the girl's "lip – a rose-bud from the thorn" and fantasy of "happiness that never flies . . . whispering of promise." Like "The Egyptian Maid," "The Armenian Lady's Love," and "The Russian Fugitive," the poem and plate exude a sensuality the more insinuating the more it is denied. As in the flirtation with the foreign other, the active role taken by women in their production, the class antagonisms visible beneath the lexicon of taste, or in the recurrent appetitive tropes, the annuals show what they would suppress. *The Monthly Repository* expatiating on the lady's boudoir and jeweled, quivering fingers renders transparent the disavowed erotic saturation that surfaces throughout the *Keepsake* and in the discourse surrounding the annuals. That Wordsworth should call in labor to interrupt this efflorescence is characteristic not only of him but also of the enterprise as a whole; but the more labor, the more the sensual image proliferated.

The eroticized and feminized universe the annuals inhabited could effortlessly absorb the edition that Wordsworth had arduously revised and spent two years in placing, the five-volume *Poetical Works* of 1827. In his article "Christmas Presents" of January 1828, Christopher North reviews recent publications by the fiction of selecting from them titles suitable for girls of his circle: "a Chosen Band of maidens, to receive from the hands of good old Father Christopher – each an appropriate volume or volumes to add to her little library, growing by degrees, year after year, like a garden that the skilful florist extends with its sloping banks towards the sunny south." In this tableau of the genial patriarch surrounded by reverent pupils the *Poetical Works* are bestowed upon Margaret Wilson:

There – hold them fast to your bosom – and let not one of all the Five slip from your embracing arms. Wordsworth's works! . . . Yes – thou mayest, unblamed, place such poetry on the very same shelf, Margaret, with thy Bible; for the word of God itself is better understood by hearts softened and sublimed by strains inspired into the souls of great Poets by devoutest contemplation of his works. Therefore, child, "with gentle hand / Touch, for there is a spirit in the leaves!"[41]

This absorption is no egregious misprision by North; as his deft invocation of "Nutting" shows, Wordsworth was more than susceptible to such an interpretation.[42] In specifying the source of poetry in the preface to the *Lyrical Ballads* as "the spontaneous overflow of powerful feelings" (*PW*, 740) Wordsworth located poetry in a territory traditionally belonging to women. Though combatted by the chivalric action of Scott's romances, the potent sexual imago of Byron, the philosophic complexity of Coleridge, and Wordsworth's repeated emphasis on his "manly" style (*PW*, 739) and ethical gravity (not facile emotion but "emotion recollected in tranquillity" [*PW*, 740]), the identification with women of the passions Romantic poetry placed at its center remained. As Stuart Curran has wittily phrased it, the suspicion would not die that the real language of men was the language of women.[43] From Charlotte Smith and Helen Maria Williams to Felicia Hemans, Letitia Landon, and Joanna Baillie, moreover, the realm of poetry was dominated by a series of successful professional women; in the novel, the predominance was yet more marked.

Defining poetry in terms of inwardness, as Wordsworth's grateful convalescent John Stuart Mill was shortly to do, thus produced a diminishing relegation to the private and the feminine that the Romantic writer recuperated by staging scenes in which he might figure as authoritative instructor to the women with whom he feared he was joined. Nowhere is this tactic more brilliantly exposed than in Charlotte Brontë's *The Professor*, initially titled *The Master* (posthumous; 1857). Her schoolteacher hero, the aptly named William Crimsworth, marries a Swiss seamstress who occasionally violates domestic decorum and teases him "with a wild and witty wickedness":

This was rare, however, and the elfish freak was always short: sometimes when driven a little hard in the war of words – for her tongue did ample justice to the pith, the point, the delicacy of her native French, in which language she always attacked me – I used to turn upon her with my old decision, and arrest bodily the sprite that teased me. No sooner had I grasped hand or arm than the elf was gone; the provocative smile quenched in the expressive brown eyes, and a ray of gentle homage shone under the lids in its place. I had seized a mere vexing fairy, and found a submissive and supplicating little mortal woman in my arms. Then I made her get a book, and read English to me for an hour by way of penance. I frequently dosed her with Wordsworth in this way, and Wordsworth steadied her soon; she had a difficulty in comprehending his deep, serene, and sober mind; his language, too, was not facile to her; she had to ask questions, to sue for explanations, to be like a child and a novice, and to acknowledge me as her senior and director. Her instinct instantly penetrated and possessed the meaning of more ardent writers. Byron excited her; Scott she loved; Wordsworth only she puzzled at, wondered over, and hesitated to pronounce an opinion upon.[44]

The vignette epitomizes the themes of nationalism and class that this chapter has touched upon; most of all, it epitomizes the recurrent drama of the paradoxically erotic virgin doubled with the male writer as her teacher – Wordsworth in earnest with Dorothy, Father Christopher with his band of maidens in extravagance (perhaps also sending up Alaric Watts as Father of the Annuals). Wordsworth proves a discipline more effective and satisfying than corporal pressure. But as the scene was imagined by a woman who would have published under a masculine pseudonym, the instability of the hierarchical oppositions remains: no wonder North became so arch.

The *Keepsake* provides the kind of fascinating success story that enlivens the chronicles of Victorian entrepreneurship: the rapid exploitation of technological advance, the cross-country tour of Reynolds and Heath to sign contributors and steal a march on rivals like Cunningham, the fearless risking of capital to permit business on an unheard-of scale, the mobilization of extensive publicity, the mushrooming circulation of the product, and the financial rewards commensurate with such tireless activity. But this production depended upon a vision of woman as domestic, decorous, and decorated, the target audience and the site for the profit-generating consumption. To the degree that the middle-class woman developed taste, her desires ("hers" here covering "those aroused in her") functioned as the motor of the system from which her male counterparts derived their income, even as she was figured as the virtuous domestic antithesis to the marketplace. In that role she converged with the aristocracy, for it was they who embodied magnanimous culture against philistinism and *laissez-faire* economics. The alliance between titled names and women in the pages of the *Keepsake* points on the one hand to the suasive hegemony they sought to establish, the "beauty" that dignified by disguising their "sublime" competitive nature and rewrote class as gender; on the other, the values they represent perpetually rebuke the commercial language of the enterprise even as that language betrays them. The annuals discomfitingly expose the homology between the productivity of the Romantic artwork, the *Bildung* it enacts and sponsors, and the mysteriously auratic commodity.

The male Romantic poet played a telling part in this cultural formation, as the eagerness of the proprietors to legitimate their enterprise by paying generously for his participation indicates. In one of the most exalted and frequently quoted passages of the preface to the *Lyrical Ballads* Wordsworth reaffirmed his mission: "For the human mind is capable of being excited without the application of gross and violent stimulants; and he must have a very faint perception of its beauty and dignity who does not know this, and who does not further know, that one being is elevated above another, in proportion as he possesses this capability" (*PW*, 735). It is a smaller step than Wordsworth would have cared to acknowledge from this rhetoric of psychic delicacy and elevation to such pronouncements as that of the *Monthly Review* that it would be impossible for anyone who had looked at the engravings of the annuals to "endure anything either common or vulgar for the remainder of the year." The annuals merchandised not goods *per se* but the elusive promise of refinement, and the magi of that intangible quality were the Romantic poets.

By persevering against hostile reviews for more than twenty-five years, Wordsworth met the task he posited as that of every great and original poet, that of "*creating* the taste by which he is to be enjoyed" (*PW*, 750). Or, at any rate, he had established a reputation for spiritual power, and consistent with a poetics that cherished an indefinable height and depth of soul abstracted from the work, his name alone could now certify its possession. Looking back on his experience, Wordsworth dismissed the "ornamented annuals" as "those greedy receptacles of trash, those Bladders upon which the Boys of Poetry try to swim" (*LY*, 2:275–76), but it was the "men," recuperatively self-constituting themselves against the women with whom they were too closely linked, rather than the "boys," who had a ware to sell. In the annuals where the poet's name became his capital, Romantic poetry realized (I use the word deliberately) itself; the consumer society that Romanticism repudiated at the level of statement made slogans of its precepts. The Romantic poet and the acquisitive bourgeois subject there stand twinned.

NOTES

1 "Christopher North" [John Wilson], "Monologue, or Soliloquy on the Annuals," *Blackwood's Edinburgh Magazine* 26 (1829), 948–76, 955. Hereafter cited parenthetically in the text as "Soliloquy."

2 This account of the annuals draws on Bradford Booth, *A Cabinet of Gems* (Berkeley: University of California Press, 1938), and Anne Renier, *Friendship's Offering* (London: Private Libraries Association, 1964). Ackermann developed continental models; for some of the English precursors, see Alison Adburgham, *Women in Print* (London: George Allen & Unwin, 1972), chapters 10 and 15.

3 S. M. Ellis, *William Harrison Ainsworth and His Friends* (2 vols.; London: John Lane, 1911), vol. 1, 160.

4 *Gentleman's Magazine*, November 1829, 442.

5 *Blackwood's Edinburgh Magazine* 17 (1825), 94.

6 *The London Literary Gazette and Journal of Belles Lettres, Arts, Sciences, etc.* 614, Saturday 25 October 1828, 688.

7 Ellis attributes this essay to Ainsworth (vol. 1, 166); Louis Landré, *Leigh Hunt* (2 vols.; Paris: Société d'Edition "Les Belles Lettres," 1935), vol. 2, 494, and Renier (8) ascribe it to Leigh Hunt. Andrew Boyle identifies it as Ainsworth's in *An Index to the Annuals* (Worcester: Andrew Boyle, 1967), 8.

8 *Monthly Review*, n.s. 3, 7 (1828), 66.

9 *Monthly Magazine*, n.s. 4 (1827), 585.

10 *Monthly Repository*, n.s. 1 (1827), 926.

11 *The Journal of Sir Walter Scott*, ed. W. E. K. Anderson (Oxford: Clarendon, 1972), 421, 441, 457.

12 *New Letters of Robert Southey*, ed. Kenneth Curry (2 vols.; New York: Columbia University Press, 1965), vol. 2, 322. Hereafter cited parenthetically in the text as *NLS*.

13 *The Life and Correspondence of Robert Southey*, ed. Charles Cuthbert Southey (6 vols.; London: Longman, 1850), vol. 5, 336. Hereafter cited parenthetically in the text as *LCS*.

14 *Letters of Robert Southey to John May 1797–1838*, ed. Charles Ramos (Austin, Texas: Jenkins, 1976), 233.

15 *Selections from the Letters of Robert Southey*, ed. John Wood Warter (4 vols.;

London: Longman, 1856), vol. 4, 103. Hereafter cited parenthetically in the text as *SLS*.

16 *The Letters of William and Dorothy Wordsworth, The Later Years, Part I, 1821–1828*, 2nd edn., ed. Alan G. Hill (Oxford: Clarendon, 1978), 583. This volume and its companion, *The Letters of William and Dorothy Wordsworth, The Later Years, Part II, 1829–1834*, 2nd edn., ed. Alan G. Hill (Oxford: Clarendon, 1979), are hereafter cited parenthetically in the text as *LY*.

17 *Letters of Dora Wordsworth*, ed. Howard P. Vincent (Chicago: Packard, 1944), 39. Hereafter cited parenthetically in the text as *DWL*.

18 Given that Jewsbury was a friend of Alaric Watts and a contributor to the *Literary Souvenir*, Dora was scarcely being tactful. In *Ambitious Heights* (London: Routledge, 1990) Norma Clarke acutely analyzes the precarious "balance between brilliance, which gained her initial entry, and the appropriate feminine behaviour which would assure [Jewsbury's] continued welcome" in the Wordsworth circle (61–68).

19 W. J. B. Owen, "Costs, Sales, and Profits of Longman's Editions of Wordsworth," *The Library*, n.s. 12 (1957), 93–107.

20 Samuel Smiles, *A Publisher and His Friends* (2 vols.; London: John Murray, 1891), vol. 2, 245.

21 Owen, 104. As I read Owen, Wordsworth would have made more money from the 1827 edition had he stayed with his arrangement of no expense but half profits: £566 rather than £422. But presumably it was Wordsworth's readiness to undertake two-thirds of the costs that persuaded Longman to risk the large edition Wordsworth wanted; had the edition been the customary 500, Wordsworth's balance (based on an admittedly crude and speculative prorating of costs and profits) would have been roughly £145 under his former contracts and £192 under the current one. The disparity illustrates John A. Sutherland's contention in *Victorian Novelists and Publishers* (London: Athlone; Chicago: University of Chicago Press, 1976) that within the profit-sharing system the interests of publishers and authors were opposed, the publisher seeking safely to cover costs in a small edition rather than to maximize his and the author's potential profit (47).

22 *Collected Letters of Samuel Taylor Coleridge*, ed. Earl Leslie Griggs (6 vols.; Oxford: Clarendon, 1956–71), vol. 6, 761. Hereafter cited parenthetically in the text as *STCL*. How overriding the display of the company and the monies spent to obtain them were to the success of the annuals can be seen in Coleridge's statement, no doubt echoing the proprietors, that Scott's story in the 1829 *Keepsake* "was to have been a Cannongate Tale, had not Mr Heath *outbid*" (*STCL* 6:757).

23 *The Letters of Charles Lamb, To Which Are Added Those of His Sister Mary Lamb*, ed. E. V. Lucas (3 vols.; London: Dent, 1935), vol. 3, 179.

24 Expansion of the preface to *Lyrical Ballads*, *PW*, 737; *The Letters of William and Dorothy Wordsworth, The Early Years 1787–1805*, ed. Ernest

de Selincourt, 2nd edn., revised by Chester L. Shaver (Oxford: Clarendon, 1967), 355.

25 The capture of Moore illustrates Reynolds's aggressiveness. As Moore narrated the episode, Reynolds first offered him "a guinea a line" for a hundred lines of poetry; when Moore "declined having any thing to do" with the *Keepsake* he upped the ante to £500 for 100 pages of prose or poetry. When Moore once more declined, Reynolds proposed "£600 for 120 pages." Moore "unreservedly" refused: "And what after all this does my gentleman do? Having got hold of some lines which I wrote one day after dinner (about ten years since) in Perry's copy of Lalla Rookh, he, without saying a single word to me, clips this doggrel into his book, and announces me brazenly on the List of his Contributors. Thus, not having been able to *buy* my name he tricks me out of it, and gets gratis what I refused six hundred pounds for." Moore "wrote up to him in a rage & demanded that the lines should be omitted," but the sheets had already been printed. *The Journal of Thomas Moore*, ed. Wilfred S. Dowden (6 vols; Newark: University of Delaware Press, 1986), vol. 3, 1161–62. A retraction stating that "Mr. Moore . . . is not a Contributor" appeared in the advertisements, but the "Extempore" is to be found on page 120 of the *Keepsake*.

26 *Blackwood's Edinburgh Magazine* 17 (1825), 96. The critical perspective on the aesthetic discourse of the annuals developed in the following pages has been shaped by Colin Campbell, *The Romantic Ethic and the Spirit of Modern Consumerism* (Oxford: Blackwell, 1987), Terry Eagleton, *The Ideology of the Aesthetic* (Oxford: Blackwell, 1990), and Mary Poovey, *Uneven Developments* (Chicago: University of Chicago Press, 1988).

27 *The Athenaeum*, 12 November 1828, 864.

28 That the epigram is pure filler is corroborated by its absence from the table of contents; so also is Reynolds's squib following "The Triad," discussed below.

29 *Monthly Review*, n.s., 10 (1829), 100.

30 *Monthly Review*, n.s., 12 (1829), 435.

31 And not just the province. Adburgham observes that because the annuals "had large sales in Britain's Indian empire, as well as in America and the Colonies, they were produced by the end of July to be shipped for the long voyage round the Cape" (261–62).

32 *Monthly Repository*, n.s., 2 (1828), 845.

33 For the rejected sonnets see *LY*, 2:14 n.4; the shying-away of the *Keepsake* from the masculine realms of the sublime and history may be judged from Reynolds's exclusion of "Roman Antiquities Discovered, at Bishopstone, Herefordshire," on which I have written in "Cleansing the Images: Wordsworth, Rome, and the Rise of Historicism," *Texas Studies in Literature and Language* 33 (1991), 271–326.

34 "You must take what comes and be content" was Wordsworth's motto

(*LY*, 1:692), but by not printing all an author's contributions Reynolds might stock material for the next year's volume gratis. On this rock the relation between several writers and the *Keepsake* foundered: though he too had supplied adequate material, Coleridge learned that because in 1829 Reynolds had selected fewer than the set number of pages he was expected to write for the 1830 volume without added remuneration (*STCL*, 6:779); Scott also disputed claims of indebtedness and ultimately withdrew: "And so farewell to Mr. Heath and [that] conceited vulgar Cockney his Editor" (*Journal*, 525).

35 *The Poetical Works of William Wordsworth*, ed. Thomas Hutchinson, revised by Ernest de Selincourt (London: Oxford University Press, 1950), 535. Hereafter cited parenthetically as *PW*.

36 Quoted by Bernard Groom, *The Unity of Wordsworth's Poetry* (London: Macmillan, 1966), 192. I follow Groom's survey of the metrical variety of this group of "fantasies" (191–93).

37 *Blackwood's Edinburgh Magazine* 19 (1826), 81.

38 Frederic Colwell has recently written that "The Triad" "domesticates and countrifies the elaborate conceit of a traditional court masque or entertainment." *Rivermen* (Kingston, Ont.: McGill-Queen's University Press, 1989), 48. Sara Coleridge was keenly alert to the contradictions of this program; while conceding that the poem was "extremely elegant, verse such as none but a great poetic artist could have produced," she dismissed it as "extravagant and unnatural as a description of three young ladies of the 19th century." In characterizing the work "as a mongrel – an amphibious thing, neither portrait nor ideal, but an ambiguous cross between the two," she trenchantly identifies the conflict that marks the poem as a product of the "19th century," or at least as a typical specimen of the *Keepsake*. Leslie Nathan Broughton (ed.), *Sara Coleridge and Henry Reed* (Ithaca, N.Y.: Cornell University Press, 1937), 68–70.

39 In *The Current of Romantic Passion* (Madison: University of Wisconsin Press, 1991) Jeffrey Robinson traces the poem's revision of "dangerous idleness" into "the exercise of prayer" (137–39).

40 Wordsworth did tell Reynolds "as a Friend" that his "Verses upon the Coquette [119] are too coarse for so fine dress'd a publication" and his "Invitation [To a Beautiful But Very Small Young Lady; 100] . . . not so happy as some light things I have seen from your Pen," but he passed Reynolds's other pieces, and their effect on him, without comment (*LY*, 2:14).

41 *Blackwood's Edinburgh Magazine* 23 (1828), 7–9.

42 North alters Wordsworth's last line, "there is a spirit in the woods," to make a pun on "leaves" that reinforces the naturalness of Wordsworth's volumes. Gene Ruoff has pointed out to me that the exclamation of the *Monthly Repository* over the annuals – "Enjoy them, or let them alone" – likewise parodies the last line of Wordsworth's

"The Redbreast and the Butterfly" (published in 1807): "Love him, or leave him alone!"

43 See Stuart Curran, "The I Altered," *Romanticism and Feminism*, ed. Anne K. Mellor (Bloomington: Indiana University Press, 1988), 185–207. On Byron's uneasy relationships with the women who made up his audience, see the incisive chapter by Sonia Hofkosh in that volume, "The Writer's Ravishment," 93–114, and my *Reading Romantics* (New York: Oxford University Press, 1990), 145–62.

44 Charlotte Brontë, *The Professor* (London: Oxford University Press, 1959), 241–42.

CHAPTER 4

Copyright and the publishing of
Wordsworth, 1850–1900

Stephen Gill

Copyrights need be hereditary, for genius isn't.

Dickens, on meeting William Wordsworth, Jr., 1839

When his own reputation was at its nadir, Wordsworth declared that support for the poet's life of "solitary and unremitting labour" would be found in "encouragement from a grateful few . . . applauding Conscience, and . . . a prophetic anticipation, perhaps of fame, a late though lasting consequence."[1] To which he might have added the hope of leaving something for one's children. Before his death, Wordsworth, Poet Laureate and Hon. D.C.L., had achieved fame, and meagre though the financial rewards were that he had enjoyed, he died with the knowledge that recent copyright legislation had secured for his family a substantial literary property.

On the shelves of any major collection of later nineteenth-century editions of Wordsworth, brightly colored single volumes advertise themselves against sober-suited multivolume sets in a quantity that discloses an important fact of literary history – that Wordsworth the great Romantic poet was a Victorian publishing phenomenon. Almost certainly, more copies of Wordsworth were sold in the ten years from 1860 to 1870 than in the fifty-seven years of his publishing lifetime, but the fact is that no one knows how many. Nor do we know exactly in what form they all appeared, for there is, astonishingly, no Wordsworth bibliography.[2] Professor Mark L. Reed of the University of North Carolina at Chapel Hill is at work on one, and he faces a Herculean task.[3] Most Victorian scholars will have seen at least the six-volume sets issued at intervals by Moxon and latterly by Ward, Lock, as well as the extraordinarily lavish editions of the late century such as William Knight's eleven massive volumes of 1882–89 with their ten-volume follow-up in 1896, and Edward Dowden's seven-volume Aldine edition of 1892/93. Alongside these grand productions range the single-volume texts from Routledge, Nimmo, Nelson, Gall and Inglis, Warne, Macmillan, and many others. But this is only the superior end of the market. What Reed will also be prospecting are provincial editions, empire editions, innumerable selections, illustrated issues of single poems (some of these using photographs), pamphlets, issued, for example, by the SPCK (the Society for Promoting Christian Knowledge), and the new phenomenon of the school text. Then there are the phantoms. Perhaps Reed will locate a copy of the pamphlet of "The Happy Warrior" struck off privately for circulation among the troops in the Crimea, not one copy of which is known to survive.[4] In short, we do not yet have a complete picture of how many Wordsworth titles were issued, or in what form or runs. What is clear is that between 1850 and 1900 Wordsworth was issued in extraordinary quantity across a wide range of publishing styles.

What determined the nature of this publishing activity, however, both its local manifestations and its overall trajectory, was the law of copyright for whose reform Wordsworth had lobbied energetically in the late 1830s. The act that was eventually passed in 1842 established copyright for the period of forty-two years from the date of a work's publication, or until seven years after the author's death, whichever was the longer; and Wordsworth died in 1850. The situation, though, was a odd one. Almost all of Wordsworth's best poetry had been published as far back as 1807, the date of his second great lyrical collection, *Poems, in Two Volumes*. This, and the two further volumes issued in 1815, it is generally agreed, mark the end of his great period. Wordsworth himself regarded them as a milestone. *The Excursion* had been published the previous year, and now all the lyrical poetry, classified according to a scheme of the poet's own devising, was presented in the substantial collected *Works*. But to him the edition was a milestone on a continuing way. We may judge that Wordsworth's real life as a poet was over by 1815, but he emphatically did not. In the two collected volumes he was tidying up, not making an end. He went on steadily issuing new volumes of original poetry until 1842 and substantially revised versions of the collected *Works* until the very last year of his life. In 1849/50 a six-volume set appeared as the poet's final authorized edition. And he left *The Prelude* ready for posthumous publication. Among his papers was also *The Recluse*, book 1, the poem now known as "Home at Grasmere," not fully prepared for publication but publishable.

So the position was this: according to agreements entered into by the poet himself in 1836 and renegotiated by his literary executors in 1856 and again in 1877, Edward Moxon & Co., followed by Ward, Lock & Tyler, had exclusive rights to all Wordsworth's copyright material, published and unpublished.[5] Until 1892 – forty-two years after the final authorized edition – they alone could claim to publish the complete poetical works. But this claim was more valuable in appearance than in fact, for after 1857, that is, seven years after the poet's death, anyone could publish the best of Wordsworth – the *Lyrical Ballads*, the 1807 poems, *The Excursion* – and they did.

Until 1892, Wordsworth's authorized publishers continued to issue the complete *Poetical Works of William Wordsworth* in six volumes and in a magnificent one-volume format, but they, and Wordsworth's heirs, his sons John and William, Jr., were haunted by the clock. One by one, Wordsworth's collected editions and separate volumes of original poetry came out of copyright protection. In 1857 the 1815 two-volume collection came out of copyright; in 1869 the 1827 five-volume collection; in 1877 the popular *Yarrow Revisited* volume of 1835; and in 1884 the last original volume, the 1842 *Poems, Chiefly of Early and Late Years*. Even the posthumous *Prelude* came into the public domain in 1892. On 4 June 1866, J. B. Payne of Moxon & Co. remarked in a gloomy letter, "we must not, however, shut our eyes to the melancholy fact that each year renders our hold on the copyrights more slender, & the literary pirates more bold & successful in their depredations." It was not necessary for him to spell it out: John and William Wordsworth, Jr. were all too well aware of their situation.

In the long term, of course, there was nothing they could do. Unlike shares in a manufacturing company, the value of a literary property can only diminish, and this was a prospect that neither of the sons could contemplate with equanimity. By succeeding his father in 1843 as official distributor of stamps, William Wordsworth, Jr. had acquired the gentlemanly income that had previously eluded him, but changes in revenue legislation eroded it so severely that by 1851 Henry Crabb Robinson was lamenting "the adversity of one deemed a prosperous man."[6] John Wordsworth was no better placed. A fortunate marriage had lifted him out of the genteel poverty he was enduring as the incumbent of a poor living, but the crash of his wife's family in 1837 reduced him to looking for pupils to supplement his income. Ever-present money worries, his wife's chronic illness, the death of one of his children, and then of his wife, all combined to make him an anxious and touchy man who was determined to make sure that at least one good fortune, his inheritance, should be exploited while time was still on his side.

His opportunity came as the agreement their father had made with Moxon for twenty-one years in 1836 neared expiry. Moxon was eager to continue the Wordsworth connection and had been talking about the desirability of a freshly edited issue of the complete *Works* for some years, but he was not prepared to publish on the old terms. In the future, he proposed, the Wordsworths should receive one-half, not two-thirds, of the profits, an arrangement he was prepared to enter into for a further twenty-one years. William Wordsworth, Jr. was discomposed, but inclined to acquiesce, for he shared his father's sense that their relations with Moxon were not merely commercial. The poet had traveled with his publisher, exchanged Christmas presents, and on one occasion commissioned Moxon to recover his false teeth from the repairers in London. For his part, Moxon, who was a poet himself, stood by Wordsworth even when sales were poor.[7] None of this cut any ice with the Reverend John Wordsworth, who was furious, both with Moxon for proposing new terms and with his brother for inclining to go along with them. He was the more furious because he knew that, ultimately, he was powerless: William was one of his father's literary executors; he was not.

At first John simply protested, leaving his brother to pass on the protest to Moxon in a letter of 20 August 1855.[8] The publisher's reply, however, dispatched the next day, only fanned the fire. Not only did Moxon insist that his terms were "fair and reasonable" but he also pointed out to William that "you and your brother ought to bear in mind that in little more than a year and half from the present time I, in common with every other Publisher, shall be at liberty to print, solely for my own benefit, two thirds of the Poems and those too the best and most popular of the collection." As it was precisely knowledge of this fact that was so agitating John Wordsworth, it is not surprising that Moxon's pointing it out made him angrier and more determined. In a letter of 24 August to William, he declared that, since Moxon's letter makes it clear "that he regards *our relations* as those of *mere business* in which every man is allowed to do the best he can for himself," the family must

look to a publisher who would offer more. The one he had in mind
was George Routledge:

as it appears to me that the time is come when we must look for the
patronage of the masses, & not depend on the middle classes or the
upper class alone, as heretofore, & as he is the head of the *Pub[lishers]*
who accommodates himself to them, & has a machinery at work all over
the world to carry out his system, which he has made so successful, I
would at once hear what he has to say, & to offer.

Now that John had a scheme of his own, his interventions looked
more dangerous, and William took a week to ponder. On 29 August
he indicated that he had carefully weighed Moxon's proposals and
believed them generous; that the past five years' total receipts of
£372 per annum would hardly be likely to tempt a publisher like
Routledge; and that feelings "becoming a gentleman" would not
allow him to engage in anything that smacked of double-dealing.[9]
It may also be that precisely what attracted John to Routledge –
his commercial push toward the lower end of the literary market –
stirred some disdain in William, as it certainly did in his coexecutor
and legal adviser, W. Strickland Cookson.[10] On 4 September 1855
Cookson assured William that they were of one mind on the matter:
"[Routledge] is not the man I should wish to have the publication
of your father's poems."

John grew angrier. On the one hand he accused his brother of
damaging the interests of the family, while on the other, sounding
like Mr. Pecksniff, he accused him of failing in his duty to the
public: "I contend that a 'People's Edition' would be a means
of enlightening & elevating the middle & lower classes, & of
promoting the pecuniary interests of the Poet's posterity" (undated
letter). Stung, perhaps, by his brother's implication that he was not
behaving like a gentleman, John Wordsworth also wrote directly to
Moxon, telling him his views, and to William's coexecutor, John
Carter. In this, the most barbed letter of the series (though he calls
it "a calm and respectful protest"), John insists that his views are
being ignored, that he and his children are being damaged, and,
taking up a higher moral ground, that the executors are frustrating
the wishes of the poet himself:

I refer you to my Father's sonnet on copyright as to his opinion respecting
his posterity *materially* profiting by his intellectual labours.[11] His feeling
was most strong on that subject – He wrote too *of*, & *for, the poor* – were

he asked, being now alive, whether his works should circulate by tens amongst the "rich" or by hundreds amongst the poor, what would be his reply do you think? Routledge's system is adapted to the latter – Moxon's to the former. (undated letter)

For the next month, William temporized. In one letter he tried to mollify Moxon, but he had to take note of his brother's protest, and on 24 October he told Moxon that the executors did not feel able to accept the new terms. The publisher's reply of 26 October was brief and to the point: no alteration in the terms proposed.

It was an impasse. What William did not know was that, dazzled by the lure of Routledge's "system," John had decided to find the way out alone. Secretly entering into negotiations with Routledge, he angled for a one-off payment (possibly up to £2,000) and a guaranteed yearly payment in addition (possibly of £400), a vision he soon floated before his brother. But John was out of his depth. The two surviving letters from George Routledge to John Wordsworth (dated 17 and 25 October 1855) make it clear that he had doubts as to Wordsworth's appeal to the popular market; that the most he was prepared to offer was £300 to £350; that he wanted Moxon's stereotype plates included in any deal; that he would not enter any agreement for more than five years; and that he did not like dealing with someone who was not an executor. Nor had John reckoned with his brother's determination to remain in charge. On 27 October 1855 William told him that as he was "anxious it should be out of your power to say I had been a means of injuring you or your children, by adhering to Moxon's offer," he would raise no further objection "if you can bring Routledge to your own terms of '£400 per annum for the next 10 years,' & get him to settle with Moxon for those copies on hand." William had read Routledge's letters and must have judged that he would agree to no such terms. John Wordsworth retired, nursing a sense of grievance, and the old alliance was reaffirmed when the new agreement with Moxon, half profits for twenty-one years, was signed on 20 June 1856.

For the remainder of the copyright term Moxon, followed by his son, and then by Ward, Lock & Tyler, tried in various ways to maintain, and if possible strengthen their position against the depredations of what Moxon always termed the "pirates." Three main strategies can be discerned. The first was the attempt to create a new copyright "complete" edition. In 1857, that is, when other publishers were first free to move into the market,

Wordsworth's literary executors brought out a new edition, a freshly edited six-volume set that included *The Prelude* (published in 1850), and, for the first time, the so-called "Fenwick Notes" that Wordsworth had dictated in 1843 as a commentary on his whole canon.[12] This new copyright edition, protected for the next forty-two years, remained the Moxon and then Ward, Lock flagship for the rest of the century.[13]

The selling power of the notes was valued highly – almost certainly too highly – by executors and publishers alike, and copyright in them was zealously guarded. In February 1870, for example, Moxon & Co. had to reassure the executors that including Wordsworth in *Moxon's Popular Poets* would not interfere with sales of the copyright edition: "Without the Notes this edition can never be more than an *avant courrier* & advertisement to the complete book" (24 February 1870). In 1874, on the other hand, it was the publishers, now Ward, Lock & Tyler, who were insisting that the notes were too valuable to be parted with. Approached by Alexander Grosart for permission to include them in a proposed collected edition of Wordsworth's prose, William Wordsworth, Jr. was at first inclined to agree, believing that "his doing so would not injuriously affect our interests in the sale of the Poems" (31 October 1874).[14] On 2 November Ward, Lock & Tyler strongly dissented:

Any other volume appearing of your Father's works containing the notes which appear in the six volume Edition would very much interfere with the sale of that Edition as the value attached to the work lies entirely in the notes and anything done to injure the book would be a great pity the work is now known and valued for the notes and we should be indeed sorry to see them appearing elsewhere.

The compromise was obvious and duly adopted. Grosart's project was kept in-house, and the three-volume *Prose Works of William Wordsworth*, including the notes, appeared with the imprint of Edward Moxon, Son, & Co. in 1876.[15]

The second strategy consisted simply of controlling, which largely meant denying, copyright permissions. In theory this might seem a straightforward matter. Permission in all copyright materials is simply denied to anyone other than the authorized publisher. In practice it proved vexatious and far from straightforward.

In 1864, for instance, a certain A. W. Bennett asked and received permission to print some copyright pieces in his forthcoming

Our English Lakes, Mountains, and Waterfall. As seen by William Wordsworth.[16] When this very handsome book came to their notice, however, the Wordsworth camp was horrified. True, Bennett had printed only a few copyright pieces and had courteously acknowledged his obligation to Moxon for permission, but he printed nothing but Wordsworth. His book was a beautifully presented Wordsworth reader, strikingly illustrated with photographs of the Lake District. The compiler's introduction brazenly referred to it as a "Selection from Wordsworth's Poetical Writings." Worse still, Bennett had included a facsimile of the poet's autograph from a scrap of manuscript he had inherited. Bennett was not a pirate. At worst he can be accused of not making his intentions clear when he applied for copyright permission. But his publication was the most piratical that the executors had yet encountered, and they reacted with vigor.

William felt on safe ground. He recollected clearly giving Bennett permission for a list that "did not appear to contain any poems but those that were out of copyright, & I remarked at the time 'that if that were so, as we could not bite, it was no use barking & we might as well make a virtue of necessity – and not refuse his application'." But Bennett had disgracefully exploited this generosity, so William thought, and he asked for Strickland Cookson's help in suppressing at the very least "his most impudent facsimile."[17] On 22 December 1864 Bennett was threatened with a Chancery injunction to prevent the sale of his book unless he undertook to remove the facsimile and all copyright pieces. The executors' position was clear; or rather, it was clear until William Wordsworth, Jr. began to waver. Bennett's book was a *fait accompli* and, moreover, it had sold 1,350 copies in only a few months. Instead of suppressing it, why not use it to make money? And so on 6 January 1865 he proposed that in return for being allowed to use a few more copyright pieces should he so wish, Bennett should hand over one-third of his existing and future profits to Moxon and the Wordsworths and add Moxon's name to the title page. Copyright, it seems, was not sacrosanct provided the sale price was right. Not surprisingly, Bennett refused to countenance William's outrageous proposal. With some protest he swallowed the executors' withdrawal of the permission that had been granted and suppressed the copyright pieces, but he still had a handsome book, and it went through three further editions without the Court of Chancery being disturbed.[18]

At one point in the correspondence Bennett unwittingly touched on the executors' most sensitive nerve. Expressing his hope on 30 August 1865 that they would not hinder another edition, he remarked to William: "should you think well to renew your permission for any or all of them to be included in a new edition, I believe it will give real pleasure to many admirers of Mr Wordsworth's poetry." The Wordsworths were all in favor of pleasing admirers of their father's poetry, but they wanted them to buy authorized editions, not scissors-and-paste productions. When William wrote a kindly letter later in the same year to another would-be anthologist, a Mr. Evans from Manchester, J. B. Payne on behalf of Moxon chided him for his generosity and urged him to hold the line of self-interest.

William Wordsworth, Jr. had to learn how to turn down such requests, but as the century rolled on, a note of desperation entered the correspondence as he recognized that his position was growing weaker every year. In August 1878 William Knight approached him for permission to include some copyright material in his little book *The English Lake District as Interpreted in the Poems of Wordsworth*. When the volume appeared in the same year, the executors were once again dismayed by how much Knight had appropriated, especially from *The Prelude*, but were mollified by the highly respectful tone in which their courtesy was acknowledged. Knight, a professor at the University of St. Andrews and a fanatical Wordsworthian, had bigger ambitions however, and as the majority of Wordsworth's poetry moved toward the end of its copyright term he stunned William, Jr. with a request on 26 March 1879 that went straight to the point. Asserting that earlier kindness "encourages me to ask a further favour at your hands," he went on:

I propose editing a complete edition of the Poet's Works, inserting all my topographical notes, & giving *all* the variations in the text in successive editions, as well as writing a biography, & a critical or expository essay. May I, in this edition which will extend to, (probably,) 8 vols. insert the I. F. "Notes and illustrations of the Poems?"

I infer from passages in the "Memoir" by the Bishop of Lincoln that there are fragments of "the Recluse" still unpublished. If this be so, will you permit me to publish these fragments? . . .

I think the time has fully come for the preparation of a complete library edition of the Poet's works, which will be the best memorial of him. I am anxious to make my edition complete.

This was just what the Wordsworths had been dreading. With sales of the complete *Works* dwindling to vanishing point, the family had for some time been been toying with the idea of a new, big edition.[19] Charles Wordsworth, the bishop of St. Andrews, had raised their hopes that John Campbell Shairp would undertake it, but when Shairp said he was too busy, the bishop had indicated that he would do it himself rather than have the project collapse "for want of an editor" (15 December 1877), and family negotiations about timing, remuneration, and even the publisher, were still in progress when Knight's request arrived. William recognized the urgency of the situation, for Knight's letter, though respectful, had overtones of reproach and even threat. He could not just be fobbed off – he was too substantial a scholar for that – but he had to be stopped; otherwise, William, Jr. foresaw, there would be no end to his "ravenous requests" (27 March 1879). The answer was to assure him that the family was well aware of its duty and had the matter in hand. But the bishop's plan was never more than the pipe dream of someone who had not the faintest idea of what the editorial task would entail, and eventually Knight won the day. He triumphed partly through perseverance and courteous assiduity, partly because he won the support of the next Wordsworth genera-tion,[20] but partly also simply because – as he hinted more than once – in a few years' time he would be free, as others would, to do as he liked. Sensing that they needed Knight almost as much as he needed them, the Wordsworths capitulated, sold *The Prelude* rights for £100 to Knight's Edinburgh publisher, William Paterson, and cooperated from 1882 to 1889 in the production of the first-ever fully edited Wordsworth. They oversaw, in other words, the transference of and care for Wordsworth's text, and the reputation of the family, into academic control.[21]

Their third strategy was to combat the "pirates" by direct competition. Moxon's first attempt was not auspicious. In 1857 – again, when other publishers were first free to enter the market – a one-volume *Earlier Poems of William Wordsworth* was issued con-currently with the six-volume complete *Works*. Edited by William Johnston, who provided some textual apparatus and a serviceable account of Wordsworth's early career, the book was well printed and laid out, but it was unfortunately titled, *The Earlier Poems* suggesting juvenilia rather than poems up to 1814, and it was rather drab. A commercial failure, it was written off in 1868 as having "no probable chance of . . . recouping itself."[22] A year after its publication Routledge showed what could be done. His one-volume Wordsworth also carried an introduction, and it included more poetry than *The Earlier Poems*, but its main appeal was to the eye. Illustrated by Birket Foster, the poems were printed within a red, single-line border on the page and cased in brightly colored, gilt-embossed boards.

Moxon & Co. could produce beautiful books – *The Princess* (1860), for example, is a high spot in any Victorian collection – but it was not until 1865 that an eye-catching production complemented the firm's stately if rather austere multivolume sets of Wordsworth. Yet although the *Selection from the Works of William Wordsworth*, edited and introduced by F. T. Palgrave, was a strikingly beautiful book, and one that the publisher believed enhanced Palgrave's reputation as "a judicious critic & as an elegant scholar," sales never took off.[23] Moxon remained hopeful, but the Wordsworths had to grow used to statements of account accompanied by assurances that the selections would soon "do something for us, & tend to make the balances more respectable" (28 March 1866).

Nor was another venture any luckier. Routledge's editions, and those of some others, generally carried a biographical memoir, cobbled together from the official biography published in 1851 and from De Quincey. In 1870 Moxon decided to launch a new edition, and he was sanguine that it would "prevent these pirates from having it so much their own way as heretofore" (17 February 1870), partly because the volume was to be prefaced by an essay from William Michael Rossetti. When the Wordsworths saw it, however, they were outraged. Not only had Rossetti made some factual errors, he had presented the poet in an unflattering light in writing whose "tone" the bishop of St. Andrews declared "so low and bad throughout that it is impossible to correct or improve it" (10 June 1871). The preface had to go. That Palgrave's preface might be substituted for Rossetti's was one suggestion made. That the family might be forced to publish a repudiation if the Rossetti offence were not suppressed was another. Moxon & Co. weakly defended themselves, claiming that Rossetti was "admittedly one of the best – if not the best – among English critics of the present day," and their legal right to resist suppression was undoubted,[24] but they could not withstand massed family and episcopal displeasure.[25]

Moxon was only one of many publishers competing with attractive editions, a fact that raises a further issue. It can be stated very simply. Wordsworth was presented to Victorian readers in a variety of packagings, but what were they getting? Many eminent Victorians – George Eliot, Mill, Ruskin, and Tennyson, for example – read Wordsworth in the collections published in his lifetime and, of course, so did many others, but I am not concerned with those editions here. Nor do I want to broach the question of what "Wordsworth" readers of varying religious and political persuasions constructed from their experience of the poetry, a topic I have explored elsewhere.[26] My question is quite straightforward: which of Wordsworth's words did someone read who bought an edition published after the poet's death in 1850?

The 1849/50 edition bore the stamp of Wordsworth's final authority. Slightly tidied up, its text remained the basis for all of the Moxon and later Ward, Lock complete poetical *Works* later in the century, and for all serious editions until the appearance of the still ongoing *Cornell Wordsworth* in the 1970s. Victorian readers who cared about these matters and wanted the genuine article, so to speak, bought a Moxon or Ward, Lock edition. Those who preferred a cheaper book, however, or a more attractive one, or who wanted a selection rather than a complete works, were confronted by textual anarchy.

Routledge in 1858, "availing ourselves of every piece which expired copyright places within our reach," reprinted Wordsworth's two-volume collection of 1815 with *The Excursion* added, and continued to do so in subsequent issues.[27] Frederick Warne's "Chandos Classics" in 1872 reprinted the heavily revised five-volume *Collected Edition* of 1827, but when it was reissued as "The Arundel Poets" in 1880 the 1835 *Yarrow Revisited* poems had been incorporated.

For his magnificently illustrated and produced selection in 1859, which featured Birket Foster and others, Robert Aris Wilmott chose to print *An Evening Walk* not from a first edition of 1793, or from the last, or from any single intervening one, but in a text he constructed himself.[28] Other editors of selections enjoyed the exercise of similar creative freedom. They excerpted passages and printed them as poems. They chose pieces from this edition or that and so produced a textual hybrid. They ignored Wordsworth's classification of his poems, preferring to group them according to systems of their own, and perhaps more damaging, they often embellished extracts with titles entirely of their own invention. The little-known Andrew James Symington was one such swashbuckler, the weightier Matthew Arnold was another.[29] For his immensely popular and influential *Poems of Wordsworth* (1879), the future president of the Wordsworth Society classified the poems according to his own sense of decorum in genre, changed and added titles, and presented a text that was neither first nor last edition, but the text of 1832 mixed with readings from later editions where they seemed preferable.[30]

What did this textual anarchy mean in practice? Those who bought the very attractive Gall & Inglis one-volume edition in 1858 read the following lines in *Michael*:

> There is a comfort in the strength of love;
> 'Twill make a thing endurable, which else
> Would break the heart: – old Michael found it so.[31]

But thirty-eight years previously Wordsworth had changed these lines in inspired revision to:

> There is a comfort in the strength of love;
> 'Twill make a thing endurable, which else
> Would overset the brain, or break the heart.

And this was the version that anyone enjoying the poem in a Moxon edition in 1858 would have read. Scores of similar examples could be given, but reading even a representative list would be tedious. One substantial illustration must serve.

The story of Margaret in *The Excursion*, now most commonly read in its early form as *The Ruined Cottage*, was a Victorian favorite. Routledge issued it in 1859 as a separate volume called *The Deserted Cottage*, with illustrations by Birket Foster, J. Wolf, and John Gilbert, and it was frequently reprinted in pamphlet form for use in schools. It appeared in its proper setting in *The Excursion*, of course, in all Moxon complete and rival so-called complete editions. The conclusion to the story of Margaret, however, is an especially important case in the history of Wordsworth's revisions. When it first appeared in *The Excursion* in 1814, exacting Christians objected that it failed to offer explicitly the consolations of Christianity – and one can see why. When the Pedlar attempts to place Margaret's suffering and death in a larger context, what he offers to his listener, the poet, is a purely "natural wisdom" as he closes his story with an evocation of the tranquillity that the dead woman now shares. So the poem stood for thirty years, but in 1845 it was radically changed. Now the poet is told not to grieve for Margaret, for she

> in her worst distress, had ofttimes felt
> The unbounded might of prayer; and learned, with soul
> Fixed on the Cross, that consolation springs,
> From sources deeper far than deepest pain
> For the meek sufferer.

Whereas in 1814 "uneasy thoughts" and "sorrow and despair / From ruin and from change" were tempered by meditation on the natural scene, in 1845 they are

> an idle dream, that could maintain
> Nowhere, dominion o'er the enlightened spirit
> Whose meditative sympathies repose
> Upon the breast of Faith.

These were the Christian words printed in all Moxon editions, of course, and in many others. But by no means in all. Reprinting *The Excursion* from pre-1845 unrevised texts, some editions continued to promulgate the "natural wisdom" version the poet had so decisively altered. This was even true of the little booklets issued for schools. Some pupils in 1865 poring over the text put out by the SPCK encountered, not surprisingly, the Christian version, whereas those in schools that had ordered the Reverend C. H. Bromby's edition ("With Full Notes and a Treatise Upon the Analysis of Sentences"), were reading the "natural wisdom" text.

On a visit to the Quantocks, where Wordsworth and Coleridge had lived during their *annus mirabilis*, William Hale White, "Mark Rutherford," reread *The Excursion*, book 1, and commented, "Much of the religion by which Wordsworth lives is very indefinite. Look at the close of this poem . . . Because this religion is indefinite it is not therefore the less supporting."[32] What he quotes in his journal is the conclusion of the Pedlar's "natural wisdom" in its pre-1845 version. In the revised text the religious consolation offered is not the least "indefinite."

Hale White was a textual scholar and a learned Wordsworthian, so we may, perhaps, assume that he was consciously choosing to read Wordsworth in the text in which he first encountered him as a young man. But for others, whether they found the religion of *The Excursion*, book 1, "indefinite" or not depended on which edition they had bought. No doubt most schoolchildren did not care one way or another. But for us, this example of textual diversity can serve to indicate that whenever discussion touches on the reception of Wordsworth in the Victorian period, caution is in order. Which Wordsworth were they reading, and which Wordsworth are we talking about?

NOTES

1 William Wordsworth, "Reply to 'Mathetes'," *The Prose Works of William Wordsworth*, ed. W. J. B. Owen and Jane Worthington Smyser (3 vols.; Oxford: Clarendon, 1974), vol. 2, 15.

2 Scholars and booksellers refer to T. J. Wise, *A Bibliography of the Writings in Prose and Verse of William Wordsworth* (London: privately printed, 1916) and George Harris Healey, *The Cornell Wordsworth Collection* (Ithaca, N.Y.: Cornell University Press, 1957), but the Wise bibliography is neither comprehensive nor accurate, and the Healey volume, though much more useful, is a catalogue of a collection, not a bibliography.

3 I am deeply indebted to Professor Reed for friendship and counsel over many years. He kindly allowed me access to his Wordsworth collection, as did Professor Paul F. Betz of Georgetown University. Scrutiny of both collections, which revealed the poverty of the holdings of even the British copyright libraries, greatly facilitated the writing of this paper.

4 "Spencer Spring-Rice . . . had copies of *The Happy Warrior* circulated among the troops in the Crimea: it was much more likely to inspire them, he considered, than pious tracts." Edith C. Batho, *The Later Wordsworth* (Cambridge: Cambridge University Press, 1933), 35.

5 Wordsworth's executors were his son William, John Carter, the long-serving clerk and factotum at Rydal Mount, and a distant relative, W. Strickland Cookson of Lincoln's Inn. Edward Moxon died in 1858, and control of the firm passed to his wife, Emma. For the next few years a Mr. Jones conducted business correspondence with the Wordsworths until a new partner, J. B. Payne, took over in 1864. Moxon's son Arthur entered partnership in 1869. Ward, Lock & Tyler took over the firm in 1871, but continued to use the Moxon imprint. On 1 September 1877 Edward Moxon, Son & Co. disappeared into Ward, Lock & Co.

6 Letter of 18 April 1851, in *The Correspondence of Henry Crabb Robinson with the Wordsworth Circle*, ed. Edith J. Morley (2 vols.; Oxford: Clarendon, 1927), vol. 2, 776.

7 For an account of Moxon see Harold G. Merriam, *Edward Moxon: Publisher of Poets* (New York: Columbia University Press, 1939), and

Patricia Anderson and Jonathan Rose (eds.), *British Literary Publishing Houses, 1820–1880* (Detroit: Gale Research, 1991).

8 The correspondence is preserved in the family papers at the Wordsworth Library, Grasmere, and in the Cornell University Library. Some of the letters are in both, the one actually sent being in one library and the copy letter or draft in the other. All other letters quoted in this paper are in the Wordsworth Library. I am grateful to the trustees of Dove Cottage for permission to quote from copyright materials and to Mark Dimunation and the staff of the Rare Books and Manuscripts division of the Olin Library, Cornell University, for their unstinted help.

9 William Wordsworth, Jr. had dealt with a similar situation before. In the year following the poet's death it became clear that Christopher Wordsworth was writing a much more substantial biography than the family had expected (published as *Memoirs of William Wordsworth*, 2 vols., 1851), and that he was trying to maximize financial advantage by offering it to John Murray. This was not in itself dishonorable – Murray was Christopher Wordsworth's own publisher – but it was dishonorable that Moxon was kept in ignorance until Edward Quillinan inadvertently let the cat out of the bag. In a remarkably strong series of letters, now in the Wordsworth Library, William expressed the executors' displeasure, leaving Christopher in no doubt that he was subject to their authority. The *Memoirs* went to Moxon.

10 For some account of Routledge and of his methods and reputation, see Anderson and Rose, and F. A. Mumby, *The House of Routledge 1834–1934* (London: G. Routledge, 1934).

11 John refers to two sonnets written during the copyright agitation of 1838: "A Plea for Authors, May 1838" ("Failing impartial measure to dispense") and "A Poet to His Grandchild" ("'Son of my buried son, while thus thy hand'").

12 For a detailed study of the construction of this important edition, see Jared R. Curtis, "The Making of a Reputation: John Carter's Corrections to the Proofs of Wordsworth's *Poetical Works* (1857)," *Texte* 7 (1988), 61–80.

13 Complementing the six-volume edition for the remainder of the copyright term was a finely produced single volume based on the 1845 one-volume edition, announced on the title-page variously as "The Only Complete Popular Edition" or "Complete Copyright Edition."

14 The Wordsworths felt some obligation to assist Grosart in his project because Henry Crabb Robinson, who died in 1867, had left money with the suggestion "that a portion of the Legacies to the Wordsworths might well be employed by them in defraying the cost of an Edition of the Prose Writings of their Ancestor the great Poet." A comical footnote to the story is that William Wordsworth found himself in

hot water with the orthodox in his family once it was discovered that the Reverend Mr. Grosart was not an Anglican but a Dissenting clergyman.

15 The "Fenwick Notes," named after a Wordsworth family friend, Isabella Fenwick, were dispersed throughout the de Selincourt and Darbishire *Poetical Works* and excluded from the Owen and Smyser edition of the collected prose. Jared Curtis's annotated edition, *The Fenwick Notes of William Wordsworth* (London: Bristol Classical Press, 1993), will, it is to be hoped, restore to due prominence Wordsworth's last great act of imaginative self-assessment.

16 A. W. Bennett, *Our English Lakes, Mountains, and Waterfalls. As seen by William Wordsworth. Photographically illustrated* (London: A. W. Bennett, 1864). The photographs are by T. Ogle. The book is arranged in sections called "Langdale," "Rydale," "Grasmere," and so on, with others called "Descriptions of Scenery," "Poems on Flowers," "Poems on Birds." It ends with the "Ode: Intimations of Immortality."

17 William Wordsworth, Jr. to W. Strickland Cookson, 1 December 1864.

18 The first three editions of *Our English Lakes, Mountains, and Waterfalls*, 1864, 1866, and 1868, appeared under the imprint of Bennett himself, but the fourth in 1870 issued from Provost & Co.

19 In a letter of 22 February 1878, William Wordsworth, Jr. spelled out the details of income received from Ward, Lock. In the previous year a half share in the profits had amounted to only £63. 7s. 10d. In addition, a royalty of one penny per copy was paid on sales of the *Moxon's Popular Poets* volume.

20 What blew apart the never-very-solid Wordsworth family front against Knight was a letter of 14 December 1879 from William Wordsworth, son of John Wordsworth and nephew of William Wordsworth, Jr. Writing from India, where he was a college principal, he staggered his seniors by announcing that he had never thought Charles Wordsworth's editorial scheme would come to anything; that he was in contact with Professor Knight and intended to give him every assistance; and that he hoped the family would do everything possible to facilitate his proposed edition. Charles Wordsworth was clearly hurt, and retired, just commenting to William Wordsworth in India on 23 June 1880: "I dare say the arrangement is the best possible *under all* the circumstances . . . and I sincerely hope that no occasion will be given for subsequent regret."

21 William Angus Knight (1836–1916), usually "Professor Knight", was the foremost Wordsworth scholar of the latter part of the nineteenth century. Accuracy in fine detail was not among his virtues, but perseverance, energy, and ambition were. For his three-volume *Life of William Wordsworth* (Edinburgh: William Paterson, 1889) he was tireless in tracking down documents and interviewing or

corresponding with those who had some Wordsworth connection. As prime mover in the Wordsworth Society he directed its projects and carried on a voluminous correspondence with members and others in the furtherance of its aims. That the *Selections From Wordsworth*, by William Knight and Other Members of the Wordsworth Society (London: Kegan Paul, Trench & Co., 1889) appeared at all was due to his efforts. His monument is the eleven-volume *Poetical Works of William Wordsworth* (Edinburgh: William Paterson, 1882–89; the last three volumes are the *Life*), the first scholarly edition and first scholarly life of Wordsworth.

Delay in publication and some misadventure meant, however, that Knight was not the first to present Wordsworth's one remaining major unpublished work, *The Recluse*, book 1, "Home at Grasmere," which was issued as a single volume by Macmillan in 1891. For an account of the circumstances in which this text escaped the control of the family and of Knight, see Beth Darlington, *Home at Grasmere* (Ithaca, N.Y.: Cornell University Press, 1977).

22 J. B. Payne for Moxon & Co., to William Wordsworth, Jr., 17 April 1868.

23 Quotation from a letter of J. B. Payne, Moxon & Co., to William Wordsworth, Jr., 11 July 1865.

24 W. Strickland Cookson pointed out to William, Jr., 1 February 1871, that as Moxon had acted on a permission given in a letter of 12 April 1870 it was now out of the question to demand "the entire suppression of Rossetti's preface." Corrections in future editions could, of course, be insisted on. After a visit from the bishop of St. Andrews, however, Cookson caved in, and in a letter to William of 11 February he agreed that the executors ought to aim for suppression.

25 In the prefatory notice to the *Poetical Works of William Wordsworth*, illustrated by Edwin Edwards (London: E. Moxon, Son, & Co., 1871) Rossetti made factual slips, such as saying that Wordsworth married his cousin and that he had taken an M.A. at Cambridge, but much more wounding was, among many tart remarks, the declaration that the poet was not "a practically self-denying or generous man" (xxi). In an emended version, which appeared in an undated edition illustrated by Henry Dell, the errors were corrected and the slight to Wordsworth's character was placed firmly at De Quincey's door, a "disputable authority." In other issues of the Dell edition the preface was suppressed altogether. It is an indication of how loose was the Wordsworths' control over publications that all of these editions of the Rossetti volume were current in the 1870s.

26 See my "England's Samuel: Wordsworth in the 'Hungry-Forties'," *SEL* 33 (1993), 841–58 and "Wordsworth and 'Catholic Truth'," *RES* 45 (1994), 204–20.

27 Quotation from the publisher's advertisement, dated April 1858,

prefacing *The Poetical Works of William Wordsworth, With Illustrations by Birket Foster* (London: George Routledge & Sons, n.d.).

28 I am indebted to Mark Reed for pointing this out to me. The volume was reissued in 1866.

29 In his *The Poetical Works of William Wordsworth* (London: Walter Scott, 1885) Symington printed extracts from *The Excursion* under such headings as "Life under the British Constitution" and "Loyalty to Church and State."

30 For a detailed study, see Jared Curtis, "Matthew Arnold's Wordsworth: The Tinker Tinkered," in *The Mind in Creation: Essays on English Romantic Literature in Honour of Ross G. Woodman*, ed. J. Douglas Kneale (Montreal: McGill-Queen's University Press, 1992), 44–57.

31 *The Poetical Works of William Wordsworth* (Edinburgh: Gall & Inglis, n.d. [1858]), 332.

32 Mark Rutherford, "Extracts from a Diary on the Quantocks," in *More Pages From a Journal* (London: Oxford University Press, 1910), 196–97.

CHAPTER 5

Sam Weller's valentine

J. Hillis Miller

On 13 February 1831, the day before the great trial of *Bardell versus Pickwick*, Sam Weller strolls through "a variety of bye streets and courts" (536)[1] in East London. He makes his leisurely way from the George and Vulture Hotel, George Yard, Lombard Street, toward the Blue Boar in Leadenhall Market to meet his father. Dickens's exact naming of streets and hotels is characteristic of his topographical circumstantiality. He assumes that his readers will have a detailed map of London in their minds and will be able to follow Sam's progress. Sam is streetwise. Dickens assumes that his readers will be streetwise too. *Pickwick Papers* as a whole depends on the reader's detailed foreknowledge not only of London's streets and buildings but also of Southern England's roads, towns, and cities. It is a good example of the way many novels assume a shared topographical inner space in the community of their readers. Many meanings are elliptically conveyed just through toponymy. If the reader does not know what sort of place the Blue Boar in Leadenhall Market is, and how it is different from the George and Vulture in Lombard Street, then an important dimension of sociological and personal meaning in this chapter will be lost. The complex array of class and gender distinctions – manners, customs, laws, ways of eating and living – are, in *Pickwick Papers*, embedded in a topography dominated by human constructive activity. Dickens's characters are surrounded and circumscribed by roads, buildings, bridges, not to speak of public and private interiors: all that men and women have built to incarnate their ways of living. These are already in place as a presupposition of the action.

As Sam saunters toward the Blue Boar in Leadenhall Market, he pauses "before a small stationer's and print-seller's window." Thereupon he smites his right leg "with great vehemence" and exclaims "with energy": "If it hadn't been for this, I should ha'

93

forgot all about it, till it was too late!" Dickens describes what Sam
sees in the stationer's window as follows:

The particular picture on which Sam Weller's eyes were fixed, as
he said this, was a highly coloured representation of a couple of
human hearts skewered together with an arrow, cooking before a
cheerful fire, while a male and female cannibal in modern attire:
the gentleman being clad in a blue coat and white trousers, and
the lady in a deep red pelisse with a parasol of the same: were
approaching the meal with hungry eyes, up a serpentine gravel path
leading thereunto. A decidedly indelicate young gentleman, in a pair
of wings and nothing else, was depicted as superintending the cooking; a representation of the spire of the church in Langham Place,
London, appeared in the distance; and the whole formed a 'valentine,' of which, as a written inscription in the window testified,
there was a large assortment within, which the shopkeeper pledged
himself to dispose of, to his countrymen generally, at the reduced
rate of one and sixpence each. (536–37)

What can be said about this admirably circumstantial description? The passage raises a cascade of questions. Was a valentine,
then or now, protected by patent or by copyright? Are valentines
printed and published or are they manufactured and sold? Is a
valentine a speech act, a performative use of language? If so, exactly
what kind of performative is it? Can a picture be a performative? If
so, what would make a picture performative as opposed to merely
constative, that is, a picture of something, say the spire of Nash's
All Souls' Church, built between 1822 and 1824 in Langham Place
at the top of Regent Street? That church is pictured in Dickens's
valentine. All Souls' was built just a few years before the action
of *Pickwick Papers*, so it would have been a spanking new church
in 1831. Is the act of publication, for example the publication of
Pickwick Papers by Chapman & Hall, a speech act? If so, of what
sort? Why does Dickens have Sam Weller sign the handmade valentine he writes to Mary the housemaid with Pickwick's name: "Your
love-sick / Pickwick"? Can a valentine be a legitimate marriage
proposal? To put this another way, can a valentine be a marriage
promise that might lead to a breach of promise suit if the promise
is not kept? What kind of performative is a promise to marry? Does
one interpret a breach of promise as another form of speech act? If
a promise is a performative, does it take another performative to
break that promise? Is it possible that "Chops and Tomata sauce"
and "Don't trouble yourself about the warming-pan" (562–63)

really do constitute a marriage promise on Pickwick's part? How could one be sure they do not? To put this another way, can one make a promise without intending to do so, for example by sending a valentine signed with someone else's name or by sending a valentine as a friendly courtesy or on a whim, taking the "privilege of the day"? Or are valentines exempt from being taken seriously, just as a man cannot be arrested for debt if he walks out of his house on Sunday, whereas on any other day of the week he would be fair game for the bailiff? Could one commit oneself by chance to a lifetime marriage partner, without intending to do so, and yet by a contract that is no less binding for being unintentional? Is commitment to a marriage partner ever anything but aleatory, a matter of chance or the drawing of lots? Does intention, to put this another way, have anything to do with the efficacy of a performative utterance? Might thinking it does be no more than another version of the "intentional fallacy," in this case the fallacious assumption not that intention controls meaning, but that it controls what speech acts do?

What, finally, is the meaning of Sam's father's objection to poetry in the scene in which he "delivers some Critical Sentiments respecting Literary Composition," as the chapter title puts it? Tony Weller comments on the style of Sam's valentine letter, putting in question anything that even "werges on the poetical" (542). Phiz's illustration shows this scene (see plate 5.1). Is Tony Weller against poetry because it is performatively efficacious and therefore might get Sam entangled into marriage? Or is it just the opposite? Is his objection to poetry that it makes the language it contaminates performatively ineffective, an infelicitous speech act? In *How to Do Things with Words* J. L. Austin firmly excluded poetry from the realm of efficacious speech acts. For a speech act to be effective, he sternly asserted, "I must not be joking, for example, nor writing a poem."[2] Is *Pickwick Papers* as a whole in poetry or in prose? Is this novel, consequently, whatever the answer to that question may be, a felicitous performative, a way of doing something with words? What difference would a "yes" to that question make to our reading of *Pickwick Papers*?

A swarm of such questions rises in the mind of a contemplative reader confronting the episode of Sam Weller's valentine. Now to try to answer them.

Valentines have always been associated with what stands on the border between the accidental and the deliberate in courtship and

Plate 5.1 Hablot Browne ("Phiz"), "The Valentine," from *The Pickwick Papers* (1836–1837).

marriage. St. Valentine was beheaded, according to his legend, on 14 February 270 AD for aiding Christian martyrs persecuted under Claudius II. His final offense was to use the occasion of his interrogation by the Emperor to try to convert Claudius rather than to save his own life by agreeing to abjure Christianity. Part of St. Valentine's legend asserts that he became friends with the blind daughter of his jailer, cured her blindness, and wrote her a letter on the eve of his execution. He signed the letter "From your Valentine," thereby sending the first valentine. All subsequent valentines, it might be said, are, like Sam's valentine to Mary, signed with another's name, since they are sent in the name of St. Valentine. Sam Weller's valentine says "Except of me Mary my dear as your valentine" (542).

Valentine's Day appears to be a Christianization of the Roman Lupercalia, a fertility festival celebrated in February, and of a Roman festival celebrated on 14 February in honor of Juno. In the latter young men drew by lot the names of the young women who would be their partners for the day. A millennium and a half later this custom of drawing by lot the name of a potential marriage partner was still carried on in England, then introduced into America, where it is reflected in the rhetoric of eighteenth-century handmade valentines. One verse, for example, given by Ruth Webb Lee in her history of valentines, reads: "Our lots we cast and, thus I drew, / Kind fortune says it must be you." On the other hand, some valentine verses make the choice deliberate: "I choose you from among the rest / The reason was I loved you best." Another combines these two sentiments in sequence: "Lots was cast and one i drew . . . kind fortune is it must be you . . . I choose you out amongst the rest . . .It was becaus I love you best" (*sic*). The verses are clearly as formulaic as our "Roses are red; violets are blue." A version of the latter already appears in these early valentines: "The rose is red the violet blue / Lilies are fair and so are you."[3] Bathsheba, in Thomas Hardy's *Far from the Madding Crowd*, writes at her servant Liddy's suggestion another version of these verses: "The rose is red, / The violet blue, / Carnation's sweet, / And so are you."[4] Though already in the eighteenth century there were "Valentine Writers" – small books of verses to be copied in the making of handmade valentines – the basic verses were undoubtedly parts of an oral tradition circulating among young people, just as such rhymes still do today. Some of these early valentines are explicitly marriage proposals: "My only wish is to make you happy and to be united with you in marriage" (this translated from a Pennsylvania Dutch valentine in German, dated about 1814; Lee, 22). The tradition of using a valentine as a proposal of marriage, serious or feigned, is registered in Bathsheba's disastrous valentine to Farmer Boldwood, with its randomly chosen seal: "Marry Me."

The history of valentines may be briefly told. The earliest valentines remaining, from the late Middle Ages and Renaissance, were letters. Valentines in England and America during the eighteenth and early nineteenth centuries were still handmade, but often incorporated elaborate cutout or pinprick lace designs, colored pictures, and handwritten verses. Commercial valentines began to be made in the early nineteenth century, first from hand-colored copperplate engravings. Then, about the time Dickens was writing *Pickwick Papers*, the method of manufacture shifted from engravings to hand-colored lithographs (see plate 5.2). Both Robert and George Cruikshank produced valentines just prior to the publication of *Pickwick Papers*. The period between 1840 and 1860 was the high point of elaborate lace-paper valentines, embossed and perforated, manufactured by such stationers as Mansell, Kershaw, and Dobbs in England and in America through home factory assembly-line production by, among others, an enterprising young woman in Worcester, Massachusetts named Esther Howland, active in the mid-nineteenth century (see plates 5.3, 5.4, 5.5). Of so-called comic valentines, a whole genre in themselves, little needs to be said here, except that the valentine Sam sees in the stationer's window is not a comic valentine. They were crudely satirical and usually did not employ the standard valentine iconography. The story thereafter is of a gradual cheapening until we reach the mass-produced valentines of today, though Kate Greenaway produced in the 1870s and 1880s some admirable valentine cards. Esther Howland's craftsperson girls making each valentine by hand were replaced in the late nineteenth century in Worcester by George C. Whitney & Company. Whitney bought her and other smaller companies out and set up a large valentine factory with "the best possible machinery . . . for embossing and making paper lace . . . giant double-cylinder presses together with all the other necessary appurtenances" (Lee, 71–72).

Several of the valentines in my illustrations bear some resemblance to the one Sam Weller sees in the stationer's window. Ruth Webb Lee reproduces, though not in color, a lithographed valentine made of paper watermarked "J. Whatman, Turkey Mill, 1842" in which, as she tells us, "the gentleman in the scene wears a dark blue coat and his prospective bride is quite dashing in a red coat lavishly trimmed with ermine" (Lee, 135). Those colors seem to have been conventional. Frank Staff reproduces a handmade valentine of 1803

Plate 5.2 English valentine, *circa* 1825–1835. From William Morton Janse, *The History of Valentines*.

Plate 5.3 English valentine by T. H. Burke, *circa* 1840. From Ruth Webb Lee,
A History of Valentines.

Plate 5.4 English valentine by Joseph Mansell, *circa* 1850. From Ruth Webb Lee, *A History of Valentines*.

Plate 5.5 English valentine by Dobbs, Bailey & Co., *circa* 1850. From Frank
Staff, *The Valentine and Its Origins*.

with a stipple engraving in which the lover's coat is blue and the girl's skirt red.[5] The Whatman valentine also has a church in the distance, as in the valentine Dickens describes. I have not found one with the motif of the skewered and cooking hearts. The cooking hearts may be Dickens's satirical invention, though two hearts skewered by an arrow and naked cupids were, of course, essential parts of the traditional iconography of valentines, as was the idea that on Valentine's Day Cupid set lovers' hearts afire with desire. Dickens's valentine is a reification of this traditional trope. The church in the background was also part of the conventional iconography of valentines. It represented the goal of matrimony, the telos of valentine courtship. Plate 5.6 is the valentine nearest to the one Dickens describes that I have found.

Answers to some of my initial questions may be approached by way of a more exact description of valentines. An enormous number and variety of them were produced, particularly as industrial revolution proceeded. The making and selling of valentines became a big business. Valentines in England in 1863 cost anything from a penny to seven shillings and sixpence, though it was possible to pay up to twenty-five pounds for a single valentine (Staff, 138–39). American prices for valentines in 1874 went from five cents to three dollars, a lot of cash in those days (Staff, 140).

Some hack writers appear to have eked out a living producing valentine verses. An advertisement in the *Boston Transcript* of 9 February 1847 for English valentines (cited by Ruth Webb Lee) gives some idea of their variety:

English Valentines. Per *Hibernia*.
A. S. Jordan, No. 2 Milk Street, respectfully informs his friends that he has just received by the above steamer, the greatest assortment of Valentines to be found in Cupid's regions, among which may be found the following kinds: Comic, Sentimental, Lovesick, Acrostic, Funny, Burlesque, Curious, Characteristic, Humorous, Beautiful, Heart-struck, Witty, Arabesque, Courting, Serio-Comical, Bewitching, Poetical, Heart-rending, Love-encouraging, Trifling, Caricature, Heart-piercing, Serio-tragical, Laughable, Silly, Spiteful, Original, Enlivening, Heart-aching, Despairing, Raving-mad, Heart-killing, High-flown, Lampooning, Romantic, Look-out, Proposal, Espousal, Matrimonial, Hen-Pecking, Suicidal, and many other varieties. Wholesale buyers would do well to call before purchasing elsewhere, as the selection has been made by one of the first London houses engaged in that particular business. (Lee, 90)

Plate 5.6 English valentine inspired by Halley's Comet of 1835.

This is an odd list, though the word "Lovesick," used in Sam Weller's valentine, appears in it. The list is almost as miscellaneous as the contents of Mrs. Jellyby's closet in *Bleak House*. One wonders if all these different kinds were kept in separate, labeled bins. Little, if any, order appears in the sequence, though if I only knew what a "Look-out Valentine" might be, I would claim to see a sad story in the final sequence that goes from Romantic to Look-out to Proposal to Espousal to Matrimonial to Hen-Pecking to Suicidal. That's not much of an advertisement! A clear warning message is given by the sequence: "Don't send or receive a Romantic Valentine! It will lead you step by step through matrimony to suicide." Farmer Boldwood finds out something like this to his sorrow. It is just what Tony Weller fears for Sam, and just what his own henpecked state forewarns. *Pickwick Papers*, like all great comic masterpieces, derives its greatest comic force from the way in which it displaces the tragic themes of human mortality and unassuageable desire (I shall return to this later). The "Wellerisms" in *Pickwick* are a case in point, as I shall show.

Most, though not all, valentines were multimedia productions. They combined words, pictures, and a purely decorative graphic aspect, such as the elaborate borders of lace and embossing popular in the mid-nineteenth century. Some valentines were mechanical contrivances that pulled out, opened up, stood up, or could be moved in one way or another. What is the meaning of the convention of the lace border to a valentine, a border around a central picture or verse often on a lower layer of superimposed sheets? Are these lace borders a covert allusion to the lace bordering feminine apparel and therefore a promise of *jouissance* when the top layer is lifted or when the looker penetrates to the picture or poem behind?

Valentines, in any case, began as a form of handmade folk art with elaborate conventions. This folk art was gradually replaced by what Walter Benjamin in the title of a celebrated essay calls "mechanical reproducibility" [*technischen Reproduzierbarkeit*]. Even in the age of reproducibility, however, handmade valentines consisting only of words or with hand-drawn pictures, still rather like the earliest surviving ones from the late Middle Ages and Renaissance, continued to be written and sent. An example is Sam Weller's valentine. Sam does not buy the cannibal valentine in the stationer's window. He laboriously writes his own valentine to Mary.

Like other multimedia productions then and now, commercially

produced valentines were and are something of a challenge to the
laws of copyright and patent. As we know, Dickens took a deep
interest in copyright law. He mounted a vigorous campaign to get
the United States to recognize international copyright and to stop
pirating his books. The original edition of *Pickwick Papers* (1837) was
dedicated to "Mr. Serjeant Talfourd, M.P.," that is, to Dickens's
friend Thomas Noon Talfourd (1795–1854). Talfourd had, in May
1837, introduced in Parliament his copyright bill. The bill finally
became law in 1842. It increased the copyright period to forty-two
years or seven years after the author's death, whichever was longer.
Dickens's dedication speaks with feeling of Talfourd's great service
to literature.

Like computer hardware and software today, a valentine could
be partly protected by patent, partly by copyright. Just as a
new process for making computer hardware can be patented,
while software programs are protected by copyright and their
titles are registered as trademarks, such as the Apple logo, ,
so the verses on a valentine could be protected by copyright,
while the sometimes elaborate procedures used to manufacture
them, for example to make so-called "mechanical valentines,"
could be protected by patent. Ruth Webb Lee mentions certain
valentines produced in New York in the mid-nineteenth century as being identifiable by the embossing along the fold in
the center: "Lang's Pat. process. Berlin & Jones, Mfrs. N.Y."

Historians of valentines sometimes speak of them as "manufactured," but more often their makers are called "publishers."
Valentines belong to the history of Victorian publishing and yet do
not quite fit within it. They were both published and manufactured
and were able, therefore, to be protected both by copyright and by
patent. Valentines show that copyright law, even at its inception in
its modern form, was mined with pitfalls and inconsistencies. That
law had to be used to protect forms of language that do not easily fit
within the ideology of single, identifiable authorship and property
ownership. It is easy to see how copyright laws are jeopardized
today when the concept of the "author" has been put into question
and when there has been a return to various forms of collaborative
or anonymous composition, for example interactive computer texts
or collaborative work by disempowered minorities. But already in
the nineteenth century copyright laws were not quite appropriate
for forms of popular art like valentines.

Copyright does not, of course, prohibit the making of copies. It prohibits the making of copies without suitable payment to the owner of the copyright. What can be copyrighted is by definition capable of being copied, word for word. If it could not be copied there would be no need for copyright. An idea may not be copyrighted, only a specific form of words or a typographical layout. Copyright protects a possible exact iteration. This would seem to exclude what can be protected by copyright from the realm of performatives, since a performative is a unique, one-time-only, unrepeatable, doing of things with words. I am married only once to this particular person on this particular occasion, even though I may be remarried on a later performative occasion. A ship is christened once and for all, even though it may be rechristened. But as Jacques Derrida has argued, however unique a speech act occasion may be it is performed by an assemblage of words, which draw their efficacy from their iterability.[6] Examples include the words of the Christian marriage ceremony: "I pronounce you man and wife"; or the traditional words naming a ship: "I christen thee the *Queen Mary*"; or the words of a promise, for example a mortgage contract, a promise to marry, or an invitation to marry, like Bathsheba's "Marry Me." Another example is a valentine: "Roses are red; violets are blue," and so on. The peculiarity of all these sorts of performatives is that they must be both unique and repeatable. In order to have meaning at all words must be iterable and at least implicitly already an iteration. There is no first and only time for words. Even the first time is already implicitly a repetition. On the other hand, a performative enters a situation at one particular time and place to change those once and for all. It uses a repetition to do the unique. This means that a combination of words and pictures capable of being used performatively, for example a valentine, might be protected by copyright. Derrida, in *Limited Inc.*, associates performatives with the question of copyright in his ridicule of Searle's attempt to control the dissemination and assert his ownership of his own essay by stamping "Copyright © 1977 by John R. Searle" on the first page, above the title.[7]

I have included valentines along with the words of the marriage and christening ceremonies among examples of performatives. It is easy to see how they fit. As the examples given from the texts of early American handmade valentines show, even a handmade valentine written on a particular occasion by one person who

intended to send it to another specified person characteristically
employed formulaic phrases for a unique purpose. Even Sam
Weller's valentine, an idiosyncratic document if ever there was
one, contains echoes of traditional valentine formulas: "the first and
only time I see you, your likeness was took on my hart"; "Except of
me Mary my dear as your valentine" (542). Commercial valentines
are even more evidently the product of an iteration. A given one
may be produced in thousands of copies. Each one is made up of an
arrangement of standardized parts: pictures, verses, and decorative
borders. Nothing could be more anonymous and impersonal than a
commercial valentine. Like a blank check or a standardized will, a
commercial valentine has performative force only when the blanks
are filled in, the valentine signed and addressed to a particular
person in a particular place: "To Mary, Housemaid, at Mr.
Nupkin's Mayor's, Ipswich, Suffolk." Then, as with Bathsheba's
valentine or Sam's, it may have performative force and make
something happen. Examples are the unintentional devastation
of Farmer Boldwood's life that follows from Bathsheba's whim,
or the implicit commitment that in the wake of Sam's valentine
leads in the end to happy marriage.

Why then, if a valentine, like a check, is only validated, activated,
charged with performative efficacy when it is signed, does Sam
sign his valentine with Pickwick's name and why does he do so
in a rhyming verse? The signature verse is given at the end of a
discussion with his father about the stylistic proprieties of valentine
signatures. To sign with a fictitious name is something like writing
poetry, a topic to which I shall return:

   "Ain't you a goin' to sign it?" [asks Sam's father.]
   "That's the difficulty," said Sam; "I don't know what *to* sign it."
   "Sign it, Veller," said the oldest surviving proprietor of that name.
   "Won't do," said Sam. "Never sign a walentine with your own
name."
   "Sign it 'Pickwick,' then," said Mr. Weller; "it's a werry good name,
and a easy one to spell."
   "The wery thing," said Sam, "I *could* end with a werse; what do
you think?"
   "I don't like it, Sam," rejoined Mr. Weller . . .
   But Sam was not to be dissuaded from the poetical idea that had
occurred to him, so he signed the letter,
   "Your love-sick Pickwick." (543)

No doubt the joke lies partly in the analogy drawn between Samuel Weller and Samuel Pickwick. Pickwick's trial for breach of promise is about to commence the next day. He can ironically be taken as a model for ardent lovers. Pickwick is about to be convicted of breach of promise on the basis of some words ("Chops and Tomata sauce") that Mrs. Bardell's lawyers convince the jury are a marriage proposal. Perhaps this is because tomatoes were once thought to be an aphrodisiac. For a man to say "Chops and Tomata sauce" to a woman is an implicit proposition. At least that is what the infamous Dodson and Fogg persuade the jury to believe. Sam's valentine constitutes another fictitious proposal of marriage by Pickwick and may get him involved in another breach of promise suit.

From the perspective of Sam's own intentions, what is the meaning of the principle he enunciates? "Never sign a walentine with your own name." That may be for two contradictory reasons. When Sam tells his father that he has written a valentine, Mr. Weller, who is unhappily married to a "perwerse, and unpleasant" (538) religious fanatic, says it'll be a trial "to see you married, Sammy – to see you a dilluded wictim, and thinkin' in your innocence that it's all wery capital." To which Sam disingenuously replies, "Nonsense . . . I ain't a goin' to get married, don't you fret yourself about that" (539). If he signs his valentine with a fictitious name, it will be no more efficacious than if I were to sign a check with someone else's name. Only the one who owns the name can use it to do something with words. Signing a valentine with someone else's name is a way to send the valentine and yet protect oneself from the consequences of doing so. Signing Pickwick's name turns the valentine into a forgery and so into an infelicitous speech act.

On the other hand, Sam's principle ("Never sign a valentine with your own name") sounds as if it might be meant to apply to serious as well as to unserious valentines. Many a forgery has functioned as an efficacious performative. It may be that the act of making a declaration of love so changes the person who makes it that he becomes another person, in this case a great lover like Pickwick, though Casanova, Romeo, or Don Giovanni might have done as well. In order to make the valentine work, Sam has to borrow the name of someone who has prowess in lovemaking, just as, it may be, he has to write it in a style that "werges on the poetical," in spite of his father's warnings (542).

The borrowing, on Valentine's Day, of a Roman custom of drawing lots for a mate, as well as the similar motif in eighteenth-century
American valentines I have cited, shows the contradictory mixture
of free choice and accident or fate in the valentine tradition. This
might be seen as a ritual institutionalization of the actual circumstances in which most marriages in our tradition are made. For us,
both the woman and the man are presumed to be free to choose,
though, of course, all sorts of social constraints "circumscribe"
that choice, to borrow a word from Sam Weller's valentine.[8] Most
marriage "choices" probably happen largely by accident. A young
woman happens to fall in a man's way or a young man in a woman's
way, one thing leads to another, and before they know it they are
married.

A comic example of that is the way Tony Weller married his
second wife. He was going to Doctor's Commons to pick up his
inheritance of four hundred pounds from his deceased first wife
when he was nabbed by a lawyer's tout. As Sam says, such people
"puts things into old gen'lm'n's heads as they never dreamed of"
(199). The next thing Tony Weller knew he was filling out a
marriage license and putting in Susan Clarke's name, though he
had had until that moment no intention of marrying her: "She'll
have me, if I ask, I des-say – I never said nothing to her, but she'll
have me, I know" (200).

The selection of a mate, even though it may always happen in
some such way, is so decisive a moment in an individual's life that
one would like to put the blame somewhere else. One would like
to make the alliance seem grounded and justified, not the result
either of a random encounter or of a free and ungrounded choice.
The traditions of Valentine's Day help us to do that by combining,
against logic, fate, and free will. The alogic, however, is hidden
because "that's the way you do it on Valentine's Day."

A valentine reveals an obscure fate. On the one hand, "Our lots
we cast and, thus I drew, / Kind fortune says it must be you." On
the other, Valentine's Day gives the lover license to express his
free choice. It allows him to use a traditional formula to express
his own particular love: "I choose you from among the rest / The
reason was I loved you best." As Sam Weller puts this: "So I take
the privilidge of the day, Mary, my dear . . . to tell you that the
first and only time I see you, your likeness was took on my hart"
(542). Sam takes advantage of the day to let Mary know that his

accidental encounter with her was fateful for his life, just as his writing of the valentine was the result of an accidental seeing of the valentine in the stationer's window. That reminded him tomorrow was St. Valentine's Day: "If it hadn't been for this, I should ha' forgot all about it" (536).

The figure Sam uses to describe how Mary's image was inscribed in his heart repeats the combination of fate and free will. "Your likeness," says Sam, "was took on my hart in much quicker time and brighter colours than ever a likeness was took by the profeel machine (which p'raps you may have heerd on Mary my dear) altho it does finish a portrait and put the frame and glass on complete, with a hook at the end to hang it up by, and all in two minutes and a quarter" (542). As Tony Weller says, "I am afeered that werges on the poetical, Sammy" (542). The profile machine was a mechanical ancestor of photography. One end of an armature followed the contours of someone's face, while a pencil attached to the other traced those contours on paper. How could Sam help falling in love with Mary? Her features were duplicated exactly on his heart, in an automatic, machinelike process over which his will had no control, though the sitter for a profile must be willing to sit still while the machine does its work. With modern photography even that complicity in one's dispossession is no longer necessary. The photograph is taken in the blink of an eye, in a "snapshot" that is as violent as a gunshot.

Bathsheba's valentine to Boldwood, in *Far from the Madding Crowd*, repeats in more somber colors this mixture of choice, accident, and the appeal to a justifying fate in order to displace responsibility. The chapter of Bathsheba's valentine is entitled "Sortes Sanctorum – the Valentine." Among the traditions of Valentine's Day was the notion that the first person you happened to see on that day would be the one you would marry. Bathsheba uses another traditional way to identify a future marriage partner. This is the custom of divination by sacred scripture. "Sortes sanctorum" meant putting a big house key on a Bible open at Ruth 1:16, tying the Bible shut, suspending it by the protruding ends of the key, repeating the verse from Ruth, fixing one's mind on the potential mate, and waiting to see if the Bible moved: "And Ruth said, Entreat me not to leave thee, or to return from following after thee: for whither thou goest, I will go: and where thou lodgest, I will lodge: thy

people shall be my people, and thy God my God." Bathsheba
thinks of Boldwood: "The verse was repeated; the book turned
around; Bathsheba blushed guiltily." (chapter 13) This prophecy
seems to justify the whim of sending to Boldwood the valentine
that was bought for a child, "little Teddy Coggan." Bathsheba's
valentine is "a gorgeously illuminated and embossed design in
post-octavo, which had been bought on the previous market-day
at the chief stationer's in Casterbridge." As for the seal, the
"pert injunction" "Marry Me" was affixed by accident, though
Bathsheba ratifies the accident by sending the letter: "Here's
one [seal] with a motto – I remember it is some funny one,
but can't read it. We'll try this, and if it doesn't do we'll have
another."

Like Dickens, though in a way that is characteristic of himself,
Hardy makes a scrupulously exact notation of the way such an
event transgresses the borders separating accident, choice, and fate.
The event arises from an inextricable mixture of the three that defies
decisive interpretation or the allocation of responsibility: "So very
idly and unreflectingly was this deed done. Of love as a spectacle
Bathsheba had a fair knowledge; but of love subjectively she knew
nothing." Poor Farmer Boldwood takes the idle valentine seriously
and is gradually driven by unassuaged desire for Bathsheba to
madness, to the murder of Sergeant Troy, and to his own indefinite
imprisonment for homicide while insane.

This combination of the fortuitous and determined in valentines
would seem inconsistent with the freely chosen enactment of
an institutionalized ritual presumed in the standard analysis of
performative speech acts. All performatives presuppose the freely
willing and choosing "I," self-consistent through time. Speech act
theory belongs to the post-Cartesian era of the assumption that
subjectivity is an a priori given. The ego is the one thing that
cannot be put into question. It survives all skeptical suspension
of belief. The paradigmatic examples of performative utterances
always involve the self-conscious subject uttering a form of words
that makes something happen: "I promise"; "I pronounce you
man and wife"; "I christen thee the *Abraham Lincoln*." Nevertheless, as Jacques Derrida and Paul de Man have in different
ways persuasively demonstrated, performatives always exceed the
intentions of their performers. They do not depend on intention for
their efficacy. A performative always makes something happen, but

it by no means always makes happen what the one who utters it intends or expects. The words work on their own, mechanically, impersonally, independently of any conscious, willing subjectivity, just as grammar does. A performative exceeds the firm and clear opposition between willed and accidental. It is the product of a machinelike power in the semantic and grammatical aspects of language that cannot be entirely controlled by intention or cognition.[9] Bathsheba did not mean to do Farmer Boldwood any harm. That did not keep much harm from befalling him as a result of the accidentally chosen "Marry Me." The phrase "marry me" is a special kind of performative, something like a bet, an excuse, or a promise, though not quite the same as any of these. To say "marry me" puts the one to whom it is said in a new situation, the situation of having either to accept or refuse the challenge. That Bathsheba does not intend the words to be taken seriously does not prevent them from working. As Hardy puts this, somewhat ponderously, apropos of Boldwood and Bathsheba:

It is foreign to a mystified condition of mind to realize of the mystifier that the processes of approving a course suggested by circumstance, and of striking out a course from inner impulse, would look the same in the result. The vast difference between starting a train of events, and directing into a particular groove a series already started, is rarely apparent to the person confounded by the issue.

(chapter 14)

In the case of Pickwick's promise to marry Mrs. Bardell, the unwitting perpetrator of the performative, not its object, is confounded by the issue. Pickwick did not mean to propose to Mrs. Bardell when he wrote "Chops and Tomata sauce." The note gets him in deep trouble anyway, as does the fact that his remarks to Mrs. Bardell about his intention to hire Sam Weller were taken by her as a proposal of marriage. Sam goes to some lengths to keep his valentine from being something he must take responsibility for having written. He assures his father that "I ain't a goin' to get married." Nevertheless, the valentine leads to his marriage anyhow. Far from disqualifying valentines from being performative speech acts, the way they mix inadvertence with machinelike effectiveness matches similar features in all performatives. This helps confirm my hypothesis that valentines are indeed a species of performative.

If so, what does this have to do with Tony Weller's abhorrence of poetry? Is Sam's valentine poetical or not? Would its being poetical inhibit it from having performative efficacy? I have referred to Austin's claim that in order for a performative to work, its utterer must not, for example, be writing poetry. Tony Weller's objection to poetry, so it seems, is not too different from Austin's. Both share with Dickens himself a pleasant but dangerous gift for irony. A little irony may even have crept across to contaminate my own discourse. Who knows? It may in principle be impossible to know. Irony is dangerous because, as de Man says, it is "the systematic undoing . . . of understanding."[10] Sam's dialogue with his father, in any case, is an admirably witty exchange of ironies. Each tries to outdo the other in a kind of ping-pong game of stroke and return, with Dickens as ironic referee or referee of ironies supervising the game.

Tony Weller approves of Sam's plainspeaking literalism in his valentine: "you *are* a nice gal and nothin' but it" (541). For Sam, in this sentence at least, a thing or person is what it is and nothing but what it is. If so, metaphorical comparisons and displacements are unveracious. The unique is not like anything else. As he says later in his valentine: "there ain't nobody like you" (542). Poetry, according to Wellerian poetics, is against nature. Nobody who is not a fraud talks poetry. An example of poetry is a poetic request for money by a low public official such as a beadle, or, alternatively, someone writing advertising copy for boot blacking or a quack medicine. "Poetry's unnat'ral," says Tony Weller to his son; "no man ever talked poetry 'cept a beadle on boxin' day, or Warren's blackin', or Rowland's oil, or some o' them low fellows; never you let your self down to talk poetry, my boy" (540). We know from *Oliver Twist* what Dickens thought of beadles. On Boxing Day, the day after Christmas, beadles went around to their parishioners chanting a poem asking for a tip. Warren's Blacking Factory was where Dickens worked as a child during those traumatic six months he makes so much of in the autobiographical fragment written at the time he was composing *David Copperfield*. Dickens's job at Warren's was to tie on the bottles the papers that bore the advertising. He had a good chance to see Warren's poetry close up. Such poetry was a precocious example of the work of art in the age of mechanical reproducibility. For Dickens as for Benjamin, poetry now is deprived of all aura and therefore meretricious. Nothing grounds its extravagant figurative transfers.

As Tony Weller's next assertion makes clear, poetry is a species of lie generated by metaphor: "Wot's the good o' callin' a young 'ooman a Wenus or a angel, Sammy?" he asks. "You might jist as well call her a griffin, or a unicorn, or a king's arms at once, which is werry well known to be a col-lection o' fabulous animals" (540–42). "Angel," it might be remembered, is just what Mr. Tupman calls Miss Wardle when he woos her (171). Poetry calls one thing by the name of another, transferring the properties of one thing to something else that does not really have them. An example is calling a young woman a Venus or an angel. Since such comparisons are not grounded in any empirical similarity, there is no way to control them or to distinguish proper from improper ones. Start calling a young woman a Venus or an angel and you might as well call her more or less anything: a griffin, a king's arms, or whatever. Since these are fabulous animals, such a comparison would add the lie of their fictionality to the lie of the ungrounded comparison, making such poetry a double lie. The examples that come to Tony Weller's mind are all characteristic names of pubs, as are "Venus" and "Angel." In Tony Weller's fertile mind calling a young woman by any of these names would be grotesquely unflattering, like comparing her to a public house.

Such lies, moreover, are the fathers of evil, as Tony's final pronouncement makes clear. If according to Samuel Johnson a man who would pun would pick a pocket, for Tony Weller a man who writes poetry is bound to be a criminal. He is certain to be a criminal of a particularly vicious kind. Tony's example is the Camberwell coachman who turned against his own profession and became a highwayman: "I never know'd a respectable coachman as wrote poetry, 'cept one, as made an affectin' copy o' werses the night before he wos hung for a highway robbery; and *he* wos only a Cambervell man, so even that's no rule" (543). Camberwell is across the Thames, almost another country. Who knows what those lawless people will do, perhaps even rob themselves? For a coachman to rob coaches is a species of self-robbery. In a similar way, the man who writes poetry or speaks poetry is defrauding his own language of power to work, to do something, to get you from here to there with something valuable you want transferred. On the other hand, to be a respectable coachman who does not write poetry is to work honestly to take people and things from one place to another. This is just what a happy performative does, for example in the transfer of real estate or other property from one owner to another in a will or a deed.

If the logic of Tony Weller's poetic theory is carried to its implicit conclusion, the opposition is seen to be not so much between poetry and prose as between lying poetry and another use of language that hardly has a name. It might be called "truth-telling poetry." Such poetry is exemplified throughout *Pickwick Papers*. It is brought especially into the open in this scene. Truth-telling poetry might be defined as an exploitation of the figurative possibilities of language that calls attention to its own operation. Such reflexivity functions to demystify lying figures that may do much harm, such as calling a young woman a Venus or a Griffin. Sam's comparison of the impression Mary made on him to the profile machine certainly "werges on the poetical," by Tony Weller's definition. This metaphorical comparison, however, is grotesque and original enough, its hyperbole is so insisted on, that it works as a cleansing satire on the merely conventional comparisons Sam's father disdains.

The best way to understand the truth-telling poetry of Sam's valentine, of the entire episode, and of *Pickwick Papers* as a whole is through an interpretation of one of Dickens's great inventions (or, rather, it was more probably a borrowing from the vigor of everyday working-class speech). I refer to the "Wellerisms" that pervade the novel like a continuously renewed and endlessly variable joke. Two punctuate this episode, one uttered by Tony Weller, the other in Sam's valentine itself. When Tony fears that his son will be married, he says "it'll be a wery agonizin' trial to me at my time of life, but I'm pretty tough, as the wery old turkey remarked wen the farmer said he wos afeerd he should be obliged to kill him for the London market" (539). In his valentine, Sam writes, in a sequence already quoted in part: "So I take the privilidge of the day, Mary, my dear – as the gen'lm'n in difficulties did, ven he valked out of a Sunday" (542).

What can be said of such locutions? They are certainly poetical by Tony Weller's definition, since they compare one thing to another. But their poetry depends on the comic incongruity of the comparison. No one thinks that a man writing a valentine is like a man who will be arrested if he leaves his house except on

Sunday, when the whole city becomes a kind of church sanctuary. The dissimilarity is a big part of the joke. On the other hand the two situations *are* alike in one way. The same form of words can be used appropriately at the right moment in both situations, two grotesquely unlike contexts. There are at least two different circumstances in which it would be appropriate to say either "I take the privilege of the day," or "I'm pretty tough." The joke and the explosion of laughter arises from seeing this strange similarity in dissimilarity. We recognize the peculiar fact that the meaning of a given group of words is not intrinsic to the words. Meaning arises from the way a given context determines one sense out of a virtually limitless number of possible different ones.[11] Seeing this liberates one momentarily from the coercive constraints of the context one is really in. We glimpse the performative role forms of language can have when those forms are inserted arbitrarily in a given context. In effecting that liberation, the Wellerism is itself a miniature performative. The Wellerism gives the one who uses it or hears it a brief power over language, a sense of language's power, and a momentary escape from its coercions. The understanding that the Wellerism gives by no means, however, prevents anyone from being the victim of unintentional performatives, as *Pickwick Papers* abundantly demonstrates. Cognition and power here are incompatible. A performative, like a Wellerism, is a form of language that works, but it works differently in different contexts. Any form of words can function as a performative if the context is right.

The Wellerisms show that it is impossible not to speak or write poetry. No form of words means just what it says. Even the most literal and referential set of words ("Chops and Tomata sauce," for example) can have a different meaning in a different context and a performative effect there. This means that whatever I say has a disquieting kind of poetry about it, and is likely to exceed my intentions and knowledge by having a quite different meaning and effect if it is taken within a different context from the one intended. You write a note saying "Don't trouble yourself about the warming-pan," meaning just what you say, and you find yourself involved in a breach of promise suit.

The central event of *Pickwick Papers*, the suit and the trial of *Bardell versus Pickwick*, is generated by an inadvertent Wellerism. The difference between an inadvertent and a deliberate Wellerism is that the former makes its perpetrator potentially the victim of false ideological forms and bad institutions like the law, whereas the latter liberates by bringing the mechanisms of language for a moment into the light. A deliberate Wellerism uses poetry against poetry, so to speak. It does this by showing how poetry works as a ubiquitous ideological power for harm within society. Poetry, like Jingle's masterly manipulation of Bouvard and Pecuchet-like clichés, tells lies and does things with them.

More can be said of the Wellerisms, however. They tend, like the two in this episode, to bring together a benign context, one involving a life-affirming situation like courtship, the other involving crime, the ruinous power of institutions, and the ever-present possibility of death. This is just what *Pickwick Papers* as a whole does, for example in the interpolated tales or in the central episode that brings Pickwick into Fleet Prison, as against the generally prevailing comedy, most often comedy arising from a perennial source: relations between the sexes. The Wellerisms, like the whole novel, assert that two apparently unrelated aspects of life are in some way alike or are inextricably involved with one another: the life drive, generated by sexual desire, and the certainty of death.

Like all great comedy, *Pickwick Papers* in the end must be defined as tragicomedy. This mixture is constantly reaffirmed by the poetico-prosaical Wellerisms. A man in love really is in some way like a man who is in danger of being imprisoned for debt. For a father to say "I'm pretty tough" when his son is in danger of marrying really is like the situation of the old turkey who may be killed and who takes pleasure in the fact that he is so tough no one will enjoy eating him. The marriage of a son is the beginning of the end for a father's patriarchal authority, though fathers, like the tough old turkey, have ways of keeping some command even beyond the grave. Marriage, to turn to Sam's Wellerism in his valentine, does have a way of putting both men and women in debt in more than one sense, needing to take the privilege of the day to get a little freedom. Marriage "circumscribes" anyone, man or woman, with a complex web of institutional and social constraints.

I asked initially whether *Pickwick Papers* as a whole may be performative. The question may now be answered in the affirmative. *Pickwick Papers* is a high-spirited reflection of early Victorian class and gender relations. It represents a wide range of English institutions and forms of behavior, along with the languages employed by them – languages scientific, historical, journalistic, political, legal, and so forth, even including the language of hunting and cricket. The novel also employs most of the narrative, dramatic, and even poetic conventions available to Dickens. But the novel also brings into the open these elements' absurdity and their potential for causing harm. It thereby puts in question the repertoire of features making up English ideology at the moment of Victoria's accession to the throne.

This comic demystification is effected by hyperbole, by irony, and by other forms of displacement that call attention to language by wresting it from its usual contexts. In this way, like all powerful critiques of ideology, *Pickwick Papers* did not merely reflect Victorian society, its institutions, and its narrative conventions. It changed them, in however small a way. Like cultural creations generally, *Pickwick Papers* is not fully explicable by what preceded it. Its biographical, historical, and social contexts do not fully explain it. As the successive monthly numbers appeared, the novel rapidly became immensely popular and widely read, particularly after Sam Weller entered the scene. Just as Sam changes Pickwick's life, so *Pickwick Papers* entered the culture of its readers to change them in all sorts of complex though not easily specifiable or verifiable ways. No one can doubt, however, that the novel had an effect on Victorian society, as did Dickens's subsequent novels.

Pickwick Papers uses poetry, as Tony Weller defines it, to criticize, demystify, and momentarily suspend the baneful efficacy of the ideological "poetry" with which its readers were surrounded, the obfuscations of the law or the low blandishments of advertisements for products like Warren's Blacking. At the same time the novel recognizes the necessity of poetry. Poetry is shown to be ubiquitous in everyday life. The novel shows this by being written in a species of poetry itself. At the beginning of the valentine episode the imaginary Sam Weller is shown walking through real East London streets. In a similar way *Pickwick Papers* throughout works its magic by presenting, as one might say, altering Marianne Moore's formula, real gardens with imaginary toads in them.

Like all performative utterances, *Pickwick Papers* exceeded Dickens's intentions. It was radically improvisatory. Dickens had no idea where the story would go when he began writing it. Moreover, neither he nor anyone else could have predicted its popularity or the effects it would have. The most he could do was to utter another kind of blind performative. This is the promise he made binding himself to go on writing the novel. Dickens did this not only in his contract with Chapman & Hall, but also in the original advertisement in *The Athenaeum* for 26 March 1836 and in the announcement at the conclusion of part 10 in December 1836. In the advertisement Dickens says "it is presumed the series will be completed in about twenty numbers" (900). In the announcement Dickens promises to "keep perpetually going on beginning again, regularly, until the end of the fair" (903). In saying this, as he confesses, Dickens uses someone else's words to make a promise. He says again "what the late eminent Mr. John Richardson, of Horsemonger Lane Southwark, and the Yellow Caravan with the Brass Knocker, always said on behalf of himself and company, at the close of every performance" (902). Dickens uses someone else's words to make a promise, just as Sam Weller signs his valentine with Pickwick's name, and just as I have borrowed Dickens's words for purposes of my own. In all three cases the language or the signature of another is used to get something done with words. No doubt the result in my case, too, will not quite be what I intended.

NOTES

1 Citations are by page number from Charles Dickens, *The Pickwick Papers*, ed. Robert L. Patten (Harmondsworth: Penguin, 1972).
2 J. L. Austin, *How to Do Things with Words*, ed. J. O. Urmison and Marina Sbisà (2nd edn.; Oxford: Oxford University Press, 1980), 9.
3 Ruth Webb Lee, *A History of Valentines* (New York: The Studio Publications, 1952), 16, 19.
4 Thomas Hardy, *Far From the Madding Crowd*, chapter 13.
5 Frank Staff, *The Valentine and Its Origins* (New York: Praeger, 1969), 43.
6 Jacques Derrida, *Limited Inc.*, ed. Gerald Graff, trans. Samuel Weber and Jeffrey Mehlman (Evanston, Ill.: Northwestern University Press, 1988), 18.
7 *Ibid.*, 30–31.
8 The word appears in the first sentence of Sam's valentine. It is prominent both because of its apparent incongruity in context and because Sam cannot read what he has written over a blot. That illegibility generates a controversy between Sam and his father over

whether "circumscribed" or "circumwented" is the better word. Sam has written: "I feel myself ashamed and completely circumscribed in a dressin' of you" (540). A little dialogue follows:

"That ain't as good a word as circumwented, Sammy," said Mr. Weller, gravely.
  "Think not?" said Sam.
  "Nothin' like it," replied his father.
  "But don't you think it means more?" inquired Sam.
  "Vell p'raps it is a more tenderer word," said Mr. Weller, after a few moments' reflection. (540)

This is, of course, sublime comic and slightly condescending nonsense, condescending to the uneducated lower classes who use big words wrongly and have foolish linguistic theories. One word does not mean more than another. It means something different. Neither word in this case seems quite right, at least at first glance. On the other hand, Sam *is* "circumscribed" in his valentine writing, not only in the sense that he is hemmed in, coerced by his feelings and by his sense of inferiority to Mary, ashamed of his temerity in addressing her, but also in the literal sense that he is "written around," narrowly enclosed on all sides by conventions of language and the specific conventions of courtship and valentine sending that constrain him to write in certain ways, even though he feels himself ashamed by the fact that she is such a "lovely creetur" (540). "Circumscribed" is uncannily the right word after all, a much better word than "circumwented." Perhaps Dickens is not so condescending to the lower classes after all.

9 Derrida's chief work on performatives, *Limited Inc.*, is cited above. De Man's most radical appropriation and reworking of the theory of performatives is the chapter on Rousseau's *Confessions*, "Excuses," in *Allegories of Reading* (New Haven: Yale University Press, 1979). See, for example, the following passages:

  Writing always includes the moment of dispossession in favor of the arbitrary power play of the signifier and from the point of view of the subject, this can only be experienced as a dismemberment, a beheading, or a castration. (296)

  Far from seeing language as an instrument in the service of a psychic energy, the possibility now arises that the entire construction of drives, substitutions, repressions, and representations is the aberrant, metaphorical correlative of the absolute randomness of language, prior to any figuration or meaning. It is no longer certain that language, as excuse, exists because of a prior guilt but just as possible that since language, as a machine, performs anyway, we have to produce guilt (and all its train of psychic consequences) in order to make the excuse meaningful. Excuses generate the very guilt they exonerate, though always in excess or by default. (299)

10 *Ibid.*, 301.

11 Or even gives meaning to what apparently has none. The stone

Pickwick finds with letters in some unknown language (+BILST/UM/ PSHI/S.M./ARK) is, when blanks are put in the right place, a perfectly readable series of English words: + BIL[L] STUMPS HIS MARK (217). The words are, as it happens, a classic example of the way a nonword can function as a performative. A cross is put by an illiterate person in place of a signature and then ratified through an explanatory note by someone who can write certifying who made the cross. The cross works as well as a signature to bind the one who makes it.

CHAPTER 6

Serialized retrospection in The Pickwick Papers

Robert L. Patten

> To understand history in the Victorian era meant to find oneself on a line running from the past through the present to the future; this sense of the linearity of time and its forward-moving nature was embodied in the serial form.
>
> *Linda K. Hughes and Michael Lund*

> Recollection of the best-ordained banquets will scarcely cheer sick epicures.
>
> *William Makepeace Thackeray*

In the 1950s when Victorian serial fiction began to be rehabilitated, it was the novels of Dickens that were most often examined by critics. They defended Dickens's work by showing that his serials were not the "loose baggy monsters" Henry James had called them but, rather, were thematically controlled. Moreover, to counter the charge made by Ouida among many others that in "the serial form . . . the writer sacrifices form and harmony to the object of attaining an exciting fragment for each division of his work," John Butt and Kathleen Tillotson demonstrated that Dickens's installments avoided the most meretricious kinds of suspensemongering at the end of each part.[1] Edmund Wilson and his successors reconceived in Freudian and New Critical terms: the serials anticipated later psychological fiction, innovated in publishing formats, and diagnosed the ills of contemporary society in advance of their more general recognition and partial amelioration. More recent theorists of parts publications have noted the affinity between forward-looking serials and Whig history, Enlightenment and Romantic paradigms of personal and social development, the capitalist induced hunger for more commodities, and changes in the speed and emphasis of "time's arrow."[2] In these revisionary interpretations Dickens's periodicals, like Victorian history and serials more generally, looked forward – to their endings, to later literature, to reform. This perspective might be said to culminate in Steven Marcus's famous formulation about the "miracle of *Pickwick Papers*": "this impulse towards transcendence," a representation, by the end of the book, "of the ideal possibilities of human relations in community."[3] Many Victorian texts issued in installments, from Thomas Carlyle's *Sartor Resartus* to William Morris's *Earthly Paradise*, traveled forward to a promised land.

Another persistent strain in the interpretation of Victorian serialization has been an appreciation of its timeliness, its representation of the *mentalité* of the day.[4] Thackeray wrote in 1840 that *Pickwick* "gives us a better idea of the state and ways of all the people than one could gather from any more pompous or authentic histories."[5] This appreciation has received powerful reinforcement from Richard Altick's magisterial study, *The Presence of the Present: Topics of the Day in the Victorian Novel*.[6] Professor Altick identifies hundreds of subjects that nineteenth-century British authors introduced into their texts as the novel strove to assimilate the currency of newspapers, gossip, legal and parliamentary forensics, and "the common fund of information, opinions, assumptions, and idea- and value-structures" that comprised the Victorian episteme.[7]

To complement these views of Victorian serials as forward-looking and time-specific, we should add a third perspective: looking backward. While Dickens's first serial, which established a model for future novels by him and by his contemporaries, is undeniably anticipatory and topical, it is also complexly retrospective. Paradoxically *Pickwick* gains propulsion as a story and a commercial venture from its suffusion of pastness, and it speaks to and about its contemporaries by articulating a nostalgia for previous modes of discursive practice, feeling, and social organization. Even its topicalities are sometimes "double-faced," as Altick puts it, looking simultaneously to the present scene and backward.[8]

Distancing the action of a text, as many Victorian novels did, achieved several ends: the story could work up to the present at its close, its incidents and settings might appeal to older readers, and in some cases, novelists wished to avoid both deeply historical accounts of the sort Scott popularized and the vulgarity of ephemerality.[9] *The Pickwick Papers*, begun according to no clear plan on the part of initiating illustrator or commissioned author, are retrospective in dating, plotting, and mood. Death is announced prior to any portion of the book, in the 26 March advertisement for the forthcoming *"Posthumous" Papers of the Pickwick Club*.[10] Death is reiterated in the concluding double number, when Mr. Pickwick dissolves the club preparatory to retiring with Sam, whose reciprocated attachment, the last words declare, "nothing but death will sever." Chronologically *Pickwick* opens with an entry in the "transactions" dated 12 May 1827; "the year of grace in which these . . . adventures, were undertaken and accomplished" (chapter 28) is nearly nine years before the 31 March 1836 publication of the first installment. The story ends in October 1828 (chapter 53), with a coda bringing the characters forward some half-dozen years. The whole of the narrative is thus set during the reign of George IV at the time of the fierce controversies aroused by Huskisson's corn bill and Catholic emancipation. Nothing takes place during the reign of Queen Victoria, and only a quarter of the text was written after she succeeded to the throne on 20 June 1837. This work so often instanced as the first Victorian serial preceded the era both in its production and in its temporal setting. The society *Pickwick* depicts, and the state of mind it reveals, Steven Marcus declares, in fact respond "to the social climate in England around the time of the Reform Bill of 1832," a social climate, therefore, four years after the novel's temporal setting but four years before its production.[11]

There are dozens of references anachronistic to the *Papers*'s internal chronology, but the dynamic of the novel is not fueled by these proleptic allusions. Indeed, "prophecyin' avay wery fine, like a red-faced Nixon" about "what's a goin' to happen" (chapter 43) gets short shrift from the Wellers and from the editor of these posthumous papers. Far more insistent, especially in the early installments, is the invocation of what *has* happened. The papers have been written, the entries of the club transactions, the Pickwick diary,[12] and Mr. Snodgrass's notebook (presented 2 December 1828) have been collected. The introduced stories are themselves old, about prior events already formulated into stories, previously written down (Dismal Jemmy's promised "curious . . . leaf from the romance of real life" [chapter 5], the Dingley Dell clergyman's notes, the Tale of Prince Bladud) or at the time of telling in the novel consigned to paper from a well-rehearsed narration (the Bagman's and Jack

Bamber's tales). The stories are then retold, retranscribed, added to the "multifarious documents" (chapter 1) the editor has searched out, and re-reinscribed in this edition of the papers.

If this serial opens like Genesis with the birth of light and keeps going by the reiterated rise of Pickwick and the sun,[13] if, as Dickens said in an address inserted midway through the numbers, borrowing the rhetoric of a showman barker, "we shall keep perpetually going on beginning again, regularly, until the end of the fair,"[14] it is equally the case that the incidents and chapters and parts repeatedly wind down and stop, that the "end of the fair" comes early and often. The club nearly breaks up in the first chapter because of Mr. Blotton, and at the end internal dissension during the absence of the members of the Corresponding Society destroys the parent institution. Death is omnipresent. During the first installments we read of the decapitation of the tall lady who, eating sandwiches while seated on the top of a coach, forgot to duck under an archway; the decollation of Charles I; the demise of Donna Christina Fizzgig and her father; the countless pilgrims and odd fellows who moulder in the ruins of Rochester Castle; and the deaths of the stroller, the father, wife, and son of John Edmunds, along with that of the returned convict himself, the brother-in-law and wife of the madman, and Quanko Samba, who bowled on, on Jingle's account, and bowled off, on his own. The clergyman's song celebrates the ivy, which "joyously hugs and crawleth round / The rich mould of dead men's graves" (chapter 6).

Later on we learn of dozens more expirations, not just in the introduced tales but also among the characters in the main story: Snodgrass is an orphan (chapter 57); Ben and Arabella Allen have only two surviving aunts; old Mrs. Wardle, Mrs. Bardell, Mrs. Pell, and Susan Weller are widows; and Mr. Wardle, Solomon Pell, and Tony Weller (twice) are widowers. Susan Weller dies, as does the Chancery prisoner. Dismal Jemmy threatens suicide; Wilkins Flasher and Frank Simmery wager that the ruined Boffer will kill himself within ten days (chapter 55).

The narrative itself is threatened by death. Many of the chapters are structured by the passage of a day, from bright beginning to cold, dark night, when Mr. Pickwick is overturned in a post chaise, caught in the rain, trapped in the garden of Westgate House where he contracts rheumatism, or wanders in the lightless corridors of the Great White Horse Inn. Travelers' inns and Inns of Court alike seem to house relics: decrepit mails, old gentlemanly chairs, musty documents, and concealed bodies. Arriving at these Gothic, and hence generically past, destinations at the end of a long day less often yields rest and recuperation than more kinds of termination: duels, real or threatened (Dr. Slammer, Mr. Magnus), altercations (Pott and Slurk), exile (Winkle at Bath), and more stories of worn-out lives (told by Jack Bamber and Mr. Perker's clerks), stories whose "somniferous influence" (chapter 7) puts auditors and readers to sleep. Mr. Miller dozes during the clergyman's verses; Mivins and Pickwick slumber through Smangle's recitation of his romantic adventures; Sam drops off while the cobbler explains how an inheritance ruined him.

The novel as material object confronted death repeatedly. Dickens predicted its termination in "about twenty numbers" before he had written more than two,[15] and restated that limit half-way through.[16] Robert Seymour's death made a "blank," a "void," which, Dickens announced in part 2, "we can hardly hope to see supplied" unless some time elapses.[17] The paucity of commercial returns on the first parts almost doomed the project. After Robert Buss spoiled the etchings for the third part he was succeeded by "Nemo," no one, a blank that time was supposed to supply, and that was subsequently filled by overwriting "Phiz," the second pseudonym of Hablot Knight Browne. Mary Hogarth's death precluded the timely composition of part 15 for June 1837, and that suspension, that void, led to rumors that the "editor" had been killed, gone mad, been imprisoned for debt, decamped to the United States, or gone into an irreversible coma.[18]

Each part enacted a kind of *petit mort*. The early ones conclude at the end of the day or with an incident implying no further new beginning or continuing story. In later ones the very chapter endings themselves are foregrounded as artificial stops, subject to the scythe of the compiler: "But bless our editorial heart, what a long chapter we have been betrayed into! We had quite forgotten all such petty restrictions as chapters, we solemnly declare. So here goes, to give the goblin a fair start in a new one!" (chapter 28) And yet the next chapter, so arbitrarily devised, retained in serialization the same number as the preceding one, so that there were two chapters 28 and no numerical distinction between the first, about Christmas at Dingley Dell, and its successor, "The Story of the Goblins who Stole a Sexton." There seems to be here and elsewhere, despite editorial foregrounding of chapter ends and beginnings, no clear-cut difference between winding down and winding up.

Moreover, when Dickens finished the book, he went back to its origins for the subject of all three of his prefaces, recounting in great detail the circumstances that led him to undertake the menial assignment of composing letterpress to accompany already sketched illustrations, his determination to take his own course, and the effect the death of Seymour had on the book's format and direction. As the years passed between composition and new editions, Dickens's prefaces became more and more retrospective, measuring the social improvements since the *Papers* were originally written, and prophesying, though in the subjunctive mood, that in the near future "a few petty boards and bodies . . . [may not] always . . . keep their jobbing little fiddles going, for a Dance of Death."[19] Looking backward to Death as the origin and propulsion of these *Papers* is thus embedded in many different features of the text and its accessory documents.

Much has been made, and rightly so, of the ways Dickens incorporated seasonal references in his monthly parts.[20] The July 1836 number tells of a "pleasant afternoon in June" (214), the September one recounts August events, in October the original audience could read about September shooting, the January 1837 part contains the Pickwickians' Yuletide celebrations, the March one treats of valentines and breach of promise, and the final November double number is set in October.[21] Many critics have pointed to this mensural dating as one of the ways in which contemporary readers found topicality in the numbers.[22] They might speculate during the month on what the Pickwickians were doing (as indeed letters of the time demonstrate), and on magazine day at the end of that month they could buy the postdated installment and discover whether their speculations were correct.[23] Dickens's audience certainly sensed, throughout his career, that the installments were being manufactured concurrently; people wrote letters advising the author to change his future course, and sometimes he did. When there was an interruption of routine, speculation raged just as much, if not more, than when regular periodicity was observed.

Although the production of the novel, along with its dated wrapper and advertising inserts, periodic announcements of changes, and regular reviews in the newspapers and magazines, contributed to the public's sense of a work issued in progress, the fact that the numbers recount the previous month's events – previous by a month and by nine years – is not such unambiguous evidence for contemporaneity as has been maintained. We who are accustomed to soap operas expect serials to take place on the day of viewing, and Christmas is celebrated proleptically from Thanksgiving forward. Dickens's readers rarely got such up-to-the-minute synchronicity; even the Christmas books and later Christmas stories printed in *Household Words* and *All the Year Round* came out at best a week prior to the holiday.

For all the apparent currency of the Pickwickians' adventures, the book subtly but insistently pushes its events backward in time. Humphry House may have been the first modern critic to call attention to "ante-dating," the distancing of Victorian fiction by placing the action a decade or more earlier than publication; Kathleen Tillotson illustrated the process in *Novels of the Eighteen-Forties*; and Richard Altick concludes from a wider survey of fiction between 1830 and 1890 that "the technique [of 'ante-dating'] proves to be less incidental than almost characteristic."[24] Yet virtually nowhere in the contemporary notices, according to Altick, is there any mention of such distancing. Dickens's fiction in particular is notable for the "extensive and peculiar blend" of past and present.[25] The backward look was thus present and absent, emphasized and obscured, to Dickens's first audience; the blend of present with "ante-dating" and distancing and retrospection takes the edge off any sharp sense that the Pickwickians' adventures are merely, or simply, contemporary.

Pickwick's readers looked back beyond the previous month. There were references to older books and events: Edward Jesse's third series of *Gleanings in Natural History* (1835), from which Jingle's story of the sagacious dog is taken,[26] and the travel accounts of visiting foreigners, Friedrich von Raumer (1835) and Prince Pückler-Muskau (1826–29), prototypes of Count Smorltork. Repeated allusions are made to the Society for the Diffusion of Useful Knowledge founded in 1826,[27] and there is one to the assassination of Prime Minister Spencer Perceval in 1812. The allusions extend still further back in time: predominantly to eighteenth-century literature (Lillo's *George Barnwell*, Defoe's *Robinson Crusoe*, Fielding and O'Hara's *Tom Thumb*, Sterne's *Sentimental Journey*, Smollett's picaresques, and Pope's and Watts's verse) and to famous personages (the Marquess of Granby, Daniel Lambert). At some level

The Pickwick Papers, like Tennyson's poetry, acknowledges through reiterations of death and past times a sense of belatedness, of coming after the time of great literary forefathers.[28]

Pickwick's story is not only set a decade earlier, it also reinscribes familiar types, scenes, and incidents already formulated.[29] "The wit of the writer," the *Atlas* lamented in a review of the first installment, "has no wider range than through that melancholy region of comicality, which Hood and Poole and Smith and Cruikshank have reaped until they have not left a single laugh behind."[30] Pickwick and Sam were instantly recognized as versions of Don Quixote and Sancho Panza, versions that, as N. N. Feltes emphasizes, by their "difference in class and historical period, interpellate that specifically bourgeois Victorian sense of self"[31] – that "peculiar blend" of past and present in yet another example. "Tupman and Snodgrass," Harvey Peter Sucksmith and James Kinsley note, "are typical variants (amorous and poetical) of the late eighteenth-century Man of Feeling and, with Seymour's Cockney sportsman, make up a simple version of the old comedy of humours."[32] The Gothic legends of ghostly suitors at love and law were being refurbished simultaneously by Dickens's closest friend, Harrison Ainsworth, whose novels of Augustan rogues were enlivened by the anecdotes and tales collected by a Manchester antiquary, James Crossley, and by the mother of the author of *Tom Brown's School Days*, Mrs. Hughes. Sam Weller recites one of Ainsworth's reworked ballads, "Bold Turpin vunce, on Hounslow heath." Although the editor alleges the legend "is not generally known" (chapter 43), it had been retold countless times, recently in Horace Smith's 1825 *Gaieties and Gravities* and again a decade later in Ainsworth's *Rookwood*.

Robert Seymour's cast of characters was familiar from the comic journals and graphic albums of previous decades. Incidents and persons Dickens added to the stock in the course of composition refurbished materials having a long pedigree, and recently renovated in the productions of Thomas Hood, Charles Mathews, and George Cruikshank, whose etchings and aquatints of "fun – London life" and of London characters were widely disseminated and copied not least by the *Pickwick* illustrators.[33]

Reading about such London types as they were freshly rendered by Boz and Phiz entailed a kind of looking backward to figures and incidents already codified in lexical and graphic formulas. And, in an era that commercialized the duplication of "originals" through steam-powered presses, etching, lithography, and photography, and the manufacture of piracies, plagiarisms, parodies, sequels, and multiple dramatizations, these formulas could be replicated again and again; new products that repeated the past.[34]

Looking backward, I am arguing, is a way of reading, possibly the way of reading. There is much about reading in this serial.[35] The Pickwickians learn to read the signs around them more accurately – with or without enabling or obscuring spectacles, to distinguish appearance *as* appearance.[36] They do not continue to mistake the mark of a man, physical or alphabetical, as Mr. Pickwick mistakes Bill Stumps's mark, or rather makes it into another kind of story.[37] "Ocular demonstration" of the sort that Mr. Magnus requires (chapter 22), or that leads the scientific gentleman in Clifton to compose a treatise on electricity (chapter 39), proves not to be the only or optimal way of interpreting or communicating. Observant lady readers, the narrator remarks, might deduce satisfactory inferences from sighs, abstinence from alcohol, and gloomy looks (chapter 30); tears may not be proof of distress (chapter 45). Mr. Pickwick manages to decipher Jingle's "system of stenography" (chapter 7). The Wellers communicate through an "alphabet of winks," "a complete code of telegraphic winks and gestures" (chapter 43),[38] while the Fat Boy tries to assure the ladies of his fidelity through smirks and grins (chapter 54). Pott and Slurk illustrate one kind of interpretive activity – the partisan sort that led Matthew Arnold to urge a "disinterested criticism." Sam and his father, discussing poetry and alibis, enact another. The point is that learning, too, comes after, from looking backward, not just at a prior system of signs but also for alternative interpretations more consonant with outcomes and experience.

> "Oh Pott! if you'd known
> How false she'd have grown,
> When you heard the marriage bells tinkle;
> You'd have done then, I vow,
> What you cannot help now,
> And handed her over to W * * * * *." (chapter 18)

"Ven you're a married man, Samivel," Tony Weller admonishes, "you'll understand a good many things as you don't understand now; but vether it's worth while goin' through so much, to learn so little, as the charity-boy said ven he got to the end of the

alphabet, is a matter o' taste" (chapter 27). The serial and the
editor of these documents read backward too, from the end of the
alphabet and the end of the transactions. Serialization fixed prior
episodes more or less unamenable to revision – although Dickens
tinkered with his text until 1867. But periodical publication did not
prevent Dickens and his successors from reading back into earlier
episodes and rewriting them differently, more fully, in unexpected
ways, as the narrative progressed. Indeed the illusion of progress is
itself dependent on a backward look, a measuring of the difference
between then and now, as the 1847 preface to *Pickwick* clearly
demonstrates. The thematic organization that Dickens planned
at the outset for *Martin Chuzzlewit* and *Dombey and Son* grew in
Pickwick out of the nexus of characters and incidents that Robert
Seymour had adapted from earlier instances and that Dickens had
composed in the opening numbers. Implicitly, in the multiplication
of scenes of disruption and resolution, death and new beginnings,
and explicitly, in such reflections as Mr. Pickwick's on the tendency
of his fellow members to "disturb the peace of mind and happiness
of some confiding female" (chapter 18), or the late revelation that
Dismal Jemmy "could assume anything" and would have been
"even a more dangerous acquaintance" than Job Trotter (chapter
53), the text reexamines its premises, its persons and actions,
having in a sense got to the end of the alphabet of types and
situations quite early on and then subjected them to revision, to
what J. Hillis Miller calls the "simultaneous plurality" of the same
story and characters encountered in multiple ways.[39] Perhaps it is
not Pickwick who grows wiser or Snodgrass and Winkle who grow
younger, but rather the serial installments that reconsider their own
materials, and in so doing grow up, change from an assemblage
of disconnected documents, like the monthly parts themselves,
into a story, one marked always by the same wrapper design
yet continuously reexamining its initial alphabet in the light of
the experience of reading. For we make up stories about where
we are by telling stories about where we have been – indeed, we
cannot make up a story while in the midst of an action, but only
from the vantage of its end, when we can look back and make out
of that occluded, packed initiation the beginning of the tale we
tell.[40] Beginnings are determined by endings; death is the mother
of invention.

   Recollection, then, is essential to story telling. It is the process by which a story gets told; it is also the mood of telling. In complex ways the Romantics, especially Wordsworth, reformulated the role of recollection in narrative. Wordsworth's diagram, set forth in the 1802 preface to *Lyrical Ballads*, uses recollection as the means for reconsidering prior personal experience, bringing it back to mind and feeling, and inciting the recollector to composition. During that composition, Wordsworth maintains, associations called up from the writer's own experience, and through simple language "arising out of repeated experience and regular feelings," may expand the private and unique remembered event into something paradigmatic and sharable with others, "the primary laws of our nature . . . the general passions and thoughts and feelings of men."[41] Dickens also founds his communication on recollection, but recollection begins in his case not with the solitary and personal memory but rather with the socially shared recollections of a common alphabet of mediated experiences – mediated particularly through literature, theater, law and news reporting, and graphic art. Not surprising, therefore, is the centrality of Dingley Dell to the writer's project, for there especially the force of recollection as a mood, an emotional and memorial bond shared among characters and between text and readers, is most elaborately evoked. Recollection, reinforced and somatically registered by partaking of viands and spirits, by the arousal and satisfaction of appetite, is then converted into a commodity, a substitute memory and meal many times multiplied, which the shilling parts make available for general consumption.

"The happiest moments of my life have been passed at this old fire-side," Mr. Wardle muses, and recollections of her own girlhood bring tears to his mother's eyes (chapter 6). Mrs. Wardle often compares current events to incidents associated with her friend Lady Tollimglower, deceased, recitation of which may extend above three hours (chapter 57). Christmas at Dingley Dell is celebrated in the old-fashioned way, Christmas being "quite a country gentleman of the old school" (chapter 28). The season awakens "many old recollections, and . . . many dormant sympathies" (chapter 28), not less for the Dingley Dellers than for Gabriel Grub. The depiction of Manor Farm is an exercise in emotive figural recollection – that is, the text articulates an old-fashioned kind of manor house celebration unlikely to have been experienced in person by Dickens or most of his readers, but known to them as a powerfully resonant myth figured in the literature and art of preceding ages. Dingley

Dell is the place where in recollecting the past the old become
younger, the young become amorous, and differentiations of class
and economic resources are temporarily and partially erased by
communal feeling. The servants are still servants, the poor relations
still poor, and Mrs. Wardle cannot stand up for the whole dance;
but the entire community assembles in the kitchen, beguiling the
time with forfeits and old stories according to the immemorial
custom of Wardle's forefathers (chapter 28).

Old-fashioned too are the coaches that drive through the novel,
connecting places far apart and singleness to matrimony. As is
well known, by 1836 railways had begun to replace the coaches
of earlier eras. "There is indeed," James Kinsley comments, "a
calculated nostalgia about *Pickwick Papers* – dated, perhaps, just to
keep the railways out."[42] Mr. Weller and his cohorts were a dying
breed, and the old galleried inns had, the narrative informs us, "in
these times . . . degenerated into little more than the abiding and
booking places of country wagons" (chapter 10). These might be
up-to-date topical references, except that the demise of the grave
and solemn old coaches had been a staple of popular imagery for
some time. Coach travel also was figured as a time for stories, for
feasting and drinking, for fellowship: all those things that in the
present degenerate times have been neglected.

Coaches not only look backward, they lead backward, in two
senses. They take travelers to a past time in their own right,
as ancient vehicles, and also by virtue of their destinations:
old inns, Manor Farm, the legendary inn Tom Smart acquires,
Tony Weller's "Marquis of Granby," and, most symbolic and
resonant, the dream journey of the Bagman's Uncle back to
eighteenth-century Edinburgh – a realization through fantasy
in the last interpolated tale of the ideal destination of many
of these coaching journeys. Moreover, at arrival one encounters
the other destination of coaches – matrimony, or bedrooms, where
at the end of the day or in the dark of night, sexual encounters
figured as sexual violations are repeatedly enacted: at the Bull
Inn, in the girls' school garden, in Miss Witherfield's chamber,
in the abduction of Arabella Allen, and, paradigmatically though
in the manner and style of the eighteenth-century picaresque this
protobourgeois parody revises, in the Bagman's Uncle's chivalric
rescue of the "dazzling beauty." After spiking the heir of the
Marquis of Filletoville (Dickens's onomastic play on abduction

and rape, "girl to town"), the Bagman's Uncle rides off in the old mail with the lady, swearing to love and marry no one but her. In that ghostly mail, pursued by men, horses, and dogs, he rides, in a sense, forever; in another sense, awake and a perpetual bachelor thereafter, he is, like the dead letters carried by those phantom coaches, a last exemplar of an earlier, dead text of sexual pursuit and heterosexual bonding, forever distant from the undelivered valentines, failed chivalry, and farcical abductions of the present. These *Posthumous Papers* both copy and skewer past texts.

There is not only a retrospective but also a regressive aspect to *Pickwick*. Travel into the past and into stories often culminates in a state of idyllic bachelorhood, whether it be the Bagman's Uncle or Pickwick, ensconced at Dulwich with his faithful attendant Sam. Master Bardell acts for all the men in the novel who don't want their parents to remarry – or themselves to be saddled with an adult female companion. Some of the text's psychological pressures, as I will demonstrate shortly, are directed toward regression, toward the bliss of orality and maternal feeding.[43] In some ways *Pickwick*'s "impulse towards transcendence" leads to the promised land of infantilized satisfactions, the legendary past of stories and food. In other ways, the novel strives for maturation and community, forged amid the darkness and privations brought about through temporal progression.

The breach of promise trial plays with many of the same ingredients as the Dingley Dell Christmas, but to different ends. The court is another site of immemorial custom, of storytelling, and of the display of appetites (desire, food, marriage, spectacle), but the dynamic is division rather than consolidation. A breach of promise is another kind of retrospective tale, one that can be told only when, from the perspective of the end, its beginning is reinterpreted to disconfirm continuity, to make a breach in the promise of a future union. The trial depends, among other things, on memory, past sight, and prior writing, all of which must be perceived by readers and writers innumerable. That process of reading backward extends not only to those in the courtroom but also to "author" and "audience": Dickens reread and reinscribed the action brought by Mr. Norton against the Prime Minister Lord Melbourne for "criminal conversation" (adultery) with his wife Caroline Norton, which had been tried in June 1836 (according to narratives already laid down by traditional court practice), and which he had reported in twenty-six tightly printed columns of the *Morning Chronicle*.[44] Readers unfamiliar with newspaper accounts might still have recollected other, more comic trials, such as the one in Robert Smith Surtees's *Jorrocks's Jaunts and Jollities* (1831). And the text, torn between the comedy of romance and regressive orality, both punishes the breach of promise (Pickwick is fined and goes into the Fleet) and celebrates it (by freeing Pickwick forever from having to settle down into domesticity with Mrs. Bardell).

One medium for the circulation and satisfaction of the desire for community is physical consumption, feasts and drinks. These are prominent among the immemorial customs of Dingley Dell, and the "Chops and Tomata sauce" text of the trial encodes, even in Serjeant Buzfuz's retrospective (and contextually carica-tural) reading, an intimacy, a connection through appetite, that is eroticized (warming pans, "hidden fire") and satiated. If the *Pickwick Papers* alternates between sunrise and sunset, between harmony and discord, between singleness and matrimony, it does so often through ceremonies of feast and famine. Men hunger in this book, and women feed them. "Women after all, gentlemen," Snodgrass rhapsodizes to the commercial travelers in the Peacock Inn, "are the great props and comforts of our existence." "When they're in a good humour," adds the red-faced man (chapter 14). If no food is provided, men may consume themselves, their clothing (as Jingle lives off his boots for a fortnight), or other men, ground up in the patent "sassage"-grinding machine. Women hunger too, for husbands as much as for material possessions, or for husbands as material possessions, or in order to have them. But females are largely the providers, males the consumers in this fantasy

Food, story, and eroticism wonderfully coalesce when Bob Saw-yer, recollecting his youthful wooing of Arabella Allen, remembers carrying two caraway-seed biscuits and a sweet apple, folded into a circular parcel and wrapped with a leaf from a copybook, in his trouser pocket, where the apple grows too warm for Arabella to eat. So Bob and Ben consume the apple themselves, in alternate bites. This story makes clear in marvelously devious ways – including wrapping the apple in a copied text – what the novel articulates time and time again: that though females may provide nourishment, the feasts and celebrations ratify male–male pair bondings. No valued marriage takes place in this book unless it preserves male friendship, between master and man, father and son, or fellow Pickwickians. Sam does not wed until Mary can move in as Pickwick's housekeeper; Weller's sons-in-law live on the estate; Job refuses to leave Jingle, so the "worthy couple" (chapter 53) embark together for the West Indies. Pickwick's festal board is set for men and consumed by men; female hunger is sublimated, caricatured, or, as in Susan Weller's case, repented. Mrs. Bardell is obtusely right: Pickwick was promising a kind of marriage when he asked if two could live as cheaply as one, and she was right again in charging that his periphrastically announced purpose is a breach of the societal promise that marriage is between woman and man, provider and provided for, keeper and kept, owner and debtor. She just got the gender of Pickwick's partner wrong.

There is something comically cannibalistic about the conjunction of love and food, apple and serpent, hunger and marriage, and the conjunction of desire and consumption is figured in another of *Pickwick*'s backward glances, the comic valentine. After all, the medico Bob Sawyer identifies the "stomach" as the primary cause of disease (chapter 48). Comic valentine writers were another staple of the petty-commodity trade[45] of preceding decades: these were luridly illustrated "how-to" books for aspiring wooers, meant to be purchased and "consumed" and laughed over by those striving for greater literacy and by their middle-class superiors. What prompts Sam to his "unnat'ral" poetry is

a highly coloured representation of a couple of human hearts skewered together with an arrow, cooking before a cheerful fire, while a male and female cannibal in modern attire, the gentleman being clad in a blue coat and white trousers, and the lady in a deep red pelisse with a parasol of the same, were approaching the meal with hungry eyes, up a serpentine gravel path leading thereto. (chapter 33)

This picture exemplifies the wares of a shopkeeper who announces a large assortment within, available for sale at the reduced price of one and sixpence. Like the monthly part, which for the even cheaper price of a shilling recounted February events, the valentine was marketed seasonally, and like the skewered hearts imaged on the picture, the valentine and the monthly part were to be consumed by happy cannibals in modern attire, the male wearing a coat of the hue so identified with the Pickwick Club.

Thus recollection is connected to appetite, and consumption in this novel ratifies male hunger and male friendship. The same thing might be said about serial production. Henry Fielding elaborately compared the contents of a novel to a collation at an eating house or tavern;[46] parts publication realized that principle of consumption. Every banquet, every monthly number, solicited a community of readers to feast again on recollections of posthumous papers, as Bob Sawyer and Ben Allen discuss minced veal and future prospects by recollecting their past project to obtain Arabella's one thousand pounds (chapter 48). Satiated, hung over from the "salmon" and the "Perambulations, Perils, Travels, Adventures, and Sporting Transactions of the Corresponding Members," the readers slowly recover. Because of the memory of those experiences they hunger for the next "feast of reason, sir, and flow of soul," as Mr. Leo Hunter, borrowing from a sonneteer who commemorated his wife's public breakfasts in the words of yet another poet (Alexander Pope) translating a third (Horace), characterizes Eatanswill entertainment. No wonder that *Pickwick* did not generate an audience until the fourth number; it took that long for the story to be consumed, digested, and recollected. Or, in other words, it was memory of past incidents, discussed by *Pickwick*'s readers along with minced veal and future prospects, that prompted the purchase and consumption of the next installment.

Consuming memories of the past in male-centered communities is what makes these *Posthumous Papers* go forward as a narratorial and commercial venture. Developing an appetite for the past, in a sense battening on mouldy graves like the ivy green, was one secret of the success of serial fiction. Thackeray exploited reminiscence as feeling and narrative strategy and used the repetitious cycle of serial parts as an analogue to history. Wilkie Collins generated nervous suspense out of unraveling a past event over many installments. Anthony Trollope went one step further, compulsively reiterating in *Phineas Redux* a moment – a variant on a breach of promise – in an earlier serial, *Phineas Finn*. And George Eliot, reinvoking a past time in the service of a humane understanding of historical processes, consummated and exploited the backward-looking dynamic of periodical fiction. *Pickwick* in manifold ways is the first text to discover, play with, and anatomize the retrospective potential of serialization. By looking backward the text is a forerunner of later narratives. It also provides an up-to-date treatment of the nostalgic mood of early Victorian England, poised between a conventionally represented, shared, and idealized past and an apprehensively viewed future.[47] The serial parts of *The Posthumous Papers of the Pickwick Club* do not breach their promise. They marry what is already united: past and present and future, documents and editor and consumers.[48]

NOTES

The epigraphs are from Linda K. Hughes and Michael Lund, *The Victorian Serial* (Charlottesville: University Press of Virginia, 1991), 60, and William Makepeace Thackeray, *Vanity Fair*, ed. Geoffrey and Kathleen Tillotson (London: Methuen & Co., 1963), chapter 19, 180.

1 "Ouida," undated (*circa.* 1882) letter to *The Times* on "English Novels," quoted in Eileen Bigland, *Ouida: The Passionate Victorian* (New York: Duell, Sloan & Pearce, 1951), 163; John Butt and Kathleen Tillotson, *Dickens at Work* (London: Methuen, 1957); see also Elliot Engel's introduction to his *Pickwick Papers: An Annotated Bibliography* (New York: Garland, 1990), ix–xxix.

2 For a summary of recent work, see Hughes and Lund, especially chapter 1.

3 Steven Marcus, *Dickens: From Pickwick to Dombey* (New York: Basic Books, 1965), 17.

4 Examples are, for Dickens, Philip Collins, *Dickens and Crime* (London: Macmillan, 1962) and *Dickens and Education* (London: Macmillan, 1963), and for Thackeray, Rowland McMaster, *Thackeray's Cultural Frame of Reference: Allusion in "The Newcomes"* (London: Macmillan; Montreal: McGill-Queen's University Press, 1990).

5 William Makepeace Thackeray, *The Paris Sketch Book*, 1840, in *Works* (biographical edn., 13 vols.; New York: J. Y. Crowell, 1898–99), vol. 5, 80, quoted in Engel, xii.

6 Richard Altick, *The Presence of the Present: Topics of the Day in the Victorian Novel* (Columbus: Ohio State University Press, 1991).

7 Altick, 2.

8 *Ibid.*, 160.

9 *Ibid.*, 100–101.

10 All citations unless otherwise noted are to the edition by James Kinsley (Oxford: Clarendon, 1986). I provide chapter numbers for the convenience of readers using other editions.

11 Marcus, *From Pickwick to Dombey*, 44–45.

12 So in a 26 March *Athenaeum* advertisement, reprinted in *The Pickwick Papers*, ed. Robert L. Patten (Harmondsworth: Penguin, 1972), 899; "note-book" in Dickens's text.

13 See J. Hillis Miller, *Charles Dickens: The World of His Novels* (Cambridge,

Mass.: Harvard University Press, 1959), 4–5, and Garrett Stewart, "Quarantine," chapter 2 of *Dickens and the Trials of Imagination* (Cambridge, Mass.: Harvard University Press, 1974), 30–54, especially 30–31.

14 Kinsley edn., 881–82.

15 In the 26 March advertisement, Patten edn., 900.

16 Kinsley edn., 881.

17 *Ibid.*, 879.

18 See address inserted in part 15, Kinsley edn., 882.

19 Kinsley edn., 888, 1867 preface.

20 Butt and Tillotson, 62–75; David M. Bevington, "Seasonal Relevance in *The Pickwick Papers*," *Nineteenth-Century Fiction* 16 (1961), 219–30; Kinsley edn., xlvii–xlviii.

21 As Simon Eliot notes in "Some trends in British book production, 1800–1919," *supra*, "the size and importance of the Christmas season grew dramatically in the period from 1850 to 1890" (34). Dickens did not anticipate Christmas sales by publishing about the holiday prior to it until *A Christmas Carol* in 1843.

22 Altick, 63–64.

23 Butt and Tillotson, 73.

24 Altick, 131.

25 Kathleen Tillotson, *Novels of the Eighteen-Forties* (1954; Oxford: Oxford University Press, 1961), 110–11; quoted in Altick, 132.

26 Kathleen Tillotson, "*Pickwick* and Edward Jesse," *Times Literary Supplement*, 1 April 1960, 214.

27 Altick, 107–8 and 108n.

28 See Herbert F. Tucker, *Tennyson and the Doom of Romanticism* (Cambridge, Mass.: Harvard University Press, 1988).

29 Extensive work tracing forerunners of the Pickwickian melange has been done by virtually every major critic of the book. One summary of "influences" is provided throughout Kinsley's introduction, another by Marcus, *From Pickwick to Dombey*, 22–30.

30 Quoted in Kinsley, xxix.

31 Norman N. Feltes, "The Production of a Commodity-Text: The Moment of *Pickwick*," in *Modes of Production of Victorian Novels* (Chicago: University of Chicago Press, 1986), 16.

32 Harvey Peter Sucksmith, *The Narrative Art of Charles Dickens: The Rhetoric of Sympathy and Irony in His Novels* (Oxford: Clarendon, 1970), 318–19; reformulated by Kinsley, xxiii.

33 *Life of Mary Russell Mitford*, ed. the Rev. A. G. K. L'Estrange (2 vols.; New York: Harper & Brothers, 1870), vol. 2, 198. Miss Mitford, writing to her friend Emily Jephson in Ireland, identifies the subject of *Pickwick* by alluding to *Life in London*, the serial (October 1820 to July 1821) written by Pierce Egan and illustrated in aquatints by Robert and George Cruikshank. The Cruikshank brothers published

twenty-four etchings of urban types, called *London Characters*, serially in the *Gentleman's Pocket Magazine* for 1827 and 1829.

34 A pioneering and in many ways still seminal essay is by Walter Benjamin, "The Work of Art in the Age of Mechanical Reproduction," *Illuminations*, ed. Hannah Arendt, trans. Harry Zohn (1955; New York: Schocken, 1969), 217–51. Feltes works out the principle of replication and surplus value in a commodity text in *Modes of Production*, 1–17.

35 See treatments of this subject by Steven Marcus, "Language into Structure: Pickwick Revisited," *Daedalus* 101 (1972), 183–202; James R. Kincaid, "The Education of Mr. Pickwick," *Nineteenth-Century Fiction* 24 (1969), 127–41; and "The *Pickwick Papers*: The Vision from the Wheelbarrow," in *Dickens and the Rhetoric of Laughter* (Oxford: Clarendon, 1971), 20–49; also the books by Marcus and Stewart cited earlier.

36 That appearances are superficial does not necessarily prove, in the epistemology of this text, that the world is "pure surface" (Miller, 12), or that "intrinsic identities" (Miller, 25) and "innate characters" (Miller, 28), have a psychological and psychic authenticity and independence concealed behind facades or that the characters are entirely constructed by their circumstances. The book is ambiguous about such ontological matters. For more on the development of characters, through language, out of caricatures, see my essay "'I Thought of Mr. Pickwick, and Wrote the First Number': Dickens and the Evolution of Character," *Dickens Quarterly* 3 (1986), 18–26.

37 Garrett Stewart points out (6) that just before Pickwick reads Bill Stumps's mark, a sign, according to Steven Marcus, that this book too is "writing about writing," Mr. Pickwick throws an inkstand at Jingle, leaving his mark on the wall in what Sam Weller glosses as "Self-acting ink" (chapter 10). Stewart argues that the book is not about writing or language in general, but about self-aware and self-serving expression. Learning to read, I would add, is necessary to distinguish among the tones, intentions, references, covert allusions, dissembling, and suppressions of language and its wielders.

38 The telegraph was a particularly timely reference; see Altick, 210 and 787.

39 Miller, 13: "The world of *Pickwick Papers* is a swarming plurality of isolated centers of vitality . . . But the plurality of the world . . . is not always simply successive. It is also a simultaneous plurality."

40 See Frank Kermode, *The Sense of an Ending: Studies in the Theory of Fiction* (New York: Oxford University Press, 1967).

41 Quoted from M. H. Abrams *et al.* (eds.), *The Norton Anthology of English Literature* (4th edn., 2 vols.; London: W. W. Norton, 1962), vol. 2, 160–74.

42 Kinsley edn., lv.

43 I am indebted to John Glavin's "misreading" of the novel, "Pickwick

on the Wrong Side of the Door," delivered at the Dickens Project summer conference, University of California at Santa Cruz, August 1991, and subsequently in *Dickens Studies Annual*, 22 (1993), 1–20.

44 The trial was reiterated in subsequent retellings, Thackeray's in *The Newcomes* (1853) and Meredith's in *Diana of the Crossways* (1885); Altick, 148–51.

45 See Feltes, 8, for the distinction between petty-commodity trade and the full-blown "commodity-text" of capitalism.

46 Henry Fielding, *The History of Tom Jones, A Foundling*, ed. Fredson Bowers (2 vols.; Oxford: Clarendon, 1974), vol. 1, chapter 1, 31–34.

47 For the conflicting moods of *1837–38*, see Richard L. Stein, *Victoria's Year: English Literature and Culture, 1837–1838* (New York: Oxford University Press, 1987).

48 Paul Ricoeur revises Martin Heidegger's theory of temporality as "being-toward-death" in "Narrative Time," in *On Narrative*, ed. W. J. T. Mitchell (Chicago: University of Chicago Press, 1981), 165–86; he offers there the possibility that analysis of narrative might show the unity of "having-been," "coming-forth," and "making-present."

CHAPTER 7

Textual/sexual pleasure and serial publication

Linda K. Hughes and Michael Lund

While best known as a medium for male authors, the serial novel's intrinsic form more closely approximates female than male models of pleasure. Rather than inviting sustained arousal of attention until the narrative climax is reached, spending the driving energy of narrative and sundering the readers from the textual experience, the installment novel offers itself as a site of pleasure that is taken up and discharged only to be taken up again (some days or weeks later), and again, and again. Moreover, the engagement and discharge of pleasure in each installment is always oriented toward the future, toward new beginnings and sustained connections with the text, since an installment ends but the narrative continues, "to be continued" until the novel's serial run concludes. Finally, this rhythm of textual pleasure is not entirely controlled by serial readers; no matter how much they might want to sustain interest and pleasure in the text, they must wait until the next installment is scheduled to appear.

Considerations of serial publication have traditionally discounted the extended time frame and periodic structure it imposed on narrative. Modern studies of reading place great emphasis on narrative endings, resolutions that retrospectively validate patterns throughout a text. Thus, critical assessments of serial texts have generally downplayed the experience of first readers who spent months without an ending to authorize response. Yet installment literature and extended reading times dominated nineteenth-century literary experience, not just in England, but in America, France, Russia, and elsewhere. Installment readers enjoyed the parts of Dickens's *Pickwick Papers* (March 1836 to November 1837) and Gaskell's *North and South* (2 September 1854 to 27 January 1855) for the many months they received installments without endings. The critically authoritative texts today, however, are the volume editions

143

in which the hesitations, speculations, reversals, and surprises of the serial text are lost in a form retrospectively defined from the point of closure.

The preference for volume editions and whole texts is, however, related to a traditional, masculinist critical paradigm. Susan Winnett argues that male sexual experience has provided the pattern for contemporary critical models of pleasure in reading. Many narrative plots do rise in tension, peak, and return to equilibrium. Winnett notes, however, that such a definition of plot structure encourages the interpretation of "a particular action in the light of what it *will have meant* at a future moment that it is simultaneously determining and resisting."[1] Furthermore, other, generally unexplored aspects of plot involve excitement that does not end in quiescence, arousals that look forward as beginnings and are not dependent on later endings or resolutions. Winnett explains that experiences of tumescence and detumescence associated with female sexuality – pregnancy and breast feeding – are ultimately oriented not toward reestablishing the state of quiescence that preceded arousal (as in male sexuality) but toward inaugurating and sustaining new beginnings and connections. Moreover, the rhythm of female tumescence/detumescence is partly controlled by forces and an individual (the nursing child) outside the mother. Winnett concludes that new models of plot and pleasure need to be constructed: "I want to explore the different narrative logic – and the very different possibilities of pleasure – that emerge when issues such as incipience, repetition, and closure are reconceived in terms of *an* experience (not *the* experience) of a female body."[2]

The serial has traditionally been viewed, then, as an inferior artistic form that fractures or impedes unified plots driving toward endings that confer meaning on entire novels. More recently it has been shown to be an expression of capitalist practices that appropriate storytelling and intimate audience relations to mask rationalized production of text and the creation of additional demand for the product.[3] We suggest that the serial form also can be reconceptualized in relation to feminine issues, especially the material and cultural conditions of Victorian women readers, and feminist theoretical paradigms. Though the financial control of serial publication rested with Victorian men,[4] the prevalence of women as readers and writers of fiction played a significant role in the serial's popularity. In this sense the serial can be said to "have it all," since it does not subvert dominant economic structures or aesthetic paradigms but nonetheless can offer particular pleasure to women readers.[5] This can be so for serials written by male and female writers alike, but it will be instructive to look at the principal unit of the serial – the part – to see how major writers' conceptions of part structure are manifested along gender lines.

Though women were a major presence among novelists in the first third of the century, and though some prominent women (for example Harriet Martineau) emphatically rejected serialization as a suitable medium for fiction, women's entry into the literary market as mass readers and popular writers and the emergence of serial fiction as a dominant publication mode in the nineteenth century can be seen as related phenomena.[6] So great was the association of novels with female authorship that, as Gaye Tuchman and Nina Fortin discovered in examining the Macmillan publishing archives, "in the 1860s and 1870s men submitting fiction were more likely to assume a female name than women were to use either a male or neuter name."[7] And male serial authors regularly inscribed the expectation of female readership even when subject matter might seem to dictate male readership.[8] Women readers and writers, then, dominated the fiction market when serial publication flourished, and cultural conditions as well as models of female pleasure on the lines Winnett suggests could have fostered women's pleasure in the serial form.

Victorian and twentieth-century commentators have often noted the sense of intimacy and connection serial publication created between audience and text, or audience and author. This result of serial publication, besides helping to perpetuate Victorian domestic ideology, could have worked to extend female readers' associations of pleasure with renewed and sustained relationships, as they met and came to know characters in part after part over as much as a two-year period.[9] And at least one serial female novelist has recorded that her own close relation to the audience affected her production of text. Mary Elizabeth Braddon revamped the ending of her adaptation of Flaubert's *Madame Bovary* because in the process of writing she found herself "so apt to be influenced by little scraps of newspaper criticism, & by what people say to me."[10]

The intimacy encouraged between text and audience by serial publication could have suited women readers on additional grounds.

Recently Mary Field Belenky and others have argued that women best respond to what the authors term "connected knowing," learning in which women develop a relationship to what they study and integrate material with their lived experience to construct personally empowering knowledge. Belenky *et al.* do not suggest that men are excluded or fail to profit from this kind of learning process but only that women resist being forced into other learning modes, for example those requiring them to consider material as separate and autonomous, subject to impersonal procedures.[11] Serial publication fostered a similarly "connected" relation of readers to fiction, since, as we argue elsewhere, "readers and reviewers engaged in provisional assumptions and interpretations about the literary world, which then shaped the evolving understanding of works as they continued to unfold part by part. And a work's extended duration meant that serials could become entwined with readers' own sense of lived experience and passing time."[12] Because authoritative pronouncements were not available on a work of fiction in process, moreover, serial fiction offered women – even within the confines of dominant male social structures – a space in which to explore and discover their own reactions to a literary work.

The material format of the serial was also adapted to the material conditions of middle-class female readers. Though the issuing of fiction in parts has sometimes been related to increasing pressures on time and leisure in the male-dominated commercial world of Victorian society, female lives were also defined by their vulnerability to interruption. In *Cassandra*, Florence Nightingale has given perhaps the most famous statement of this condition:

Women are never supposed to have any occupation of sufficient importance *not* to be interrupted, except "suckling their fools;" and women themselves have accepted this, have written books to support it, and have trained themselves so as to consider whatever they do as *not* of such value to the world or to others, but that they can throw it up at the first "claim of social life." They have accustomed themselves to consider intellectual occupation as a merely selfish amusement, which it is their "duty" to give up for every trifler more selfish than themselves.[13]

If this condition held for the single, upper-middle-class Nightingale, married women and mothers of small children, even with the help of servants, could hardly have immersed themselves all day long in a novel. Conduct books nonetheless encouraged women to maintain reading programs. Isabella Beeton urged that the "mistress of the house" save time late in the morning for, among other things, "the pleasures of literature"; regarding domestic evenings, Beeton stated, "It has often been remarked . . . that nothing is more delightful to the feminine members of a family, than the reading aloud of some good standard work or amusing publication."[14] Short stories, of course, could have responded to the demand for reading in restricted units of time, but short stories feature the gathering and dispersal of narrative energy in a single burst rather than the slowly accreting and intimate form of the serial novel – itself a form defined by its interruptions in the text.

The periodicity of the serial narrative could also have functioned to make such literary work congenial to women while not excluding or marginalizing male readers. The scheduled release of literary parts should bring to mind the monthly scheduling of a female bodily activity also not subject to willed intentions, menses. As a nineteenth-century American physician at Harvard remarked, "Periodicity characterizes the female organization, and develops feminine force. Persistence characterizes the male organization, and develops masculine force."[15] The serial novel, which incorporated periodicity as well as persistence, may have been an ideal mass-market strategy not only because it was attuned to capitalism and gender ideology but also because it presented structures attuned to actual female experience in an era when women were major consumers of literature. Of course, novels appeared in weekly, biweekly, and bimonthly installments as well as in monthly parts, but the cyclic periodicity that typifies serial fiction differs significantly from the model of the whole volume and should remind us that periodicity suppressed in critical discourse has an analogue in the biological periodicity that was an important part of every Victorian woman's life – an experience outside the confines of accepted social or literary discourse in the Victorian age.[16]

Serial fiction did not serve, and most likely could not have served, as a medium for what today is called *écriture féminine*, but the form did, in certain instances, allow women authors to inscribe the female body in the silent spaces between numbers that answered to the silencing of female experience in the larger culture. In *Daniel Deronda* George Eliot (who practiced some form of birth control while living in extralegal union with George Lewes) raised the possibility of unwanted pregnancy for Gwendolen after

Grandcourt's death in the novel's book 7, published August 1876. Serial readers had to wait a full month, until book 8 was published in September 1876, to learn this crucial element of Gwendolen's fate. For women readers this month-long interval could have gestured toward bodily functions signalling pregnancy or menses so familiar as not to require verbal articulation.

Though not as striking as in *Daniel Deronda*, Elizabeth Gaskell also made use of the interval between parts to indicate female bodily change and the introduction of physiological cycles. Between the first and second parts of *Wives and Daughters* (published from August 1864 to January 1866 in the monthly *Cornhill Magazine*), Molly Gibson underwent puberty. A young girl of twelve in the first part (August 1864), Molly was a postpubescent young woman of seventeen who attracted sexual attention in the second installment (September 1864). Gaskell used the space between parts to indicate a change that may be said always to occur offstage, but one that is dramatic and certain nonetheless. By calling attention to this physical change in a young girl's body at the same time she omitted to narrate it, Gaskell exemplifies Elaine Showalter's point that a female subculture emerged from a whole array of physical experience, "increasingly secretive and ritualized," that was shared but could not be openly articulated.[17] The inherent periodicity and silent spaces between parts that characterized serial fiction could have enabled women writers and readers to indicate and recognize female bodily experiences that were not permitted direct articulation.

Although the serial may not be a form of *écriture féminine*, many of the distinctive features of serial fiction are analogous or even homologous with models of feminine narrative developed by a number of theorists and critics.[18] As Hélène Cixous remarks in "Sorties," if a woman "is a whole, it is a whole made up of parts that are wholes, not simple, partial objects but varied entirety, moving and boundless change, a cosmos where eros never stops traveling"; similarly, a woman's "writing also can only go on and on, without ever inscribing or distinguishing contours . . . she goes and goes on infinitely."[19] Estelle Jelinek has advanced a comparable argument about the structuring of feminine, as opposed to masculine, autobiographies. Feminine autobiographies, she proposes, tend to be irregular and fragmentary, "organized into self-sustained units rather than connecting chapters," thus mirroring the "pattern of diffusion and diversity" in women's social (and socially constructed) lives.[20] A serial novel is itself a whole made up of parts that at once function as self-contained units and as building blocks of a larger aesthetic structure. Though the serial eventually ends and takes its place within the literary establishment as an entire, completed work awaiting interpretation and judgment, the long middle of a serial form approximates in significant terms the patterns identified by Cixous and Jelinek. Indeed, as Margaret Beetham remarks of the periodical genre as a whole:

"Closed" or "masculine" forms are seen as those which assert the dominant structures of meaning, by closing off alternative options and offering the reader or viewer only one way of making sense of the text and so, by analogy, of the world and the self. By contrast the "open" form, the form which refuses the closed ending and allows for the possibility of alternative meanings, is associated with the potentially disruptive, the creative, the "feminine."[21]

She terms the periodical "a potentially creative form for its readers," though noting as well that the regular issue and format in the periodical implicitly position readers in social groups and in given vantage points.[22]

Many patriarchal terms used to describe the female rather than male body have been used to describe the serial novel as well. As Rachel Du Plessis and others remark, masculine terms are often those used to describe "good writing" – "lean, dry, terse, powerful, strong, spare, linear, focused, explosive" – versus the feminine terms often associated with "bad writing": "soft, moist, blurred, padded, irregular, going around in circles."[23] The serial has often been censured for padding, digression, and irregularity, all evoked in Henry James's famous term for Victorian novels, "baggy monsters." It is precisely the bag, however, that Ursula Le Guin advances as a preferred, feminist model of narrative in her "Carrier Bag Theory of Fiction." She repudiates the notion that "the proper shape of the narrative is . . . the arrow or spear, starting *here* and going straight *there* and THOK! hitting its mark (which drops dead)." Instead, she proposes that "the natural, proper, fitting shape of the novel might be that of a sack, a bag." In this model of narrative, conflict is only one of many possible elements in shaping plot, not *the* determinant, since the purpose of "narrative conceived as carrier bag/belly/box . . . is neither resolution nor stasis but continuing process." She argues that her own plots are "full of beginnings without ends, of initiations, of losses, of transformations and translations."[24] Le Guin's terms can also be usefully applied to serial fiction, to stories that depend on beginnings that end only provisionally, at the end of a part, before the narrative is further transformed in additional parts.[25]

Yet even if, from material, cultural, and theoretical vantage points, serial fiction has particular relevance to female readers, the serial form did not subvert or exclude dominant male experience or ideology; an individual installment, viewed as an independent entity, was both an apt commercial product and a single instance of aroused and discharged interest and textual pleasure. And, of course, the name most closely associated with the serial form was that of a male: Charles Dickens. Tuchman suggests that the history of nineteenth-century fiction can be viewed as a story of the displacement (by men) of women as authors and the elevating of the aesthetic prestige of the novel. Although she focuses on the customary volume editions rather than serial novels, Tuchman's account of the prevalence and then decline of women novelists in the publishing industry roughly coincides with the heyday and decline of serial fiction. Citing 1840–79 (when serialization also flourished) as the period in which women dominated the submission and acceptance of novels, Tuchman argues that 1880–99 marked the redefinition of the novel, when the number of submissions and acceptances was distributed evenly between men and women, whereas men dominated submissions and acceptances between 1900 and 1917 – the latter period, we argue, also a time when modernist aesthetics caused the serial to decline as a preferred form for "high" literary art.[26] Tuchman's detailed research on Macmillan's publishing archives may suggest as well, then, that the serial form was a particularly congenial medium for women writers and readers. Indeed, she notes that when the aesthetic paradigm shifted to the shorter, "high art" novel in the 1890s, women were either unwilling or unable to abandon the long form of the novel that flourished in mid-century.[27]

Two traditional accounts of serial composition and response – one success story and one apparent failure, the former masculine and the latter feminine – serve to illustrate further how certain concepts of plot have shaped critical understanding of serial form and neglected important elements of literary experience. The rocketing sales of Charles Dickens's *Pickwick Papers* after the fifth monthly number in July 1836 (from 400 to 40,000) represent the achievement of genius as his narrative captured the first genuine mass audience for literature. The pattern of this development, from slow start to later explosion, has dominated our understanding of this particular text and of literary history in the nineteenth century. However, the sustained appeal of *Pickwick* through the remaining fourteen months of its publication needs additional exploration; and here the sources for prolonged reading pleasure suggest a different dynamics, one perhaps more accessible in the fiction of a Dickens contemporary.

Elizabeth Gaskell serialized *North and South* in Dickens's weekly *Household Words* (2 September 1854 to 27 January 1855). But she and Dickens disagreed about what constituted proper and effective structure for individual installments.[28] This battle about editorial policy involved different narrative aims and rival assumptions about readers' pleasure. While Dickens wanted each part to be self-contained – with a clear climax and resolution – Gaskell wanted a more leisurely pace for the development of plot and the entanglement of her audience.

North and South was not the first serial fiction Gaskell published under Dickens's editorship. "Lizzie Leigh," a story serialized in three parts in *Household Words*, opened the inaugural number of the magazine on 30 March 1850. Each part of "Lizzie Leigh" was certainly self-contained. The story's subtitle is "In Four Chapters," and the first and second parts "contained" one chapter each. The first part, moreover, ended on a distinct note of suspense. Anne Leigh, whose husband James dies at the beginning of the part, rents out the farm and moves the family of two sons to Manchester to look for their "fallen" sister Lizzie; Will, the eldest, has fallen in love with Susan Palmer and feels inhibited in his courtship by his mother's quest to reclaim Lizzie. The part ends with him poised to encounter his mother. But if the part ends on a note of suspense, it looks forward, not to an event or action, but to a conversation, a relationship, between a mother and her son. It is easy to see why this part construction might satisfy both the editor Dickens and the author Gaskell. The ending of the second part is not skewed toward suspense, since the ending of this part coincides with the end of a revelatory conversation between Mrs. Leigh and Susan Palmer, during which Mrs. Leigh learns that Susan's "niece" is the daughter of Lizzie. Yet because Mrs. Leigh has yet to encounter her daughter, the part also looks forward to a final part, and a final meeting, suggested by the story's title. In this short serial, then, Gaskell maintained a balance between "connectedness" and suspense, self-containment and anticipation, as forms of narrative pleasure; and Dickens was pleased enough to solicit more work from her for his periodical.

The successful serialization of *Cranford* in *Household Words* owed much to its special character as a series of related tales and to the fact that, as Winifred Gerin writes, Gaskell was able to write for once "under no professional or personal pressures."[29] This work has long been a favorite among Gaskell's readers, and Dickens's major concern was to secure additional parts for *Household Words*. Were it not for the novel's rich, quiet humor and engaging characters, an editor's delight with it might be surprising, for this work is an unusually clear instance of "arousal" and "desire" in plot emerging in patterns contrary to traditional concepts. The first four installments presented assorted vignettes of life in Cranford but neglected a sustained "rising action"; rather than a forward-driving plot, the four parts appearing from 13 December 1851 to 3 April 1852 invited renewed and deepening acquaintance with a community. There followed a nine-month hiatus in *Cranford*'s publication;[30] when it resumed in the 8 and 15 January 1853 issues of *Household Words*, the fifth part quickened with an advancing plot and concluded on a note of suspense as the still-unnamed narrator wondered if the Aga Jenkyns could be Matty Jenkyns's lost brother Peter. Thereafter *Cranford* became in large part Matty's story, with a clearly advancing plot, until the work concluded in the 21 May 1853 issue. Yet even here, as readers later discovered, *Cranford* had not reached a definitive climax that cut off the text from author and audience, for a separate sketch entitled "The Cage at Cranford" appeared in the November 1863 *All the Year Round*. In 1853 and 1854, meantime, *Cranford* pleased Gaskell, Dickens, and the readers of *Household Words*. Some parts of *Cranford* manifested the suspense and rising action traditionally associated with Dickens's own parts structure; but in other respects the novel's larger plot, serial issue, and parts structure resembled the model of feminine narrative pleasure offered by Winnett and others. The publication of Gaskell's next serial work, however, revealed conflicting ideas about literature and its pleasures.

When Dickens first reviewed the manuscript of *North and South*, he praised its "character and power" and noted especially "a strong suspended interest in it (the end of which, I don't in the least foresee)." However, Dickens's advice about the work's serialization was presented in absolute terms: "let me endeavor to shew you as distinctly as I can, the divisions in which it must fall."[31] In an outline, he presented what he thought should be the first six installments; each entry began with the phrase "I would end No. [ ] with . . .," showing his concern that each part have an effective conclusion. In another letter Dickens also insisted, "I believe you are aware that it will at least be necessary to begin every weekly portion as a new chapter."[32] Although Dickens summarized the content of three of the proposed first six installments, he identified the last event to be narrated in every case. Thus, the rhythm of reading, as it was shaped by the sense of each part's beginning in a precise place and coming to a felt conclusion, may have been more important to Dickens as editor than what element of the narrative's subject should be presented by the author every week. Dickens also stated unequivocally that "if it were divided in any other way – reference being always had to the weekly space available for the purpose in *Household Words* – it would be mortally injured."[33] Dickens, of course, was the magazine's editor; but he seemed to assume that Gaskell was unable to conceive on her own of an appropriate division into parts.[34]

Dickens's plan for the novel rearranged some of Gaskell's material; and his efforts almost always were directed at creating self-sufficient units with powerful conclusions.[35] He even offered to take over the matter of parts structure completely, including "sometimes" writing "a word or two of conclusion" for the author. Even as he admits, "I hope these remarks will not confuse you," Dickens's letter ends with additional stress on the absolute necessity of turning the parts structure over to him as editor: "I am bound to put before you my perfect conviction that if it did not [follow this pattern], the story would be wasted – would miss its effect as it went on – *and would not recover it when published complete*" (Dickens's emphasis).[36] For Dickens, the entire life of this novel through all its editions would be a product of the rhythm of its first appearance, a rhythm he was intent on controlling.

The entire plot of *North and South* reveals important distinctions from traditionally conceived (masculinist) plots. The opening number hardly contained within itself the germ of its resolution.

The first two chapters, in fact, were so carefully crafted that they constitute a brilliant, complete short story. It is also difficult to argue that the novel's end point determined or conferred sole meaning on this beginning when there was no hint of the removal to Milton or of John Thornton. And after even the first five parts of the novel had appeared, so astute a reader as Charlotte Brontë thought the novel was to focus on religious doubt.[37] This discontinuity between beginning and end has been one basis for censuring the novel, but if we recur to Cixous's or Le Guin's notions of transformations and ongoing process, or Winnett's model, in which narrative arousal can occur at unforeseen (and even arbitrary) moments, this larger narrative shape is less disturbing.

The shape of an individual part could also, in Gaskell's hands, diverge from Dickens's emphasis on "strong suspended interest" or from the traditional, linear emphasis on event. Interest in the affective lives of characters, more than in events' outcomes, often characterizes individual parts of *North and South*. The twelfth part, for instance, takes the shape of "woman's work" as identified by Margaret Hale in that installment: "If I saved one blow, one cruel, angry action that might otherwise have been committed, I did a woman's work."[38] The part opens when tension during the strike has built to a point of impending explosion, and the thrust of the narrative seems to be toward explosive violence. But the tension building toward a cataclysmic event is deflected into the connectedness of a courtship plot instead. When workers threaten Thornton, Margaret throws her arms about him and is the one wounded (not seriously, as it turns out) rather than John. This protective action then initiates the forward movement of the courtship plot, and the part ends looking ahead, not to another explosive event but to the developing relationship of Margaret and John. In this installment, too, then, Gaskell "saves a blow," prevents an "angry action," and focuses on "woman's work" of nurturing and affection instead.[39]

The divergence between Dickens's and Gaskell's notions of serial publication, however, is most evident in the major textual variant between the serial version, over which Dickens exercised some authority, and the volume edition, which Gaskell could superintend with less external interference. The volume edition differed from the serial *North and South* primarily in its conclusion, where the final four chapters were expanded by Gaskell to make eight. Most of this addition involved a return visit paid by the heroine Margaret Hale from England's industrial North to her old home in the country's rural South. The life of her father's old friend, Mr. Bell, is nicely extended (he had died suddenly in the serial text) so that he can accompany her on the trip. But what was kept out of the narrative by Dickens and *Household Words* was not so much event as commentary and reflection.[40]

The entire novel of *North and South* had progressed through a series of stages in understanding as different or opposing perspectives clashed: North against South, Church of England against Methodism, men against women, worker against employer, servant against mistress. Each installment, then, constituted a debate from different positions: capital versus labor, wealth versus poverty, age versus youth, old versus new, agriculture versus industry. And the completion of every number generally represented a new moderation of views, as characters (and readers) slowly but steadily moved closer to shared values.[41]

The expanded conclusion was needed less to complete a sequence of action than to provide one more stage in the dialectical evolution toward a new, transforming perspective.[42] In the expanded last chapters Margaret sees the limits of her past life against the promises of a new. And the most memorable passages from the new text involved more time devoted to acknowledging and coming to terms with contraries. Margaret, for instance, recognizes that even in "timeless" old England, represented by her native village of Helstone, "There was change everywhere; slight, yet pervading all" (481). She admits to continual change within herself as well: "And I too change perpetually – now this, now that – now disappointed and peevish because all is not exactly as I had pictured it, and now suddenly discovering that the reality is far more beautiful than I had imagined it" (489). One of the most frequently cited passages from Gaskell's revision is Margaret's long meditation after Mr. Bell's death, the passage that concluded chapter 48 in the volume edition. The heroine uses this occasion to moderate her estimate of life's opportunities: "On some such night as this she remembered promising to herself to live as brave and noble a life as any heroine she had ever read or heard of in romance . . . And now she had learnt that not only to will, but also to pray, was a necessary condition in the truly heroic" (502). Such balancing of opposed principles, such extended description of a character's relation to her environment and circumstances, were important enough to Gaskell's novel that they figured prominently in her revisions of the serial text.

In her own account of composition and serialization, Elizabeth Gaskell felt the need to extend both the time of her own work on the novel and the length of the story's natural form.[43] In January 1855 she complained to her friend Anna Jameson of not having "happy leisure hours" for her own work, and she insisted that, if "the story had been poured just warm out of the mind, it would have taken a much larger mould." She wrote to Anna Jameson late in the process of composition that the

story is huddled & hurried up . . . But what could I do? Every page was grudged me, just at last, when I did certainly infringe all the bounds & limits they set me as to quantity. Just at the very last I was compelled to desperate compression. But now I am not sure if, when the barrier gives way between two such characters as Mr. Thornton and Margaret it would not go all smash in a moment.[44]

However, Gaskell also seemed to accept Dickens's judgment about the necessities of magazine publication and to admit to her own inability to work within this mode. She wrote, for instance: "I have tried to shorten & compress [the 20 January 1855 installment] . . . but, there were [sic] a whole catalogue of events to be got over . . . but, *if you will keep the MS for me, & shorten it as you think best for HW*, I shall be very glad. Shortened I see it must be."[45] Later letters and comments show that Gaskell resented, even if she could not escape, the magazine's shaping of her novel.[46] The ways in which her own structuring of *North and South* attempted to avoid sharp divisions of plot into chapters or installments suggest that Gaskell felt the pleasure of reading a text derived from more than engaging well-constructed individual parts. She faced similar pressures to compress material in her masterpiece, *Wives and Daughters*, serialized in the monthly *Cornhill*. However, the installment shape of all Gaskell's serial fiction derives from fundamental patterns of narrative that complement and expand traditional, masculinist formulations.

A final element of *North and South* deserves attention in an exploration of sexual and textual pleasure in the serial form, one that has often been censured in critical estimates: the novel's eroticism. Beginning with part 12, when Margaret casts her arms about John Thornton, a pattern of erotic tension begins to develop and is sustained until the novel's final pages, when it is released in the couple's second embrace that mirrors the first: "he gently disengaged her hands from her face, and laid her arms as they had once before been placed to protect him from the rioters" (529–30). From the moment John is first touched by Margaret he becomes intensely aware of her physical presence and returns again and again to the memory of their embrace:

Mr. Thornton remained in the dining-room, trying to think of the business he had to do at the police-office, and in reality thinking of Margaret. Everything seemed dim and vague beyond – behind – besides the touch of her arms round his neck – the soft clinging which made the dark colour come and go in his cheek as he thought of it. (244; see also 274)

Yet because Margaret spurns with stinging words his marriage proposal offered the next day, Thornton thereafter combines apparent indifference to Margaret's presence with intense erotic awareness: "[Margaret] fancied that, from her being on a low seat at first, and now standing behind her father, he had overlooked her in his haste. As if he did not feel the consciousness of her presence all over, though his eyes had never rested on her!" (276). Margaret eventually realizes she has fallen in love with Thornton, but a number of obstacles prevent their union until the final page: Thornton's mistaking Margaret's brother Frederick for her lover, Margaret's lie to the police to protect Frederick, the hurt Margaret and John inflict on each other by their forthright (if not ingenuous) comments, and more. This strand of the novel is a familiar one: it is the erotic plot that characterizes romance fiction.

The eroticism in romance fiction, as in Gaskell's work, consists of the feminine desire of being desired, and the impetus toward, yet prohibition of, desire for a male erotic figure. This structure prolongs and intensifies erotic arousal, making desire, more than its release, the focal point. It is of course a model of desire predicated on cultural norms for middle-class women. If they are encouraged to attract an erotic partner and to form intimate emotional bonds made possible in part by the postponement of sexual activity, they are also prohibited from directly expressing their own desire for a heterosexual partner. Such a structure suggests male control of female sexuality to ensure paternity but also a feminine quest for emotional security and protection from abandonment.

This Victorian pattern has persisted into twentieth-century romance fiction, as Janice Radway makes clear in a study based on interviews with readers of the genre. According to these readers, Radway explains, the middle of a romance narrative "must create some form of conflict to keep the romantic pair apart until the proper moment[;] many authors settle for misunderstanding or distrust as the cause of the intermediary delay of the couple's happy union." The heroine should be "strong" or "fiery," and possessed of "intelligence, a sense of humor, and independence." The romance hero should be "strong and masculine, but equally capable of unusual tenderness, gentleness, and concern for [the heroine's] pleasure."[47] The plot of the romance must above all be developmental and filled with anticipation, traits linked by Radway to the form's eroticism:

[Readers] want to identify with the heroine . . . The point of the experience is the sense of exquisite tension, anticipation, and excitement created within the reader as she imagines the possible resolutions and consequences for a woman of an encounter with a member of the opposite sex . . . In all their comments about the nature of the romance, the Smithton women placed heavy emphasis on the importance of *development* in the romance's portrayal of love. [Thus,] It matters little whether that care and attention [from the hero] are detailed in general terms or presented as overtly sexual as long as they are extensively described. However, this focus on his attention to her is in itself erotic, for even the most euphemistic descriptions of the heroine's reception of his regard convey the sensual, corporal pleasure she feels in anticipating, encouraging, and finally accepting those attentions of a hero who is always depicted as magnetic, powerful, and physically pleasing.

Though scholars offer varied reasons for romance readers' attraction to this genre, most agree that the eroticism it offers is defined by "waiting, anticipation, anxiety."[48]

The features of waiting, anticipating, and postponing fulfillment are also salient features of serial fiction. The serial might be said to further prolong the duration of desire; and, since this prolongation is identified as a central feature of romance fiction, the prolonged narrative of the serial form may lead to erotic intensification in a feminine economy of desire. In the case of *North and South*, serial issue, moreover, could have allowed erotic tension to fade in the intervals between parts only to revive and extend its duration with each succeeding part.[49] Winnett's narrative model is again relevant here, especially her reminder that female arousal can occur at any time during the sexual act and can resurface again and again and again. Margaret remarks in part 19, when she realizes she loves Thornton, "it [her love for him] has come upon me little by little, and I don't know where it began" (401). The frequently expressed impatience with Gaskell's deflection of an industrial novel plot into a romance plot is a shrewd critique from the vantage point of political strategies and concerns, but it may also be useful to assess this narrative structure in terms of feminine sexuality and patterns of pleasure.

Serial publication by male and female authors in the Victorian age could "have it all" in its ability to integrate female and male structures of experience. Readers could have the pleasure of each installment read as a satisfying unit, with the bound whole volume always the final product of the publication process. Or readers could, without threatening the status quo, enjoy a serial text's pleasure by having all the parts over the months of publication, thus making of reading a prospective and ever-renewed experience until the end was reached long after the text began. This was so even when women read fiction by the age's best-known male authors, such as Dickens. But their pleasure in serial fiction could have been heightened in installments by writers like Elizabeth Gaskell, whose handling of individual parts suggests approaches to plot that lie outside traditional, masculinist norms of textual pleasure, and whose distinctive strategies in a given part remind us why serial publication as a whole may have been a pleasure to its female readers.

NOTES

1 Susan Winnett, "Coming Unstrung: Women, Men, Narrative, and Principles of Pleasure," *PMLA* 105 (1990), 515.

2 *Ibid.*, 509.

3 Norman N. Feltes, in *Modes of Production of Victorian Novels* (Chicago: University of Chicago Press, 1986), has provided the fullest assessment of the serial's effects from a Marxist perspective. See also Mary Poovey's chapter on Dickens and the serial in *Uneven Developments: The Ideological Work of Gender in Mid-Victorian England* (Chicago: University of Chicago Press, 1988).

4 Gaye Tuchman with Nina E. Fortin, *Edging Women Out: Victorian Novelists, Publishers, and Social Change* (New Haven: Yale University Press, 1989), 209.

5 Elaine Showalter proposes a model for gynocentric criticism that never loses sight of the appearance of women's writing within dominant social structures; see "Feminist Criticism in the Wilderness," in *Writing and Sexual Difference*, ed. Elizabeth Abel (Chicago: University of Chicago Press, 1982), 31–33.

6 For further evidence that women functioned as major forces in the production and consumption of nineteenth-century fiction, see Elaine Showalter, *A Literature of Their Own: British Women Novelists from Brontë to Lessing* (Princeton: Princeton University Press, 1977), 20–21; G. D. Klingopulos, "The Literary Scene," in *From Dickens to Hardy*, ed. Boris Ford (1958; Harmondsworth: Penguin, 1972), 71; Elizabeth K. Helsinger, Robin Lauterbach Sheets, and William Veeder, *The Woman Question: Society and Literature in Britain and America, 1837–1883* (3 vols.; Chicago: University of Chicago Press, 1983), vol. 3, 8; and Tuchman, 7.

7 Tuchman, 53. By the 1880s this pattern had changed, and women were more likely to use male pseudonyms (Tuchman, 54).

8 Thus, Edward Howard paused in the midst of his largely nautical *Life of a Sub-Editor*, serialized in *Metropolitan Magazine* from 1834–1836, to explain the finer points of naval rigging for his female readers.

9 Elizabeth Gaskell's letter to an aspiring woman novelist with young children is usually cited to illustrate women's enforced subordination of personal achievement to domestic responsibility. Yet Gaskell's remarks also suggest that she perceived her relation to fictional characters in much the same way she did her relation to her family: "When I had *little* children I do not think I could have written stories, because I should have become too much absorbed in my *fictitious* people to attend to my *real* ones." J. A. V. Chapple and Arthur Pollard (eds.), *The Letters of Mrs. Gaskell* (Cambridge, Mass.: Harvard University Press, 1967), 694–95.

10 David Skilton, introduction to *Lady Audley's Secret* by Mary Elizabeth Braddon (Oxford: Oxford University Press, 1987), xi.

11 Mary Field Belenky, Blythe McVicker Clinchy, Nancy Rule Goldberger, and Jill Mattuck Tarule, *Women's Ways of Knowing: The Development of Self, Voice, and Mind* (New York: Basic Books, 1986).

12 Linda K. Hughes and Michael Lund, *The Victorian Serial* (Charlottesville: University Press of Virginia, 1991), 8.

13 Florence Nightingale, *Cassandra* (New York: Feminist Press, 1979), 32.

14 Janet Murray (ed.), *Strong-Minded Women and Other Lost Voices from 19th Century England* (New York: Pantheon, 1982), 84, 88. For the dilemma of interruption for women writers, see Helsinger, Sheets, and Veeder, 3:10, 3:12; and Dale Spender, *The Writing or the Sex? or Why You Don't Have to Read Women's Writing to Know It's No Good*, Athene Series (New York: Pergamon Press, 1989), 127–30.

15 Helsinger, Sheets, and Veeder, 2:83. The physician was Edward H. Clarke. Dr. Clarke's pronouncement is notorious because he went on to argue that women's periodicity, rather than persistence, meant that women were unsuited either for intensive study associated with higher education or for sustained professional work outside the home. Elaine Showalter and English Showalter, in "Victorian Women and Menstruation," *Suffer and Be Still*, ed. Martha Vicinus (Bloomington: Indiana University Press, 1972), 42, as well as Helsinger, Sheets, and Veeder (2:86–88, 2:104), record contemporary refutations of this strand of Clarke's argument. Yet the works they cite also assert the periodicity of feminine physiology, though noting that such biological functions did not preclude persistence of intellectual or physical energies.

16 Murray, 211; Spender, 113, 117.

17 Showalter, *A Literature of Their Own*, 15.

18 We are particularly interested in the analogy between the serial and notions of feminine form as process-oriented and open. However, because the nonverbal spaces between parts are a fundamental part of the form, the serial's enfolding of silence into the text might usefully be examined in relation to the notion of the preverbal (the "semiotic," according to Julia Kristeva) that has been identified with the feminine in Lacan's and related theorists' work.

19 Hélène Cixous, "Sorties," in Hélène Cixous and Catherine Clément, *The Newly Born Woman*, trans. Betsy Wing (Minneapolis: University of Minnesota Press, 1986), 87, 88.

20 Estelle C. Jelinek, "Introduction: Women's Autobiography and the Male Tradition," in *Women's Autobiography: Essays in Criticism*, ed. Estelle C. Jelinek (Bloomington: Indiana University Press, 1980), 17.

21 Margaret Beetham, "Towards a Theory of the Periodical as a Publishing Genre," in *Investigating Victorian Journalism*, ed. Laurel Brake, Aled Jones, and Lionel Madden (New York: St. Martin's Press, 1990), 27.

22 Beetham, 27–29; see also Poovey, 104.

23 Mary Eagleton (ed.), *Feminist Literary Theory: A Reader* (Oxford: Basil Blackwell, 1986), 228.

24 Ursula K. Le Guin, "The Carrier Bag Theory of Fiction," in *Dancing at the Edge of the World* (New York: Grove Press, 1989), 169–70.

25 Susan Morgan argues that nineteenth-century British heroines embody the virtues of change and connectedness that may be celebrated in novels but have been "traditionally undervalued and labeled as feminine." *Sisters in Time: Imagining Gender in Nineteenth-Century British Fiction* (New York: Oxford University Press, 1989), 17.

26 Linda K. Hughes and Michael Lund, "Linear Stories and Circular Visions: The Decline of the Victorian Serial," in *Chaos and Order:*

Complex Dynamics in Literature and Science, ed. N. Katherine Hayles (Chicago: University of Chicago Press, 1991), 167–94; see also *The Victorian Serial*, 229–74.

27 Tuchman, 7–8, 188.

28 In *Elizabeth Gaskell* (Boston: Twayne, 1984), Coral Lansbury says that serialization was "a mode of publication that she detested, scrambling to fit the work into twenty separate numbers, instead of the twenty-two that she insisted Dickens had promised her" (36). See also Angus Easson, *Elizabeth Gaskell* (London: Routledge & Kegan Paul, 1979), 88.

29 Winifred Gerin, *Elizabeth Gaskell: A Biography* (Oxford: Clarendon, 1976), 124.

30 As Gerin explains, the nine-month hiatus in *Cranford*'s serialization was most likely occasioned by Gaskell's turning from this story to the composition of *Ruth*, issued as a whole novel in January 1853, after which *Cranford* resumed (126).

31 David Paroissien (ed.), *Selected Letters of Charles Dickens* (Boston: Twayne, 1985), 320.

32 In a letter dated 26 July 1854 which discusses five later installments, Dickens again explains his idea of parts structure by stressing how each must "close." Paroissien, 322.

33 *Ibid.*, 320.

34 Dorothy Collin, in "The Composition of Mrs. Gaskell's *North and South*," *Bulletin of the John Rylands University Library of Manchester* 54 (1971), notes how Dickens assumed that he, rather than Mrs. Gaskell, would take care of the whole question of parts structure. She cites Dickens's 18 February 1854 letter, written before he received any manuscript:

> Don't put yourself out at all as to the division of the story into parts. I think you had far better write it in your own way. When we come to get a little of it into type, I have no doubt of being able to make such little suggestions as to breaks of chapters as will carry us over all that easily. (70)

35 Collin compares the parts endings proposed by Dickens to the conclusions of installments actually published, which, presumably, were approved by Mrs. Gaskell (89–91). J. Don Vann, in "Dickens, Charles Lever and Mrs. Gaskell," *Victorian Periodicals Review* 22, 2 (Summer 1989), 67, explains that Dickens was guided not only by his notion of effective parts structure for fiction but by concern for the overall shape of each issue of *Household Words*.

36 Paroissien, 320.

37 Martin Dodsworth, introduction, *North and South* by Elizabeth Gaskell, ed. Dorothy Collin (Harmondsworth: Penguin, 1970), 7.

38 Elizabeth Gaskell, *North and South*, 247. Subsequent citations will be given in the text.

39 Gaskell's emphasis on social relations and characters' contexts is evident in the title she preferred. Her choice for the novel's title, *Margaret Hale*, roots the story in personal circumstances, whereas Dickens's choice of title, which prevailed, emphasizes conflict, abstraction, and ideological issues that rest on but supersede given individuals.

40 In August, Dickens was angered to find proofs returned from Mrs. Gaskell "*'unaltered'*" by the author (letter dated 20 August 1854). The editor had wanted "a great condensation and a considerable compression, where Mr. Hale states his doubts to Margaret." Paroissien, 323. Mrs. Gaskell apparently did not want to reduce this kind of narrative, which presents argument and counterargument rather than advancing the story's action.

41 See also Rosemarie Bodenheimer, "*North and South*: A Permanent State of Change," *Nineteenth Century Fiction* 34 (1979), 281–301.

42 Mrs. Gaskell asked several of her friends if she should revise the serial text for volume publication. To Mrs. Anna Jameson she wrote, "I can not insert small pieces here & there – I feel as if I must throw myself back a certain distance in the story, & re-write it from there; retaining the present incidents, but filling up intervals of time &c &c." Chapple and Pollard, 329. Mrs. Jameson responded that "there should be more gradation in effect [in the novel's conclusion], and the rapidity of the incidents at the close destroys the proportions of your story as a work of art." Cited in Collin, "Composition," 88. Bodenheimer argues "it may be that the difficulty of ending [the novel] had something to do with the stubbornly open presentation of character and social change in the main part of the story" (301).

43 Deirdre David, in *Fictions of Resolution in Three Victorian Novels* (New York: Columbia University Press, 1981), says that Gaskell wrote this novel "feeling perhaps that her woman's knowledge was not the 'correct knowledge,' and it was a painful experience for her" (9). See also Lansbury, 36.

44 Gerin, 154; Chapple and Pollard, 330, 328–29.

45 Chapple and Pollard, 323.

46 Although not all of Mrs. Gaskell's letters to Dickens about serialization have survived, Dorothy Collin argues "it may be shown that disregard was not [Gaskell's] attitude to serial divisions in the case of *North and South*," but "there is evidence that the disagreement between Dickens and Mrs. Gaskell was bruited abroad at least among the circle of her correspondents" (73–74).

47 Janice A. Radway, *Reading the Romance: Women, Patriarchy, and Popular Literature* (Chapel Hill: University of North Carolina Press, 1984), 65, 54, 77, 81. Just as Margaret Hale is displaced from her family homes in London and Helstone at the novel's outset, so the ideal romance, according to Radway's study, "begins with its heroine's removal from a familiar, comfortable realm usually associated with her

childhood and family" (134), a move that allows the heroine to adopt unconventionally assertive behavior and to encounter the hero.

48 *Ibid.*, 64–65, 105; Ann Barr Snitow, "Mass Market Romance: Pornography for Women is Different," *Radical History Review* 20 (1979), 146.

49 Cixous indicates the regressive politics of such desire, which she perceives as a masculinist strategy: "The good woman [in patriarchy], therefore, is the one who 'resists' long enough for him to feel both his power over her and his desire . . . to give him the pleasure of enjoying, without too many obstacles, the return to himself which he, grown greater – reassured in his own eyes, is making" (79–80). But John Thornton does not return to his single, same self as a result of desire; like Margaret, he changes over the course of the novel, spurred in part by his vulnerability to Margaret's attacks or praise.

CHAPTER 8

The disease of reading and Victorian periodicals

Kelly J. Mays

> Reading, it is safe to say, is a lost art. And what has killed it
> is the spread of reading.
>
> *Arnold Haultain*

The changing dimension and character of the reading public
and the ever-greater productivity of the publishing industry were
subjects of urgent debate in England throughout the nineteenth
century. Such debates helped to establish a common vocabulary
of terms and assumptions that are crucial to understanding the
shape and meanings of literacy and reading for nineteenth-century
readers. Between roughly 1860 and 1900, men of letters took up
the task of shaping those meanings with a new directness and a
sense of urgency born of what they insisted were problems unique
to their times – an explosive expansion of the arena of "knowledge"
that was signified by an overwhelming abundance of printed matter
and an equally dramatic increase both in the number of readers and
in the amount of time such readers devoted to reading. In these
years hundreds of articles on the subject of reading and readers
were published in the monthlies and quarterlies, while the weeklies
– particularly the *Pall Mall Gazette* after 1865 and the *Athenaeum*
– provided a major forum for a more directly confrontational
exchange. "The subjects of Books and Reading," as a *Quarterly*
reviewer commented in the watershed year 1886, "is *in the air* at the
present time."[1] Lectures and books, as well as the pages of periodicals, were devoted to answering the questions of how, why, and
what readers were and should be reading, while they individually
and collectively urged the vital social importance of such questions
and of the practices they sought to define. As presently practiced,
they insisted, reading was threatening not only individuals but also,
through them, the entire social fabric. Together these writers and

speakers thus constructed and meditated upon a reading problem
not unlike what we might call the "television problem" of our own
day, a disease of the individual and social system produced and
signified in practices of textual consumption.[2]

While twentieth-century studies of the period have focused on
the questions of who was reading what, the "how" and "why"
of reading practices became much more vital questions by the
second half of the nineteenth century.[3] As a result, what was
"in the air" was much more than a semantic struggle over the
various meanings of the terms *reader* and *reading*. As in Haultain's
economical formulation, men engaged in that struggle aimed their
efforts both at removing current practices from the rubric of "reading" by diagnosing the systemic ill such practices produced and
at crafting more narrow definitions of the term and the practices it
signified. Agreeing upon a rhetorical framework of diagnosis and
cure, such efforts together comprised a project aimed, to borrow the
terminology of Jon Klancher, at "manipulating" and "dismantling"
the sign *reading* in order to define, or "fabricate," a single, healthy
reading practice for middle-class readers.[4]

The discussion reached its greatest intensity in the year 1885/86. In
that year there were published: *The Pleasures, the Dangers, and the Uses of
Desultory Reading* by the Earl of Iddesleigh,[5] G. J. Goschen's *Hearing,
Reading and Thinking*,[6] and Frederic Harrison's *On the Choice of Books;
and Other Literary Pieces*;[7] while the *Pall Mall Gazette*'s publication
of John Lubbock's list of "the best hundred books" elicited so
much (solicited and unsolicited) response that the journal printed
upwards of thirty articles on the subject before republishing these
and more in an "Extra" edition entitled *The Best Hundred Books. By
the Best Judges*.[8] Escaping the pages of the *Pall Mall*, the discussion
continued simultaneously in most of the other major journals and
reviews and in less publicized lectures and books.

A variety of media thus played host to this project, and we can
best understand such well-known works as John Ruskin's *Sesame
and Lilies* (1864–65) in the context of this larger, and less familiar,
discussion.[9] Yet, as the *Quarterly* reviewer's description of how
the "discussion" was "carried forward from Newspaper to Journal,
and from Journal to Magazine" suggests, its primary vehicle was
the periodical press.[10] The periodicals were the natural home for
such efforts, for the essays on reading published in their pages
may best be understood as the place where the periodicals most

directly engaged their implicit generic task: mediating between increasingly numerous and diverse readers and a field of print commodities that was itself constantly increasing in both quantity and diversity.[11]

While periodicals had developed and multiplied in the eighteenth and early nineteenth centuries explicitly as a mechanism for guiding readers in their selection of appropriate reading matter, they implicitly functioned to create readers and appropriate, class-specific reading practices as well. James L. Machor's characterization of reviews in early nineteenth-century America applies equally to their English counterparts:

Reviews . . . were the primary vehicle for the dissemination and assimilation of ideas about . . . ways of reading. Appearing in magazines with circulations that, for the time, were large or in periodicals of national influence, reviews enjoyed a publicly sanctioned authority buttressed by the institutional imprimatur of the publishing industry itself . . . reviews were not merely individual assertions of aesthetic values but expressions whose content was corporate and communal. . . .

To say this is not to imply that reviewers controlled or precisely mirrored the reading practices of the mass audience; however, the gap between the two was not as large as it is today . . . Reviewers and magazine essayists were not professional critics but "moral and intellectual leaders in the community," who shared a common "social standing, education, and opinion" with the . . . [reading] public.

As Klancher argues in his study of early-nineteenth-century periodicals, it was in the very (corporate) texture of middle-class periodical prose that "this audience learns to operate those interpretive strategies through which it can 'read' a social world, a symbolic universe, a textual field. . . . Manipulating or fabricating signs, this public both learns and asserts what it means to be 'middle class' in the nineteenth century."[12]

In England, the corporate character of the periodical text was exemplified formally in the practice of not identifying the authors of particular pieces or of doing so only with pseudonyms.[13] This feature, as well as the sense of continuity between authors and readers, also took material form in the "we" endemic to the middle-class periodical. Such practices, as essayist Eneas Sweetland Dallas (anonymously) argued in 1859, were the distinctive "cornerstone" of "the English system" of "class journalism." Through these mechanisms, he insisted, the periodicals not only were the representatives and creators of public opinion but also were "to a very large extent . . . in fact – the public."[14]

In the later-nineteenth century, middle-class periodicals and those who wrote for them became increasingly self-conscious about the task of producing readers. That very self-consciousness may be seen as registering a discomfort that accompanied important changes in the social role of periodicals, in the relation between individual publications and their contributors, and in the format of the periodical text. Dallas's argument comes, for example, as a defense; as such, it testifies to the increasing contestation in the second half of the century over traditional periodical practice and format and over the social role the press assumed and performed through these mechanisms. The practice of anonymity, challenged only sporadically throughout the century, began to give way completely as a standard in the 1860s. Where *Macmillan's*, founded in the latter part of 1859, "made a practice of signature without proclaiming it as deliberate policy," the founders of the *Fortnightly* (1865), *Contemporary* (1866), *Academy* (1869), and *Nineteenth Century* (1877) made such proclamations from the outset, insisting that the policy of signature defined both the character and value of their publications. Following the lead of these newer journals, most of the established journals, reviews, and magazines gradually embraced the new policies.[15]

While the arguments that underwrote the new orthodoxy were multiple, the overarching ideological rationale and effect was to transfer authority from the corporate text to the individual contributor and thus to understand authority as properly the outgrowth of individual personality and competence, or – as George Lewes put it – individual "sensibility and culture." As *Academy* founder and editor Charles Edward Appleton emphasized, only when "the honesty and competence of the reviewer should be vouched for by his signature" could a journal claim to act as an arbiter "on which the general reader might rely for guidance." The reviewer's "competence" and authority now rested precisely upon his difference from, rather than on his similarity to, that "general reader," for the latter needed guidance, according to Appleton, because he had "neither the time nor perhaps the ability to guide himself."[16]

Appleton's particular distinctiveness from the general reader was guaranteed, not least, by his status as a new-style Oxford scholar, advocating specialist research not only at the university but also in the pages of the *Academy*. Here a reviewer's competence was guaranteed not only by his signature but also by his publicly sanctioned expertise in a specific "province" of study.[17] And that public sanction, the "culture" Lewes identified, would increasingly be seen to derive as did Appleton's, not from experience in reviewing but from educational training. In this way, the periodicals began to operate less as sociocultural authorities in their own right than as forums for the exercise of a sociocultural authority derived elsewhere – chiefly from the universities – that was vested in the university-trained individuals who exercised it as periodical editors and contributors.

The debates about reading not only occurred simultaneously with these redefinitions and redistributions of cultural authority but also served as an important site for these larger struggles. As the *Pall Mall*'s "extra" title suggests, at issue was not only what and how readers should read, but also who were the "best judges" of such matters. Or, as the title of a *Temple Bar* essay implies, defining the "well-read man" was an effort simultaneously to shape the practices of the reading public and to articulate in qualitative, characterological terms the difference between that public and those with the capacity and duty to oversee and guide it.[18] This double function should be kept in mind in order to understand the specific diagnoses of the reading problem to which I now turn.

The first symptom of the problem was the sheer abundance of reading matter. One essayist marveled, "about 20,000 separate works are annually added to the shelves of the British Museum . . . amounting in a normal life period of seventy years to the prodigious total of 1,400,000 books. And this leaves wholly out of account the vastly greater mass of journalistic literature which consumes part of everybody's time and attention."[19] Another averaged the output at "a ratio of publication (Sundays excepted) of about ten per diem."[20] Yet most described the phenomena in cataclysmic rather than numerical terms, emphasizing the unquantifiable monstrousness of the thing that resulted. "Urged on by the power of steam," the press became "as prolific as Berecynthia, the fabled mother of the gods," and its issue a "remorseless cataract,"[21] a "dense jungle," "an eddying torrent,"[22] an "avalanche," an "overwhelming multitude."[23] Though metaphors varied, they all shared an insistence upon the physicality of what amounted to an assault on readers, as Frederic Harrison's mixture of metaphors suggests: "We read nowadays in the market-place – I would rather say in some large steam factory of letter-press, where damp sheets of new print whirl round us perpetually – if it be not rather some noisy book-fair where literary showmen tempt us with performing dolls, and the gongs of rival booths are stunning our ears from morn till night."[24] Such highly physical metaphors figured readers as being swept up in the machinelike pace of the steam-driven press or the railway with which it was so often linked and as being crushed, drowned, "buried alive" or "suffocate[d]" beneath the sheer weight of its products:[25] "The present age is denominated a 'fast' one; 'fast' living, very fast dying, viâ mines and railways . . . But of the many chariots entered on the modern race-course, literature seems making the swiftest, most noticeable career . . . with a circulation quickening every moment . . . we are only afraid the pace may be too killing."[26] Abundance, then, was problematic insofar as it was figured as sensually inundating, physically "overwhelming," even "killing," readers: "books of travel, science, poetry, history, fiction, succeed and overwhelm one another with such alarming rapidity, that the man who stops for a moment to take breath and reflect, is lost."[27]

It was rarely suggested that the press should produce less.[28] But that readers were reading too much was a constant refrain: "The danger in this much written-for age is of reading too much . . . We read too much, and too little. The former of the two excesses is, I think, the more new and remarkable"; "it is this habit of ceaseless reading . . . that bodes so much danger to our modern system of enlightenment."[29] Alfred Austin provided an almost hysterical description of this evil and its effects:

We have nakedly entitled this paper "The Vice of Reading"; for we are unable to dispel the conviction that Reading . . . has become a downright vice, – a vulgar, detrimental habit, like dram-drinking . . . a softening, demoralising, relaxing practice, which, if persisted in, will end by enfeebling the minds of men and women, making flabby the fibre of their bodies, and undermining the vigour of nations.[30]

Ultimately, neither the quantity nor the quality of the products of the press distressed essayists so much as the related changes first in the habits, second in the character, of readers.

While the overconsumption of certain genres – especially fiction and periodicals – was targeted by Austin and others for censure, that censure fell mainly on the kinds of reading practices or habits such genres seemed to encourage. Focusing on the particular vice of "novel-drinking" and arguing that "this habit" may well have been "the principal cause of the general Vice of Reading," Austin nonetheless insisted that the "general Vice" was that "of which we complain" most vehemently.[31] Another essayist decried the "method" by which readers habitually went about "gleaning intelligence from a newspaper" only to insist that this process was "merely a sample of what is going on very extensively in all the paths of literature."[32] Similarly, though the debate of 1886 was inspired initially by the publication of book lists that attempted to tell readers what they should be reading, many participants emphasized the inadequacy of an approach that privileged the issue of reading matter over that of reading practices. As Edward Dowden insisted:

It would have been more profitable for us had we been advised [by those participating in the "hundred best books" debate] how to read any one of the hundred; for what, indeed, does it matter whether we read the best books or the worst, if we lack the power or the instinct or the skill by which to reach the heart of any one of them?[33]

More generally, the continuous insistence upon the quantitative magnitude of the press's output functioned to indicate the extent to which, in practice, all qualitative distinctions between texts, including genre itself, effectively disappeared.

The quantitative and qualitative aspects of the reading problem were summed up in the oft-repeated tag borrowed from the Latin: "We read too much, and too little." As that phrase indicates, the concern that readers were reading excessively entailed a worry that readers were reading incorrectly. Not least, readers were reproducing the speed of production in the speed of their own reading, and this "hurried, careless, method of reading" represented "one of the chief dangers":[34]

Some books are so exciting to the attention, to the imagination, to the passions, that they produce a mental debauch . . . in reading the mind is often in nearly a passive state, like that of dreaming or reverie, in which images flit before the mind without any act of volition to retain them. In rapid reading [the mind] is nearly in the same state as yours is when you are whirled through a country in a railway-carriage or post-chaise.[35]

Yet this pace was being reproduced not only in the reading of particular books but also, and more surely, in the way readers turned from book to book. As one essayist insisted, "The 'Run and Read Library' only too accurately fits the popular feeling. It is here that the multitude of books tells injuriously. Really, the more books, the better possible selection for the readers; but each fills so little time in an age when every one reads, that it is natural to turn to the next on the table."[36] "Having finished" one book, readers immediately "hunger for another."[37]

The "omnivorous" reading practices that resulted were automatic, no more deliberate than the motions of the machines they mimicked; and, indeed, essayists portrayed the subject produced by such reading as a nonhuman, inanimate object.[38] Such a reader was a "machine," a "sausage of a man," "a living lexicon, a walking encyclopaedia," an "animated book-case," "his mind" a "kaleidoscope": "Their minds, their whole natures, have become subdued to what they work in. They have become of the books, booky."[39] Such dehumanized individuals resembled rather than managed technology and its products, mirrored rather than controlled the machines that produced their reading matter and hurtled both it and them through space. In this sense, the discussions of reading participated in escalating debates about the ultimate effects of technological progress.[40] Though contemporary reading practices seemed to render humans indistinguishable from machines and their inanimate issue, they equally seemed to destroy the characterological distinctions between civilized, modern Britons and more primitive peoples, and between humans and animals. Thus, the subject produced by such reading could also be described pejoratively as an animal – a "bookworm" or, even worse, a "book-butterfly" – and as a "savage."[41] While reading habits resembled the automatic motions of the machine, they were also and more consistently described with reference to bodily ingestion – eating, drinking, and drug-taking. Like these, reading was an act guided by the most primitively sensual urges – "thirst," "hunger," and "craving."[42] Born of an "inborn" "intellectual appetite" that was "a characteristic of [the human] race down to the lowest stages" and thus also present in "rude savages," the urges that drove readers represented at best a return to the lowest common denominator of humanity, at worst to an animalistic entrapment in bodily impulses.[43]

The dehumanization of readers was thus portrayed as the potential, catastrophic culmination not only of a process of technological evolution but also of a devolutionary or degenerative process that worked in tandem with the former. Like the other addictions – "dram-drinking," "tobacco-smoking," and "opium-eating" – with which it was associated and as the semantic move from "hunger" to "craving" (even "artificial cravings") suggests, the reading habit also represented the perversion of the natural urges of thirst and hunger, an unyoking of the relation between such appetites and material needs and a disruption of the boundaries and balance between mental and physical impulses and acts.[44] As essayist after essayist stressed, contemporary reading resembled not eating merely but "overfeeding,"[45] "devouring,"[46] a "mental gluttony" that was itself an addiction.[47] Even in eating, ideally, the higher powers of the mind – will, reason, and judgment – were in full control, the mind acting as "the co-ordinating centre," assessing the needs of the body and determining what food best satisfied those needs.[48] Overindulgent "book-devouring," however, aimed at pleasure rather than sustenance, so that "Hedonism, then – the doctrine . . . which sets pleasure as the right aim of existence – seems to be the spirit ruling the readers of books."[49] Driven by sensual attraction rather than a rational calculation of nutritional value, such reading confused the proper hierarchical relation between body and mind:[50]

[A "large class of readers"] feel attracted to the page of a book or to the column of a newspaper, just as they are to a garden of flowers, or to a winding river. They have no purpose in view; they have no object to be accomplished. The act of reading terminates in itself, so far as any end is concerned. It is just a matter of present gratification, of present amusement.[51]

As such and like other addictions, reading produced nothing beyond more of itself, "fatiguing our minds without enriching them," "clogging the spirit without satisfying it."[52] This confusion of the proper body–mind relation was potentially, essayists warned, a permanent rather than temporary effect of such reading, "impairing the intellectual vigour," "weakening the moral power so as to disqualify you for study or labour," destroying "the firm tone of the mind, and render[ing] it fitful and inefficient in its exertions," "rapidly destroying all thinking and all powers of thought."[53]

The healthy balance between body and mind was also endangered by the mere fact that in the lives of most readers the

mental exercise of reading displaced bodily exercise. As Austin
complained:

> books are used as an excuse for coddling and laziness . . . and women
> who would take a good long walk on a winter's day [or] grub in their
> gardens . . . if there were nothing else they could do, do none of these
> things because they can sit over the fire and read a new novel or pore
> over a dreary journal. Thus they are defrauded of their proper amount
> of exercise, get their muscles relaxed and their health out of gear.[54]

Excessive reading also cut into the time needed for resting, and
thus restoring, the body. As one essayist warned, "reading should
be avoided when it interferes with necessary repose . . . To read
when you ought to be in bed, especially to read when in bed, is to
inflict a great evil on yourself without an equivalent. It is to injure
your eyes, your brain, your nervous system, your intellect."[55]

Doubly threatening the balance of body and mind crucial to
health, such reading and the urges that drove it were represented
as manifestations of a distinctly modern illness. While one essayist
suggested that there is at least "a question whether the craving
for books may not be a disease,"[56] others indicated that such a
connection was far more than speculative:

> With printing and the promiscuous circulation of books the mischief
> that had broken out in Germany was spread everywhere by insidious
> contagion, like the Black Death of the fourteenth century. But unlike
> that subtle and deadly plague, it has gone on running its course ever
> since, and diffusing itself gradually through all classes of the community.
> The ferment of thought, the restless craving for intellectual excitement
> of some kind, have been stimulated; till now, in the last quarter of the
> nineteenth century, we are being driven along at high-pressure pace; and
> it is impossible for any one who is recalcitrant to stop himself.[57]

In similar and no less dire terms, another essayist figured this
disease as a "wide-spread and desolating dyspepsia."[58] Spread
through the "promiscuous circulation" of books and the urges
and acts these inspired but never quite satisfied, the addiction to
reading was a social disease that contributed to the enfeebled body
and mind peculiar to modern men and women. As these essayists
insisted, however, the correlation between reading and disease
was far from merely metaphorical. That correlation was instead
both literal and directly causal. By virtue of reading habits that
uniquely distinguished them from men of the "dark ages," modern

Britons were subject to a "wear-and-tear of the mental fibres," to the impaired "digestion" of stomachs strained and "troubled by abstruse thought," to "far-fetched anxieties," and to "those painful brain and nerve diseases that fill our asylums, and are transmitted by descent."[59]

This essayist and others thus called upon readers to see their reading habits as directly contributing to a society-wide process of degeneration. Austin, for one, ended his essay by declaring that any one individual reader's unhealthy reading habit ultimately endangered the whole nation because that nation resided in the very "fibre" of the individual:

We should be glad to think that our observations had led even one person to pause and consider, and had acted as a note of warning to him. So surely as he surrenders himself to mere printed matter, to mere books and newspapers, so surely will he end by being, like most of his neighbours, a poor creature, with a flabby, flaccid, aqueous, unstable sort of a brain; – a mere copy of somebody else, such as our truly Chinese civilisation occupies itself with producing . . . that such reading as at present prevails has, by reason both of its quality and quantity, led to a deterioration of the human species, physically, mentally, and morally, we entertain no doubt; nor do we see how, unless the vicious habit be somehow corrected, the race can escape from being ultimately divided into two sections, the members of one of which will be little removed from invalids, and the members of the other scarcely distinguishable from *crétins*.[60]

The *Quarterly* reproduced Austin's terms almost exactly: "In every rank of life the book-devouring vice abounds . . . This thoughtless, fragmentary, reading has debilitated the contemporary mental fibre of the nation."[61] National integrity, conceived as racial integrity, was lodged in the integrity of its individual members. As those individuals engaged in the "softening, demoralising, relaxing practice" of reading, they thus undermined not only their own integrity, but also and necessarily that of their nation and their race.

While not always calling upon the figure of nation specifically, other essayists nonetheless insisted equally upon the threat to individual integrity and identity posed by reading habits. The craving for reading might indeed be a disease, one essayist argued, because through it we may "live too little in ourselves, and too much in others," always seeing "things reflected in another man's mind"; as a result, even "a savage in a state of primeval nature" had "advantages over" a modern Englishman because the former's "thoughts and feelings are [his] own."[62] Using reading to "kill time," readers made an "escape from themselves" that amounted to "suicide."[63] Through the oft-criticized practice of "desultory reading" in particular, the individual reader, having no principle of organization, no self-coherence, came to mirror the indiscriminate, unorganized chaos of texts he read:

How can the well-regulated and healthy mind skip with sobriety from the "Latest Discovery of Gold-fields in Sutherlandshire" . . . to the "Largest Haul of Whales in Greenland," and the "Roasting of a Missionary in the Sandwich Islands." What mind is not is not [sic] likely to be thrown into a state of nightmare and ferment by this dancing among disconnected items of temporary intelligence, this hurrying at lightning speed from one part of chaos to another?[64]

The "sausage of a man," "walking encyclopaedia," "animated bookcase," or mental "kaleidoscope" produced by desultory reading was thus not merely any inanimate object, but one without coherence, integrity, wholeness, or the individuality these qualities guaranteed.[65] Such reading produced, in other words, a subject that was not one.

The link between progress and devolution central to these scenarios of individual and collective dissolution was equally central to nineteenth-century depictions of "the Orient." Thomas De Quincey, for one, described China as "a torpid blob of life," "an inorganic mass," a "vast, callous hulk," because it was merely the chaotic amalgamation of a huge population within which "man is a weed," as plentiful and as undifferentiated as vegetable matter.[66] The social critic Fourier likewise insisted "the Chinese" desire for "monotony and uniformity" deviated from nature's search for "variety": "as a consequence, the Chinese are, from their habits of stagnation, the most perverted of races and the farthest removed from the paths of nature."[67] Thus, in diagnosing the "wide-spread and desolating dyspepsia" produced by the mental "overfeeding" of British readers, *Victoria Magazine* essayist C. H. Butterworth unfavorably compared the "highly civilised condition of [English] society" with that of "semi-civilized [sic] people, such as the inhabitants of India, Turkey or China."[68] Just as a perverse, monotonous China figured in Mill's *On Liberty* (1859) as the potential future of a maldeveloped European culture, so "Chinese" figured in Austin's essay as the adjective that crystallized fears of the dissolution of individual and national identity.[69] The fears of degeneration that framed the reading problem thus rested upon fears of the instability and fragmentation of the individual self that was figured as the "Orientalizing" of English readers.

Such fears about the Englishness, understood as the subjective integrity of individual English readers, were inseparable from fears about gender and class instability. For the masculinity of the reading public was as endangered as its Englishness by the confusion of body–mind relations and the concomitant loss of individual integrity that were caused by excessive and incorrect reading. The feminization of the reading public was in one sense quite literal. Women readers were not only numerous, but also were understood to be desultory readers *par excellence*. Asserting that "it is always, by the bye, the ladies" who perpetrate readerly crimes, one essayist offered sketches of typical offenders.[70] From "a lady" reading a periodical inside a brougham and a "maiden aunt" exchanging gossip while reading a novel to a mother reprimanding children from behind her book and "a lady" "reading and knitting at the same time," all women readers committed the same offense.[71] Intermixing the texts they read "with domestic recollections, with snubbings of children," and with "questions about washing-bills," these women readers managed to "chaw up" even ostensibly coherent texts "into small fragments" and to "jumble" them up – to borrow another essayist's terms – "higgledy piggledy" with "disconnected items of temporary intelligence."[72] Lest his readers missed the point, this essayist performed this process of textual dismemberment himself, showing what a text looks like when broken up – as he worried it usually was – with women's words.[73]

The particular worries about mothers expressed here suggest, moreover, that the degenerative trajectory launched by reading habits was being passed along not only by descent (as other essayists suggested) but also through the distinctly unexemplary example being set by women, the primary caretakers responsible for cultural reproduction. "Mothers, who have sons who will one day write books themselves, have a knack of reading and *watching* at the same time . . . a practice unbecoming to a British matron . . . Is this the way to bring up children? What sort of reverence will they feel in after life for a volume which they look upon as a kind of domestic ambush?"[74]

Clearly at stake was a gendered division of production and consumption that defined literary labor and authority as male prerogatives. But equally and inseparably, so was the genderedness of subjectivity itself. Within descriptions of the reading problem there was a continual slippage between criticisms of women readers per se and of the feminine quality of mind they exemplified. In his *Subjection of Women* (1869), John Stuart Mill summed up the traditional view of the distinctive mental (in)capacities that characterized women: "women's minds are by nature more mobile than those of men, less capable of persisting long in the same continuous effort, more fitted for dividing their faculties among many things than for travelling in any one path to the highest point which can be reached by it."[75] Or, in the words of a *Blackwood's* essayist, women were "desultory, restless, incorrigible interrupters, incapable of amusing themselves or of being amused by the same thing for five minutes together."[76] Ironically or not, this essayist also happened to be a woman.

Emergent medical theories of sex difference, popularized through debates over women's higher education in the 1870s, lent scientific credence to such descriptions. According to Henry Maudsley, M.D., F.R.C.P., Professor of Medical Jurisprudence, University College London, woman "labours under an inferiority of constitution."[77] "Their nerve centres being in a state of greater instability, by reason of the development of their reproductive functions," women were "more susceptible by nature" to external stimuli, and thus their "organizations" were "more easily" and "more seriously deranged." The periodicity of their reproductive cycles both produced and signified an inability to sustain continuous mental or physical effort without serious risk to proper reproductive functioning and the general health predicated on those functions.[78]

Nonetheless, such theories effectively split off innate sex difference from acquired gender differences. While the former resided ultimately in the physiological distinctiveness of reproductive systems, the proper development of the latter, "those qualities of mind which correlate the physical differences of her sex," depended on the proper environment and training.[79] Opening up the possibility of a derangement of proper gender organization through inappropriate training and habits, medical theory thus also opened up the possibility that these feminine "qualities of mind" could be produced in men. Such theories supported the fear evinced by the writers on reading that this "feeble and indecisive" order of mind was being produced more generally, becoming as typical of men as of women, as these indiscriminate, "desultory and omnivorous reading" practices themselves became the habit of all.[80]

Entailed in definitions of the normative categories of Englishness and masculinity, the integrity of class was equally at issue. The extension of "the literary franchise" to include more and more working-class men had, since the 1790s, shaped the concerns over the size, character, and habits of the reading public.[81] As R. K. Webb argues, the specter of the working-class reader organized the reading problem of the early nineteenth century and primarily mobilized efforts from above to shape reading habits.[82] Yet, as with women readers, the working-class man functioned as at once a quite real social entity and as the embodiment of a certain model of subjectivity. Just as gendered subjectivities were always understood in relational terms in the nineteenth century, so the character of lower-class mentality was consistently described with reference to an upper-class norm. And, as Steven Shapin and Barry Barnes suggest, such depictions had a remarkable similarity to those of the female mind. Like that of women, the thought of the lower orders was represented as simplistic, "sensual and concrete," and their minds as "actually or potentially *unbalanced*" and unstable.[83] Seen to lack as much as did a woman's the balance and integrity of self characteristic of middle-class and upper-class men, the working-class "organization" also represented the threatening endpoint of desultory reading.[84]

While the specter of working-class readers clearly organized the reading problem of the early nineteenth century, the very different focus of this late-century reading problem is aptly demonstrated by the occasional invocation of the ambitious laborer, mechanic, and artisan as an ideal reader and a potential model for middle-class readers. A. Innes Shand, for example, called up the image of the "intelligent mechanic" with a "hearty enjoyment" in reading that "must be taken by fits and starts" as a foil to that of the modern "*blasé* book-buyer who can spend as he pleases, and has the run of libraries that are pretty nearly exhaustive."[85] The palm, in this case, clearly went to the former, for the working-class reader was guided by a rational purpose that middle-class readers were seen to lack, while his material constraints reproduced the conditions of scarcity essayists associated with a more innocent age, in both the individual and collective sense: "short commons are the best substitute for the freshness of intelligent boyhood."[86] Like the male child, who here and elsewhere also figured as an ideal reader, the working-class reader's innocence of the literary marketplace was a virtue. So also was the fact that, unlike the middle-class reader, the laborer was threatened neither by an excess of leisure time nor by a lack of physical exercise. In an essay that originated as a lecture to a primarily working-class audience, John Lubbock avowed that:

> the great readers of the next generation will be, not our lawyers and doctors, shopkeepers and manufacturers, but the labourer and mechanic. Does not this seem natural? The former work mainly with their head; when their daily duties are over the brain is often exhausted, and of their leisure time much must be devoted to air and exercise. The labourer or mechanic, on the contrary . . . have in their work-time taken sufficient bodily exercise, and could therefore give any leisure they might have to reading and study.[87]

Nonetheless and especially in an essay that also invoked the Darwinian model of "survival of the fittest," such visions of a future dominated by working-class readers must have seemed a nightmarish threat to some.

Thus, like railway travel with which it was so often compared, reading endangered a number of crucial social boundaries – between man, machine, woman, and animal; between Occidental and Oriental, civilized and primitive, man; between laborer, doctor, and manufacturer. Because of its perceived agency in producing subjectivity – or, in more properly Victorian terms, in molding character – reading threatened those boundaries by threatening the characterological distinctions that secured them. The linkage between reading and character had always operated, as Thomas Laqueur argues, as the cornerstone of the "culture of literacy" that developed in England during the late eighteenth and early nineteenth centuries. The cause–effect relation between reading habits and subjectivity was, in turn, predicated upon linkages between the achievement and use of reading skills, rationality, economy, productivity, and the achievement and development of a full humanity conceived as simultaneously individual and national. The late-nineteenth-century reading problem clearly drew from, and depended upon, such well-established links. Indeed, the recognition that these correlations were woven into the very fabric of common sense motivated many essayists. Harrison, for one, noted the extent to which "books as books, writers as writers, readers as readers" were considered "meritorious and honourable, apart from any good in them, or anything that we can get from them." Yet he argued against such de facto assumptions: "Why," he asked, "do we pride ourselves on our powers of absorbing print, as our grandfathers did on their gifts in imbibing port?"[88] Harrison and other diagnosticians of the reading problem thus attacked this common sense by effectively reversing some of the connections it assumed. Where, for example, reading had been consistently opposed to more sensual, less rational, and less productive uses of leisure time, and especially to drinking and gambling, these essays represented it – as did Harrison's analogy between "print" and "port" – as precisely too like these if practiced incorrectly. Thus, essayists worked to dismantle the term *reading* and to remove certain practices from that category, often supplanting "reading" with the term "study" as in the following: "There is often reading, in the common sense of the word, when there ought to be study . . . There is . . . a temptation to substitute the pleasure of negligent reading for the pain of study. Reading is often identical with study, as when one is said to *read* law."[89] Dismantling the "common sense of the word" *reading* and the multiplicity of practices to which, they argued, it indiscriminately referred, essayists worked to create distinctions among those practices and to insist that the word should rightly refer only to the normative practice they aimed to define for readers.

The truly literate, well-read man was, quite simply, the man who read well, which is to say correctly in the normative terms established by these essayists. He was distinguished neither by the sheer ability to read nor by what he read but by how he did so, for it was in the process of his reading (*qua* study) that his character was produced and demonstrated. In casting the dangers and promises of reading and literacy in these terms, the discursive construction of the reading problem thus functioned to establish and sanctify social boundaries in new terms. This function becomes visible, for example, in the contributions of working-class journalists who entered the fray by asserting their mental equality as both readers and men. Invoking gender, they distanced themselves from their female counterparts. Far more than an accident of phrasing came into play when "The Journeyman Engineer" declared that the "well-read working man can and *does* . . . feel himself equal to any man."[90] Counting as not equal both "those who are utterly unable to read at all" and those who read only "penny weekly journals and 'numbers'," the "Engineer" made claims only on behalf of a select class of readers. That class was circumscribed largely by gender, for, he insisted, such "worthless, contemptible, enervating trash" was read only by "the women and girls of those classes" and by a few, pitiable "grown and bearded men."[91] Similarly, Thomas Wright countered the diatribes of Wilkie Collins and James Payn against "the unknown public," the penny press readers they assumed to be working class, by arguing – from experience – that this public was a female "tribe."[92] While admitting that penny journals were "not without men readers," Wright insisted that such men were "only led to read them from the circumstances – accidental so far as they are concerned – of their being brought into their homes by their women folk."[93] More significantly, he stressed that male readers read these journals exactly the same way that middle-class and even professional readers would do so: "Many a time and oft, too, I have heard such working-men readers . . . get as hearty amusement out of the folly suggested by . . . [penny journals] as any that could have been extracted from them by more polished critics."[94]

These working-class journalists clearly recognized the connection implicit in the project of readerly diagnosis between social and cultural inclusion and authority, and they joined their male, middle-class peers in employing gender to define the boundaries of the literary domain. On these terms working-class men were granted a kind of inclusion – as audiences for lectures, as ideals offered up within them, and as occasional contributors. As such, however, even their inclusion was of a limited kind. The contributions of these two journalists, at least, were as reports from the trenches and the hospitals; they spoke as foot soldiers or as nurses rather than as the literary generals and doctors who directed the wars over reading and watched over readerly health.[95]

While these and other nineteenth-century texts indicate that "general readers" and their reading practices were affected by such concerns, the overarching and more accessible effect of the reading problem was the construction of a gulf between common and ideal readers, introducing a need for intervention in the former's readerly acts, specifying the particular modes that intervention should take, and defining the character of those best suited to take up this cultural work.[96] In other words, whether or not readers and reading habits were "directly" affected, the mechanisms by which the producers and arbiters of literary culture were defined and through which they acted to produce culture for readers certainly were. In this sense, the constant use of a medical schema was far from arbitrary. Alongside the doctor, with whom they aligned themselves and their project, such men articulated their task as one of diagnosis and cure and, in the process, legitimated their own ability and right to oversee the literary health of both the individual reader and a reading public imagined to be coextensive with the nation. In this sense, the alliances rhetorically established with the profession of medicine articulated deeper material and ideological ties. Making both individual readers and the reading public over into patients, men of letters defined and shaped the contours of their expertise and legitimated their own authority in distinctly professional terms. As such, this project was part of an ongoing professionalization of intellectual labor that included the closure of existing learned societies to amateurs, the formation of numerous professional associations proper, the introduction of standardized examinations as the prescribed route to professional work, and the transformation of "clergyman" into "don" within the universities.[97]

The professional men produced and authorized by those institutional structures, moreover, began to take up and to take over the medical–pedagogical tasks set forth by these essayists. In these years the universities began to assert control over, systematize, nationalize, and professionalize the rather ad-hoc lectures and mutual-improvement societies that had been a mainstay of provincial literary communities and a primary means of their self-education. Through University Extension beginning in the 1880s, Oxbridge sent out university-affiliated lecturers and, along with them, select libraries and instructions for supplementary reading.[98] A related organization founded in 1887–88, the National Home Reading Union, established more permanent reading circles throughout the country, its central office distributing a monthly newsletter with reading lists and detailed instructions. As described by John Churton Collins, the Union's goals were to counter the "evils that result from aimless and ill-regulated reading" by promoting "continuous and systematic home reading among all classes of people in such a way as to make it truly educational."[99] Above all it aimed to ensure that for "boys and girls," and "artisans" in particular, "the gift of reading" should prove "the greatest of blessings" where "without guidance" it might prove "one of the greatest of curses." The much-needed system that the union sought to bring to readers' reading was equally central to its organizational structure; it could only "be disseminated" "by missionaries from a common centre, and that not casually, by one here and one there, but systematically, and as the reflective result of system."[100]

At the same time, the production of literary history and anthology volumes and series increased at a rate never before seen.[101] Such efforts were aimed explicitly at creating and guiding readers in a more informal, but no less systematic and authoritative fashion, organizing both what and how general readers read. Whereas earlier publishing ventures of this kind, such as Robert Chambers's *Cyclopaedia of English Literature* (1843–44), had been as informally put together as provincial lectures, publishers now sought out professional men of letters as the editors and writers uniquely suited to the planning, management, and enactment of these projects. Of the authors whose essays are cited here, at least three – Alfred Ainger, Edward Dowden, and Frederic Harrison – were among those John Morley chose as having the "respectability" and "capacity" he required of contributors to what was perhaps the most influential of these ventures, the English Men of Letters series.[102] As a recent historian of this project argues, the series worked, in tandem with many others, "to empower a specific strategy for reading . . . one formulated by a new class of professionals, that of the Victorian man of letters."[103]

Such authoritative publications, University Extension, and the National Home Reading Union thus became the primary institutional mechanisms for the project of readerly instruction that was called for by the periodical essayists' dire diagnoses and that had traditionally been a definitive mission of the periodical press. Those very diagnoses had helped to undermine the cultural authority of the periodicals themselves: while the genre had not produced the kinds of reading habits censured in its pages, it certainly had encouraged them in both readers and writers, as these essayists and others were quick to point out. The innovative periodical policy of signature and the increasing specialization of expertise with which it was associated could only tangentially address these problems.

In this light, it is of great significance that periodicals always figured as the other in calls for university reform, for it was the university thus reformed that could produce professionals, specialized expert readers rather than desultory generalists:

There comes a time when you must choose between that dispersion and fragmentariness, which is the habit of journalism and life in a hurry, and the concentration and completeness which is the habit of serious literature and life at leisure . . . Our society being what it is, we do not need more intellectual talk at dinner-tables, or classical allusions in leading articles; we need more science and "special learning"; and of science and special learning the universities should be the centres.[104]

Institutionalizing English literature as itself a distinct kind of "exact and thorough" special learning with "its own methods," universities could produce for the nation "a body of trained scholars," "the intellectual aristocracy of a democratic age," and ultimately the specialized "critic of literature" who would displace the heroic man of letters.[105] While, as Haultain lamented, reading may have been forever lost as an art in the nineteenth century, it had been simultaneously gained as both a discipline and a profession.

NOTES

Reading is far from being "a lost art" among the following people, whom I thank for their generous contributions to this chapter: Andrew Bell, Shaleen Brawn, Bud Bynack, Alexandra Chasin, Regenia Gagnier, Anahid Kassabian, Herbert Lindenberger, William McPheron, and Robert Polhemus. Equally vital was support in the form of fellowship grants from the Whiting Foundation and the Mabelle McLeod Lewis Memorial Fund. The epigraph is from Arnold Haultain, "How to Read," *Blackwood's Magazine* 159 (February 1896), 250.

1 [John Murray], "Books and Reading," *Quarterly Review* 162 (April 1886), 501.
2 Alex Zwerdling – a reader of an early version of this chapter – suggested, one has only to substitute throughout this chapter *television watching* for *reading* in order to make these nineteenth-century texts and the problem they articulate more familiar than they might otherwise appear.
3 When literary or social historians have made nineteenth-century British readers the subject of inquiry, their guiding questions have tended to be what was read (or even what was owned or what circulated) and who read (or even, the very different question, who was able to read). See, for example: Richard D. Altick, *The English Common Reader: A Social History of the Mass Reading Public, 1800–1900* (Chicago: University of Chicago Press, 1957);

Amy Cruse, *The Victorians and Their Reading* (Boston: Houghton Mifflin, 1935), published in England as *The Victorians and Their Books*; Louis James, *Fiction for the Working Man, 1830–1850: A Study of the Literature Produced for the Working Class in Early Victorian Urban England* (London: Oxford University Press, 1963); Roger Schofield, "Dimensions of Illiteracy in England, 1750–1850," *Explorations in Economic History* 10 (1973), 437–54; Lawrence Stone, "Literacy and Education in England 1640–1900," *Past and Present* 42 (February 1969), 69–139; and R. K. Webb, *The English Working Class Reader, 1790–1848: Literacy and Social Tension* (London: George Allen & Unwin, 1955). For a study of periodical readership specifically, see Alvar Ellegård, "The Readership of the Periodical Press in Mid-Victorian Britain," Göteborgs Universitets Årsskrift, 63, 3 (1957).

Like all historical studies, however, these necessarily privilege certain questions over others. J. R. R. Adams offers a uniquely forthright statement of the model that often underlies such efforts: "popular reading habits, if accurately determined, can form a reliable mirror in which we can see the mind of past generations at work and play. The past may be a different country, but it *is* possible to travel there and meet, and understand, the natives." J. R. R. Adams, *The Printed Word and the Common Man: Popular Culture in Ulster 1700–1900* (Belfast: The Institute of Irish Studies, 1987), 6. The mirror analogy assumes that the difference between the scholarly reader of the present and the common readers of the past resides solely in the kinds of reading materials they encounter and that the modern scholar's paradigm of interpretive reading produces essentially the same texts out of those raw materials as the natives themselves would have, employing other reading practices and paradigms. Such a historiographical practice assumes first and foremost that interpretation constitutes both the practice and goal of reading for all readers, regardless of their sociohistorical location.

More recent studies, however, have begun to focus on the socially and historically specific uses of literacy. See especially, Ian Hunter, *Culture and Government: The Emergence of Literary Education* (London: Macmillan, 1988); Thomas Laqueur, "The Cultural Origins of Popular Literacy in England 1500–1850," *Oxford Review of Education* 2, 3 (1976), 255–75; and David Vincent, *Literacy and Popular Culture, England 1750–1914*, Cambridge Studies in Oral and Literate Culture, 19 (Cambridge: Cambridge University Press, 1989). Also relevant are Robert Darnton, "First Steps Toward a History of Reading," *Australian Journal of French Studies* 23, 1 (January to April 1986), 5–30; and Roger Chartier, "Frenchness in the History of the Book: From the History of Publishing to the History of Reading," *Proceedings of the American Antiquarian Society* 97, 2 (1988), 299–329.

4 Jon Klancher, *The Making of English Reading Audiences, 1790–1832* (Madison: University of Wisconsin Press, 1987), 51.

5 First Earl of Iddesleigh (Sir Stafford Henry Northcote), *The Pleasures, the Dangers, and the Uses of Desultory Reading: An Address delivered to the Students of Edinburgh University on Nov. 3, 1885* (London, 1885). Reprinted as "Desultory Reading," in *idem, Lectures and Essays* (Edinburgh: Blackwood, 1887), 118–53. As the full title suggests, the book reproduced Iddesleigh's speech as Lord Rector. Acting in precisely the same capacity, Thomas Carlyle addressed students on much the same topic in 1866. See Thomas Carlyle, *On the Choice of Books* (2nd edn.; London: Hotten [1872]).

6 Goschen's monograph also originated as a lecture, his to students attending the lectures of the London Society for the Extension of University Teaching. The text of this speech was also printed in the *Pall Mall Gazette* in the midst of the "best hundred books" debate described below. See "How to Speak, How to Read, and How to Think," *Pall Mall Gazette*, 1 March 1886, 11–12.

7 Frederic Harrison, *On the Choice of Books; and Other Literary Pieces* (1886; London: Macmillan, 1907). The title essay of the book originally appeared in an 1879 issue of the *Fortnightly Review*, and it is to the latter that I refer in the remainder of this chapter. Perhaps the best-known English proponent of positivism, Harrison described his essay as based entirely on the library of August Comte and urged readers of that essay to consult the catalog published in English translations of Comte's *Catechism* (1858) and *Positive Polity* (1877). In his book, Harrison himself provided the catalog. This list also became part of the *Pall Mall* debate described below. See "Mr. Frederic Harrison on the Best Books," *Pall Mall Gazette*, 2 March 1886, 5; "The 'Best Books' for Positivists," *Pall Mall Gazette*, 7 July 1886, 1–2.

8 Lubbock's list also appeared in print in the February 1886 volume of the *Contemporary Review* as an addendum to his essay "The Pleasures of Reading" (cited below). The essay, in turn, originated as a speech delivered at the London Working Men's College, portions of which were printed in the *Pall Mall Gazette* and, according to that source, in the *Morning Advertiser*. See "Sir John Lubbock's Liberal Education," *Pall Mall Gazette*, 11 January 1886, 4; "Sir John Lubbock on the Pleasures of Reading," *Pall Mall Gazette*, 11 January 1886, 7. Though I have not been able to locate a copy of the *Pall Mall* "Extra," it apparently appeared on 17 February 1886. It contained, according to the issue that day, the material already published in the *Gazette*; additional, previously unpublished responses; and "an alphabetical price list, giving particulars of the best and cheapest editions of all the principal books – over 400 in number – mentioned by one or other of our distinguished correspondents." "Carlyle on the Best

Books. An Unpublished Letter," *Pall Mall Gazette*, 17 February 1886, 1. The debate in the *Pall Mall Gazette* extended from the January publication of Lubbock's speech and list into the November issues. Despite (or because of) the controversy Lubbock's list did come to material fruition as a series of volumes. Norman N. Feltes offered a more thorough treatment and very different reading of the Lubbock phenomenon in his "Commodifying Literary Value: Lubbock's 'Hundred Best Books'" (paper delivered at Masterpieces in the Marketplace: Victorian Publishing and the Circulation of Books, Kresge College, University of California at Santa Cruz, 11 August 1991).

9 Indeed, in one of his contributions to the *Pall Mall* debate, Ruskin referred readers to this earlier effort. See "'The Best Hundred Books.' I – By Mr. John Ruskin," *Pall Mall Gazette*, 23 February 1886, 3–4.

10 Murray, 501.

11 The best general description of the development of literary periodicals remains Walter Graham, *English Literary Periodicals* (New York: Thomas Nelson & Sons, 1930). While the eighteenth-century reviews, dominated by the *Monthly* and *Critical*, aimed at noticing all new publications for the information of their readers, the different tenor of nineteenth-century reviews was signaled by the original advertisement for the *Edinburgh Review* in 1830, which emphasized the editors' wish that their new journal "be distinguished, rather for the selection, than for the number of its articles." Quoted in John Clive, *Scotch Reviewers: The Edinburgh Review, 1802–1815* (London: Faber & Faber, 1957), 35.

12 James L. Machor, "Historical Hermeneutics and Antebellum Fiction: Gender, Response Theory, and Interpretive Contexts," in *Readers in History: Nineteenth-Century American Literature and the Contexts of Response*, ed. James L. Machor (Baltimore: Johns Hopkins University Press, 1993), 64; Klancher, 51.

13 Writing in 1853 Frederick Oakeley described the effects of this practice in Machor's terms: "the benefit of editorial protection . . . consist[ed] . . . in the sanction which it gave to individual opinion. The regular contributors to a Review, constitute a kind of corporation, each member of which derives an immense accession of weight from the fact of his forming an integral part of the whole." [Frederic Oakeley], "Periodical Literature," *Dublin Review* 34 (June 1853), 550. Similarly, six years later Eneas Sweetland Dallas attributed the "life and power" of the great journals solely to "the continuity of thought and sentiment" and "degree of harmony" produced by "the anonymous": "a certain power is gained as the result of mystery. A journal has a right to acquire as much power as it can; it desires to give to every contribution the prestige and momentum which belong to it as a whole." [Eneas Sweetland

Dallas], "Popular Literature – The Periodical Press," *Blackwood's Magazine* 85 (February 1859), 183.

14 Dallas, 184.

15 Oscar Maurer, Jr., "Anonymity vs. Signature in Victorian Reviewing," *University of Texas Studies in English* 27, 1 (June 1948), 4.

16 *Ibid.*, 22, 7.

17 *Ibid.*, 7.

18 [F. H. Madan Mayers], "A Well-Read Man," *Temple Bar Magazine* 76 (April 1886), 539.

19 Herbert Maxwell, "The Craving for Fiction," *Nineteenth Century* 33 (June 1893), 1047.

20 E. Noble, "Readers and Writers," *Colburn's New Monthly Magazine*, n.s. 3, 12 (1877), 34.

21 "Reading as a Means of Culture," *Sharpe's London Magazine*, n.s. 31 (December 1867), 322; Frederic Harrison, "On the Choice of Books," *Fortnightly Review*, n.s. 25 (April 1879), 497.

22 Murray, 504.

23 "Choice of Books," *Pall Mall Gazette*, 11 February 1886, 11; Maxwell, 1046.

24 Harrison, 496.

25 "Choice of Books," 11; [E. C. Whitehurst], "What and How to Read," *Westminster Review*, n.s. 70 (October 1886), 111. The term is quoted from Iddesleigh.

26 Noble, 33.

27 C. H. Butterworth, "Overfeeding," *Victoria Magazine* 14 (November to April 1870), 501.

28 The only such "Malthusian" suggestion came in the pages of the *Pall Mall Gazette*, where it was argued that the year of the Queen's Jubilee could also profitably be declared "A Literary Jubilee Year" in which "the literary soil should be allowed to lie fallow." According to this plan, only newspapers would publish "new matter on new subjects," while "reviews and other periodicals" could "occupy themselves with criticism and discussion" of "the literary giants" of the past, and all other "publishing energy" would be directed at "the production of cheap, annotated reprints of the whole range of British prose, poetry, and drama." "A Literary Jubilee Year," *Pall Mall Gazette*, 12 January 1886, 4.

29 [Alfred Ainger], "Books and Their Uses," *Macmillan's Magazine* 1 (December 1859), 110; Butterworth, 501.

30 [Alfred Austin], "The Vice of Reading," *Temple Bar Magazine* 42 (September 1874), 251.

31 *Ibid.*, 253–54.

32 Butterworth, 503.

33 Edward Dowden, "The Interpretation of Literature," *Contemporary Review* 49 (May 1886), 701.

34 Murray, 513.
35 "Reading as a Means," 317.
36 F. T. Palgrave, "On Readers in 1760 and 1860," *Macmillan's Magazine* 1 (April 1860), 489.
37 Austin, 253.
38 Murray, 517.
39 Butterworth, 502; "Reading as a Means," 317; Murray, 517; Butterworth, 501; Austin, 256.
40 For the history of such debates, see Martin J. Weiner, *English Culture and the Decline of the Industrial Spirit, 1850–1980* (New York: Cambridge University Press, 1981); and Raymond Williams, *Culture and Society, 1780–1950* (1958; New York: Harper & Row, 1966).
41 "Reading as a Means," 317, 322; [A. Innes Shand], "Contemporary Literature, VII: Readers," *Blackwood's Magazine* 126 (August 1879), 246; Iddesleigh, quoted in Whitehurst, 110; Ainger, 111.
42 For an examination of the operation and effects of such metaphors of ingestion in twentieth-century scholarship, see Janice Radway, "Reading Is Not Eating: Mass-Produced Literature and the Theoretical, Methodological, and Political Consequences of a Metaphor," *Book Research Quarterly* 2, 3 (Fall 1986), 7–29.
43 E. Tylor, quoted in Maxwell, 1048.
44 Austin, 251; Shand, 239.
45 Butterworth, 500.
46 *Ibid.*, 501; Murray, 517–18; Austin, 253; Ainger, 111.
47 "Reading as a Means," 317; Murray, 506.
48 Henry Maudsley, "Sex in Mind and in Education," *Fortnightly Review*, n.s. 15 (April 1874), 469.
49 Maxwell, 1046.
50 *Ibid.*, 1052; C. A. Ward, "Books, Libraries, and Reading," *Bookworm* 3 (1890), 20; "Reading as a Means," 317, 321; Murray, 502, 506.
51 "Reading as a Means," 316.
52 Harrison, 497.
53 "Reading as a Means," 317; Austin, 252.
54 Austin, 256.
55 "Reading as a Means," 317.
56 Ainger, 110.
57 Shand, 238–39.
58 Butterworth, 503.
59 Shand, 236.
60 Austin, 257.
61 Murray, 517–18.
62 Ainger, 110–11.
63 *Ibid.*, 111; "Reading as a Means," 316.
64 Butterworth, 503.
65 *Ibid.*, 502; "Reading as a Means," 317; Murray, 517; Butterworth, 501.

66 Robert Maniquis, "Lonely Empires: Personal and Public Visions of Thomas De Quincey," *Literary Monographs* 8 (1976), 106.

67 *Ibid.*, 108.

68 Butterworth, 500.

69 John Stuart Mill, *On Liberty* (1859; Arlington Heights, Illinois: Harlan Davidson, 1947), 73.

70 Charles Alliston Collins, "Our Audience," *Macmillan's Magazine* 8 (June 1863), 162.

71 *Ibid.*, 161–62.

72 *Ibid.*, 162–63; Butterworth, 501, 503.

73 Charles Alliston Collins, 163. In this context, it is worth remembering that "castration" was commonly employed in the nineteenth century to refer to the expurgation of a literary text and that such expurgation was most often rationalized with reference to female, and especially "young lady," readers. In this way, the shape of texts was indeed determined with regard to, if not by, female readers. Such practices were often cited as the source of the peculiar Englishness of English literature. Margaret Oliphant, for example, explained that the "very high reputation" of "English novels" rested on their peculiar "sanity, wholesomeness, and cleanness," qualities that, in turn, derived from and encouraged "that perfect liberty of reading which is the rule in most cultivated English houses." [Margaret Oliphant], "Novels," *Blackwood's Magazine* 102 (September 1867), 257. Increasingly, however, such connections were turned on their head by authors vying for more autonomy, self-determination, and power in the literary marketplace. George Moore's *Literature at Nurse* was one of the many sustained attacks on that market that focused on Mudie's power to control it. Moore invoked gender to shape his attack, and like the essayists on reading, constantly oscillated between attacking women readers themselves and invoking gender to caricature Mudie's practices. "You are popularly believed," Moore chided Mudie, "to be an old woman." George Moore, *Literature at Nurse; or, Circulating Morals* (1885; New York: Garland, 1978). For more on Mudie's and late-century attacks, see Guinevere L. Griest, *Mudie's Circulating Library and the Victorian Novel* (Bloomington: Indiana University Press, 1970).

74 Charles Alliston Collins, 162.

75 John Stuart Mill, *The Subjection of Women* (London, 1869). Reprinted in John Stuart Mill and Harriet Taylor Mill, *Essays on Sex Equality*, ed. Alice S. Rossi (Chicago: University of Chicago Press, 1970), 197. Mill was, of course, summing up such traditional views in order to refute them.

76 [Anne Mozley], "On Fiction as an Educator," *Blackwood's Magazine* 108 (October 1870), 457.

77 Maudsley, 479.

78 *Ibid.*, 473, 479–80.

79 *Ibid.*, 472.

80 [William Maginn], "Note-Book of a Literary Idler, No. I," *Blackwood's Magazine* 17 (June 1825), 736. For more on such theories, see Joan N. Burstyn, "Education and Sex: The Medical Case Against Higher Education for Women in England, 1870–1900," *Proceedings of the American Philosophical Society* 117, 2 (April 1973), 79–89. For a more general treatment of Victorian medical theories and their impact on literary critics and criticism, see Bruce Haley, *The Healthy Body and Victorian Culture* (Cambridge, Mass.: Harvard University Press, 1978).

81 Montagu Gattie, "What English People Read," *Fortnightly Review*, n.s. 46 (August 1889), 321.

82 "For the first time [i.e., in the 1790s] the working class reader had specifically to be reckoned with." Webb, 36.

83 Steven Shapin and Barry Barnes, "Head and Hand: Rhetorical Resources in British Pedagogical Writing, 1770–1850," *Oxford Review of Education* 2, 3 (1976), 232–33.

84 Also relevant here is Andreas Huyssen's general characterization of the mutual operation of gender and class in representations of mass culture in nineteenth-century Europe:

> The fear of the masses in this age of declining liberalism is always also a fear of woman, a fear of nature out of control, a fear of the unconscious, of sexuality, of the loss of identity and stable ego boundaries in the mass . . . Male fears of an engulfing femininity are here projected onto the metropolitan masses, who did indeed represent a threat to the rational bourgeois order. The haunting specter of a loss of power combines with fear of losing one's fortified and stable ego boundaries, which represent the *sine qua non* of male psychology in that bourgeois order.

After the Great Divide: Modernism, Mass Culture, Postmodernism (Bloomington: Indiana University Press, 1986), 52–53.

85 Shand, 251–52.

86 *Ibid.*, 252, 253. The working-class "Journeyman Engineer" urged much the same thing, insisting that though "working men have sufficient time at their own disposal to enable them to make themselves well-read, well-informed members of society . . . the environments of their daily life are such that there can be no danger of their reading causing them to degenerate into mere bookworms, or making them dreamy or impracticable, when called upon to encounter the 'stern realities' of life." The Journeyman Engineer, "Readers and Reading," *Good Words* 17, 317.

87 Lubbock, "On the Pleasure of Reading," *Contemporary Review* 49 (February 1886), 245.

88 Harrison, 493.

89 "Reading as a Means," 317.

90 Journeyman Engineer, 318.

91 *Ibid.*, 318–19.

92 [Wilkie Collins], "The Unknown Public," *Household Words* 18 (21 August 1858), 217–22; James Payn, "Penny Fiction," *Nineteenth Century* 9 (January 1881), 145–54.

93 [Thomas Wright], "Concerning the Unknown Public," *Nineteenth Century* 13 (February 1883), 282.

94 *Ibid.*, 283.

95 References to readers as an "army" were common, one occurring in Wright, 279.

96 The essays of working-class journalists themselves testify to the extent to which "common readers" felt called upon to address the charges launched against them in the periodicals. Aside from those of Wright and the Journeyman Engineer, other essays also by men identifying as working-class appeared sporadically in middle-class journals during this period. See, for example: George R. Humphrey, "The Reading of the Working Classes," *Nineteenth Century* 33 (April 1893), 690–701; "A Working Man's View of It," *Pall Mall Gazette*, 24 November 1886, 11–12; [William Brighty Rands], "The Penny Magazine," *St. Paul's Magazine* 12 (January to June 1873), 542–549. The latter is particularly interesting because the author defends himself against charges, once made by a friend of his father, that his early reading was dangerously "desultory" (545). Such an account at least suggests that this terminology infiltrated the experience of readers, operating as a norm through or against which individual reading practices and identities were defined.

97 Burstyn, 88; A. J. Engel, *From Clergyman to Don: The Rise of the Academic Profession in Nineteenth-Century Oxford* (Oxford: Clarendon, 1983).

98 J. F. C. Harrison, *Learning and Living 1790–1960: A Study in the History of the English Adult Education Movement* (London: Routledge & Kegan Paul, 1961), 232–45.

99 John Churton Collins, "The National Home Reading Union, and Its Prospects," *Contemporary Review* 58 (August 1890), 200, 196. Collins was also (in)famous for championing and popularizing the campaign for a school of English literature at Oxford, and this article ended with references to these related efforts. For an account of Collins's activism, see D. J. Palmer, *The Rise of English Studies: An Account of the Study of Language and Literature from its Origins to the Making of the Oxford English School* (New York: Oxford University Press, 1965), 78–103.

100 John Churton Collins, 196, 204.

101 John Gross, *The Rise and Fall of the Man of Letters: Aspects of English Literary Life Since 1800* (London: Weidenfield, 1969), 193–96.

102 John Morley, quoted in John L. Kijinski, "John Morley's 'English

Men of Letters' Series and the Politics of Reading," *Victorian Studies*, 34, 2 (Winter 1991), 206.

103 Kijinski, 205.

104 Sidney Colvin, "Fellowships and National Culture," *Macmillan's Magazine* 34 (June 1876), 141, 142.

105 Edward Dowden, "Hopes and Fears for Literature," *Fortnightly Review*, n.s., 45 (February 1889), 182, 177; *idem.*, "Interpretation of Literature," 717. Dowden's essays expound his view of this "exact and thorough" method and argue that, through it, the "critic of literature" should ideally serve not – like periodical reviewers – as an evaluative judge, but as a "professional interpreter." "Interpretation," 703. Dowden's essays, then, make visible the historical emergence of interpretation as the definitive process and product of professional reading.

CHAPTER 9

How historians study reader response: or, what did Jo think of Bleak House?

Jonathan Rose

Do not be misled by the title of this chapter. This is not an essay in reader-response criticism, for it does not deal with "implied readers," "informed readers," "qualified readers," "superreaders," or any other kind of hypothetical reader. My subject – which has been remarkably neglected by reader-response critics – is the response of the actual ordinary reader in history.

This is one of the newest fields of historical inquiry, opened as recently as 1957 by Richard Altick's *The English Common Reader*. Of course reception histories, which traced the reading responses of literary critics and other professional intellectuals, were being written long before Altick entered the arena; but he attempted something much more difficult. After all, if you are tracking the reactions of London reviewers to Charles Dickens, source material is hardly a problem; but if you want the opinions of the general reading public, where would you begin to look? Altick confessed that he could not penetrate very far into this mystery – only one chapter of his book actually deals directly with the "common reader." Until recently, many historians of reading despaired of ever finding a way to enter the mind of that reader.[1]

In fact, the history of the common reader, at least after 1800, is recoverable. Like any other scholarly enterprise, the historiography of reader response will require the cooperative efforts of an organized body of scholars. But the necessary source materials for a history of ordinary readers are already available. Taking the audience for Charles Dickens as a case study, I want to illustrate here some of the resources, methods, and theoretical problems involved in exploring that audience.

One's first thought upon entering this field might be to check the borrowing records of public libraries. Unfortunately, these are not often broken down by author. An exception is a report by the

Belfast Public Library shortly after its opening in 1888, and as
one might expect, *The Pickwick Papers* and *David Copperfield* were
among the most requested books, along with Frederick Marryat's
Mr. Midshipman Easy.[2]

Somewhat more revealing are reader surveys, which date back as far
as the 1830s. Several of the earliest studies published by the Statistical
Society of London were surveys of book ownership and readership
among the working classes.[3] In 1888 Edward Salmon reported the
responses of 790 boy pupils and just over 1,000 girl pupils, aged
eleven to nineteen, who had been asked to name their favorite
authors and books. Salmon claimed that his respondents ranged
"from the ordinary Board schoolboy to the young collegian," but
since few working-class children continued to attend school into their
teens, they were probably vastly underrepresented in this sample. In
any case, the results are listed in tables 9.1 through 9.4, with many
respondents naming more than one author.[4]

Unsurprisingly, Dickens was the favorite author among both
sexes, with Scott not far behind, but some other results are more
unexpected. No work by Dickens heads either list of favorite books.
Among boys, *The Pickwick Papers* is pushed down to third place by
two desert island tales. Jane Tompkins will be pleased to know that,
among girls, *The Wide, Wide World* beat out every work by Dickens,
with *David Copperfield* only in sixth place; but they were both topped
(astonishingly) by Charles Kingsley's preposterous *Westward Ho!*
Salmon was even more surprised by the finding that "hardly one
of the recognised writers for girls is in high favour." There were
only four votes for Sarah Doudney, one for Mrs. Ewing, none at all
for Anna Sewell. Note also the poor showing of Louisa May Alcott,
Mary Elizabeth Braddon, Harriet Beecher Stowe, Lewis Carroll,
Mrs. Gaskell, and Charlotte Brontë. The other Brontë sisters do
not even appear on the charts, nor does Jane Austen. Overall, just
under 30 percent of the girls' votes (and a negligible proportion of
the boys' votes) were cast for female authors, although nearly half
of the girls mentioned favorite books written by women.

Any attempt to explain why these girls voted the way they did
will serve to illustrate the tricky interpretive problems involved in
studying reader response. Salmon suggested that the results had
been skewed in favor of Dickens and Scott by three factors: their
novels were more available in home and school libraries, their
names were more recognizable than the authors of generic girls'

Table 9.1: *Boys' favorite authors*

Charles Dickens	223
W. H. S. Kingston	179
Walter Scott	128
Jules Verne	114
Frederick Marryat	102
R. M. Ballantyne	67
Harrison Ainsworth	61
William Shakespeare	44
Mayne Reid	33
Bulwer Lytton	32
Charles Kingsley	28
Daniel Defoe	24
James Grant	12
J. Fenimore Cooper	12
T. B. Macaulay	11
Charles Lever	11
W.M. Thackeray	10
Lord Tennyson	10
H. C. Adams	10
Charles Reade	9
M. E. Braddon	9
George Eliot	9
Rev. J. G. Wood	8
William Cowper	8
Whyte Melville	7
Wilkie Collins	6
Hans C. Andersen	6
H. W. Longfellow	6
A. R. Phillips	5
Lord Byron	4
John Bunyan	4
Thomas Carlyle	3
Mark Twain	3
Alexandre Dumas	3
Dean Farrar	3
Aimard	3
A. R. Hope	2
G. Stables	2
Erckmann-Chatrian, G. A. Henty, Thomas Hughes, John Ruskin	1

Table 9.2: *Boys' favorite books*

Robinson Crusoe, Defoe	43
Swiss Family Robinson, Wyss	24
Pickwick Papers, Dickens	22
Ivanhoe, Scott	20
Boys' Own Annual	17
The Bible	15
Tom Brown's Schooldays, Hughes	15
Valentine Vox, Henry Cockton	13
Vice Versa, F. Anstey	12
St. Winifred's, Farrar	11
Arabian Nights	10
Westward Ho!, Kingsley	9
Oliver Twist, Dickens	9
The Three Midshipmen, Kingston	8
Charles O'Malley, Lever	7
Around the World in Eighty Days, Verne	7
Midshipman Easy, Marryat	7
David Copperfield, Dickens	7
Every Boy's Annual	6
Ernie Elton, C.J. Eiloart	6
Peter Trawl, Kingston	6
Scalp Hunters, Reid	6
Nicholas Nickleby, Dickens	6
Eric, Farrar	6
Uncle Tom's Cabin, Stowe	5
Peter Simple, Marryat	5
Twenty Thousand Leagues under the Sea, Verne	5
Masterman Ready, Marryat	5

stories, and many girls may have voted for them because they thought their elders would approve. Perhaps, but that last source of bias was eliminated in a 1906 survey of 200 secondary-school girls: they were asked for anonymous responses and assured that these would not be shown to their teachers. The results did not change much over twenty years, except that a new crop of contemporary novelists had become fashionable: Edna Lyall, Marie Corelli, L. T. Meade, and E. E. Green. Dickens and Scott remained the only "standard novelists" who scored well. Thackeray, Jane Austen, Mrs. Gaskell, Mrs. Ewing, Mrs. Oliphant, Mrs. Craik, Louisa May Alcott – none of them rated more than a few mentions. Charlotte Yonge was now dismissed as juvenile, and Charles Kingsley too had fallen precipitously from grace.[5]

Table 9.3: *Girls' favorite authors*

Charles Dickens	355
Walter Scott	248
Charles Kingsley	103
C. M. Yonge	100
William Shakespeare	75
Mrs. Henry Wood	58
Elizabeth Wetherell	56
George Eliot	50
Bulwer Lytton	46
Hans C. Andersen	33
H. W. Longfellow	32
A.L.O.E.	32
Hesba Stratton	27
Dean Farrar	27
Grace Aguilar	23
Jules Verne	22
Brothers Grimm	20
W. M. Thackeray	20
Mrs. O. F. Walton	20
W. H. G. Kingston	19
Whyte Melville	18
Diana Mulock Craik	15
T. B. Macaulay	15
Louisa May Alcott	14
Mary Elizabeth Braddon	13
Harrison Ainsworth	13
Miss Worboise	12
John Bunyan	11
Harriet Beecher Stowe	11
Lord Tennyson	10
Miss Montgomery	9
R. D. Blackmore	9
Miss Havergal	9
William Black	8
Daniel Defoe	8
Mark Twain	8
Charlotte Brontë	8
Frank Smedley	7
Thomas Carlyle	7
John Ruskin	7
Maria Edgeworth	6
R. M. Ballantyne	6
Lewis Carroll	5
Elizabeth Gaskell	5
Felicia Hemans	5
Mrs. E. Marshall	5
Frederick Marryat	5
F. Anstey	5

Table 9.4: *Girls' favorite books*

Westward Ho!, Kingsley	34
Wide Wide World, Wetherell	29
The Bible	27
Peep Behind the Scenes, Walton	27
John Halifax Gentleman, Craik	25
David Copperfield, Dickens	22
Little Women, Alcott	21
Ivanhoe, Scott	18
The Days of Bruce, Aguilar	16
The Daisy Chain, Yonge	13
The Heir of Redcliffe, Yonge	12
Kenilworth, Scott	12
Pickwick Papers, Dickens	11
Little Meg's Children, Stretton	10
Good Wives, Alcott	9
Christie's Old Organ, Walton	8
Queechy, Wetherell	8
Scottish Chiefs, Jane Porter	8
The Channings, Wood	8
Uncle Tom's Cabin, Stowe	8
Lorna Doone, Blackmore	8
Eric, Farrar	8
St. Winifred's, Farrar	8
Hereward the Wake, Kingsley	8
Pilgrim's Progress, Bunyan	8
Mill on the Floss, Eliot	7
The Lamplighter, Dickens	7
Swiss Family Robinson, Wyss	6
John Inglesant, J. Shorthouse	6
Last Days of Pompeii, Bulwer	6
Last of the Barons, Bulwer	6
The Heroes, Kingsley	6
Two Years Ago, Kingsley	5
Little Dot	5
Melbourne House, Wetherell	5
Home Influence, Aguilar	5
The Newcomes, Thackeray	5
Hypatia, Kingsley	5
East Lynne, Wood	5
Vanity Fair, Thackeray	4
The Talisman, Scott	4
Dove in Eagle's Nest, Yonge	4
Arabian Nights	4
Old Curiosity Shop, Dickens	4
The Prince of the House of David, J. H. Ingraham	4
Tales from Shakespeare, Lamb	4
Robinson Crusoe, Defoe	2
Alice in Wonderland, Carroll	1

We can uncover an important dynamic of Victorian reader response by analyzing the popularity of *Westward Ho!* among girls. Some of them may have actually enjoyed Kingsley's bombastic anti-Catholicism: as one young lady of eighteen reported, *Westward Ho!* "abounds in truly *noble* characters, men who are marked by their loyalty and love for the English Church." A better explanation, however, jumps out at us when we look back at table 9.3. We normally regard Jules Verne, W. H. G. Kingston, Whyte Melville, Harrison Ainsworth, Daniel Defoe, R. M. Ballantyne, and Frederick Marryat as adventure writers for boys, but they also had a considerable female following. Salmon reported that girls rated *The Girls' Own Paper* their favorite magazine (315 votes), but *The Boys' Own Paper* (with 88 votes) took second place. All this suggests that many girls found "girls' stories" insipid and read *Westward Ho!* – or *A Tale of Two Cities* – for the action and adventure, the blood and thunder, the swashing and buckling. As one woman told Salmon:

Charlotte Yonge's stories are pretty, and if they were not quite so goody-goody, would be very nice stories of home and everyday life. Anne Beale is still more goody-goody in her style. I think if *The Wide, Wide World* and *Queechy* had been English stories, they would not have gained a quarter of the popularity they have – the American writing is so much more life-like than the English. American stories for girls are always more true to nature than English stories. A great many girls never read so-called "girls' books" at all; they prefer those presumably written for boys. Girls as a rule don't care for Sunday-school twaddle; they like a good stirring story, with a plot and some incident and adventures – not a collection of texts and sermons and hymns strung together, with a little "Child's Guide to Knowledge" sort of conversation . . . People try to make boys' books as exciting and amusing as possible, while we girls, who are much quicker and more imaginative, are very often supposed to read milk-and-watery sorts of stories that we could generally write better ourselves. . . . When I was younger I always preferred Jules Verne and Ballantyne and *Little Women* and *Good Wives* to any other books, except those of Charles Lever.

Salmon concluded that many girls' books sold well only because they were given as presents by adults: "If girls were to select their own books, in other words, they would make a choice very different from that which their elders make for them." In fact, when London elementary schoolchildren of both sexes selected prize books in 1910, the only "girls' book" high on the list was *Little Women* (1,625 choices), along with *Robinson Crusoe* (2,283), *The Old Curiosity Shop* (1,390), *David Copperfield* (1,114), *Ivanhoe* (1,096), and *Westward Ho!* (1,136).[6]

The children in this last survey would have been mainly working-class. A historiography of reading certainly must attempt to isolate class as a variable, and it is possible to focus specifically on proletarian readers. The reseacher can, for example, look to the numerous libraries maintained by trade unions in Britain during the late nineteenth and early twentieth centuries. In 1879 the Alliance Cabinet Makers' Association printed a catalogue of their 1,500-volume library, in which Dickens was among the most heavily represented authors, along with Scott, Carlyle, Macaulay, Thackeray, Bulwer-Lytton, Marryat, and Lord Brougham. Evidently the cabinet makers were thoroughly respectable, for they included hardly any radical literature: nothing by Marx, nothing by Charles Bradlaugh, and only an occasional volume by Tom Paine.[7]

Of course, catalogs tell us nothing about borrowing frequencies, which is an exceedingly difficult riddle to crack when one is dealing with working-class readers. At the South Wales Miners' Library in Swansea, Hywel Francis tried the approach of counting the due dates stamped inside particular volumes. He reported no figures on Dickens, unfortunately, but he did find that Welsh colliers were reading Marx in the 1920s and 1930s. Remarkably, Sigmund Freud and Herbert Spencer were checked out just as often, Bernard Shaw and Sidney and Beatrice Webb were rather more popular, and popular texts on Communism and psychoanalysis were among the most frequently requested books.[8] Few borrowing ledgers have survived from the hundred-odd miners' libraries that once flourished in the South Wales coalfields, but the records we have recovered suggest a modest but steady demand for Dickens. In 1941, the Tylorstown Workmen's Institute Library loaned out *A Tale of Two Cities* seven times and *David Copperfield* three times – well ahead of Marx, but far behind the seventeen loans of P. G. Wodehouse's *Right-Ho Jeeves*.[9]

Gauging the reactions of proletarian library users is more difficult still, but not impossible. Granted, you would have to station investigators with questionnaires at library checkout desks – and that is exactly what was done by Mass Observation, a British social survey organization. In early 1940 Mass Observers queried fifty patrons of the Fulham Public Library, nearly all of them working class, and not one of them borrowed anything by Dickens. Mostly they were interested in light contemporary fiction, and barely one in ten took out anything that could be called a classic – *Jane Eyre*, *Sense and Sensibility*, *Antic Hay*, *Les Misérables*, Emile Zola's *The Downfall*. Nevertheless, this survey does reveal something important about responses to Dickens: it tells us why these people were not reading him, and it shows that they still placed him at the top of the canonical hierarchy. As one man explained his choice of a whodunit, "Well, it's written snappy, you see . . . Modern writers may not be up to the standard of the old writers, Dickens, Thackeray and Scott, but they're snappy – they're quick reading."[10]

Dickens may have had a greater impact on the leaders of the British working class. When the first large cohort of Labour Party MPs was elected in 1906, the *Review of Reviews* asked them to name the books and authors that had most deeply influenced them. Their responses are listed in table 9.5.[11] Dickens is just nosed out of first place, but is still more popular than the Bible. The most remarkable revelation in this table, however, is that most of the authors are canonical: whatever ordinary working people may have read, their representatives hailed the classics as sources of political enlightenment.

Still, it could be argued that these MPs were all male, all politicians, all on the political left. What if the sample were more representative of the working class as a whole? In 1918 Arnold Freeman, the founder and warden of the Sheffield Educational Settlement, published a remarkable investigation into what we would now call "cultural literacy." He compiled detailed questionnaires from 816 Sheffield working people, evenly divided between men and women and carefully distributed among the various economic strata within the working class. Unfortunately, he did not quantify his results, which are exasperatingly impressionistic, but he did reproduce fifty-six of his completed questionnaires, and from them we can draw some rough inferences.[12]

Freeman and his coinvestigators asked their subjects to identify a long list of writers and other cultural figures, including Aristotle, Beethoven, Darwin, Raphael, Bernard Shaw, and Charles Dickens. They also asked questions about home life, work, knowledge of local government and national politics, familiarity with trade union affairs and the Cooperative movement, use of leisure time, tastes

Table 9.5: *Labour MPs' favorite authors*

John Ruskin	17
Charles Dickens	16
The Bible	14
Thomas Carlyle	13
Henry George	12
Walter Scott	11
John Stuart Mill	10
William Shakespeare	9
Robert Burns	8
John Bunyan	8
Lord Tennyson	6
Giuseppe Mazzini	6
Charles Kingsley	5
T. B. Macaulay	5
J. R. Lowell	5
Sidney/Beatrice Webb	4
Adam Smith	4
William Cobbett	4
W. M. Thackeray	4
J. R. Green	4
Charles Darwin	4
Henry Drummond	4

in music and art, attendance at the theater, use of public libraries, religious and ethical beliefs, education, and reading habits. Those who answered most of these questions satisfactorily – according to the investigators' subjective and rather stringent standards – were classified as intellectually "well-equipped," and they made up about 23 percent of the total. About 70 percent scored less well, and they were labeled "inadequately-equipped"; while about 7 percent, who flunked most of the questions, were judged "mal-equipped."

Extrapolating from the fifty-six published questionnaires, I estimate that between a quarter and a third of adult Sheffield working people had read at least one work by Dickens, and most everyone could identify him correctly. Out of eight "well-equipped" men, at least six and possibly seven had read him. That is a very tiny sample, to be sure, but it suggests that Dickens might have been a special favorite among self-educated workingmen active in politics and trade union affairs – precisely the sort who might eventually become Labour MPs.

If we want to measure the popularity of a given author, why not simply look at his sales figures? Certainly, one of the objectives of a historiography of reading would be to uncover those kinds of statistics, but too many nineteenth-century publishers' archives have been lost to waste-paper dealers or the Luftwaffe. Even reliable sales records don't tell us who was buying those books or how widely they were being read. To take the subject of my own research, self-educated Victorian working people might read over a lifetime a vast array of books, but very few of those books would be bought new. They would be gifts or school prizes or family heirlooms, or borrowed from public libraries, relatives, or workmates. Labor activist Manny Shinwell picked up Dickens, Meredith, Hardy, Keats, Burns, Darwin, Huxley, Kant, Spinoza, and literally hundreds of other volumes from rubbish heaps and tuppenny bookstalls.[13] Publishers' ledgers don't record any of that, nor do they tell us anything about reader response. We should bear that fact in mind when we are tempted to generalize too easily about the "commodification" of literature: a huge portion of the Victorian book-reading public scarcely participated at all in the publishers' marketplace.

We should likewise be wary of the assumption, widely shared among students of popular culture, that the influence of a given book is directly proportional to its circulation. In his day, the sensational novelist G. W. M. Reynolds outsold Dickens, but he does not even register in any of these reader surveys. Evidently some books are a kind of literary chewing gum – though widely consumed, they leave no taste behind.

If we want to discover which books changed the lives of their readers, then we must study those lives directly, and the source that best gives us an entree into the mind of the common reader is autobiography. Richard Altick recognized that, but few memoirs of common people were available to him in 1957: "If only we had the autobiography of [a] pork-butcher!" he lamented.[14] Today, I am delighted to report, we have a good deal more than that. For his 1981 book *Bread, Knowledge and Freedom*, David Vincent was able to assemble 142 memoirs by early-nineteenth-century British workers and showed that they could be used to reconstruct a detailed history of reading response.[15] Together with John Burnett and David Mayall, Vincent has compiled an immensely useful bibliography, *The Autobiography of the Working Class*, with nearly 2,000 entries.[16] And William Matthews's old volume on *British*

Autobiographies lists more than 6,000 works, mainly by middle-class and upper-class writers.[17] It is encouraging to note that some literary researchers, such as Virginia Berridge and Kirsten Drotner, are beginning to draw upon autobiographical sources to illuminate reader response.[18]

Working-class memoirists are remarkably forthcoming about the books they read and enjoyed, and they frequently pay tribute to Dickens. A typical paean is offered by a London leather-bag-maker: "Two names were held in great respect in our home, and were familiar in our mouths as household words, namely, Charles Dickens, and William Ewart Gladstone."[19] George Acorn recalled that, growing up in extreme poverty in London's East End, he scraped up 3 1/2d to buy a used copy of *David Copperfield*. His parents soundly thrashed him when they learned he had wasted so much money on a book, but later he read it to them:

And how we all loved it, and eventually, when we got to "Little Em'ly," how we all cried together at poor old Peggotty's distress! The tears united us, deep in misery as we were ourselves. Dickens was a fairy musician to us, filling our minds with a sweeter strain than the constant cry of hunger, or the howling wind which often, taking advantage of the empty grate, penetrated into the room.[20]

Now this passage, some may object, itself sounds suspiciously Dickensian. If we are going to use memoirs as a historical source, shouldn't we be wary of the fictive elements in autobiography? After all, autobiographers can forget, misremember, remember selectively, embellish, invent, lie outright, and rearrange events in the interest of creating an engaging story. If Acorn was so enthralled by Dickens, couldn't he have recast his childhood memories in a Dickensian mode?

You are certainly not going to find unalloyed truth in an autobiography. The problem is even more acute with working-class memoirs because we usually have no other sources to check them against. When historians do have an opportunity to double-check the facts – as Joel Wiener did in his biography of Chartist William Lovett, and as Barbara English did for Flora Thompson's *Lark Rise* – just enough discrepancies show up to make us cautious.[21] Still, if they are used carefully, autobiographies can reliably tell us a great deal about reader response. For our purposes, it does not really matter if George Acorn's little melodrama did not happen in precisely the way he related it. We want to measure Dickens's influence on working-class readers, and if Acorn thought *David Copperfield* was important enough to place at the center of his story, and possibly used it as a literary model, then that influence was clearly very great and deep. It may be objected that "the book that changed my life" is a very common motif in autobiographies, and perhaps Acorn fabricated his story to follow that literary convention. In that case, let us shift our attention away from these grand epiphanies – which may indeed be embellished – and look instead at the casual, passing allusions to Dickens, for it may be that the novelist's true influence is revealed in a memoirist's offhand comments.

And here it becomes apparent that Dickens spoke directly to the workers, for they repeatedly called upon him to describe their own life experiences. They remember attending a school out of *Nicholas Nickleby*,[22] or one like Dr. Blimber's Academy.[23] *A Tale of Two Cities* took them out of a "confused kitchen, that reeked still of fish and chips . . . to France and the Revolution."[24] And the fate of Mr. Wopsle in *Great Expectations*, they assure us, accurately illustrates the treatment of inferior actors by the patrons of cheap theaters.[25]

On the other hand, when Dickens got his sociology wrong, his working-class readers were not shy to offer professional criticisms. What did the Artful Dodger think of *Oliver Twist*? Arthur Harding, a professional criminal who grew up in the East End slum known as "the Jago," was quite impressed by *A Tale of Two Cities* and *Dombey and Son* when he read them in prison, and confirmed that he had learned pickpocketing just as Fagin's boys had. But Oliver Twist, as a character, he judged not credible: someone so lacking in street wits could not have survived a moment in the East End, he argued.[26] What did Sleary think of *Hard Times*? Journalist Thomas Frost put that question to circus performer Willie Francisco, and his response was an unqualified "Rot!" He noted that Dickens clearly did not know the actual size of an average circus company, since he squeezed Sleary's entire troupe into one small tavern: "They must have been as thick as herrings in a barrel!" As for "all the men's wives riding bare-becked horses and dancing on the tight-rope," very few circus women would attempt any such thing. "Then Dickens was not well up in circus life?" Frost asked. "Can know very little about it," came the answer. "As for the circus slang he has put into the mouths of Sleary's people, it is all new to me."[27]

Moreover, while many ragged readers cried over Dickens's descriptions of poverty, some of them found it difficult to share his anguish over the hardships of the clerkly classes. Growing up in the depressed steelworks town of Merthyr Tydfil between the world wars, some poor schoolboys were a bit baffled when their teacher read them *A Christmas Carol*: "For one thing, we never could understand why it was considered that Bob Cratchit was hard done by – a good job, we all thought he had. And the description of the Christmas party . . . didn't sound bad at all – great, it must have been in Dickens's day!"[28]

Let us then not speak too glibly of Dickens or any other writer imposing some kind of cultural hegemony on his readers. When Victorian workers read things that contradicted their own experience, they were quite willing to talk back to the author. True, many of those workers passively accepted the social order as it existed, but one printer had a very revealing way of describing that kind of deference. Before the First World War, he recalled, the workers were not yet willing to "demand a bit more, like Oliver Twist."[29] Far from being reconciled to the status quo, working-class readers were likely to extract a very radical lesson from Dickens.

This is not to suggest that Dickens's influence was invariably progressive. He was only a delightful entertainer for many if not most readers. Sometimes he seems to have reinforced their prejudices, as revealed in a passing remark by Chartist Robert Lowery: "he was cold and calculating, and of a 'Fagin-like' Jew appearance, and seemed fitted for any dark deed."[30] All the same, the reader surveys conducted by the *Review of Reviews* and Arnold Freeman, along with Robert Roberts's memoir *The Classic Slum* and David Vincent's investigations, all confirm that the workers who were most active politically were usually those who had read Dickens, Carlyle, Ruskin, and even that arch-Tory Sir Walter Scott.[31]

The history of reader response, then, can and should tell us something about the political influence of authors: the impact of Dickens on class attitudes, of Conrad on imperial ideologies, of Hardy on women's social roles. But here I should raise some serious misgivings about the political criticism of literature and art as it is currently practised. Too often it demands the same intellectual skills that would make a good censor: measuring an author against a one-dimensional ideological yardstick and grading him pass/fail. Too often it misrepresents the work and its historical context.

My most serious objection, however, is methodological. In recent years we have become accustomed to the idea that each reader brings a unique reading to a particular book. That fact introduces an uncertainty principle into the study of reader response: How do we know that the common reader is picking up the same political messages that we perceive in a Dickens novel? Literary critics still frequently commit what might be called the receptive fallacy: that is, they try to discern the influence of a text on an audience simply by examining the text. They are looking in the wrong place. If you want to know how Dickens shaped attitudes toward women in the minds of his readers, you are not going to find the answer in *The Pickwick Papers* or anything else Dickens wrote. You must interrogate the readers, because they all read unpredictably. To put it bluntly, a large body of recent literary criticism, based as it is on the receptive fallacy, should be scrapped and done over again, using a very different method – perhaps one of the methods outlined here.[32]

I have one last misgiving about political criticism: that it may be crowding other perspectives in literary studies. There is no question that literature influences the politics of common readers; but it also shapes their aesthetic sensibilities, psychological traits, religious beliefs, and literary skills. A history of reading should be sensitive to these dimensions of response – even if they are not, strictly speaking, political. Perhaps Dickens's most important gift to the British working classes was the role he played, not in converting them to any particular ideology, but in making them articulate. He provided a fund of allusions, characters, tropes, and situations that could be drawn upon by people who were not trained to express themselves on paper. In 1869 the *People's Journal*, which had a huge circulation among Scottish workers, sponsored a Christmas story competition: readers submitted over 1,000 entries (about one for every hundred subscribers) and many of them clearly reflected the influence of *A Christmas Carol*.[33] If George Acorn did try to write something like *David Copperfield*, he was offering a great testament to Dickens, who provided working people with the inspiration and the generic literary conventions they needed to tell their own life stories. How would the daughter of a Dudley shoe repairer know how to begin her memoirs? She could follow David Copperfield and write, "I am born."[34] What convinced a Devonshire farm boy that his experiences were worth recording? He had read, in chapter 6 of *The Pickwick Papers*, that even a "homely and ordinary life" may deserve a biography.[35] Cotton operative Joseph Burgess was so deeply shocked by the death of Dickens that he was driven to compose a poem, and that creative act began his long career as a labor poet and journalist.[36] Thanks to Charles Dickens, Jo was not only thinking: he was beginning to write.

NOTES

1 See for example Robert Darnton, *The Kiss of Lamourette: Reflections in Cultural History* (New York: Norton, 1990), 177, 212.
2 J. R. R. Adams, *The Printed Word and the Common Man: Popular Culture in Ulster 1700–1900* (Belfast: Institute of Irish Studies, Queen's University of Belfast, 1987), 168–69.
3 For example, F. Liardet, "State of the Peasantry in the County of Kent," and G. R. Porter, "Results of an Inquiry into the Condition of the Labouring Classes in 5 Parishes in the County of Norfolk," in *Third Publication of 1839* (London: Central Society of Education, 1839).
4 These tables, as well as the information in the next few paragraphs, are all culled from Edward Salmon, *Juvenile Literature as It Is* (London: Henry J. Drane, 1880), chapter 1. The survey was reported by Salmon but actually carried out by Charles Welsh.
5 Florence B. Low, "The Reading of the Modern Girl," *Nineteenth Century* 59 (February 1906), 278–81.
6 "What Children Read," *Co-Partnership* (April 1911), 55.
7 Stan Shipley, "The Library of the Alliance Cabinet Makers' Association in 1879," *History Workshop* (Spring 1976), 181–84.
8 Hywel Francis, "The Origins of the South Wales Miners' Library," *History Workshop* (Autumn 1976), 183–205.
9 Jonathan Rose, "Marx, Jane Eyre, Tarzan: Miners' Libraries in South Wales, 1923–1952," *Leipziger Jahrbuch zur Buchgeschichte* 4 (1994).
10 "Selection and Taste in Book Reading" file 48; Tom Harrisson Mass-Observation Archive, University of Sussex, 1940.
11 "The Labour Party and the Books That Helped to Make It," *Review of Reviews* 33 (June 1906), 568–82.
12 [Arnold Freeman], *The Equipment of the Workers* (New York: Macmillan, 1919), chapters 8 to 10.
13 Emanuel Shinwell, *Conflict without Malice* (London: Odhams Press, 1955), 24–25.
14 Richard Altick, *The English Common Reader* (Chicago: University of Chicago Press, 1957), 244.

15 David Vincent, *Bread, Knowledge and Freedom: A Study of Nineteenth-Century Working Class Autobiography* (London: Methuen, 1982), part 3.

16 John Burnett, David Vincent, and David Mayall (eds.), *The Autobiography of the Working Class* (3 vols.; New York: New York University Press, 1984–89).

17 William Matthews (ed.), *British Autobiographies* (Hamden, Conn.: Archon Books, 1968).

18 Virginia Berridge, "Popular Sunday Papers and mid-Victorian Society," in George Boyce, James Curran, and Pauline Wingate (eds.), *Newspaper History from the Seventeenth Century to the Present Day* (London: Constable, 1978), especially 251. A concise and useful discussion of the theoretical problems involved in analyzing reader response may be found in Kirsten Drotner, *English Children and Their Magazine, 1751–1945* (New Haven: Yale University Press, 1988), 7–12.

19 Charles H. Welch, *An Autobiography* (Banstead: Berean Publishing Trust, 1960), 33.

20 George Acorn, *One of the Multitude* (London: Heinemann, 1911), 28–35.

21 Joel Wiener, *William Lovett* (Manchester: Manchester University Press, 1989), 2; Barbara English, "Lark Rise and Juniper Hill: A Victorian Community in Literature and in History," *Victorian Studies* 29 (Autumn 1985), 7–35.

22 John Sykes, *Slawit in the 'Sixties* (Huddersfield: Schofield & Sims, n.d.), 23–29.

23 Alfred Gilchrist, *Naethin' at A'* (Glasgow: Robert Gibson & Sons, n.d.), 14.

24 Elizabeth Flint, *Hot Bread and Chips* (London: Museum Press, 1963), 163.

25 Thomas Wright, *Some Habits and Customs of the Working Classes* (London: Tinsley Brothers, 1867), 166.

26 Raphael Samuel, *East End Underworld: Chapters in the Life of Arthur Harding* (London: Routledge & Kegan Paul, 1981), 47, 74–75, 274. The same criticism is offered in the anonymous "Autobiography of a Journeyman Shoemaker," *Saturday Evening Commonwealth*, 22 November 1856, 3.

27 Thomas Frost, *Reminiscences of a Country Journalist* (London: Ward & Downey, 1886), 151–53.

28 R. L. Lee, *The Town That Died* (London: Author, 1975), 88.

29 Arthur Fredrick Goffin, "A Grey Life" (typescript; Brunel University Library), chapter 7.

30 Brian Harrison and Patricia Hollis (eds.), *Robert Lowery, Radical and Chartist* (London: Europa Publications, 1979), 134.

31 Robert Roberts, *The Classic Slum* (London: Penguin, 1990), 177–79; Vincent, chapters 8–9.

32 For a fuller discussion of the receptive fallacy and its implications,

see Jonathan Rose, "Rereading the English Common Reader: A Preface to a History of Audiences," *Journal of the History of Ideas* 53 (1992), 47–70.

33 William Donaldson, *Popular Literature in Victorian Scotland* (Aberdeen: Aberdeen University Press, 1986), 32.

34 Nora Hampton, "Memories of Baptist End, Netherton, Dudley in the Period 1895–1919" (typescript; Brunel University Library), 1.

35 Richard Pyke, *Men and Memories* (London: Epworth Press, 1948), 9.

36 Joseph Burgess, *A Potential Poet?: His Autobiography and Verse* (Ilford: Burgess Publications, 1927), 61–62.

CHAPTER 10

Dickens in the visual market

Gerard Curtis

During the Victorian period two markets conflated to produce a new merchandising strategy, a strategy ready made for the developing industry of advertising. The two markets were publishing and the fine arts, and a pivotal figure around which this union developed was Charles Dickens. Intrinsic to this fusion of markets and strategies were three cultural mechanisms on which Dickens and his publishers avidly capitalized: the Victorian emphasis on the role of observation or "the art of seeing," the "sister-arts" tradition, and the increasing importance of portraiture. Not only do these connected cultural developments aid in showing the relation of the mercantile and publishing worlds with the fictive in the nineteenth century, but they also point to a type of subsidiary reading/visualizing process underlying the Victorian book.

The phrase "the art of seeing" describes the Victorian passion for observation and for refining the skills of looking and seeing. Ruskin best stakes the claim for the superiority of "the art of seeing" when he notes that "the first distinct impression which fixed itself on me was that of the entire superiority of Painting to Literature as a test, expression, and record of human intellect, and of the enormously greater quantity of Intellect which might be forced into a picture – and read there – compared with that which might be expressed in words."[1] The artist was the dominant master of communication for Ruskin – for "the greatest thing a human soul ever does in this world is to *see* something . . . To see clearly is poetry, prophecy, and religion, – all in one."[2]

This cultivation of the art of seeing supplied a continuing impetus for the sister-arts tradition. Summed up by Horace's famous maxim *ut pictura poesis* – as is painting, so is poetry – it linked painting and literature together as being "almost identical in fundamental nature, in content, and in purpose."[3] One of the principal reasons for this association was that art was celebrated by theorists like Ruskin as the ultimate refinement of observation – part of a universal code of seeing and representing. In painting, as Dickens noted, literature found "a new expression, and in a universal language."[4] While Whistler might complain of a growing tendency to see art as literature's hieroglyphic handmaid, the visual arts provided what was believed to be a universally acceptable representation of reality that transcended the limitations imposed by a culturally specific language/text experience.[5] Thanks in part to the emphasis supplied by the sister-arts tradition, Victorians were keenly aware that the act of reading required typographical seeing, an acknowledgment of the visual value and visual semiotics of material signifiers, print, and the book itself. For Victorians there existed a visual typographic awareness, along with a correspondent association of word and visual image – notably in the revival and development of illuminated lettering and art bindings.[6]

The desire to read the material world also powered a growing popular passion for portraiture and for reading character in the human face. The Victorians' desire to taxonomically classify the world with a scientific precision joined with a widespread belief in physiognomic analysis and phrenology to make the face itself a text. Portraiture in popular works and illustrated series catered to a belief that the human race could be anthropologically classified down to the evolutionarily lowest peoples. A prime example is Henry Mayhew's classic series *London Labour and the London Poor*, which combined Lamarckian evolutionary theories with illustrations identifying characteristics of the various peoples and workers of the lower classes.

The advertisements that appeared in the original serial installments of Dickens's novels provide sources for a critique of this Victorian art of seeing, as well as of the related phenomena of the sister-arts tradition and the increasing popular importance of portraiture in the Victorian cultural marketplace.[7] Since Bernard Darwin's light-hearted examination of these adverts in the 1930s, they have been ignored, though Darwin himself noted they might be of use to future historians.[8] Advertisements are, as the *Quarterly Review* in 1855 noted: "the very daguerreotypes cast by the age which they exhibit, not done for effect, but faithful reflections of those insignificant items of life and things, too small it would seem for the generalizing eye of the historian, however necessary to clothe and fill in the dry bones of his history."[9]

It is hard now to appreciate both the rapid graphic developments made in advertising in the nineteenth century and the immense impact these advances made. Adverts made public literacy and the value of the word visual, with text becoming an overwhelming feature of the streets and their new urban semiotics. *Punch* complained that adverts blocked the very thoroughfares, with street-vans exhibiting "letters six feet long" hemming in urbanites with "bold black letter assertion."[10] In 1847 *Punch* complained about how one could no longer escape "ads"; they were all-pervasive – everywhere capturing the eye with novel techniques and formats.[11] The period saw a dramatic rise in the design of advertising typefaces and display types to attract and entice the reading eye into text and image. By 1921 Roland Hall could claim that advertising worked by "appeal to the eye alone . . . the eye is the window to the mind."[12] Hall represented this visually through a diagram that showed an eye placed between the words "advertising" and "consumer." Advertising, as it developed in the Victorian period, thus exemplified a conflation of word and visual image that was central to the conflation of the markets for literature and the fine arts.

Victorian advertisers did not forget the diagrammatic eye (plate 10.1) as a medium to bring to consciousness the process of looking in reading, the link between the mind's eye and the physical eye. These eyes act as a reminder that even in the act of reading, a reader is involved in the process of looking; they make readers hyperconscious of their own eyes observing. This ocular self-consciousness was part of a whole culture of increased scientific and artistic observation, a culture that was promoted through the book trade.

The Education of the Eye, with Reference to Painting, by John Burnet (1837) argued that eye training and drawing should be two essential aspects of child and adult education, with drawing accompanying "the elements of reading and writing."[13] Thomas Dunman, in an article titled "The Art of Observing" in the 1880s self-help series *The Universal Instructor*, stressed the need and value of observation for Victorian education, particularly as it applied to the natural sciences.[14] Books and journals advertised in Dickens's serials catered to the recreational aspects of looking and to eye training, particularly journals like "Microscopic Teachings" (advertised in *Our Mutual Friend*, number 1, 1864), "The Grammar of the Five Senses" (*Nicholas Nickleby*, number 16, 1839), "The Intellectual

Plate 10.1. "Come and See!!!" *Nicholas Nickleby*, numbers 19 and 20, 1839.

Observer" (*Our Mutual Friend*, number 1, 1864), and for children, "The Observing Eye" (*Little Dorrit*, number 2, 1856).

One could also buy from ads in the Dickensian serial the instruments necessary for observation, from optical glasses to cameras, telescopes, projection devices, binoculars, optical instruments, and microscopes. Sam Weller, in *Pickwick*, comments on these new products in Pickwick's trial when Sergeant Buzfuz questions Sam's sight: "Yes, I have a pair of eyes," replied Sam, "and that's just it. If they was a pair o' patent double million magnifying gas microscopes of hextra power, p'raps I might be able to see through a flight o' stairs, and a deal door; but bein' only eyes, you see, my wision's limited."[15]

Observation became commodified by these products. This commodification both allowed and made it fashionably obligatory to see the world in new ways – from the photographically frozen three dimensional reality of the stereoscopic photograph (advertised in *Little Dorrit*, January 1856, with the Shakespearean proviso of "Seems Madam! Nay, it IS!"), to the formerly microscopic world made macroscopic via the Stanhope Lens. In the latter case, the lowly flea is illustrated, magnified so that it takes on the dimensions of a monstrous organism. Even water was magnified (in an ad for water filters) to show the impurities and organisms causing disease – and to show that water, and the world, were not all they appeared to be.

If nothing else, however, the effect of these ads and the commodification of observation was not unsettling. They put in popular circulation a reassuring epistemological realism. They told the public that there exists an observable and real world beyond their standard field of vision. Charles Knight, in his *Pictorial Gallery of Arts*, noted that the "humble classes have *their* observatories, too, as well as the learned," in the itinerant astronomers who "dispense out, in penny-worths, a share of that sublime pleasure which results from a view of the beauties presented by the 'starry firmament.'"[16] By the 1860s microscopes had become a minor craze. After-dinner parties often featured microscopic examinations of the abstract patterns to be found in nature, and Elgar is said to have kept three microscopes on his billiard table.[17] Such devices and new skills spelled a dramatic change in the practices of visual communication and visual understanding in the nineteenth century. It was as dramatic in effect as the rise of textual literacy.

Dickens's texts were of course a dominant part of this new culture of seeing, of realistic and naturalistic observation. His observant manner and ways had long been noted, with friends like Macready mentioning that he had an acute sense of perception and a "clutching eye."[18] The *Spectator* magazine, in attempting to decipher Dickens's genius, noted the essential quality of "a power of observation so enormous that he could photograph almost everything he saw."[19] The *Quarterly Review*, in June 1839, stated that "Boz sketches . . . with the power of a camera lucida." These reviewers, in a not uncommon comparison, equate Dickens's observational manner to the instruments of precise optical inquiry. And the most common analogy made of Dickens's work and his observational manner by his contemporaries repeated this pervasive association of written word, observing eye, and visual image: Dickens was a painter or portraitist. As the *Quarterly Review* of 1839 stated, he "sees with the eyes and writes with the pen of an artist."[20] Similarly, nineteenth-century critics like Frederic Kitton and John Forster described Dickens's style by using a sister-arts analogy: "word-painter."

Both the fiction and the adverts in the Dickens serials repeat the reassuring appeal to realism produced by the commodification of observation. Dickens himself stated that "some beneficent power shows it all to me . . . I don't invent it – really do not – but see it, and write it down."[21] This echoes Ruskin's praise that "the greatest thing a human soul ever does in this world is to *see* something, and tell what it *saw* in a plain way."[22] In his preface to *A Tale of Two Cities* Dickens clearly states that in writing he puts himself in the imaginative role of an "observant spectator,"[23] placing himself in that protomodernist viewing position that Baudelaire too had adopted. Walter Benjamin labelled both with the stance of the modernist – the consumer *flâneur*.[24]

A prime example of how the ads themselves produced this effect, an example that shows a sophistication of advertising design and merchandising acumen that antedate what has generally been accepted as the advent of graphic advertising design, is an ad for Hill's Seal Wafers in *Nicholas Nickleby* (numbers 19 and 20, 1839) that incorporated a series of actual wax seals (plate 10.2) stamped onto the advert page as a product sample, much like modern perfume sample strips. In *Edwin Drood* (number 2, 1870) a half-page piece of paper-thin cork with an engraving on it was enclosed to promote cork-lined hats.

It is important to note that these adverts, like their modern

Plate 10.2. Hill's Seal Wafers, *Nicholas Nickleby*, numbers 19 and 20, 1839.

counterparts, were part of the original reading process of the serial, an integral part of its framing device and of its effects. Recovering this reading process allows us insights into the novel, its construction, and publication concerns. For example, the almost continuous use of the then famous green covers for the Dickens serials – with their pictorial cover illustration designed to be read, as the *Spectator* magazine noted, as a visual primer to the story line – served to make the serials an eye-catching feature on Victorian bookstalls.[25] In turn, this pictorial wrapper design was mimicked by an enterprising advertiser in *Bleak House* as a way of catching the reader's eye through visual echoing (plate 10.3). This type of correspondent association served to link the claims of advertiser and novelist in a way that served the marketing interests of both. Other advertisers capitalized on the associated value of Dickens's name by addressing their ads directly to Dickens. The Dakin Tea Company, for example, had a full-page ad on the first page of the "Bleak House Advertiser" (number 3, May 1852) disguised as a letter addressed to Chas Dickens, Esq., and reading: "Sir, We thank you for your new work. Though its name is 'Bleak House,' we know well that its inmates will be warm and life-like . . . but we thank you on more solid grounds; we thank you for it as a matter of business." The letter goes on to note that the reader will profit from reading both the serial and the ad, and to acknowledge Dickens's own prodigious sale of stories. Other advertisers might be more subtle, incorporating a reference to the serial title within the ad itself. In turn, the novel was related directly to the ad, creating a type of textual interchange. Inside the serials' pictorial wrappers the advertising supplements were always named after the serial they occurred in (thus adverts were placed or foregrounded in the "Nickleby Advertiser" section of *Nicholas Nickleby*, serving to link the ads and products by name with the successful serial text and its author).

Dickens himself was not immune to utilizing ads, both inside his text and out. Indeed, ads and text might meet in complementary ways. In number 2 of *Our Mutual Friend*, Dickens incorporates within the novel's body an illustrated version of Silas Wegg's small card ad, as it would appear in life.[26] *Our Mutual Friend* (number 8) had a quarter-page bright orange ad (for a new book release) placed between two pages of text, interrupting the narrative flow and forcing the eye back out of the internal text and into the external market of books for sale. Or a green ad insert (imitating the green

Plate 10.3. Dakin & Co., *Bleak House*, number 6, 1852.

color of the serial cover) advertising Dickens's own *Household Words* might get a prime and rarely utilized advertising slot immediately after the illustrations and just prior to the main text of *David Copperfield* (number 13, 1850). The serials also featured ads by Chapman & Hall promoting book and serial editions of Dickens's and other authors' works. In these cases a reader was reminded of the release of future offerings from the same authorial voice that would soon be leading them into the novel's text. The acts of flipping and pausing to look at promotional pages in order to reach the novel, while being reminded of the authorial voice in both ad and fiction, served to conflate the mercantile and publishing world with the fictive, and to equate the fictive with the real.[27]

The original reader of the serials might be reminded of this flow between the ads and the text and the realism they both claimed by the repetition of certain products from the ads in the serial. For example, Rowland's Kalydor complexion cream, advertised extensively in *Martin Chuzzlewit* and *Nicholas Nickleby*, appears, as Michael Slater has noted, in *Nicholas Nickleby* when an old man proclaims that the miniature portrait painter Miss La Creevy is more beautiful than "Mrs. Rowland who every morning bathes in Kalydor."[28] Yet the same Miss La Creevy might exit the text and become an actual portrait painter in the "Nickleby Advertiser" in a promotional ad for the publication of an engraving series, *Heads From Nicholas Nickleby*, by Robert Tyas. In this advert Miss La Creevy is actually portrayed in the act of painting, with a list of her illustrated heads for sale beneath (plate 10.4).

Dickens might enter the advertising market himself, employing the effects it developed to claim authenticity for his own products, as in an ad on which he places his signature (plate 10.5) in the reissued serial version of *Sketches by Boz* (number 5). Here "Boz" himself announces, using eye-catching legal typography, a warrant against pirates of his serials (some of whom advertised in the serials), while also puffing the forthcoming release of his *Nicholas Nickleby* series. In this case, novel, advert, authorial voice, and real world merge in an advertising jumble that links the pseudonymous author "Boz" with Dickens's own, very real publishing concern regarding copyright. The reader is let into this extrafictive world of Dickens's concerns over piracy (and sold a bit of puffery on the side) as a participant buyer of authentic editions instead of possible forgeries.

This flow between the word and the image of the author

TO THE READERS OF NICHOLAS NICKLEBY!

This Day is Published, No. I. **PRICE SIXPENCE,** (to be continued Monthly) of

HEADS
FROM
NICHOLAS NICKLEBY

ETCHED   DRAWINGS

BY   BY

A. DRYPOINT   MISS

FROM   LA CREEVY.

These "HEADS" will comprise Portraits of the most interesting individuals that appear in "THE LIFE AND ADVENTURES OF NICHOLAS NICKLEBY," selected at the period when their very actions define their true characters, and exhibit the inward mind by its outward manifestations. Each Portrait will be a literal transcript from the accurate and vividly minute descriptions of this able and most graphic author; and will present to the eye, an equally faithful version of the maiden simplicity of KATE NICKLEBY—the depravity of Sir MULBERRY HAWK—the imbecility of his dupe—the heartless villany of the calculating RALPH—the generosity of the noble-minded NICHOLAS—the broken spirit of poor SMIKE—and the brutality of SQUEERS. These and many others furnish subjects for the display of the artist's genius, and will form an interesting and most desirable addition to the work.

No. I. CONTAINS

KATE NICKLEBY	**SIR MULBERRY HAWK**
RALPH NICKLEBY	**NEWMAN NOGGS.**

LONDON: ROBERT TYAS, 50 CHEAPSIDE:
J. MENZIES, EDINBURGH; MACHEN AND COMPANY, DUBLIN.

Plate 10.4. "Heads from Nicholas Nickleby," *Nicholas Nickleby*, number 12, 1839.

credulous, by producing cheap and wretched imitations of our delectable Works. **And Whereas** we derive but small comfort under this injury, from the knowledge that the dishonest dullards aforesaid, cannot, by reason of their mental smallness, follow near our heels, but are constrained to creep along by dirty and little-frequented ways, at a most respectful and humble distance behind.

And Whereas, in like manner, as some other vermin are not worth the killing for the sake of their carcases, so these kennel pirates are not worth the powder and shot of the law, inasmuch as whatever damages they may commit, they are in no condition to pay any.

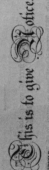

This is to give Notice.

FIRSTLY,

TO PIRATES.

THAT we have at length devised a mode of execution for them, so summary and terrible, that if any gang or group thereof presume to hoist but one shred of the colours of the good ship NICKLEBY, we will hang them on gibbets so lofty and enduring, that their remains shall be a monument of our just vengeance to all succeeding ages; and it shall not lie in the power of any Lord High Admiral, on earth, to cause them to be taken down again.

SECONDLY,

TO THE PUBLIC.

THAT in our new work, as in our preceding one, it will be our aim to amuse, by producing a rapid succession of characters and incidents, and describing them as cheerfully and pleasantly as in us lies; that we have wandered into fresh fields and pastures new, to seek materials for the purpose; and that, in behalf of NICHOLAS NICKLEBY, we confidently hope to enlist both their heartiest merriment, and their kindliest sympathies.

THIRDLY,

TO THE POTENTATES OF PATERNOSTER-ROW.

THAT from the THIRTIETH DAY of MARCH next, until further notice, we shall hold our Levees, as heretofore, on the last evening but one of every month, between the hours of seven and nine, at our Board of Trade, Number ONE HUNDRED and EIGHTY-SIX in the STRAND, LONDON; where we again request the attendance (in vast crowds) of their secretaries, agents and ambassadors. Gentlemen to wear knots upon their shoulders; and patent cabs to draw up with their doors towards the grand entrance, for the convenience of loading.

Given at the office of our Board of Trade aforesaid, in the presence of our Secretaries, EDWARD CHAPMAN & WILLIAM HALL, on this Twenty-eighth day of February, One Thousand Eight Hundred and Thirty-eight.

(Signed)

Boz.

Plate 10.5. "Proclamation," *Sketches by Boz*, number 5. 1838.

under the sign of the "real" world, the observed world, would find its greatest manifestation in the publishing and advertising market's conflation of the fine arts and literature – exploiting the sister-arts tradition. In institutions like the working men's colleges and free libraries, the arts were taught side-by-side with literature. This analogous relationship of the sister-arts in education meant textual literacy was taught along with visual literacy. Dickens, in a speech to the students of the Birmingham and Midland Institute (6 January 1853), noted that the institution's art gallery, library, and models gallery seemed well designed for that new age of men, the men of "the inquiring eye."[29]

The relationship between the sister-arts, particularly between the visual arts and literature, was never more incestuous, or more accepted, than in the mid-Victorian period. Juliet McMaster has noted that it was as if "Horace's maxim of *ut pictura poesis* [was taken] quite for granted."[30] Richard Altick has found that while the aesthetic debates and controversy over the doctrine of *ut pictura poesis* died away in the century, it was in paintings from the novel that "it flourished on a more demotic level as a statement of a demonstrable fact, [in] the joining of painting and the written word."[31] English popular tradition thus directly challenged Lessing's proscription of the sister-arts analogy in the name of painting's purity, its fundamentally static quality. Pantings lacked literary expressiveness but possessed visual beauty, which Lessing opposed to the purity of poetry and to its narrative temporality. Popular tradition saw the arts together. This is particularly evident in the popularity of Hogarth's narrative painting schemes, to which Dickens's writing was often compared.

Because the visual system, and not the word, was considered the universal language of Victorian culture, text aimed for that visually descriptive value. This is the thrust of Martin Meisel's arguments in his monumental cataloguing of the visual semiotics of Victorian culture in *Realizations*. Pictorial realization, as Meisel's evidence amply points out, was the dominant and desired mode of expression in Victorian (and, to an extent, European) writing, drama, and art.[32] Juliet McMaster has studied the visual systems operating in the Dickensian text in *Dickens the Designer*, and also finds extensive evidence that the visual operates as the dominant stylistic tool in Dickens's work. McMaster points to Gerard Manley Hopkins's opinion that "word-painting is, in the verbal arts, the great success of our day" as supporting evidence of the widespread orientation toward the visual by writers of the period.[33] And, as if to tie the commodification of observation to the commodification of text, there is Proust's statement that "the Book is only a sort of optical instrument which the writer offers to the reader."[34]

In these halcyon days, prior to the development, with increased literacy, of a more overtly literary culture, both sister-arts, the textual and visual, shared the same pedestal, as the *Illustrated London News* was willing to point out when it depicted on its volume covers a statue of art and literature as sisters (with the required attributes of pen, brush, and palette), arm in arm, surveying London and the world (plate 10.6). Here, as elsewhere, the two arts are conflated within the dimensions of the book/serial in a visual advert selling both text and image.

Adverts capitalized upon the design potential of both dynamic typography and image. This was particularly true in the Dickens serials, where early attempts at incorporating typographic design and image antedate previously catalogued examples of the genre. These early graphic ads point to the role of the Dickens serial in promoting the new advertising culture (the serials escaped the advertising tax placed on newspapers) and illustrate the close link between the serial and the development of a market-oriented conflation of text and imagery. This advertising art also stresses the fundamental links existing between the sister-arts at very basic levels in the Victorian economy. The rise of the professions of the commercial artist, copywriter, and graphic designer (professions that continue to join the two arts in popular imagery) can be traced back to this period.

As if to compliment this market-driven conflation of text and image in publishing, at Royal Academy exhibitions throughout the century there was a steady rise of longer, descriptive and narrative titles for paintings, coupled to a remarkable growth in that genre of paintings depicting scenes from the novels.[35] A growth in publishing catalogues and descriptive indexes to exhibitions and collections also developed (a specialized branch of publishing that has grown, hand-in-hand with exhibitions, into the twentieth century). Painters like Ford Madox Brown, Holman Hunt, Luke Fildes, and particularly W. P. Frith and Vincent van Gogh were all influenced by Charles Dickens's writings; and there was a plethora of artists exhibiting scenes from Dickens's novels at Royal Academy exhibitions and other venues.[36]

Plate 10.6. Volume cover for *Illustrated London News*, number 21, 1852.

Dickens himself was keen to exploit the relationship between these sister-arts in order to promote the dignity of the "Grub Street" writer. In his Royal Academy of Art speeches he spoke of and promoted the idea of the "great magic circle" of art and literature, linking the respectability of the Royal Academy to the Grub Street writer's sister-art.[37] In Dickens's and Bulwer-Lytton's promotion of the Guild of Literature and Art (which actually existed more for the benefit of literature than of its sister, art), both advocated a new and dynamic organization, based on the model of the Royal Academy of Art, to replace the stagnant and aristocratic Royal Literary Fund.

While Dickens publicly advocated the links between the sister-arts (*Bleak House* was dedicated to the Guild of Literature and Art), a number of publishers advertising in his serials were busy selling wares to a middle class concerned about visual literacy. Charles Knight noted, in his ads for volume issues of *Knight's Pictorial Works* in *Bleak House*, that he was attempting through fine art engraving and high-minded text to help "the expansion of the intellect of all who see and read."[38] Innumerable guides and catalogues to the art works of Great Britain and continental Europe were made available through the Dickensian serial, and there were books and journals that sought to satisfy the public thirst for art knowledge – texts on art instruction, hints on engravings, and books on perspective, art tools, and drawing: *The Artist* (*Nicholas Nickleby*, numbers 19 and 20, 1839), *The Art Journal* (*Little Dorrit*, number 2, 1856), *Painting in Oil and Watercolours* (*Nicholas Nickleby*, number 16), or *The Artist or Young Ladies Instructor*.[39] *Hannah Bolton's First Drawing Book* (advertised in *Bleak House*, number 9, 1852), would aid the school master in his or her instructions, giving "intelligent assistance to the scholar; and while training the hand will instruct the mind."

The foundational basis that linked writing and drawing, visual image and word, was disseminated through the essence of the line. In drawing and writing copybooks students were taught the proper use of the line, its proper route and proper form in pencil or pen.[40] In *Elementary Drawing Copy Books* (plate 10.7), a copybook series advertised in *Our Mutual Friend* (number 12, 1865), a student could learn drawing and improve his or her writing at the same time. Here both types of line were fundamentally and structurally linked, with the student starting with copying out the alphabet, "learning the different kinds of lines by drawing Italian letters," and progressing through the series

ELEMENTARY DRAWING COPY BOOKS.

INTRODUCTORY REMARKS.

The present Series of Seven Elementary Drawing Copy Books is intended to aid in making instruction in *Drawing* to children as general as that of *Writing*. They are therefore to be used in the same manner as the usual writing copy books—viz., the copy being set at the top or at the side of the page (as the case may be), is to be copied on that same page, either below or on a line with the copy.

A power of marking lines and curves with precision, and imitating the outlines of forms with accuracy, is the first step towards a proper training of the hand and eye; and when it is obtained, the child will readily pass into the next step of drawing objects themselves; just as in writing, the imitation of letters and words must precede his writing out thoughts. But, though this power of imitation is essential to drawing accurately, its practical use is limited when it is copied with a power of applying it in drawing the *forms* of nature. Copying by itself is not worthy to be called drawing.

The set of Seven Books is made up as follows:—No. 1, Letters of single lines. No. 2, Letters of double or parallel lines. No. 3, Geometrical and ornamental forms. No. 4, Objects. No. 5, Single leaves. No. 6, Leaves, flowers, and sprays. No. 7, Animals, insects, reptiles, fishes, and boats. Learning to draw these kinds of forms by the children, and in the order here named, something with which the child is already acquainted, will be found easier and far more interesting than drawing abstract lines.

The First Book is made up of the Alphabet, in large and small printing letters of single lines. The letters are arranged in order, beginning with vertical and horizontal lines, and passing on to oblique and curved lines. Letters of small size are placed first, as being less difficult to draw accurately than the larger ones. Lines of letters of the same character are increased by the letters being in double or parallel lines.

Book III.—*Geometrical and Ornamental Forms.*—These copies will be found much more difficult, and will require to be drawn with great care and accuracy.

Book IV.—*Objects.*—After the letters and forms in Book III. this set of copies will be found easy, and it will always appear more easy to the child; but it must not be forgotten that the same care is equally necessary in drawing the objects, as in the more simple and rigid copies, whose faults are more easily seen and detected.

Book V.—*Leaves.*—These copies should lead the child to look at natural leaves, and to understand somewhat their growth and construction. As great a variety of leaves as possible has been given.

Book VI.—*Leaves, Flowers, and Sprays.*—This book gives the extent to which it is necessary the child should go in drawing copies in outline from nature.

Book VII.—*Animals, Insects, Reptiles, Fishes, and Boats.*—This last book is really the most difficult of the series; and, though from the greater variety and interest of subjects it may not be so tedious as the preceding copies, the utmost care in drawing them must be given.

A child who has already learnt to write, by passing on through this series of books, will gradually acquire, without any trouble, an appreciable power of drawing from objects. The same remark equally applies to an adult wishing to acquire the power of drawing. But if at the first essay the student cannot accomplish the exercises of the first, or any other books well, it is desirable that the copies should be repeated until the end is obtained. With this object a metre of blank copy books has been prepared; to be used either for second copies or for drawing other things.

After each of the last four books the same or similar objects may be drawn direct from nature. The copy previously drawn will serve as a guide to the manner in which to set about the same subject from nature. It will also be found very useful to cause the child to practise any of the copies from memory on a slate between the respective lessons.

to end by drawing animals and insects. In this case drawing was structured from an alphabetic source, linking the structure of drawing through the structure of writing. It is in the now largely forgotten copybook exercises, and the tradition of the writing master (who taught the essence of proper line), that Victorian students learned the fundamental structure of a line that was seen as the common source for both art and writing or printing.[41] This was a necessary linking in a period in which commerce and communication were traced and recorded via the skills of fine penmanship and fine line making. The view linking these two types of line has a long history, pointing to the sister-arts tradition as arising out of other sources than just the rhetoric of Horace's *ut pictura poesis*.[42]

One could also buy, advertised through the Dickens serial, such elaborate conflations of the sister-arts tradition as Clarkson Stanfield's renowned art engraving/literary production *Coast Scenery* (Smith Elder, 1836). In this case advertising and publishing created a mutually beneficial market: while painters promoted literature through scenes from the novel, artists and engravers gained increased sales and a wider audience via the lucrative literary market. Thomas Boys's eight-page ad of "select" art engravings sold engravings with the added inducement of lottery prizes in an attempt to attract customers to what was becoming, as Boys himself noted, an extremely competitive market (*Martin Chuzzlewit*, number 2, 1843). Illustrated examples of John Cassell's engravings (specimen engravings) were available for perusal in the final part of *Bleak House* (plate 10.8). Or, more importantly for the linking of literature to art, a reader could be induced in *Martin Chuzzlewit* (number 1, 1843), with Dickensian quotes, to purchase an engraved copy of Frith's own version of *Dolly Varden* from a bookseller/printseller (an occupation merging the two arts in the marketplace through their mutual process of printing). In this last ad, the fine art and publishing markets absorb the fictive world.

From a previously upper-class domain, the market for fine art engravings had rapidly shifted to the middle and lower classes by mid-century. This was due to cheaper reproduction techniques, highly competitive marketing through lotteries and other inducements, and advertising through journals like Dickens's serials. This, along with print sales in magazines such as *The Art Union/Art Journal*, and the rougher and cheaper prints produced by magazines like *The*

ILLUSTRATED AND OTHER WORKS
PUBLISHED BY
JOHN CASSELL, LUDGATE-HILL, LONDON.

SPECIMEN OF THE SMALLER ENGRAVINGS IN THE "WORKS OF EMINENT MASTERS."

THE BEGGARS.—FROM REMBRANDT.

[*For particulars, see next Page.*

Plate 10.8. *The Beggars, Bleak House*, numbers 19 and 20, 1853.

Penny Magazine, all served to widen the market. Publishers, particularly in the case of *The Penny Magazine*, believed themselves to be socially responsible in catering to the lower and middle classes' desire for visual arts education. (*The Penny Magazine*, for example, offered a cheap engraved portrait series to its readers.) The increasing accessibility to such prints made them a type of visual inducement, for the lower classes, to upper-class aesthetic pretensions.[43]

The popular market for portraits had followed a similar course. Serially issued portraiture developed out of the tradition of fine art engraved portraiture popularized through such eighteenth-century works as the Rev. James Granger's *A Biographical History of England . . . Adapted to a Methodological Catalogue of Engraved British Heads and Help to the Knowledge of Portraits* (1769–74). As Gertrude Prescott has pointed out, this work in particular popularized portrait collecting and the fine art portrait book. Given impetus by the Victorian passion for classifying all things, including the face, popular enthusiasm for portraits led to an expanding market that "British publishers avidly exploited" with such releases as Charles Knight's *The Gallery of Portraits: with Memoirs* (1833–37).[44] Robert Tyas's publication of engraved "Heads of the People," advertised in the *Nicholas Nickleby* serial, was meant to appeal to the new "philosophic observer" and to challenge the false pictures and portraits of the English "dreamt of by the fashionable novelmonger" by providing accurate images of the various workers of the new urban environs.[45] Tyas, though, while challenging the "novelmonger's" portraits, was only too willing to sell serialized portraits from *Nicholas Nickleby* (plate 10.4). Textual portraits here work their way out of the novel, into the market for "real" portraits.

The reading of the "portrait/face" underwent dramatic changes in this period. The face was, in effect, democratized: new, cheap reproduction technologies (most notably the dropping price of photographic portraits), coupled to aggressive merchandising, commodified the face in new markets. Anyone's face could now be mass-engraved or reproduced at little cost, and in various media, even, as *Punch* jokingly observed, down to portraits being reproduced in pats of butter.[46] Portrait mania reached such a point that, as *Punch* put it, soon the Royal Academy exhibitions would consist of rooms of just portraits of every conceivable type (plate 10.9).[47] The reviewer of an 1859 *Blackwood's Edinburgh Magazine* article entitled "London Exhibitions – Conflict of the Schools," complained that the Royal Academy exhibition of that year was dominated by "portraits of a gentleman and portraits of a lady . . . [all] tributes to vanity, wealth, and mere position – [they] upsurge the place of higher art, and give to the Academy more than ever the aspect of a shop."[48]

A number of series and volumes were published attempting to catalog the famous of the past and the present through portrait biography.[49] A monthly called *Photographic Portraits of Men of Eminence*, for example, offered a monthly *carte-de-visite* and biographical essay, with Dickens's image being its January 1866 offering.[50] And R. H. Horne attempted to imitate Hazlitt with his portrait/biography series entitled *New Spirit of the Age* (1844). This featured Dickens in both the frontispiece engraved portrait and as the preeminent writer of the New Age, points of particular significance in establishing Dickens's emerging literary status.

James White, in a satirical article entitled "Your Life or Your Likeness" published in Dickens's journal *Household Words*, chronicled the continuous demand made on public figures by artists and writers seeking permission to create new portrait/biographical epics. White felt the market was becoming so saturated with these series that they would soon be degenerating into such titles as "Lives of Yachters," or "Notes on Potato Growers."[51] He viewed the portrait "taker" as the greater of the two villains involved in the process, for he felt that people more quickly pass judgment on the basis of the immediacy enforced by seeing another's image than on the basis of reflection occasioned by reading a biography. In a similar vein, there was an article in *All the Year Round* entitled "Engraved on Steel" featuring the fictitious Great Bunglebutt, M.P., author of "Our Empty Coal-Cellars."[52] This article traces the vicissitudes of Bunglebutt, who, for the twenty-second edition of his book, seeks an engraved frontispiece portrait in "the highest style of art." While the article is mainly an account of the processes involved in producing this portrait, the processes mingle with a sardonic attack on Bunglebutt's (and any vain author's) attempts to achieve a frontispiece portrait that will accurately portray the narrative voice. In this case Bunglebutt's image is seen to serve two ends: it is believed by Bunglebutt to provide an image of the author to a demanding and admiring public, and it serves Bunglebutt's (and his family's) vanity by having his face captured and placed before the public.

Punch, indeed, noted that the price of fame meant one had to sit

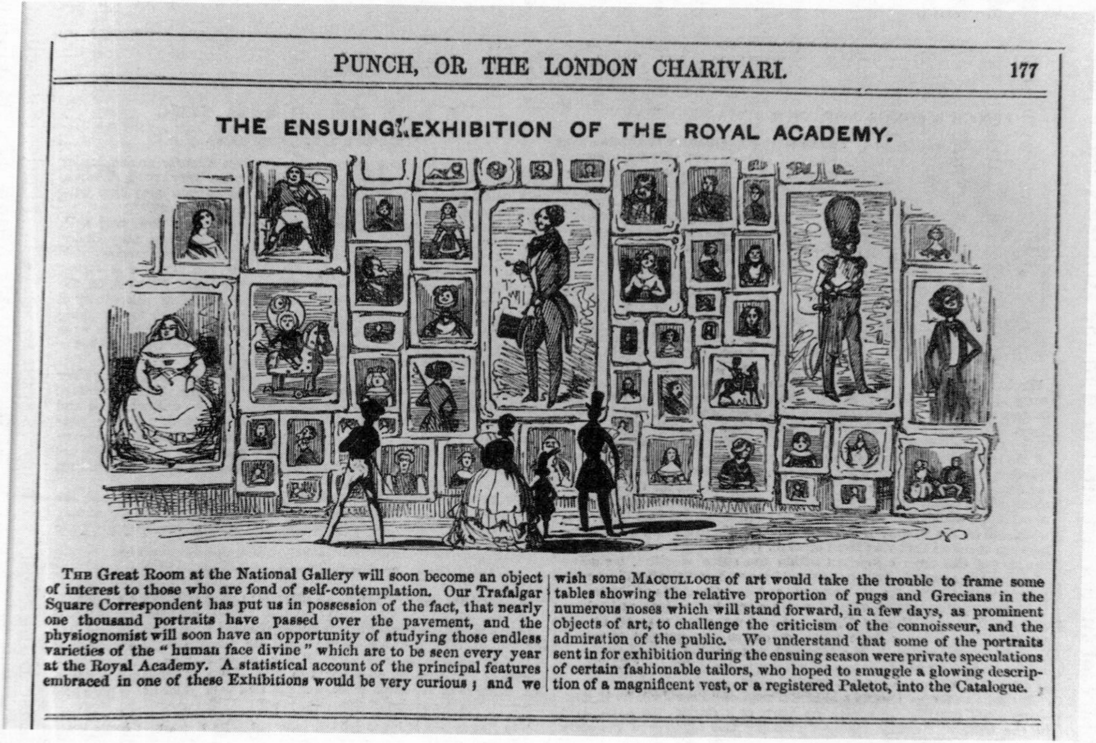

PUNCH, OR THE LONDON CHARIVARI. 177

THE ENSUING EXHIBITION OF THE ROYAL ACADEMY.

The Great Room at the National Gallery will soon become an object of interest to those who are fond of self-contemplation. Our Trafalgar Square Correspondent has put us in possession of the fact, that nearly one thousand portraits have passed over the pavement, and the physiognomist will soon have an opportunity of studying those endless varieties of the "human face divine" which are to be seen every year at the Royal Academy. A statistical account of the principal features embraced in one of these Exhibitions would be very curious; and we wish some Macculloch of art would take the trouble to frame some tables showing the relative proportion of pugs and Grecians in the numerous noses which will stand forward, in a few days, as prominent objects of art, to challenge the criticism of the connoisseur, and the admiration of the public. We understand that some of the portraits sent in for exhibition during the ensuing season were private speculations of certain fashionable tailors, who hoped to smuggle a glowing description of a magnificent vest, or a registered Paletot, into the Catalogue.

Plate 10.9. "Portraits at the Royal Exhibition," *Punch*, volume 12, 1847, 177.

for portraits to Royal Academy members, have *cartes-de-visite* taken, and then suffer seeing one's photograph on display in shop windows (usually that of a bookseller).[53] In the window, according to Gertrude Prescott, celebrities risked the vicissitudes of popular ranking according to placement in the window front, or the embarrassment of ignominy when the image was removed due to poor sales.

These portrait passions are a common motif in Dickens's works. Sitting uncomfortably for what he saw as a particularly bad portrait to Ary Scheffer (and constantly desiring to get back to work on *Little Dorrit*), he incorporated the experience into Mr. Dorrit's own desire for a portrait, a portrait that turns out to be as poor a counterfeit as Dickens's own was.[54] There is also the pretentious Tite Barnacle looking as if he had "been sitting for a portrait to Sir Thomas Lawrence all the days of his life."[55] In *Oliver Twist* a portrait serves to establish Oliver's lineage, as do the animated portraits that line the Dedlock household in *Bleak House*; or there is Rosa Bud's portrait in *Edwin Drood*. Painted portraits serve as types of soul traps throughout Dickens's works (when they are painted well), animated voices from the past that serve as ghosts and moral rejoinders, haunting the memories of those in the present.

Portraits and character portraiture are such a common motif for Dickens that Horne, in 1844, stressed their importance to show that Dickens (like Hogarth before him) had an "eye for art" through "an observing eye for externals."[56] Horne's opinion follows a common sister-arts analogy of the time with regard to Dickens's abilities: nineteenth-century critics saw his characters as either textual "fine art portraits" or, in adverse criticism, as mere "caricatures." Dickens himself clearly states his use of portraiture as a literary tool in the preface to *Martin Chuzzlewit* (numbers 19 and 20). Here he notes that his characterizations are portraits, "sketches" in which a "character is delineated," and that "Mrs. Gamp considers her own portrait to be quite unlike, and altogether out of drawing," while she does have praise for "the picture of Mrs. Prig."[57] Such literary portraiture was a necessary element to the successful marketing of time-delayed serial publications. J. Donn Vann, in his *Victorian Novels in Serial*, notes that "vivid portraiture is needed to help the audience recall characters from month to month" and that this "led Dickens to create characters who are easily visualized or identified with a tag."[58]

Nor did Dickens himself escape the portrait marketplace and its public eye. Rather, he seems to have been remarkably capable of exploiting it for his own benefit, particularly the photograph. While Dickens might warn Angela Burdett-Coutts never to sit for a photograph, "having suffered dreadfully"[59] from the experience himself, he continued to sit for over eighty photographs in his life. The *Quarterly Review* in October 1837 noted that poster portraits were used in omnibuses to promote authors – with Dickens's image replacing the previous favorites.[60] In 1837 Dickens had used his image as a promotional tool when he took over the editorship of *Bentley's Miscellany*, producing an advertising blurb that bore his caricatured visage (likely the *Quarterly Review* omnibus portrait: plate 10.10). He also used a caricature portrait of himself, done by Phiz, in the original advertising prospectus to *Master Humphrey's Clock*.

In 1867 Dickens's image was again a promotional tool when he agreed to an exclusive sitting for the photographer Gurney in New York to promote his American reading tour.[61] The *New York Herald* saw this exclusivity as a blatant attempt by Dickens and his promoters to both capitalize on and battle against pirated and counterfeit images by creating a profit making portrait trademark – an image along the lines of the crude trademark portraits used on patent medicines as stamps of authenticity:

Since the dust of the Pharaohs was sold as a nostrum and mummy became merchandise there has been nothing so precious and so wonderful in the market as the face of Charles Dickens. Hence it is natural there should be danger from counterfeits, and that the happy merchant who possesses a monopoly of the real article should take all pains to prevent deceptions. Even in commodities of a viler stamp such precautions are necessary . . . Surely, Mr. Dickens' face is his own, and he has as good a right to make a cent a piece on his pictures.[62]

By the mid-Victorian period portrait imagery was a necessary promotional mechanism both for products and for figures in the public eye. In an ad for The Poor Man's Pills in *Nicholas Nickleby* (plate 10.11), for example, miniature portraits of seven eminent doctors were both reproduced in the ad and included with each pill case, to verify the pills' worth. These portraits are an endorsement, and like Dickens's portraits they mark a broad change, shifting the portrait from its iconic position as a luxury item of wealth and power and moving the face/portrait toward the status of mass-produced likenesses and promoted commodities in the market economy.

Plate 10.10. Advertising leaflet portrait of Dickens for *Bentley's Miscellany*, 1837.

These various market and cultural forces come together in a linchpin portrait of Dickens that occurs as a preliminary frontispiece to the final installment of *Nicholas Nickleby* (plate 10.12).[63] It was engraved by William Finden in 1839 from a portrait by the then well known artist Daniel Maclise.[64] The Maclise portrait of Dickens had originally been commissioned by Chapman and Hall to be presented to Dickens at a banquet in his honor. However, it was not only a commemorative gift but also a "masterpiece" utilized as a marketing tool by Dickens's publishers. For one thing, on the otherwise blank recto page to this engraved frontispiece, there is, at the bottom, small type noting that the portrait is for sale as an engraving: thus the image was both frontispiece and advertisement. Strategically placed after the serial illustrations, and yet with adverts still occurring after it (including one for Dickens's latest serial release), it acts as advert and promotional frontispiece of the author's face. It was advertised (but not illustrated) in other serial issues, including *Martin Chuzzlewit* (number 1) where it appeared for sale in an advertisement for volumes of Dickens's works. By commissioning the portrait, Chapman and Hall of course maintained copyright over the image, thus profiting from its sale. Forster tells us that the painting was commissioned by Chapman and Hall "with a view to an engraving for Nickleby,"[65] and Kitton tells us that the image was so popular that the plate quickly deteriorated.[66]

There is a second point to consider. This image is a central piece in that subtle change from the popular writer of caricature sketches to cultural icon and writer of dignified novels. The image iconographically follows a long portrait tradition, one showing poetic genius with the light of inspiration striking the eyes. This "fine art" portrait thus helps give an aura of respectability to "Charles Dickens," the writer of artistic portraiture, versus, as some critics were wont to label him, "Boz," the mere popular caricaturist. It appeals also to the growing middle-class taste for "fine art." And whereas Boz had always appeared to the public before as a mere caricatured portrait or sketched outline (as in the *Master Humphrey's Clock* poster), here, Dickens, concerned with establishing respectability for the writers of Grub Street, comes out with the light of respectability shining in his eyes.[67] Since volume three of the bound edition of *Oliver Twist*, Dickens had, in fact, been in the process of changing his name over from Boz.[68] The appeal to the real that was a central feature of Victorian advertising in the

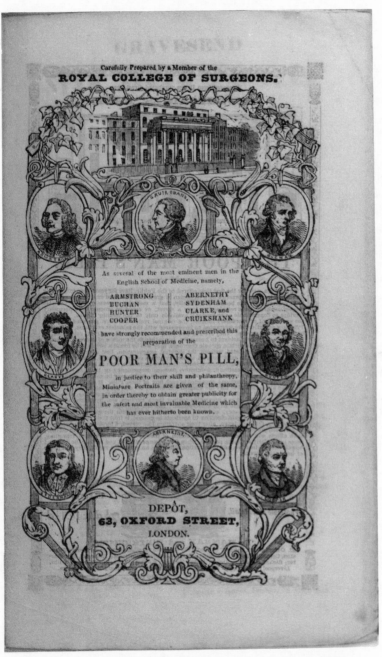

Plate 10.11. Poor Man's Pills, *Nicholas Nickleby*, number 4, 1838.

Plate 10.12. *Portrait of Charles Dickens*, engraved from the painting by David Maclise, *Nicholas Nickleby*, numbers 19 and 20, 1839.

markets for literature and the fine arts is here used to market the real man instead of the formerly "pseudonist" caricature. There is now this "looking-glass . . . facsimile"[69] face (as Thackeray called the original Maclise portrait), with its well-flourished signature of "Charles Dickens."

That is the third point regarding this portrait: the image is signed. It is an "authentic" image and recalls the striving for verification and authenticity displayed by two ads mentioned earlier, for wax seals (which themselves act as stamps of authenticity) and for medical portraits serving to verify an authentic product. Similarly, the signature and portrait were coming to be a trademark feature for certain products in the period, acting as stamps or seals in order to protect against fraudulent imitators. The use of a signature in this manner can be found in an ad in *Little Dorrit* (number 8, 1856) for Dr. De Jongh's Cod Liver Oil, where authenticity against imitators, the ad states, is insured by the facsimile signature and stamp on the bottle. Immediately before the publication of *Nicholas Nickleby* there was an advertised proclamation by Boz warning off would-be impostors and pirates of his serials (and selling the forthcoming release of *Nicholas Nickleby*); here, Charles Dickens's name/signature and "real-life" portrait serve as a seal of authenticity. Indeed, Forster tells us that the telltale flourish of Dickens's signature had become "familiar to everyone" – with the implication that it was a conscious trademark. (Dickens himself apologizes to Forster for leaving the flourish out in a letter he writes.[70]) The value of Dickens's name as a promotional device was realized by one of his former teachers, who obtained permission to use Dickens's name as an endorsement on adverts for a new school.[71]

In this linkage of portrait and signature, image and word are also linked through the perspective of ownership: one owns one's face as one owns one's signature, and the two together are taken as autobiographical trademark/stamp guaranteeing the authenticity of a published work. And as with the copybook tradition where word and image are united by their source in a common line, here portrait and name are united in a shared visual (engraved) and textual (signature) line.[72]

Finally, this portrait placed Dickens's face directly in the eye of the public, a public who wanted to see a representation of the ultimate "point of view" in the novels – the author. In the first issue of the *Spectator*, Addison attempted to handcuff this popular enthusiasm for the visual reading process by mentioning it directly from the visually anonymous position that "the Spectator" cannily occupied: "I have observed, that a Reader seldom peruses a Book with Pleasure 'till he knows whether the Writer of it be a black or a fair Man of a mild or cholerick Disposition, Married or a Bachelor, with other Particulars of the like nature, that conduce very much to the right Understanding of an Author."[73] That such demands cannot be so easily foreclosed is revealed in the portrait done of Addison by Michael Dahl in 1719, where he posed, quill in hand, in the iconographic posture of the writer. Dickens's frontispiece portrait thus points to the long publishing history of actively providing for the passion of the reading public to see a visual representation of an image behind the authorial voice.[74]

For the Victorians the "art of seeing" meant a dramatic rise in the use of frontispiece portraits – reflecting a desire to observe the ultimate voice of creation and an almost biblical belief in a connection between fiction, a nonfictive voice, and a real world. They believed that visual images of the nonfictive face offered insights into Dickens's fictive world. Like Dickens's suggestion to John Forster that "I don't invent it – really do not – but see it, and write it down," there was a reciprocal effect in which readers did not accept an invented world of fiction without the reassuring image, so common to ads in the conflated markets of Victorian literature and art, of a nonfictional face that "writes it down." Dickens's frontispiece portrait produces the effect of an extranarrative voice and point of view operating within the epistemology of the text's marketplace, a marketplace in which realism and authenticity were created by the marketing of images.[75] But this is not the final market. The Bank of England's decision to include Dickens's portrait on its £10 note serves to link the trademark value of Dickens as cultural icon to the ultimate market of monetary exchange. It seems a fitting end that the first heavily promoted face of literature should become the currency of his books' purchase.

NOTES

This research was funded in part by a Sir James Lougheed Scholarship and a Commonwealth Scholarship Commission award. I would like to thank Dr. David Parker, Curator, and Andrew Bean, Assistant Curator, along with Stewart Slade and Angela Hockley, for their advice and assistance while I was working at the Dickens House

Museum. I would also like to express my thanks to Dr. George Wing, who first guided me in my research on Dickens, to Dr. Sarah Symmons Goubert, and especially to Chris Short. This work is dedicated to John Curtis.

1 John Ruskin, "Notes on the Louvre," 8 September 1849, in Joan Evans (ed.), *The Lamp of Beauty* (Ithaca, N.Y.: Cornell University Press, 1959), 41.

2 John Ruskin, quoted in Robert Hewison, *John Ruskin – The Argument of the Eye* (Princeton: Princeton University Press, 1976), 7.

3 Rensselaer W. Lee, "*Ut Pictura Poesis*: the Humanistic Theory of Painting," *Art Bulletin* 22, 4 (December 1940), 197.

4 Charles Dickens, "Royal Academy Banquet Speech," 30 April 1853, quoted in K. J. Fielding (ed.), *The Speeches of Charles Dickens: A Complete Edition* (Hemel Hempstead: Harvester Wheatsheaf, 1988), 164.

5 James McNeil Whistler, *Ten O'Clock Lecture* (London: Chatto & Windus, 1888), 17–18.

6 Owen Jones, for example, supplied the illuminated text from Shakespeare that hung in the entrance hall of Dickens's Gad's Hill home. The hanging and display of illuminated passages of text was a common feature in the Victorian home, and it represents the highly visual and decorative value placed on the textual experience in Victorian culture.

7 There is no consistent page numbering for adverts in the Dickens serials, and ads will often appear in different sequences in each serial. All adverts were photographed from the Sydney A. Henry and Miss M. Henry Collection of Dickens serials in the Dickens House Museum, London. I would like to thank Andrew Bean and Dr. David Parker for allowing me to photograph these works: copyright remains with the Dickens House Museum.

8 Bernard Darwin, *The Dickens Advertiser: A Collection of the Advertisements in the Original Parts of Novels by Charles Dickens* (New York: Macmillan, 1930). See Darwin's preface.

9 *Quarterly Review*, June 1855, quoted in Blanche B. Elliott, *A History of English Advertising* (London: Business Publications Ltd./B. T. Batsford Ltd., 1962), 158.

10 "The Real Street Obstructions," *Punch* 19 (1850), 30.

11 See "Sibthorpe's Gallant Attack," *Punch* 20 (1851), 189; "A Nation of Advertisers," *Punch* 12 (1847), 31; and "St. Paul's Exhibition," *Punch* 12(1847), 164.

12 Roland Hall, *The Advertising Handbook* (New York: McGraw Hill, 1921), 14.

13 John Burnet, *The Education of the Eye, with Reference to Painting* (London: James Carpenter, 1837), 1.

14 Thomas Dunman, "The Art of Observing," *The Universal Instructor* (3 vols.; London: Ward Lock & Co., 1880–84), vol 1., 486–87.

15 Charles Dickens, *The Posthumous Papers of the Pickwick Club*, ed. Robert L. Patten (Harmondsworth: Penguin, 1972), 573.

16 Charles Knight, *The Pictorial Gallery of Arts* (2 vols.; 1845–47; London: The London Printing & Publishing Co. Ltd., 1885), vol. 1, 375. Knight provides an illustration of an itinerant observatory (1:373, illus. 1518) and has a section of the *Pictorial Gallery* dealing with lenses and optics.

17 Nicolette Scourse, *The Victorians and Their Flowers* (London: Croom Helm, 1983), 137.

18 William Charles Macready quoted in Lady Juliet Pollock, *Macready As I Knew Him* (London: Remington & Co., 1884), 59. Macready was here warning the artist Maclise that to travel with Dickens meant little time for an artistic or contemplative looking. Macready noted that given Dickens's rapid visual assimilation, he rarely lingered in one spot.

19 "The Genius of Dickens," *The Spectator*, 18 June 1870, 750.

20 "Oliver Twist by Boz," *Quarterly Review* (June 1839), 90.

21 Charles Dickens, quoted in John Forster, *The Life of Charles Dickens* (3 vols.; Philadelphia: J. B. Lippincott Co., 1911), vol. 2, 305. This quote is extensively cited as indicating Dickens's visual source for his writing.

22 Ruskin, quoted in Hewison, 7.

23 Charles Dickens, preface of *A Tale of Two Cities*, combined numbers 7 and 8, December 1859.

24 Walter Benjamin sees both Baudelaire and Dickens as qualified "*flâneurs*" – not merely observers, but writers who stamped their impressions (quoting G. K. Chesterton) on the age. See his *Charles Baudelaire: A Lyric Poet in the Era of High Capitalism*, trans. Harry Zohn (London: NLB, 1973), 49, 69. Baudelaire coins the term *flâneur* in discussing the work and style of Constantin Guys, as a reference to the passionate spectator: see Charles Baudelaire, *The Painter of Modern Life and Other Essays*, ed. and trans. Jonathan Mayne (New York: Da Capo Press, 1964), 9. Yet as Dr. Sarah Symmons Goubert has pointed out, Baudelaire found Dickens to be an obsessively "myopic" observer, one who was inordinately fixed on detail; Charles Baudelaire, *Oeuvres Complètes*, ed. Claude Pichois (2 vols.; Paris: Gallimard, 1976), vol. 2, 58–59.

25 The cover color ranged from a drab olive green to a blue-green. The reissued *Sketches by Boz* was sold using a light pink cover, a color that Thomas Hatton and Arthur Cleaver, in *A Bibliography of the Periodical Works of Charles Dickens* (London: Chapman & Hall, 1933), speculate may have caused lost advertising revenues because it reduced the commodity's visual impact and violated the then-familiar association of the green serial cover with Dickens's name (104). Such color values have continued publication and market value and iconic significance.

The color is still utilized to trade on the Dickens association on the covers of journals like *The Dickensian*, original issues of *Dickens Studies Annual*, and the "Garland Dickens Bibliographies" series. *The Spectator*, 1 October 1870, 1176–77.

26 Charles Dickens, *Our Mutual Friend* (1864), number 2, chapter 5, 33.

27 The mercantile world of Victorian society, both in product manufacturing and publishing (particularly in the critical puffery of the period), are thus strongly linked. Ads for book sales dominated the bulk of advertisements in the early Dickens serials, with medicinals and quack cures a strong second. By mid-century there was a notable rise in the advertising of domestic products – notably silver goods, luxury items, and various household products. This shift in advertised products seems to reinforce the view that in the middle to late nineteenth century there was a broadening out of the middle-class domestic market for luxury goods.

28 Michael Slater, in Charles Dickens, *Nicholas Nickleby* (Harmondsworth: Penguin, 1978), 972, n.7.

29 Charles Dickens, "Presentation to Dickens and Banquet to Literature and Art: Birmingham," in Fielding (ed.), *Speeches of Charles Dickens*, 160.

30 Juliet McMaster, *Dickens the Designer* (London: Macmillan, 1987), xii.

31 Richard Altick, *Paintings from Books* (Columbus: Ohio State University Press, 1985), 57.

32 Martin Meisel, *Realizations: Narrative, Pictorial, and Theatrical Arts in Nineteenth-Century England* (Princeton: Princeton University Press, 1983), 33. Meisel sees the creation of the *Illustrated London News* as one of the major and representative cultural occurrences of the nineteenth century.

33 Gerard Manley Hopkins, quoted in McMaster, xii.

34 Marcel Proust, quoted in Ellen Winner, *Invented Worlds: The Psychology of the Arts* (Cambridge, Mass.: Harvard University Press, 1982), 247.

35 See Altick. By the late eighteenth century the Royal Academy was allowing the inclusion of poetic quotes with painting titles in their descriptive catalogues.

36 See Catherine Gordon, *Paintings from the Novel* (London: Garland, 1985), for a full list to 1870 of paintings from Dickens's novels.

37 Charles Dickens, "Royal Academy Banquet Speech," 3 May 1862, in Fielding (ed.), *Speeches of Charles Dickens*, xxv.

38 *Bleak House*, number 10, page 11 of advertisements.

39 Also advertised were *The Gallery of British Art* in *Martin Chuzzlewit*, number 1, 1843, and Ruskin's *Modern Painters* and *The Seven Lamps of Architecture*. "The Artist," along with *The Pictorial Album or Cabinet of Paintings for* 1837, is mentioned by Darwin in *The Dickens Advertiser*,

34–35. One could find advertised in *Dombey and Son* (number 14, 1847) the products of a consortium of artists/designers (headed by Henry Cole) called "Felix Summerly's Art Manufacturer" that sought to refine the public taste by producing artistically designed products at accessible prices.

40 Copybooks are a long-neglected area of research for this structural foundation of word and image association. There is Vivian Henry Crellin's history of the copybook: "The Teaching of Writing and the Use of Copybooks in Schools" (M.Phil. dissertation; University of London, 1976). Molly Nesbit of Columbia University has presented some research on the subject: "The Language of Industry" (The Lawrence Lectures, University College London, May 1991).

41 For a linking of painting to the drawn line, see also John Sloan, *Gist of Art: Principles and Practise* (1939; New York: Dover, 1977), 109, 53, 57.

42 See, for example, Desiderius Erasmus's "Dialogue on Handwriting" on the links between writing and drawing in Albrecht Dürer's geometric line examples of the alphabet: Desiderius Erasmus, *Erasmus on Handwriting: An Extract from the Dialogue of Desiderius Erasmus De Recta Latini Graecique Sermonis Pronuntiatione*, trans. A. S. Osley (Surbiton, Surrey: The Glade Press, 1970), 16; 4, 7, 14, 15.

43 While the Dickens serial supplied the middle classes with the tools, texts, and engravings of their pretensions to cultured visual refinement, Dickens was only too willing to satirize these affectations. *Little Dorrit*, for example, is replete with instances of this aesthetic posturing.

44 Gertrude Mae Prescott, "Fame and Photography: Portrait Publications in Great Britain, 1856–1900" (Ph.D. dissertation, University of Texas at Austin, 1985), 17, 181–82.

45 In *Master Humphrey's Clock* part 1, 4 April 1840.

46 "New Design," *Punch* 13 (1847), 20.

47 "Portraits at the Royal Exhibition," *Punch* 12 (1847), 177.

48 "London Exhibitions – Conflict of the Schools," *Blackwood's Edinburgh Magazine* (August 1859), 128.

49 Prescott does an extended survey of Herbert Fry's failed serial *The National Gallery of Photographic Portraits*.

50 *Photographic Portraits of Men of Eminence* (London: Lovell Reeve & Co., 1866). The photographs are by Ernest Edwards; Dickens featured on 93–99.

51 James White, "Your Life or Your Likeness," *Household Words*, 25 July 1857, 73–75 (titles noted on 75).

52 "Engraved on Steel," *All the Year Round* 16 (27 October 1866), 372–76.

53 "Comfort for the Lowly," *Punch*, 30 April 1870, 169.

54 W. Dexter (ed.), *The Letters of Charles Dickens* (3 vols.; Bloomsbury: Nonesuch Press, 1938), vol. 2, 734. Dickens mentioned that he

"suffered from sitting to Scheffer every day . . . I can scarcely express how uneasy and unsettled it makes me to sit, sit, sit, with Little Dorrit on my mind, and the Christmas business too . . . And the crowning feature is, that I do not discern the slightest resemblance, either in his portrait or his brother's!"; Dickens to John Forster, November 1855, *Letters*, 2:710.

55 Charles Dickens, *Little Dorrit*, ed. John Holloway (Harmondsworth: Penguin, 1967), 152.

56 R. H. Horne, *New Spirit of the Age* (2 vols.; London: Smith Elder & Co., 1844), vol 1, 4. See also 1:6, 1:25, 1:52, 1:72. Again using the "sister-arts" concept to develop the analogy of this observing eye, Horne notes that Dickens "first paints his portrait at full length; sometimes his dress before his face, and most commonly his dress and demeanor. When he has done this to satisfaction, he fills in the man" (1:25). For Horne these portraits are "drawn" with the equivalent visual effect of a Hans Holbein image (1:52–53).

57 Dickens, preface to serial edition of *Martin Chuzzlewit*, numbers 19 and 20 (London: Chapman & Hall, July 1844), vii–viii. McMaster has provided a more contemporary update of Horne's opinion, concentrating specifically on the role of the face, of phrenology and physiognomy, in Dickens's character portraits.

58 J. Donn Vann, *Victorian Novels in Serial* (New York: Modern Language Association, 1985), 4.

59 Charles Dickens, letter dated 23 May 1841 in *The Letters of Charles Dickens*, ed. Madeline House and Graham Storey (7 vols.; Oxford: Clarendon, 1969), vol. 2, 284.

60 "The Pickwick Papers," *Quarterly Review* (October 1837), 484. The article goes on to point out the consumer merchandising of Boz's name and characters: "Pickwick chintzes" in linen drapers' windows, and "Weller corduroys" in breechesmakers' advertisements; "Boz cabs might be seen rattling through the streets" (484).

61 Quoted by N. C. Peyrouton in "The Gurney Photographs," *Dickensian* 54 (September 1958), 145–55.

62 *New York Herald*, 1867, quoted in Andrew J. Kappel, "The Gurney Photograph Controversy," *Dickensian* 74, 386 (September 1978), 170.

63 The same image was used as a frontispiece to the first bound edition of *Nicholas Nickleby* (London: Chapman & Hall, 1839).

64 Maclise made his name early in his career through an engraved portrait of Sir Walter Scott sold in a local bookstore in Cork. He later went on to generate a popular series of sketch/caricature portraits of "Literary Characters" that appeared in *Fraser's Magazine* between 1830 and 1838 and that served to identify a new generation of London writers.

65 Forster, *Charles Dickens*, 1:156.

66 F. G. Kitton, *Charles Dickens by Pen and Pencil* (3 vols.; London: Frank T. Sabin, 1890), vol. 1, 29.

67 A caricatured sketch of Dickens by Phiz, much along the style of Maclise's *Fraser's* engravings, had appeared in the *Court Magazine* 10, 4 (April 1837). Samuel Laurence also did a chalk portrait sketch in 1837 that was sold as a lithographed print prior to the Maclise/Finden engraving (and that featured the pseudonymous signature of "Boz" beneath). Neither of these images appears to have matched the audience or popularity of the Finden engraving.

68 Quoted in Kathleen Tillotson (ed.), *Oliver Twist* (Oxford: Oxford University Press, 1966), ix-xi, and mentioned in Walter E. Smith, *Charles Dickens in the Original Cloth: a Bibliographic Catalogue* (Los Angeles: Heritage Book Shop, 1982–83), 35.

69 Thackeray noted that the Maclise portrait of Dickens captured the image of both the inward and the outward man. William Makepeace Thackeray, "A Pictorial Rhapsody: Concluded," *Fraser's Magazine* 22 (1840), 113.

70 Forster, *Charles Dickens*, 1:119.

71 Philip Collins, *Dickens and Education* (London: Macmillan, 1963), 11.

72 The origins of this value placed on facsimile trademark signatures linked to portraits can be traced back to late-eighteenth-century portrait series like John Thane's *British Autography, a collection of fac-similes of the handwriting of Royal and Illustrious Personages, with their authentic Portraits* (3 vols.; 1793).

73 Joseph Addison, *The Spectator*, 1, 1, 1. Forster, in *Charles Dickens*, noted that he included in his book a drawing by Maclise of Dickens in order "to help also the reader's fancy to a complete impression" (2:156).

74 Opposite Martin Droeshout's 1623 first folio portrait of Shakespeare was Ben Jonson's blatant warning "To the Reader" not to seek more in the face than existed in the plays: "*Reader*, look / Not on his *Picture*, but his *Book*." This warning recognizes the reader's desire to read the face – to slip behind the images supplied by the narrative voice to try to find some grounding in images of an authorial visage. And while Milton, in the 1645 Moseley edition of his poems, sought redress on a poor frontispiece portrait done of him (and the visual immortality of the subsequent voice captured), Dickens does not appear to have shown a similar concern or vanity. Even though he himself was not keen on the engraved version of the Maclise image, he was willing to tell acquaintances that they could order an enlarged copy from any bookseller. See Charles Dickens's letter to George Brightwen of 28 May 1840, in House and Storey (ed.), *Letters*, 2:74. Dickens also notes that the engraving is being published separately by Chapman & Hall and that Brightwen can order "it of any bookseller. There is another published with the signature of 'Boz,' which I am told is not so good." House and Storey think Dickens is here referring to the Samuel Laurence chalk portrait (*Letters*, 2:75, n.2).

75 The publishing tradition of using the frontispiece portrait in this

way maintained some popularity well into the 1920s, until the subsequent moving of the authorial face to the dust jacket or back cover of the book and its subordination to blurbs. Such a shift points to a conceptual change in the twentieth century toward popular acceptance of the separation of narrative voice from authorial presence also insisted on by literary critics during the professionalization of reading. As a marketing tool, authorial presence became de-essentialized, disposable, like the dust jacket itself, and was replaced by testimonials claiming to represent the experience of other readers.

CHAPTER 11

Male pseudonyms and female authority in Victorian England

Catherine A. Judd

It has become a critical commonplace to assert that the use of male pseudonyms by Victorian women writers, especially domestic novelists, illustrates the repression and victimization of the female writer. Male pseudonyms, so the argument goes, bespeak the struggle of women writers for authority and acceptance. By shrouding the "disability" of femininity, male pseudonyms offered a way for women to overcome the prejudices of the marketplace. Patricia Lorimer Lundberg, for example, asserts that "female writers, especially those nineteenth-century novelists struggling to write in a patriarchal society, often have taken male pseudonyms to disguise their identities."[1] In specifying "especially . . . nineteenth-century novelists" as needing to hide behind a male pseudonym, Lundberg's assertion dodges the question of why femininity would disable domestic novelists more than it would women writing in other genres.

In fact, the pervasive notion that many Victorian women writers published under a masculine *nominis umbra* skews our understanding of the nineteenth-century literary marketplace, for most of these women writers did not use pseudonyms. Furthermore, of the small number who did hide their identities, the majority used female pseudonyms or published anonymously. Basing her analysis of patterns and trends in mid-Victorian publishing on her study of the Macmillan archives, Gaye Tuchman, for example, determines that "pseudonymous submissions in general were rare" during the mid-nineteenth century. She concludes that women writers were no more inclined to use pseudonyms than were their masculine counterparts, and that both male and female authors were far more likely to adopt a pseudonym from their own gender than to cross over. Surprisingly, of the writers who published under *noms de plume*, men apparently were more likely than women to use a cross-gendered pseudonym. Tuchman writes that "solid data seem to support the assumption that many male writers masqueraded as women in the novel's heyday . . . in the 1860s and 1870s men submitting fiction were more likely to assume a female name than women were to use either a male or a neuter name."[2]

The discrepancy between the historical record of women writers' publication trends in the nineteenth century and modern perceptions of those patterns indicates the existence of a cluster of mythic images surrounding the Victorian woman writer – especially the Victorian domestic novelist. This cluster has three major components. The first stems from a belief in the gender bias of the marketplace – that is, that the male pseudonym was a necessary mask due to the prejudices and exclusions of the literary marketplace. This reading results in a conception of the woman writer caught in a heroic struggle against male prejudice and exclusion. The second component derives from the notion of the domestic novelist as at once family protector and family martyr – that is, she shields her name both to protect her family honor and to protect herself from the wrath of her disapproving family. The third explanation of the need for the male pseudonym stems from twentieth-century readings which claim that the male pseudonym is a mark of the androgyny of the female domestic novelist and a symptom of her need to feel somehow masculinized before she could pick up the "phallic" pen. As we shall see, these readings of the male pseudonym were born and promoted during the nineteenth century by women writers themselves.

In reexamining the myth of the origins of the male pseudonym, I am not trying to diminish or deny the very severe legal, social, medical, political, educational, or vocational discrimination suffered by women in the nineteenth century. Nor am I trying to reinforce another fiction – that of the open and equitable marketplace. The inclusions and exclusions of the literary marketplace are vexed and complex topics, and there is little doubt that women writers experienced prejudice in the largely masculine world of publishing. There were inequities in rates of pay and no doubt many women writers were rejected for publication, or had their publications reviewed unfairly, based solely on their gender. One reads with exasperation, for example, Robert Southey's famous letter discouraging the young Charlotte Brontë, a letter that simultaneously acknowledges her unusual literary talents and dissuades her from attempting to become a professional writer because "literature cannot be the business of a woman's life, and it ought not to be."[3] Nonetheless, it was during the nineteenth century that the female voice gained authority and dissemination, more than in any previous century. Tuchman argues that the "edging out" of women occurred toward the end of the nineteenth century when men began to regain the literary marketplace after a brief field victory by their female rivals.[4]

For mid-Victorian women writers, publishing under a male pseudonym was a choice – it was not forced or deemed necessary solely by the publishing climate – and it was a choice that few writers made. Nonetheless, the enormous amount of emphasis given to the infrequent phenomenon of the male pseudonym is not misplaced, for the masculine *nom de plume* does have great import despite its rarity. Sandra Gilbert and Susan Gubar write that "certainly, as we all now recognize, by the mid-nineteenth century the male pseudonym was quite specifically a mask behind which the female writer could hide her disreputable femininity."[5] As we shall see, the male pseudonym was quite patently a mask, but the "disreputability" resided in the mask itself. Conversely, the feminine self that the pseudonym veiled was believed to be at once domestic, heroic, creative, sacred, and martyred. Thus the "veiling" of the female writer's identity by a male pseudonym, exceptional as it was, helped a certain group of Victorian women writers establish important claims of possessing a moral and social authority within the context of the ideological separation of the public and the domestic realms and the Romantic notions of creativity and genius that separation supported. For the remainder of this essay, I will examine the origins and the use of the male pseudonym by its most significant employers – Charlotte Brontë and Mary Ann Evans.[6]

There is an element of happenstance in the fact that the four most canonical nineteenth-century female novelists – Jane Austen, Charlotte Brontë, Emily Brontë, and Mary Ann Evans – published under pseudonyms, and that three of these writers used a masculine or a masculinized name (Jane Austen's "A Lady" was the pseudonym used most frequently in both the eighteenth and nineteenth centuries by women writers).[7] Yet, as we shall see, Evans and the Brontës decided to use male pseudonyms for reasons other than general difficulties in finding a publisher or a fear of being unjustly attacked by critics or dismissed by the reading public because of their gender.

In her 1850 preface to *Wuthering Heights* and *Agnes Grey*, Charlotte Brontë gives a detailed account of the reasons behind her decision to use a male pseudonym. She writes that adopting a masculinized pseudonym was an unsophisticated decision based on a "vague impression."[8] However, Brontë's apprehensions did not stem from the fear that her gender would thwart her quest for a publisher. Rather, she worried that her work would be dismissed as typically "feminine" writing. The Brontë sisters perceived themselves to be mavericks, but not because they were breaking into a male-dominated field. On the contrary, they wanted to distance themselves from the large group of women who were then writing domestic fiction: "we veiled our own names . . . because – without at the time suspecting that our mode of writing and thinking was not what is called 'feminine' . . . we noticed how critics sometimes use for their chastisement the weapon of personality, and for their reward, a flattery, which is not true praise."[9] In a letter written only a few years after Brontë's preface to *Jane Eyre*, Evans gives further evidence of a commonly held belief in the proliferation of women writers and the sense of an ease, approaching laxity, with which their works were published and critically evaluated. Here she wonders "how women have the courage to write and publishers the spirit to buy at a high price the false and feeble representations of life and character that most feminine novels give."[10]

The fear expressed by Charlotte Brontë and Mary Ann Evans of being judged as women writers does not indicate their apprehension of being silenced as women in the marketplace but rather their dread of being judged by a "class standard." Ironically, this standard was believed to grant excessive license to female writing, and it was this critical permissiveness that Brontë and Evans claimed to loathe more than uncharitable appraisal. In 1868, for example, Emily Davies wrote: "That the greatest of female novelists [that is, Charlotte Brontë and Mary Ann Evans] should have taken the precaution to assume a masculine nom de plume for the express purpose of securing their work against being measured by a class standard, is significant of the feeling entertained by women."[11]

Yet these statements seem to be in direct conflict with the abundance of gender-based attacks then appearing in many English periodicals.[12] It helps to clarify this conflict by recognizing the context of nineteenth-century England's misogynistic critical legacy. With the exception of a few serious literary critics (including, of course, Evans herself and George Henry Lewes), the art of Victorian literary criticism consisted largely of partisan puffery or attacks based on the politics of the writer, his or her publisher, and the journal reviewing the work.[13] From this viewpoint, femininity became one more weapon in the arsenal of biased literary criticism. Furthermore, male authors were not exempt from this critical vituperation – recall, for example, Shelley's assertion in his preface to "Adonais" that Keats was murdered by John Wilson Croker's harsh review of *Endymion*. In 1857, Mary Ann Evans wrote to Sara Sophia Hennell:

> Don't let your soul be moved by newspaper criticisms. If you knew well what sort of books the Spectator praises . . . you would not care about its blame. It is only as a question of sale that such notices are at all important, and even in that light, they can't stop the sale of a book that really lays hold of the readers' minds. One person who has admired and enjoyed tells another, and by and bye Athenaeum, Spectator and Co. are forgotten. On the other hand, no dithyrambs . . . can make a bad book successful.[14]

Evans herself made it a rule never to read reviews of her own fiction: "I have found this abstinence necessary to preserve me from that discouragement as an artist which ill-judged praise, no less than ill-judged blame, tends to produce in me."[15]

Indeed, this issue of "ill-judged praise" being given to women writers seemed to trouble Evans more than did "ill-judged blame." In "Silly Novels by Lady Novelists," for example, Evans wrote that "we are aware that the ladies at whom our criticism is pointed are accustomed to be told, in the choicest phraseology of puffery," that their novels are brilliant, well drawn, fascinating, and lofty.[16] Evans claimed that this puffery was especially evident in reviews of inept women writers. She felt that talented women writers kindled far less critical enthusiasm: "when a woman's talent is at zero, journalistic approbation is at the boiling pitch; when she attains mediocrity, it is already at no more than summer heat; and if ever she reaches excellence, critical enthusiasm drops to the freezing point. Harriet Martineau, Currer Bell, and Mrs. Gaskell have been treated as cavalierly as if they had been men."[17] Thus, rather than the expected denunciation of the biased condemnation of women writers by the press, Evans instead begged journalists to "abstain from any exceptional indulgence towards the productions of literary women" so that women writers would be forced to write toward the same higher standards applied to their male counterparts.[18]

Accompanying the explanations of gender bias as a motivation for the use of male pseudonyms by Victorian women writers in general, those critics who have focused specifically on the personal situations of the Brontës and Evans have often concluded that the male pseudonym served as a strong shield of privacy for these writers, all of whom had extraordinary personal lives that would not bear the public scrutiny that comes with fame. Although Charlotte Brontë, Evans, and their biographers laid claim to their urgent needs for privacy, these accounts overlook the fact that they had made the decision to become public women, and to become a popular writer in England during the mid-nineteenth century was to renounce all claims to anonymity, as the examples of Scott, Dickens, or any number of celebrated writers would have shown.[19] Charlotte Brontë and Evans were professional writers, and as professionals they had (or sought to obtain in the case of Charlotte Brontë) a real sense of the literary marketplace.[20] This awareness of a professional identity held true especially for Evans, who became a novelist only after years of work as a translator, critic, and editor in London. As professional writers, both Brontë and Evans had some awareness of the significance of putting their names in the marketplace, and to believe that any sort of pseudonym would long protect an illustrious writer's identity from the curiosity of the press and the reading public would be an ingenuous hope at best. Jane Austen, for example, who was not even very popular during her lifetime compared with writers such as Walter Scott and Maria Edgeworth, gave up any attempts to conceal her identity very early in her career and desired instead to profit from her fame:

the Secret has spread so far as to be scarcely the Shadow of a secret now – & that I beleive [*sic*] whenever the 3d [volume] appears, I shall not even attempt to tell Lies about it. – I shall rather try to make all the Money than all the Mystery I can of it. – People shall pay for their knowledge if I can make them.[21]

The cult of authorship and the commodification of the signature had been growing throughout the nineteenth century, the two key examples of the marketability of the personal name in literature being Walter Scott and Charles Dickens. No doubt both Brontë and Evans learned lessons in authorial commodification from these two celebrated examples, both male, one using pseudonyms and the other publishing under his given name after briskly dropping his original pseudonym of "Boz." Mary Poovey writes that "the commercial marketing of books by linking a writer's name to a

unique and recognizable image" was one of the "critical components" in the advent of the expansion of the mass-marketing of the
book trade, and that this unique image of the writer, the writer as
celebrity, was "often an 'autobiographical' image derived from the
writer's work."[22] In Charles Rowcroft's 1844 novel *The Man Without
a Profession*, an experienced London journalist, Mr. Seedy, gives a
young novelist advice about the publishing industry:

> the sale of a work depends not on the merits of the book, but on the
> personal reputation of the author . . . so that an author must write
> several works . . . before his name becomes popular. Then, when his
> name is up, he may for some time sell anything that is not positively
> and glaringly bad . . . When the name of an author is well up, he can
> obtain easily a thousand pounds and upwards for a new work.[23]

Evans's business acumen is well known, and her letters exhibit
a sophisticated awareness of the commodification of the name
described by Mr. Seedy. In 1877 Evans wrote to her future
sister-in-law Mary Finlay Cross that "I read your touching story
aloud yesterday . . . Your Brother wrote to me that you had doubts
about giving your name. My faith is that signature is right, in
the absence of weighty special reasons against it."[24] Several years
earlier, in 1862, she wrote far more vehemently to her close friend
Sara Sophia Hennell after Hennell wondered if Eliot had written
a recently published anonymous piece:

> I am NOT the author of the Chronicles of Carlingford. They are written
> by Mrs. Oliphant . . . A little reflection might, one would think, suggest
> that when a *name* is precisely the highest-priced thing in literature,
> any one who has a name will not, except when there is some strong
> motive for mystification, throw away the advantages of that name. I
> wrote anonymously while I was an unknown author, but I shall never,
> I believe, write anonymously again.[25]

The irony that this name she justified so ardently is a pseudonym does
not seem to have occurred to Evans – by this time, the pseudonym
had become the mainstay of her sense of a public self. Yet as crucial
as "George Eliot" was to Mary Ann Evans's life, the pseudonym was
not meant to usurp or replace the woman who had existed for close
to forty years before she had invented her public persona.[26]

Rather than displace her personal name with her pseudonym,
Evans rarely referred to herself in private life as "George Eliot."
Indeed, her earliest letters to her publisher, John Blackwood, were

signed "George Eliot," but once she revealed her identity she signed the rest of her professional correspondence as "M. E. Lewes." To friends, family, and fans she continued to be known as "Marianne Evans Lewes," or by one of the nicknames generated among her intimate acquaintances (Pollian, Polly, Clematis, Mother, Madonna, and Mutter were among the most common at different periods in her life).[27] In one of the very few personal letters that she signed with her pseudonym (in this case simply "G.E."), Evans added an insistent postscript: "my *name* is Marian Evans *Lewes*."[28]

Nonetheless, the Brontë sisters' and Evans's professional identities were inexorably bound up with their male pseudonyms. They never published under their own names even though their identities were well known within several years of their debuts as novelists. Thus the division between the Brontë sisters' and Evans's professional and personal life seems not only emphatic, but gendered as well. With the adoption of male pseudonyms, the Brontës' and Evans's writing and public persona appear to derive from a "masculine" sphere or a masculine aspect of their characters. Gilbert and Gubar give this reading to the Brontës' and to Evans's use of the pseudonym – that they were uncomfortable being women writers, that writing was an exclusively male enterprise, and that the male pseudonyms bespoke both an attempt at acceptance and a need to feel somehow masculinized before they could legitimately pick up the phallic pen: "the most rebellious of [Behn's and Cavendish's] nineteenth-century descendants attempted to solve the literary problem of being female by presenting themselves as *male*. In effect, [Evans and the Brontës] protested not that they were 'as good as' men but that, as writers, they *were* men."[29]

Yet, as with George Sand, Evans's and the Brontës' audiences did not think of them as men; rather, they perceived them to be women almost from the beginning of their careers. *Jane Eyre*, for example, was seen as a revolutionary book in terms of the history of the British novel precisely because it articulated the passions and desire of a specifically feminine experience. In examining the question of why Charlotte and Emily Brontë "should occupy a place of such prominence in the British cultural consciousness," Nancy Armstrong believes that this centrality derives from their skill at "formulating universal forms of subjectivity" and converting history into desire.[30] Raymond Williams states that with Charlotte and Emily Brontë there came "an emphasis on intense feeling, a commitment to what we must directly call passion, that is in itself very new in the English novel."[31] Thus, what seemed so exhilarating or threatening to many readers in the late 1840s was *Jane Eyre*'s giving voice to a previously unarticulated realm of feminine desire, and it was this voice that seemed to open the door for the establishment of a new kind of female authority. In 1855, Margaret Oliphant wrote that "suddenly, without warning, *Jane Eyre* stole upon the scene, and the most alarming revolution of modern times has followed th[is] invasion."[32]

Ironically, rather than averting or dissipating this authority, the male pseudonym actually served to enhance feminine domestic authority and reinforce the split between the public and private realms. In 1853, Elizabeth Gaskell characterized Brontë's life as being "divided into two parallel currents – her life as Currer Bell, the author; her life as Charlotte Brontë, the woman," thus underscoring the way that the male pseudonym helped to create a distinct and emphatic division between Brontë's professional and domestic selves.[33] As a mechanism for literary production this division functioned in the following way: Charlotte Brontë the artist was seen to conceal herself in a feminine, domestic, and hidden space, thereby invoking the Romantic image of creativity as an idio-pathic and clandestine enterprise. By presenting her public self as both masculine and a known fiction, this division between the public and the domestic, the masculine and the feminine, also becomes aligned with a division between false and authentic selves. Since it was in this private, feminized, creative realm that the masculine public self was invented and then brought forth for public display and consumption, women writers who used male pseudonyms implied that the private space was the realm of origination that took precedence over the public and the masculine. Therefore the "arti-ficial" male identity served to shelter the woman writer's "real" (feminine and domestic) self from the corrupt public realm.[34]

As with Brontë, Evans's use of a male pseudonym became not a pathway to androgyny but a means of protecting and emphasizing what the ideology of Romantic literary production identified as her specifically feminine creativity. In her 1856 essay "Silly Novels by Lady Novelists," Evans touches on her belief in a creativity accessible only though female genius, a belief that was more fully articulated by Lewes in his 1852 essay on female novelists.[35] Lewes argues that great literature depicts "universal truths" of "the forms and orders of human life," hence the "universality and immortality of Homer, Shakspeare [*sic*], Cervantes, Moliere." For Lewes, literature is "essentially the expression of experience and emotion – of what we have seen, felt, and thought." Yet the "universal and immortal" authors Lewes lists are all men, and he raises the question: "What does the literature of women mean?" In answering this query, Lewes claims that "while it is impossible for men to express life otherwise than they know it – and they can only know it profoundly according to their own experience – the advent of female literature promises woman's view of life, woman's experience: in other words, a new element." Lewes believes that this new element derives from women's special knowledge of the human heart. Using rigid notions of sexual difference, he asserts that the "Masculine mind is characterized by a predominance of the intellect, and the Feminine by the predominance of the emotions":

Woman, by her greater affectionateness, her greater range and depth of emotional experience, is well fitted to give expression to the emotional facts of life . . . To write as men write, is the aim and besetting sin of women; to write as women, is the real office they have to perform . . . To imitate is to abdicate. We are in no need of more male writers; we are in need of genuine female experience. The prejudices, notions, passions, and conventionalisms of men are amply illustrated; let us have the same fulness [*sic*] with respect to women.[36]

According to Lewes's logic in "The Lady Novelists," the greatest literature tells universal truths about human emotions; women are more emotional than men and are more able to depict those emotions. Consequently, women are more privy to universal truths and are thus more likely to write great literature. Lewes argues that this has not happened quite yet because most women writers are busy trying to imitate men, but the few who have tapped into the emotional truths of humanity (Maria Edgeworth, Jane Austen, George Sand, Currer Bell, and Elizabeth Gaskell) are the pioneers of a profoundly emotional literary voice – a voice that is at once universal and feminine.

Thus Evans's and the Brontës' use of the male pseudonym is not a usurpation of the patronym, rather it is a creative appropriation of the possibilities inscribed in the nineteenth-century myth of subjectivity's division into distinct public and private realms. Gilbert and Gubar, for example, contend that this pseudonymic self functions as "a name of power, the mark of a private christening into a second self, a rebirth into linguistic primacy," but I would maintain that for these novelists the power was seen to rest with the private self.[37] Like the Brontës, Evans employed the pseudonym as a fictional creation and a detachable identity, locating the source of power – the "real" self who was responsible for the creation of the pseudonymic self – in the private, domestic self, a self sheltered from the contamination of the marketplace in part through the pseudonym itself.

The conflict between the didactic or messianic aspirations of Victorian writers and the commercial aspects of publishing and marketing was profound during the mid-nineteenth century. George Meredith conveys a sense of this uneasiness in *Rhoda Fleming*: "You can buy any amount for a penny, now-a-days – poetry up in a corner, stories, tales o'temptation."[38] In *Lucretia*, Francis Edward Paget expresses this fear even more harshly: "Most of the worst sensational novels are republished, vile type and vile paper combining to secure for the dissemination of still viler sentiments a very low price."[39] Mary Poovey writes of the confusion felt by male writers during the mid-nineteenth century over their place in society, the status of their profession, and their ancestry of not only medieval court scribes and Renaissance intellectuals but also "early and mid-eighteenth-century hacks who sold ideas by the word and fought off competitors for every scrap of work."[40] Brontë and Evans, I would argue, found a partial solution to the conflict that all Victorian writers felt over their profession by exploiting the potentially crippling oppositions of Romantic ideology, by splitting the self into the public, male writer and the private, female genius.

In her essay on Aphra Behn, Catherine Gallagher makes an argument similar to the one that I am making here when she writes of Behn's construction of an innocent self that existed above the exchange of writing:

authorship for the marketplace and self-hood are here dissevered, for the author that can be inferred from the work is merely a 'way of writing' dictated by the Age, an alienable thing below the true self. . . . Aphra Behn constructs the effect of an authentic female self on the basis of the very need to sell her constructed, authorial self. By making her authorial self an emanation of the marketplace, then, she saves this putative authentic self from contamination.[41]

Yet, as Gallagher notes, Behn's tainted professional identity was construed as "woman writer as prostitute," not as a male as with Brontë and Evans. By the nineteenth century, the "woman writer as whore" had transmuted into the "woman writer as man."

Behn may have aimed for a sense of purity and decorum existing in the realm of her "true self," while her marketable self was a whore, but for both Evans and Charlotte Brontë, the "true self" was a complex construction of domestic angel and messianic leader, martyred daughter and sibyl. Furthermore, all of these "private" selves were understood to be specifically feminine, the domestic self obviously so, but even the oracular teller of universal truths was believed to speak with a woman's voice. Thus the domestic self and the self of genius worked in tandem to create what Lewes and Evans had defined as "great" literature – the domestic self gave women writers the emotional authority that derived especially from domestic martyrdom. The self-sacrificial experiences of the mother, wife, daughter, and sister were then recreated in the crucible of literary genius – a hidden, ultraprivate self that transformed the everyday emotional events of women into "universal truths."

What, then, of the commodified, marketable author – the public self? This was the self that was most tainted and ephemeral: a self who writes, as Evans puts it, "drivel for dishonest money."[42] The commercial self, interested in profit and bargaining and business deals, certainly would dilute a writer's claims of possessing a disinterested, universal voice marked with the stamp of Romantic genius. Thus in order to separate fully the public from the private self, the public self becomes a masculine mask – a mask that shields the private, feminine self from the tarnish of the marketplace.

NOTES

I would like to thank Otto Drawer, Fran Michel, Teresa Faherty, Thomas Goodman, Tassie Gwilliam, Catherine Gallagher, and my editors for their criticisms and suggestions.

1 Patricia Lorimer Lundberg, "George Eliot: Mary Ann Evans's Subversive Tool in *Middlemarch?*," *Studies in the Novel* 18, 3 (Fall 1986), 270.

2 Gaye Tuchman with Nina E. Fortin, *Edging Women Out: Victorian Novelists, Publishers, and Social Change* (New Haven: Yale University Press, 1989), 53. Some female pseudonyms used by male writers include Kate Phusin (John Ruskin), Margaret Nicholson (Percy Bysshe Shelley), Theresa MacWhorter (William Makepeace Thackeray), Ellen Alice (Col. Thomas Bangs Thorpe), Sappho of Toulouse (Clarence Isaure), Clara Gazul (Prosper Mérimée), Fiona

Macleod (William Sharp), and Mrs. Horace Manners (Algernon Swinburne).

3 Robert Southey to Charlotte Brontë, March 1837, quoted in *The Brontës: Their Lives, Friendships, and Correspondence*, ed. T. J. Wise and J. A. Symington (4 vols.; Oxford: Oxford University Press, 1931–38), vol. 1, 154–56. As Margot Peters points out, these words of discouragement are to be expected from an archconservative like Southey, yet she also speculates that during the 1830s very few men would have encouraged any woman to become a professional writer. See Margot Peters, *Unquiet Soul: A Biography of Charlotte Brontë* (New York: Atheneum, 1975), 55.

4 For a fascinating reading of the competitions of the nineteenth-century British literary marketplace that takes class (but, uncharacteristically, not gender) into account, see Mary Poovey, *Uneven Developments: The Ideological Work of Gender* (Chicago: University of Chicago Press, 1987), 101–16.

5 Sandra Gilbert and Susan Gubar, "Ceremonies of the Alphabet: Female Grandmatologies and the Female Authorgraph," in *The Female Autograph*, ed. Domna C. Stanton (New York: New York Literary Forum, 1984), 28.

6 Although I will, at times, include Anne Brontë and Emily Brontë in my discussion of Charlotte Brontë's use of a male pseudonym, my focus remains on Charlotte Brontë for two reasons. The first is that Charlotte Brontë was in charge of the business of getting published and therefore evinced a greater awareness of publication practices than did her sisters. The second reason I highlight Charlotte Brontë is that although Ellis Bell now shares Currer Bell's eminence, during the mid-nineteenth century, it was Currer Bell alone who raised the Brontë sisters to fame.

7 The problem of what name to use for Mary Ann Evans arises early in this chapter. Evans's pseudonym displays a profound tenacity that is entirely lacking with the Brontës. We associate Evans's pseudonym very closely with her historical identity in a way that is not extended to many other authors who published under pseudonyms. We do not, for example, think of Charles Dickens as "Boz," Walter Scott as "Jedediah Cleishbotham," or Jane Austen as "A Lady." Similarly, no one deems Charlotte, Anne, and Emily Brontë to be primarily "Currer, Acton, and Ellis Bell." Yet in the same way that Amandine Aurore Lucie Dudevant is always "George Sand" and Marie Henri Beyle is simply "Stendhal," we think today of "George Eliot" and never consider Mary Ann Evans to be Mary Ann Evans. Perhaps this is the fault of critical conventions and the habits of modern publishers: all of her novels continue to be marketed under Evans's pseudonym and almost all critical commentary about Evans designates her "George Eliot." Evans herself set this precedent. In 1879 she wrote

to the editor of the *Oxford English Dictionary*, in answer to his inquiry about what name she preferred to be cited by, that "I wish always to be quoted as George Eliot . . . Yours very truly, M. E. Lewes." George Eliot, *The Yale Edition of the George Eliot Letters*, ed. Gordon S. Haight (9 vols.; New Haven: Yale University Press, 1978), vol. 9, 279.

Nor is it easy, having once discarded the pseudonym, to decide what to call Evans, since her given first name is Mary Anne (on the baptismal record and in her first signed letter) or Mary Ann (from 1837 to 1850 and then again in 1880, her last year of life), and her two married names are "Lewes" and "Cross." For the purposes of this chapter, I have decided to use Evans's somewhat altered given first name of "Mary Ann." One could argue for the use of "Marianne" largely because "Marianne Evans" is the name she used when she began her career as a professional writer and editor for the *Westminster Review*, and further, the first known manuscript of Evans's is a school notebook from 1830 signed "Marianne Evans" in "large, ornate script." Gordon Haight believes that this experimental spelling stems from Evans's "recent introduction to French." Gordon Haight, *George Eliot: A Biography* (Oxford: Oxford University Press, 1968), 552. Nonetheless, I have settled on "Mary Ann Evans" because this was the name she was using when she translated Strauss's *Leben Jesu* and is thus her first professional name.

8 The full quotation is: "we had a vague impression that authoresses are liable to be looked on with prejudice." Quoted in Elizabeth Gaskell, *The Life of Charlotte Brontë*, ed. Alan Shelston (New York: Penguin, 1975), 286.

9 *Ibid.*, 285–86.

10 Eliot, *Letters*, 3:86.

11 Quoted in Eliot, *Letters*, 8:429, n.9.

12 For a good sense of the debate over gender and writing in mid-Victorian England, see, Miriam Allott (ed.), *The Brontës: The Critical Heritage* (London: Routledge & Kegan Paul, 1974); Elizabeth K. Helsinger, Robin Lauterbach Sheets, and William Veeter, *The Woman Question: Society and Literature in Britain and America, 1837–1900* (3 vols.; New York: Garland, 1983); Elaine Showalter, *A Literature of Their Own: British Women Novelists from Brontë to Lessing* (Princeton: Princeton University Press, 1977); Carol Ohmann, "Emily Brontë in the Hands of Male Critics," *College English* 32 (May 1971); and Walter E. Houghton, *et al.* (eds.), *The Wellesley Index to Victorian Periodicals, 1824–1900* (5 vols.; Toronto: University of Toronto Press, 1966–89).

For nineteenth-century essays on women and writing, see George Henry Lewes, "Currer Bell's *Shirley*," *Edinburgh Review*, 91 (April 1850); W. R. Greg, "The False Morality of Lady Novelists," *National Review* 15 (January 1859); John Eagles, "A Few Words about

Novels," *Blackwood's* 64 (October 1848); Harriet Martineau, "Review of *Villette*," *London Daily News*, 3 February 1853; W. G. Clark, "New Novels," *Fraser's* 40 (December 1849); Margaret Oliphant, "Modern Novelists – Great and Small," *Blackwood's* 77 (May 1855); and "Women in the Domain of Letters" *Sharpe's* 40 (1864).

13 For an excellent overview of the state of Victorian literary criticism, see the editors' introductory essay in Edwin M. Eigner and George J. Worth (eds.), *Victorian Criticism of the Novel* (Cambridge: Cambridge University Press, 1985).

14 Eliot, *Letters*, 2:305.

15 *Ibid.*, 6:378.

16 George Eliot, "Silly Novels by Lady Novelists," *The Westminster and Foreign Quarterly Review* 6, 2 (October 1854), 460. See, also, Emily Davies's letter to Jane Crow where she writes that Evans "thinks people who write regularly for the Press are almost sure to be spoiled by it. There is so much dishonesty, people's work being praised because they belong to the confederacy [i.e., because they are friends of the reviewers]." Quoted in Eliot, *Letters*, 8:466.

17 Eliot, "Silly Novels," 460.

18 *Ibid.*, 460.

19 The Brontës and Evans did indeed have compelling personal reasons for concealing their identities. The Brontë sisters apparently wanted to hide their literary projects from their father until public judgment was over. However, this stemmed from a fear that they were writing second-rate works, not because any sort of literary production was forbidden and unladylike – no doubt Patrick Brontë (who, as a self-made man, had changed his own name from the Irish peasant patronym of "Brunty" to the more aristocratic "Brontë" with its pretentious umlaut) had long ago resigned himself to the fact that his daughters would have to work for a living. Perhaps even more pressing was their desire to hide their publications from their dying brother Branwell, whom they felt would be tormented by his sisters' successes.

   Evans also published under a male pseudonym for a number of reasons that included the need to conceal familial or provincial sources, her fear of humiliating herself in a new genre until the critical verdict was in and, perhaps most of all, because of the scandal surrounding her relationship with George Henry Lewes.

20 In Gaskell's *Life of Charlotte Brontë*, for example, one gets a sense of Brontë's struggle to grasp the workings of the publishing industry. In 1845 Brontë wrote to the publishers Aylott & Co.:

It is evident that unknown authors have great difficulties to contend with before they can succeed in bringing their works before the public. Can you give me any hint as to the way in which these difficulties are best met? For instance, in the present case, where a work of fiction is in question, in what form would a publisher be most likely to accept the MS.? Whether offered as a work of three vols., or as tales which might be published in numbers, or as contributions to a periodical? (Quoted in Gaskell, *Life*, 293)

Gaskell, who experienced numerous difficulties with her editors, especially with Dickens, aims a few wily blows at male editors when she writes of this period in Brontë's life as one of an heroic struggle to gain the acceptance and recognition that she deserved from British publishers:

among the dispiriting circumstances connected with her anxious visit to Manchester, Charlotte told me that her tale came back . . . curtly rejected by some publisher . . . But she had the heart of Robert Bruce within her, and failure upon failure daunted her no more than him . . . 'The Professor' had met with many refusals from different publishers; some, I have reason to believe, not over-courteously worded in writing to an unknown author, and none alleging any distinct reasons for its rejection. (Gaskell, *Life*, 305, 315)

21 Quoted in Mary Poovey, *The Proper Lady and the Woman Writer: Ideology as Style in the Works of Mary Wollstonecraft, Mary Shelley, and Jane Austen* (Chicago: University of Chicago Press, 1984), 211. In *The Tutor's Ward*, Felicia Skene depicts the inevitable loss of privacy that women writers faced:

She has gone beyond her own province, and therefore she must consent to belie her own nature. It would be a mockery to talk of shrinking from observation when of her own will she has met the rude stare of strange eyes; absurd to say that she trembles to trust her own judgment or to guide her own faltering steps, when she who should have done the bidding of others has come forth to govern and influence the minds of many. She has quitted the stronghold of her womanly reserve and privileges, and henceforth she dare not turn . . . from the personal remarks, the fulsome flattery, and the impertinent scrutiny to which she has exposed herself; she has given herself as fair game to be hunted down for the public amusement, and she has no right to complain if the noise and turmoil of the chase fill her with terror, and with a weary longing for the unnoticed retirement which is her rightful sphere. (Felicia Skene, *The Tutor's Ward: A Novel* (London: Colburn, 1851, 24)

22 Poovey, *Uneven Developments*, 108.

23 Charles Rowcroft, *The Man Without a Profession* (3 vols.); 1844, vol. 3, 157, 160; quoted in Myron F. Brightfield, *Victorian England in its Novels (1840–1870)* (4 vols.; Los Angeles: University of California Library, 1968), vol. 1, 157.

24 Eliot, *Letters*, 5:171.

25 *Ibid.*, 4:25.

26 Eliot, *Letters*, 2:91. Many commentators see Evans's choice of the name "George" as a tribute to both George Henry Lewes and George Sand. See, for example, Penny Boumelha, "George Eliot and the End of Realism," in *Women Reading Women's Writing*, ed. Sue Roe (Brighton,

Sussex: The Harvester Press, 1987), 16; and Nancy L. Paxton, *George Eliot and Herbert Spencer: Feminism, Evolutionism, and the Reconstruction of Gender* (Princeton: Princeton University Press, 1991), 12; or Gillian Beer, *George Eliot* (Bloomington: Indiana University Press, 1986), 22.

Evans's decision to use the last name of "Eliot" has presented more of a puzzle to critics. Ruby V. Redinger has suggested that "Eliot" is another tribute to Lewes, in other words, that Eliot functions as a puzzle whose solution is "To L[ewes] I owe it." Ruby V. Redinger, *George Eliot: The Emergent Self* (New York: Knopf, 1975), 331. This idea has been forwarded by Michal Peled Ginsberg in "Pseudonym, Epigraphs, and Narrative Voice: *Middlemarch* and the Problem of Authorship," *ELH* 47, 3 (Fall 1980), 544, and discarded by Beer, *George Eliot*, 22. Noting the importance of weaving and women's writing, Beer points out that Eliot spelled backwards is "toile" (*ibid.*, 22). Evans, herself, claimed that she chose Eliot because it was an old-fashioned, stolid "mouth-filling name." (Quoted in Ginsberg, 544.)

As to the issue of Evans's tribute to the "Georges," I would also like to add, along with George Sand and George Lewes, William Makepeace Thackeray. In 1857, Evans wrote that: "I may have some resemblance to Thackeray, though I am not conscious of being in any way a disciple of his, unless it constitute discipleship to think him, as I suppose the majority of people with any intellect do, on the whole the most powerful of living novelists." *Letters*, 2:349. Thackeray's most famous pseudonym was George Savage Fitz-Boodle, Esq., his nom de plume for all of the work he contributed to *Fraser's Magazine*, including *The Luck of Barry Lyndon*.

27 Please refer to note 7 above for a discussion of Evans's uses of "Mary Anne," "Mary Ann," and "Marianne."

28 Eliot, *Letters*, 3:217, her emphasis. This letter was written to her old friend Charles Bray in 1859 when she was quite angry with him for betraying her pseudonym to Chapman. She also felt ire because he continued to address her by her maiden identity – Mary Ann Evans.

29 Gilbert and Gubar, "Ceremonies," 65.

30 Nancy Armstrong, *Desire and Domestic Fiction: A Political History of the Novel* (Oxford: Oxford University Press, 1987), 186.

31 Raymond Williams, *The English Novel from Dickens to Lawrence* (London: Hogarth Press, 1984), 60.

32 Quoted in Sandra Gilbert and Susan Gubar, *The Madwoman in the Attic: The Woman Writer and the Nineteenth-Century Imagination* (New Haven: Yale University Press, 1979), 337.

33 Gaskell, 334.

34 Evans, too, wrote about Brontë as a person with multiple selves. In a letter to her close friends the Brays written in 1853, she equates Charlotte Brontë with George Sand: "Lewes was describing Currer

Bell to me yesterday as a little, plain, provincial, sickly-looking old maid. Yet what passion, what fire in her! Quite as much as in George Sand, only the clothing is less voluptuous." Evans's easy comparison of Brontë to Sand derives, in part, from the unusual use of male pseudonyms by both authors, yet Evans's image of a fiery interior beneath a dull facade underscores Brontë's status of living a dual existence and possessing a multiplicity of selves – her "real" self, i.e., the self of passionate emotions, being hidden except in and through her art. (Eliot, *Letters*, 2:91.) Evans had a complex sense of indebtedness to both George Sand and Charlotte Brontë. Although she probably esteemed Sand's art more than she did Brontë's we can speculate that she shared Lewes's estimation of the major women writers of the nineteenth century. (See, for example, George Henry Lewes, "Lady Novelists," *Westminster Review* 2 [July and October 1852], 450–53.) I would argue that Evans felt more affinity with Brontë. Unlike Sand, who was spirited, aristocratic, and beautiful, Evans saw Brontë as someone who had written herself out of being a "plain, provincial, sickly-looking old maid": attributes that Evans felt she was likewise overcoming through her intellectual labor.

Throughout the middle and late nineteenth century, there continued to be an intriguing comparison of George Sand, Charlotte Brontë, and George Eliot. In 1876, for example, Emily Davies made a hostile but fascinating association between Sand and Evans when she wrote that a portrait of Evans that hung above the Lewes's fireplace in their study (Davies calls it a "staring likeness and odious, vulgarizing portrait") reminded Davies "of Couture's drawing of George Sand – and there is a strong likeness to this drawing in [Evans's] own face. The head and face are hardly as noble as George Sand's, but the lines are almost as strong and masculine . . . and the hair is dressed in a similar style, but the eyes are not so deep, and there is less suggestion of possible beauty and possible sensuality . . . Indeed one rarely sees a plainer woman." (Quoted in Eliot, *Letters*, 5:8–9.) For an extended discussion of Evans's debt to George Sand, see Valerie A. Dodd, *George Eliot: An Intellectual Life* (London: Macmillan, 1990), 132–42.

35 Nina Auerbach writes of literary women creating a "mystic free-masonry of gender" that was essentially separatist in nature. Nina Auerbach, "Woman and Nation," *Tulsa Studies in Women's Literature* 6, 2 (Fall 1987), 183. See also Virginia Woolf's seminal statement in *Three Guineas*: "as a woman I want no country. As a woman my country is the whole world." (*Ibid.*, 183.)

36 Lewes, "The Lady Novelists," 130, 131, 132.

37 Gilbert and Gubar, "Ceremonies," 29.

38 George Meredith, *Rhoda Fleming* (London: Tinsley, 1865), 73.

39 Francis Edward Paget, *Lucretia or, The Heroine of the Nineteenth Century: A Correspondence Sensational and Sentimental* (London: 1868), 302.

40 Poovey, *Uneven Developments*, 103.
41 Catherine Gallagher, "Who Was That Masked Woman?: The Prostitute and the Playwright in the Comedies of Aphra Behn," *Women's Studies* 15, 1 (1988), 30.
42 George Eliot, *George Eliot's Life as Related in Her Letters and Journals*, arranged and edited by her husband, J. W. Cross (3 vols.; Edinburgh: William Blackwood & Sons, 1885), 2: 262.

CHAPTER 12

A bibliographical approach to Victorian publishing

Maura Ives

Bibliography – the physical analysis of printed texts – is increasingly recognized as a historical and therefore an interpretive field of study relevant to the concerns of a number of other text-based disciplines, most notably literary and historical studies. Bibliographical considerations are visible in recent work in the history of the book by Cathy Davidson, Robert Darnton, and G. T. Tanselle, each of whom locates physical aspects of the book within a complex matrix of social relations among authors, printers, publishers, and readers.[1] The role of bibliography in literary scholarship has gained new emphasis as scholars such as Jerome J. McGann and D. F. McKenzie attempt to focus less on the strictly editorial applications of bibliography and more on the part that bibliography might play in establishing the cultural and interpretive significance of the physical book in literary studies.[2] One can see this shift in McGann's introduction to *Historical Studies and Literary Criticism* (1985), which presents the physical form of a book as an important factor in the production of literary meaning.[3] More recently, Donald G. Marshall's essay on "Literary Interpretation" in the Modern Language Association's new *Introduction to Scholarship in Modern Languages and Literatures* expresses a similar interest in the way that readers respond to the physical and historical circumstances of printed texts:[4]

The way a text is printed or bound, the scholarly apparatus of notes and commentary that may accompany it, the circumstances under which we first encounter it – whether we see it in a bookstore, library, or classroom or hear of it through a comment by a newspaper reviewer, a friend, a teacher, or in another book – all shape our initial orientation to it. Interpreters are therefore necessarily interested in how a text got put together and how and why it comes to us.

Marshall's comment makes no reference to "bibliography" per se, yet in these few words he introduces his readers to several important areas of intersection between bibliographical and literary studies. Bibliographers have traditionally contributed to the discovery of "how a text got put together" by considering printed artifacts analytically (in terms of their separate, or at least separable, parts). Thus the place of bibliography in discovering "the way a text is printed or bound," or in constructing the "notes and commentary" of a critical edition, has long been recognized. But Marshall also points toward a new role bibliography can play in the discovery of "why it [a text] comes to us." This role is one in which bibliographers consider texts holistically (the text as a physical/conceptual fusion) in order to provide evidence about the circumstances and intentionalities of text production.

At present, the degree to which other scholars can make use of bibliographical approaches to texts is limited, and will remain so until both bibliographers and nonbibliographers make stronger efforts to bridge the gaps between bibliography and other fields. Some researchers know so little about bibliographical analysis and description that they do not realize its potential usefulness. Noting the divisions between analytical bibliography and recent work in the history of the book, G. T. Tanselle points to misunderstandings about the supposed "narrowness" of the field and the still-present assumption that bibliography is only useful for literary, rather than historical, scholarship – an observation that will, doubtless, provoke a wry smile from bibliographers whose work has been stigmatized because it isn't sufficiently "literary."[5]

To be fair, however, one must recognize that it is no easy task for colleagues in history, literature, or other related fields to become bibliographically literate. In "What is the History of Books?", Robert Darnton likens the situation of the book historian to that of an explorer in a "tropical rain forest . . . entangled in a luxuriant undergrowth of journal articles and disoriented by the crisscrossing of disciplines – analytical bibliography pointing in this direction, the sociology of knowledge in that, while history, English and comparative literature stake out overlapping territories."[6] The interdisciplinary approaches favored by many literary scholars place them in essentially the same dilemma, which is compounded by the scarcity of courses in analytical, descriptive, and historical bibliography.[7] Since bibliography is no longer regularly taught, there is a very real lack of suitable introductory materials for new students and interested scholars, so that at present, researchers who wish to become proficient in bibliographical techniques must forge their own path through the scholarship in the field. This is not as Herculean a task as some have suggested; the bibliographical jungle is dense and challenging, but demands no greater effort than one might reasonably expect to expend in an attempt to master the basics of an unfamiliar discipline.[8] Still, Darnton's advice to historians – "Analytical bibliography may seem arcane to the outsider, but it could make a great contribution to social as well as literary history" – would be taken more frequently if bibliographers themselves would do more to clear the path for "outsiders."[9]

First, however, bibliographers must explain why this path is worth taking, and that is in part what this chapter seeks to accomplish. My observations are directed both to readers who do not know much about bibliography and to bibliographers themselves. To readers unfamiliar with bibliographical theory and practice, I offer some examples of the kinds of information that bibliography can provide, and some suggestions toward making use of that information as it is presented in one of the most common bibliographical resources, the author-based descriptive bibliography. To readers who already have some bibliographical training, I offer some suggestions toward extending bibliographical theory both "externally" (by reconsidering the intersections of bibliographical, literary, and historical approaches to texts) and "internally" (by taking bibliographical research beyond the boundary of the "book"). I begin with a short orientation to bibliographical theory and practice, followed by some examples of the theoretical and critical issues that I have encountered in my research into various printings of a set of short stories by George Meredith.

By "bibliography" I refer primarily to analytical bibliography, generally defined as the practice of examining printed artifacts as physical objects in order to determine the technological and social processes of their production, and the related practice of descriptive bibliography, which records the results of the bibliographical analysis of an individual printed object (or group of objects). Readers who are unfamiliar with the field of analytical bibliography need to know that there has been considerable debate about whether the "technical" or the "social" orientation of bibliography has (or should take) precedence. Earlier theorists tended to stress the former; W. W. Greg's 1932 definition of analytical bibliography as the study of "pieces of paper or parchment covered with certain written or printed signs"[10] continues to be the most frequently cited example of this tendency. More recent commentators have used Greg's definition to support claims that the work of Greg and Fredson Bowers, author of the influential *Principles of Bibliographical Description* (1949), has contributed to the field's neglect of historical and critical concerns. Thus D. F. McKenzie's *Bibliography and the Sociology of Texts* (1985), a work that intends to "redirect bibliographical inquiry in a fruitful response to recent developments in critical theory and practice," begins by arguing that Greg's formulation of bibliography divorces bibliographical study from historical concerns and has thus encouraged bibliographers to refrain from commenting upon the meanings – historical, literary, social, aesthetic – of the book as a physical object.[11]

McKenzie's book raises important issues for bibliography and for the diverse scholars who stand to benefit from bibliographical research.[12] There is much to gain from McKenzie's vision of a "comprehensive" bibliography that "testifies to the fact that new readers of course make new texts, and that their new meanings are a function of their new forms." Such a bibliography, while taking the physical analysis of printed artifacts as a "starting point," would also point out the cultural significance of the physical evidence that it uncovers.[13] The difficulty with McKenzie's argument is that it proceeds by misrepresenting the historical orientation of bibliography. McKenzie writes as if bibliography is somehow aimed at – and even accomplished – a surgical separation of books from the historical circumstances of their creation. The impossibility of attempting to decode the physical evidence provided by any one book without a very sound understanding of certain historical conditions is obvious; bibliography is inherently a historical pursuit. To advocate the cultural relevance of bibliographical evidence, as McKenzie does, is not to introduce historical concerns into the ahistorical sphere of bibliographical studies. It is, rather, to make the valuable suggestion that the part of history that bibliographers have traditionally focused upon – that is the history of what happens to a text up to the time that it is issued to the public – might be interpreted so that it also illuminates the history of texts after their publication.

What McKenzie sees as a limitation can just as easily be seen as an advantage. Although bibliographers have not been primarily concerned with the way in which readers apprehend various forms of the texts, bibliography has much to contribute to the study of reception precisely because it is situated within the process of production. Production always assumes, and tries to determine, reception, and for that reason it is illogical to posit a separation between the two. As G. T. Tanselle points out in his criticism of McKenzie, "there can be no question that the physical forms in which texts are presented to the public are the products of printers and publishers (and sometimes authors as well), and that they in turn affect the interpretations of readers."[14] Although Tanselle presents this as a matter of simple common sense that McKenzie has belabored, the idea deserves to be developed in some detail. Most printed texts come about as a result of the decisions and actions of a group of human beings who share a number of tasks: writing, revising, setting type, designing bindings, folding sheets, inserting advertisements. Bibliography accounts for and represents the end product of these decisions, and in so doing it not only tells us how and of what materials a printed text was constructed but also provides a great deal of information that can be used to draw inferences about the effects that the author, the publisher, and the book designer wished to produce upon the book's readers.

To clarify the point I wish to make, I will return to definitions. McKenzie defines bibliography as "the discipline that studies texts as recorded forms, and the processes of their transmission, including their production and reception."[15] I would shift the emphasis of this definition, so that we can think of bibliography as the discipline that studies texts (which, for the purposes of this chapter, are printed materials) as the physical and visual products of human intentions. This is not, of course, to say that those intentions determine the functions of print artifacts, but instead to recognize that they do contribute to them. No one can predict the range of ways in which the physical and visual phenomena that bibliographers examine might mediate the verbal aspects of texts, much less the degree to which they are also capable of producing meaning in and of themselves.

Bibliography can, however, establish the existence of certain crucially significant material features of a text. Each part of the text represents the work, and the intentions, of a particular person or persons. The author's vision of a text is most likely to be expressed in words; the intentions of designers and graphic artists are expressed through typography, layout, and covers; and the economic goals of the publisher are evident in every aspect of the text. Bibliographical awareness of each of these parts of the text enables scholars to investigate the links between production and reception, as Cathy Davidson does in her examination of the American publishing history of the novel *Charlotte Temple*. Although Davidson's work is not strictly (or primarily) bibliographical, her explanation of how the "packaging" of the novel directed the reader's interpretations demonstrates the value of what bibliographers do when they gather precise information about the nonverbal components of texts, such as binding, illustrations, and typography.[16] Davidson's essay also underscores what bibliographers could do, if, in addition to providing information about the nonverbal characteristics of texts, they also took a leading role in the interpretive assessment of them.

What I am suggesting is that bibliographical studies can and should occupy a position somewhere between the intentionalities of production and the actualities of reception. Bibliography can occupy this place because even bibliographers who insist on defining their work solely in terms of the physical and visual "inked shapes" described by Greg have the advantage of possessing more than one way of thinking about material texts.[17] In one sense, the bibliographical "book" (which need not be a book at all) is an indivisible whole, a single, material object through which the various, even at times competing intentions of those who contributed to its production are inextricably joined. Descriptive bibliographies account for the book in this way by describing each of its parts without necessarily suggesting that the words are more important than the illustrations or that the binding is less valuable than the title page. Yet descriptive bibliography always records the book as a catalogue of its separable parts – paper, binding, inked shapes – and points us toward the ways in which the physical *and* the conceptual book retain certain fissures that are the products of the never wholly identical intentions of the people who participated in the book's production and of the occasional conflicts between human wishes and historical circumstances. The inevitable disparities between the producers and the receivers of a book is also a territory that bibliography could map. A bibliographical approach to texts reiterates the fact that each part of a book tells its own story about the book's production, and has its own part to play in the history of its reception.

Nor should the bibliographical point of view be confined to the single book, newspaper, or broadside. When the Victorian literary marketplace as a whole is viewed bibliographically, it becomes a collection of artifacts, each of which displays a unique combination of the overlapping agendas of Victorian publishers, printers, writers, and even readers, who, as the consumers of printed matter, expect to find their own interests, expectations, and aspirations taken into account by those who produce the books they buy. By allowing us to identify, and subsequently to interpret, the physical manifestations of the agendas of the text, bibliography can provide a basis for critical analysis of the ideological, visual, and linguistic juxtapositions contained in a single printed text or in the entire range of texts available to a single group of readers.

A few examples from the publication history of George Meredith's three short stories, *The House on the Beach*, *The Case of General Ople and Lady Camper*, and *The Tale of Chloe*, illustrate some of the juxta-positions that a bibliographical point of view makes visible. Since descriptive bibliographies of many authors are readily available and because they contain fairly standard categories of information, I have cast my discussion in terms of the kinds of information that appear (or at least should appear) in descriptive bibliographies of individual authors, such as: quasi-facsimile transcriptions of an item's title page or wrappers; a listing of its contents; information about the way in which the sheets of a periodical or book were printed; descriptions of illustrations, typography, and binding; and other details, depending on the aims of the bibliography and the special circumstances of the items it describes. Although there are two published bibliographies of George Meredith – Maurice Buxton Forman's *A Bibliography of the Writings in Prose and Verse of George Meredith* and *Meredithiana: Being a Supplement to the Bibliography of Meredith* (1924), and Michael Collie's *George Meredith: A Bibliography* (1972) – the examples I use here are drawn primarily from my own research.[18]

I should also explain that at times my approach to Meredith's texts departs from standard bibliographical practice in order to accommodate nonbook texts such as periodicals, newspapers, and other inexpensive or ephemeral publications. There is no justification in bibliographical theory for the practice of limiting descriptive bibliography to books, and by going beyond the traditional boundaries of the field I can more accurately represent the conditions of the Victorian marketplace while also providing a more convincing demonstration of the advantages of examining that marketplace bibliographically. My discussion of Meredith's stories attempts to identify both bibliographical and critical issues typically associated with the range of publishing genres in which the stories originally appeared: a British periodical, an American newspaper, mass-market American paperbacks, and several British clothbound books.

Meredith's three stories were first published in a periodical, the British *New Quarterly Magazine*, where they appeared in 1877 and 1879.[19] Since periodical publications are by nature collaborative projects, they present particularly interesting bibliographical and textual issues, such as the interplay of editorial and authorial voices, the assimilation of a writer's words to the visual as well as the verbal style of a particular journal, and the heightened responsiveness of periodical publications to their immediate social, political, and technological environments.

The typography of a periodical indicates its particular historical, technological, aesthetic and ideological contexts. One of the first things that we might notice in a bibliographical examination of the typography of the *New Quarterly Magazine* is that a typical page of this magazine was almost indistinguishable from a page of a contemporary book. The mast title of the *New Quarterly* (the title printed at the head of the first text page of each number) was composed of ordinary letterpress, as opposed to an engraved "logo." The headlines of each page of the *New Quarterly* provide only the title of the text that appears on that page and the page number, as is customary in books; there is no reference to the issue, volume, or date of the *Magazine*, as one might find in other magazines and in most newspapers. Some contemporary periodicals, such as *Blackwood's Edinburgh Magazine*, arranged text in columns, but the *New Quarterly* does not. It also distinguishes itself from other periodicals by containing no illustrations and by avoiding unusual fonts or type ornaments. Although a Gothic font is used in the heading for each essay or story, and small and large capitals appear occasionally in the text, there are no other typographical variations. Type ornaments are nonexistent except for a device bearing the words "Arbor Scientiae" and "Arbor Vitae" that appears on the title pages of each volume, and a few small ornamental rules that appear elsewhere in the text.

To interpret this information, we must situate it historically in terms of the greatly increased technological opportunities available to periodical publishers at this time (1877–79). Some periodical publications contemporary with the *New Quarterly*, such as the *Illustrated London News* (founded in 1838), described by John Lewis as "the first periodical to devote more space to the illustrations than to the text,"[20] made extensive use of new illustrative processes and ornamental typefaces to attract the attention of contemporary readers.[21] The plainness of the *New Quarterly* may be evidence of a tight budget (and thus evidence of the extent to which the representation of texts is mediated by economic considerations), but it probably also is a visual representation of the publisher's concept of the *New Quarterly* as a "High-Class Literary and Social Periodical," as the prospectus had advertised.[22] The *New Quarterly*'s persistence in a rather old-fashioned focus on text rather than pictures, as well as its willingness to identify itself visually with books rather than with mass-market periodicals, might have carried both an aesthetic and a class connotation to readers who distinguished the staid quarterly from flashier illustrated magazines and newspapers.

A different set of issues arises when we investigate the typography of a newspaper. Daily newspapers, even more than periodicals like the *New Quarterly*, were (and are) unequivocally mass-produced, temporally conditioned texts. The practical realities of daily production create sharp visual distinctions between newspapers and less frequently produced, more expensive periodicals such as the *New Quarterly*. Each page of the *New Quarterly* is devoted to a single item, whereas the pages of a newspaper tend to contain numerous, often unrelated items, some of which are placed simply to fill up space that in the *New Quarterly* would remain blank or perhaps be decorated with a small type ornament.

If we look at the reprinting of Meredith's *The Case of General Ople and Lady Camper* in an American newspaper, the New York *Sun*, we see several typographical shifts. The last installment of Meredith's *The Case of General Ople and Lady Camper* appeared in the morning edition of the *Sun* on Sunday, 15 June 1890.[23] The space devoted to Meredith's story (it occupies nearly four columns of the page) and the noticeably larger type of its heading clearly differentiate it from the short, succinctly titled anecdotes that fill up the rest of the page. The heading that introduces the story provides a particularly good example of the kinds of information that a combination of typographical and verbal features can convey; in this instance, we can discover something about the *Sun*'s reasons for choosing this story and about the *Sun*'s assessment of its readership. The heading reads (in quasi-facsimile):[24]

'GEORGE MEREDITH, | [short rule] |GREATEST OF ENGLISH NOVELISTS, | [short rule] | Sends to The Sun this Original View | of English Life. | [short rule] | A WITTY AND INTERESTING STORY. [short rule] | THE CASE OF GEN. OPLE AND LADY CAMPER. | [short rule]'.

In this heading, 'GEORGE MEREDITH' is printed in the largest letters, while the story's title is printed in the smallest. This simple typographical fact, combined with the sequence of information (author's name first, title last) indicates that the *Sun*'s decision to print Meredith's story may have had more to do with the author's popularity (the *Sun*'s readers would recognize his name) than with the merits of the story itself. Of course, not all readers would recognize Meredith; hence the identification of him as the "greatest of English novelists." This, along with the description of the story as an "Original View of English Life," reveals that regardless of the value that the *Sun* and its audience may have placed upon Meredith's literary reputation, his nationality and the "English" nature of this story were its strongest selling points.

Bibliography has several roles to play in our consideration of serialization and the construction of the author. Serialization, as Laurel Brake has recently explained, exposes long fictional narratives "to the glare of the topical and the ephemeral, to structural rhythms of the part rather than the whole, and to disruption through juxtaposition with other discourses."[25] A list of contents identifies some of these competing discourses, while assessments of typographical elements and transcriptions of verbal cues such as headings offer information about how the *Sun* attempted to direct the reader's assessment of them. A bibliographically minded comparison between the installment of Meredith's *Case of General Ople* in the *Sun* and the short anecdote that immediately follows it, "John Smith's Luck," shows that if anything the typography and page layout of the newspaper emphasizes the disparity between the serialized story by the "greatest of English novelists" and the anonymous contribution from the *Lewiston Journal*. Meredith's story, with its elaborate heading, fills nearly half the page, and its end is marked both by the byline 'GEORGE MEREDITH' set thus in large and small capitals, and by the words "THE END." The heading for "John Smith's Luck," while slightly more elaborate than those of the other short items on the page, is still not on a par with that of Meredith's story. It reads:

'JOHN SMITH'S LUCK. | [short rule] | **Pocahontas Not the First Squaw to Get** | **Between Him and Harm.** | *From the Lewiston Journal.'*

The typographical format of this heading (italics for the title, boldface for the subtitle) is used for several other short pieces on the page, thus visually linking this item with them rather than with Meredith's story. The typography of the headings suggests visually the relative importance that the reader should place on each text: one is the last installment of a featured serial, the other is mere filler.

But the bibliographical fact of the juxtaposition of these two texts remains, and if as readers we choose to investigate it, we discover something important about the conditions of the Victorian literary marketplace. "John Smith's Luck" tells the story of Seboois, daughter of the chief of a tribe of Native Americans identified in the article as the Cabassa. Seboois, "famed among her tribe for beauty and grace," was "unfortunately smitten at once with the gallant Captain," and like Pocahontas, she supposedly protected Smith from the rest of her tribe. When the Cabassa mistakenly attacked Smith's party, Seboois "fled to him, threw her arms about his neck, and in that position received an arrow in the breast that caused instant death."

The juxtaposition of these bibliographical elements helps show some of the ways in which, from the reader's perspective, this narrative impinges upon the one that precedes it and vice versa. Meredith's story and the *Lewiston Journal's* anecdote both deal with a man whose careless "gallantry" is dangerous to women. Each breaks hearts, figuratively or (in Smith's case) literally. Both narratives link military and sexual conquest, and both represent ongoing concerns with issues of class, race, and gender in late-nineteenth-century Anglo-American culture. But the two texts also differ. Meredith's text emphasizes the moral culpability and real dangerousness of men like General Ople. Especially interesting is the fact that in this installment of *The Case*, Meredith also links the general's "sharp sarcasms upon women" to "quotations in the papers and the pulpit, his two main sources of information." According to Meredith, the problem with the misogynistic general is that he has read too many anecdotes like "John Smith's Luck," which despite its sympathy for the Cabassa expresses a certain admiration for the irresistible white male who colonizes native women along with native land. A bibliographically literate examination of the *Sun* may prompt us to question the ultimate separability of these texts. The design of the page may in some ways disconnect the two pieces, but their existence on the same page nevertheless forms a link between them.

Thus far we have seen that even if we limit ourselves to the consideration of a single publishing genre, such as the periodical, a bibliographical approach places the literary marketplace in a new perspective. Even though descriptive bibliographies do not usually engage in detailed bibliographical examination of periodicals, they often list an author's periodical publications. Such lists are inherently useful because they remind us that for nineteenth-century readers a writer's image formed not just from the first edition or from monolithic sets of collected works but from the shifting physical, social, and literary contexts of periodical contributions that in many cases count into the hundreds. If such lists were to include some bibliographical details, such as transcriptions of wrappers, lists of contents and illustrations, and descriptions of typography, they could be even more useful to readers who would like to determine how and why an author, in this case Meredith, whose stories appeared three times in the *New Quarterly Magazine*, differed from the Meredith whose poems appeared in *Once a Week* illustrated by woodcuts, or from the Meredith who published serialized novels in *Once a Week*, *Cornhill*, the *Fortnightly Review*, and the *Glasgow Weekly Herald*.[26]

One of the pitfalls of standard bibliographical practice is that the distinctions it makes between books and other publishing genres can keep us from seeing the similarities and interconnections that existed among various textual formats. But here, too, a shift in the emphasis of bibliographical research is all that is necessary to uncover what an at times narrow focus has hitherto obscured. A bibliographical examination of Meredith's publications in inexpensive paperback series allows us to identify the distinctive features of this publishing genre as well as the formal and conceptual similarities between series books, trade books, and more expensive collected "editions" of popular authors.

The first book publications of Meredith's stories took place in the United States, in series published by Harper, George Munro, and John Lovell. Book series are a hybrid publishing format that very much resembles the periodical in its juxtaposition of genres, authorial voices, and potential readerships within a fairly stable bibliographical environment. A bibliographical description of a book in a paperback series such as Lovell's would include a transcription of its wrappers (as well as its title page), thus allowing us to interpret the details by which publishers and readers recognized the book and contextualized its contents. The front cover of Lovell's *Case of General Ople* might be transcribed as follows:

Front cover (with 51 mm x 36.3 mm illustration of Westminster Abbey in upper left corner, beside lines 1–4 of text):
Nᵒ 3 25 Cts. | LOVELL'S | WESTMINSTER | SERIES | [rule, 110 mm] | *Entered at the Post Office, New York, as second class matter.* | [rule, 76 mm] | THE CASE OF | GEN'L OPLE AND | LADY CAMPER | BY | GEORGE MEREDITH | [rule, 33 mm] | NEW YORK | JOHN W. LOVELL COMPANY | 150 WORTH ST., COR. MISSION PLACE | ISSUED WEEKLY. ANNUAL SUBSCRIPTION, $12.00. JUNE 23, 1890 (EXTRA).

On the whole, the wrapper says more about the series itself (its title, frequency of publication, and subscription information) than it does about the text of this particular issue. The engraved cover design also leaves only so much space for the book title and author's name to be inserted; "General" is even abbreviated to "Gen'l" in order to fit the allotted space. Thus the design of the wrapper points toward one of the most salient features of the series format, namely, the subjugation of the individual text and author to the format and circumstances of the larger series.

A comparison of cheap series with regular trade and with limited or fine press editions uncovers additional ways in which we might consider bibliographical details as factors that publishers manipulate according to their ideas about a book's potential readership. Generally speaking, the cheaper the form of publication, the greater the emphasis placed upon the goals of the publisher and the needs of the reader, as the wrapper of Lovell's Westminster series demonstrates. In more expensive publishing genres, the goals of the publisher are presented as if they were secondary to those of the author, whose identity and authority is more likely to be expressed not only by means of the verbal text but in its physical and visual components. One can see this rather easily by comparing a wrapper like that of the Lovell edition of Meredith's *Case of General Ople* and the title page of the first British book publication of Meredith's stories by Ward, Lock & Bowden.

The title page of the British compilation of the stories (large paper issue) appears as follows:

THE TALE OF CHLOE – THE |HOUSE ON THE BEACH – | THE CASE OF GENERAL | OPLE AND LADY CAMPER | BY | *George* | *Meredith* | LONDON | WARD, LOCK & BOWDEN, LIMITED | WARWICK HOUSE, SALISBURY SQUARE, E. C. | NEW YORK AND MELBOURNE | 1894 | [*All rights reserved*]27

Here, the book's title and the name of its author occupy most of the page. The title is printed all in capital letters, with a large initial capital; Meredith's name also stands out on the page because it is spread over two lines and italicized. By contrast, the publishing information that appears after Meredith's name was minimized by especially small fonts used for the last two lines. This is a far cry from the front wrapper of Lovell's edition and even from Lovell's formulaic title page, on which Meredith is identified as the 'Author of "Chloe," "Diana of the Crossways," "The Egoist," etc,. etc.,'. While Lovell's tactic seems to outdo the Ward, Lock title page by focusing even more attention on the author, the author identification (a variation of which occurs on each of the Lovell series titles) actually works to enhance the quality of the series by playing up the accomplishments of its contributors.

The ultimate in the book as representation of its author (rather than its publisher or series) is the limited edition, which functions to remove both the verbal and the physical texts from their proximity to other works and books, not excluding other works and books by the same writer or issued by the same publisher. The purpose of a special edition is to constitute both the writer and the material text as separate from and superior to all other versions of the text and writer in question. Constable's "Edition de Luxe" of Meredith (1896–98, 1910–11) illustrates this point quite clearly. Every detail of the edition, from its words to the paper it is printed on, pays tribute to Meredith's reputation, authority, and individuality. Even though Meredith's revisions to the text, stipulated in the contract, may have been made in order to secure the American copyright for the new edition,[28] Constable's prospectus for the edition presents the revisions as proof of the Edition de Luxe's fidelity to Meredith's aesthetic intentions: "Mr. Meredith has revised his works for this edition, which he wishes to be regarded as textually final."[29]

The physical details of the Edition de Luxe, as described in the prospectus and stipulated in Meredith's contract, seem to give Meredith a physical and visual, as well as a verbal, presence in the text. Meredith's contract with Constable made plain "that the edition shall be such as to meet the author's views as to paper, type, binding and all details." No records exist to show whether Meredith actually exercised these rights, but Constable's prospectus, and the books themselves, show that someone made sure that the "details" of its construction not only proclaimed the care and expense with which it was manufactured but also took every opportunity to suggest the author's involvement. The rarity of the edition itself was expressed in its limited print run of 1,025 copies (each numbered and signed by Meredith's son William), by its typography (the prospectus said that it was to be printed from "a fount specially made for this edition"), and its paper.

A bibliographer who examined this paper would find something that the prospectus doesn't mention: a watermark comprised of Meredith's initials. The watermark is the ultimate statement of the extension of the writer's authority beyond the verbal into the material aspects of the text. The degree to which the material text not only mediates the verbal text but also participates in the reader's conception of an author is underscored by the personalization of Constable's edition. Only a bibliographical approach can make visible the full effects of this display of a writer's "authority," signified not only in words but in the type from which they were formed and the paper on which they were printed.

A bibliographically literate consideration of this text might also discover some similarities between it and other publishing genres. The set of collected works differs in many ways from cheap book series, but in some ways the two perform similar functions. Cheap and expensive texts are remarkably similar in the commodification of the works or writers that they represent, for example. A deluxe edition conferred a special status upon an author, if only because it indicated a reputation strong enough to make an expensive printing saleable. Meredith's Edition de Luxe sold well: over half the issue was subscribed before the prospectus was even printed.[30] And buyers who purchased such an edition participated in the canonization of the author in question. Ironically, Meredith, who always felt himself to be at odds with the reading public because of his refusal to give them the "rose-pink" sentimentality that they demanded, ended up in mauve boards and linen spines to suit the tastes of readers who, like the Pole sisters he had satirized in *Rhoda Fleming*, may well have valued his work only because it had become fashionable to do so, and for whom the expensive volumes served as comforting tokens of social and economic status. That Constable followed the deluxe edition with a less-expensive "Library" edition emphasizes the phenomenon of the collected edition – all the author's works in a standardized form – as a physical embodiment of Meredith as "standard" reading for the middle class.

What we see, however, is that in every format, no matter what its intended audience, Meredith is in some way being offered up, to use the *Sun*'s phrase, as the "greatest English novelist," the new Victorian sage. Purchasers of the "pocket" edition of Meredith (1902–?), a new impression of the plates of the Constable and Scribner Library edition, found Meredith's signature (British issue) or initials (American issue) stamped in gilt on the front cover, an even more visible reminder of the extent to which Meredith's name had become a late nineteenth-century publisher's version of the designer label. The variety of printed materials made available through innovations in nineteenth-century printing technology results, ironically, in a more thorough standardization of the public's conception of authors like Meredith, and the packaging of "established" authors, which brings the physical text into conformity with all of the widely varying expectations (economic, aesthetic, social) of a mass audience, demonstrates the malleability of the words and especially the public image of a popular writer. These are some of the cultural consequences of a technology that made it possible for "Meredith" to become, in any one document, whatever the publisher thought the reader might want him to be.

Those who study texts as physical embodiments of literary, historical, and cultural concerns need to realize the role that bibliographical research can play in clarifying our understanding of these concerns. In the case of Meredith, analytical bibliography can help us see how each of the physical formats through which his works met the public expressed the intentions of their producers, which in turn contributed something to the ways in which readers perceived those works and to their conceptions of Meredith himself. Bibliography also allows a greater awareness of the complexity of the marketplace in which the works of Meredith, and of his contemporaries, were produced, distributed, and read. The most cursory scan of the items described and listed in a descriptive bibliography prompts us to consider the marketplace in terms of the juxtapositions contained in any one text, as well as the juxtapositions of whole documents against each other. Careful consideration of the physical details of these printed materials is the essential first step toward discovering what those details meant to Victorian readers, and what they might now mean to us.

NOTES

1 See Cathy Davidson, "Toward a History of Books and Readers" and Robert Darnton, "What is the History of the Book?" in *Reading in America: Literature and Social History*, ed. Cathy Davidson (Baltimore: Johns Hopkins University Press, 1989); G. T. Tanselle, introduction to *Books and Society in History*, ed. Kenneth Carpenter (New York: R. R. Bowker, 1983), and "The History of Books as a Field of Study" (Chapel Hill: University of North Carolina Press, 1981).

2 See, for example, Jerome J. McGann, introduction to *Historical Studies and Literary Criticism* (Madison: University of Wisconsin Press, 1985), and "The Monks and the Giants: Textual and Bibliographical Studies and the Interpretation of Literary Works" in *The Beauty of Inflections: Literary Investigations in Historical Method and Theory* (Oxford: Clarendon, 1985), 69–89; D. F. McKenzie, *Bibliography and the Sociology of Texts*, the Panizzi Lectures, 1985 (London: The British Library, 1986), and Tanselle's commentary on McGann, McKenzie, and others in "Textual Criticism and Literary Sociology," *Studies in Bibliography* 44 (1991), 83–143.

3 McGann, *Historical Studies*, 4.

4 Donald G. Marshall, "Literary Interpretation," in *Introduction to Scholarship in Modern Languages and Literatures*, ed. Joseph Gibaldi (New York: Modern Language Association of America, 1992), 163.

5 Tanselle, introduction, *Books and Society in History*, xx–xxi.

6 Darnton, 29.

7 McGann observed as late as 1988 that "courses in textual criticism and bibliography are no longer required in most graduate schools, and often they are not even available to the student." "Monks and Giants," 70. Interested students and scholars can attend a variety of

286 MAURA IVES

bibliographically oriented courses at the Rare Book School held every summer at the University of Virginia.

8 G. T. Tanselle, in "A Description of Descriptive Bibliography," *Studies in Bibliography* 45 (1991), 1–30, and "A Sample Bibliographical Description, with Commentary," *Studies in Bibliography* 40 (1987), 1–30, offers a good introduction to the history, purposes, and methodology of descriptive bibliography; Fredson Bowers's *Principles of Descriptive Bibliography* (1949; Winchester, UK: St. Paul's Bibliographies, 1986) remains the essential advanced text in the field. Additional practical and theoretical considerations are covered in Tanselle's *Selected Studies in Bibliography* (Charlottesville: University Press of Virginia, 1979) and Fredson Bowers's *Essays in Bibliography, Text and Editing* (Charlottesville: University Press of Virginia, 1975).

9 Darnton, 43.

10 W. W. Greg, "Bibliography: An Apologia," in *Collected Papers*, ed. J. C. Maxwell (Oxford: Clarendon, 1966), 247.

11 McKenzie, x.

12 The shortcomings of McKenzie's work are discussed by Tanselle in "Textual Criticism and Literary Sociology." This chapter attempts to offer what Tanselle finds lacking in McKenzie, namely, "an illustration of the way in which format, type design, and layout can convey meanings and are thus 'textual'" (92–93).

13 McKenzie, 20, 8.

14 Tanselle, "Textual Criticism," 93.

15 McKenzie, 4.

16 Cathy Davidson, "The Life and Times of *Charlotte Temple*: The Biography of a Book," in *Reading In America*, 171.

17 I take this term from Peter Shillingsburg's "Text as Matter, Concept, and Action," *Studies in Bibliography* 44 (1991), 31–82, where it is defined as "the union of Linguistic Text and Document: A Sign Sequence held in a medium of display" (81).

18 I do this because both Forman and Collie are often sparse and even inaccurate in their descriptions of American editions and editions beyond the first. The omissions in Forman's *Bibliography* and *Meredithiana* (Edinburgh: The Bibliographical Society, 1924) primarily reflect the state of the field at that time, whereas Collie's *George Meredith* (Toronto: University of Toronto Press for Wm. Dawson & Sons, UK, 1974), published more that twenty years after Bowers's landmark *Principles of Bibliographical Description*, seems to reflect both ignorance of the advances that had taken place in the field and poor handling of data (as when he, like Forman, fails to notice the canceled leaf in the first British edition of *An Essay on Comedy*). Some of the shortcomings of Collie's work are dealt with in James Stone, "Errata in Michael Collie's Bibliography of George Meredith," *Bulletin of Bibliography* 43, 44–53, and in the

descriptive bibliography that accompanies my "George Meredith's Publications in the *New Quarterly Magazine*: A Critical Edition" (Ph.D. dissertation; University of Virginia, 1990).

19 *The House on the Beach* appeared in vol. 7, January 1877 (329–410); *The Case* in vol. 8, July 1877 (428–78); and *The Tale*, in vol. 12 old series/ vol. 2 new series, July 1879 (57–113).

20 John Lewis, *Anatomy of Printing: The Influence of Art and History on its Design* (New York: Watson-Guptill, 1970), 199.

21 My observations are based on an examination of volumes of *Illustrated London News* 70 (January to June 1877), the *Fortnightly*, n.s. 21 (January to June 1877), and the *Edinburgh* 145 (January to April 1877) at Texas A&M University, and the volumes of the *New Quarterly Magazine* at Northwestern University. All the volumes consulted had been rebound; none retained the original wrappers, an extremely important point of comparison for Victorian periodicals. My observations concerning the *Cornhill* 35 (January to June 1877) are based upon examination of a microfilm copy produced by University Microfilms.

22 Walter E. Houghton, "The *New Quarterly Magazine*, 1873–80," in *The Wellesley Index to Victorian Periodicals, 1824–1900*, ed. Walter Houghton *et al.* (5 vols.; Toronto: University of Toronto Press, 1966–89), vol. 2, 608.

23 Both *The Case* and *The Tale of Chloe* appeared in the *Sun*'s Sunday morning edition in the summer of 1891. *The Case* was printed in three installments: chapters 1–3 (no. 274, June 1, 23); chapters 4–6 (no. 281, June 8, 22) and chapters 7–8 (no. 288, June 15, 21). *The Tale* appeared in four installments: chapters 1–3 (no. 295, June 22, 18); chapters 4–5 (no. 302, June 29, 15); chapters 6–8 (no. 309, July 6, 16), and chapters 9–10 (no. 316, July 13, 15).

24 I follow the bibliographical convention of using single quotation marks to distinguish quasi-facsimile transcription from regular quotation, for which double marks are used. A description can be found in Tanselle's "A Sample Bibliographical Description."

25 Laurel Brake, "Production of Meaning in Periodical Studies: Versions of the *English Review*," *Victorian Periodicals Review* 4 (1991), 168.

26 Scott Bennett has advocated the bibliographical description of periodicals in two essays: "The Bibliographic Control of Victorian Periodicals," in *Victorian Periodicals: A Guide to Research*, ed. J. Don Vann and Rosemary T. Van Arsdel (New York: Modern Language Association, 1978) and "Prolegomenon to Serials Bibliography: A Report to the Society," *Victorian Periodicals Review* 12 (1979), 3–15. The Research Society for Victorian Periodicals has also produced an unpublished manual that offers much useful information for the prospective bibliographer: John Palmer *et al.*, Manual for the Bibliographical Description of Serials: Preliminary Draft, 1980.

27 There were four issues of the first edition of this book (the British large paper issue, British small paper, American small paper, and colonial small paper), each of which is described in my "George Meredith's Publications," 851–63. A second edition was printed by the same publisher in 1896.

28 The contract for the edition, dated 1 February 1896, is at the University of Texas at Austin; it stipulates that Meredith was "at liberty to make such additions, extracts & alterations, in all or any of his works as he may consider necessary." The correspondence between Constable and Scribner in the Scribner Archives at Princeton (author files, box 101) includes several references to Meredith's revisions. In a letter dated 2 September 1896, Otto Kyllman, a Constable representative, tells Charles Scribner that "we can furnish you with the revised final text of all the works, which you could of course copyright, I may mention that there are several alterations in the various volumes." In a subsequent letter to the Scribner firm (17 September 1886), William Meredith (George's son and literary representative, who worked for Constable) refers to "my father's alterations and corrections, which renders this copyright possible." That the revisions were both practically and aesthetically motivated is suggested by William Meredith's further comment that "in some of the volumes they [the revisions] do not amount to very much, but in the case of the others, and as it chances some of the most popular, Richard Feverel for instance, the alterations and improvements have been very considerable."

29 A copy of the prospectus is in the Beinecke Library, Yale University.

30 Otto Kyllman, letter to Charles Scribner, 2 September 1896, Scribner Archives (author files, box 101), Princeton University Library, Princeton, N.J.

CHAPTER 13

The *"wicked* Westminster," *the* Fortnightly, *and Walter Pater's* Renaissance

Laurel Brake

I shall begin with the book and the named author because that form with that authority is where "Eng. Lit." normally starts, and that is the discourse in which Pater's *Renaissance* volume has been primarily circulated. However, I want to register a protest as I commit the act: if I were writing in the discourse of publishing history, I would not begin with the book or the author but with the periodicals in which most of the articles in the book first appeared, their names and those of their editors; the titles of articles, both Pater's and the others' in the issues in which his appeared; the formats and character of the journals; how much they cost and who published them; and whether the articles were anonymous (as most nineteenth-century articles were) or signed. I shall argue that in the case of Pater's pieces in the *Westminster Review* and the *Fortnightly* the character of the two journals and what appeared in them at the time Pater contributed – their different formats (review versus article, quarterly versus monthly, anonymity versus signature), politics (radical versus liberal), and dominant discourses (philosophical/polemical versus literary), significantly affected the nature of the pieces that Pater wrote for them and then recirculated in the *Renaissance* volume.

The book form in the Victorian period was only one of the dominant forms in which literature appeared, and it was heavily dependent in all manner of ways on periodicals: economically, for adverts, for trailers, and for first whetting and then reinforcing the appetite of the reading audience for reading itself; for specific genres (the serial novel); and for works by specific authors.[1] It is not only textual critics who should be looking at periodical versions of Victorian literature, but all critics who study the subject whose interests include the dissemination and circulation of print and of ideas, different and multiple reading audiences, and publishing networks. George Saintsbury, in his 1896 *History of Nineteenth Century Literature*, written from the "inside," is quite explicit about the relation of the periodical and book forms in the period.

Perhaps there is no single feature of the English literary history of the nineteenth century, not even the enormous popularisation and multiplication of the novel, which is so distinctive and characteristic as the development in it of periodical literature . . . Very large numbers of the best as well as of the worst novels themselves have originally appeared in periodicals; not a very small proportion of the most noteworthy nineteenth century poetry has had the same origin; it may almost be said that all the best work in essay, whether critical, meditative, or miscellaneous, has thus been ushered into the world. Even the severer and more academic divisions of – history, philosophy, theology, and their sisters, have condescended to avail themselves of this means of obtaining a public audience; and though there is still a certain conventional decency in apologizing for reprints from periodicals, it is quite certain that, had such reprints not taken place, more than half the most valuable books of the age in some departments, and a considerable minority of the most valuable in others, would never have appeared as books at all.[2]

Walter Pater's *Studies in the History of the Renaissance*, which appeared in 1873, had its conceptual and material origins in the periodical press in which the bulk of it first appeared. The book is comprised of essays with two types of publishing history: those (six) written for and previously published in periodicals and those (four) written in 1872 exclusively for the *Renaissance* volume. The periodical essays in turn are distinguished from each other by the origin of the periodical in which they appeared. Two, the boldest and arguably the most weighty, are reviews. Appearing anonymously in the *Westminster Review* in 1867 and 1868, they were identified as Pater's only by their appearance in the signed *Studies*, and proved the most controversial for reviewers of the volume. The later periodical essays, published in the *Fortnightly Review* between 1869 and 1871 and free from the constraints of the review form, treated linked subjects determined by Pater's choice rather than the vagaries of book publication at a particular time. It may also be argued that the *Fortnightly*'s policy of signature elicited more discreet and possibly more conventional signed essays from Pater, on Leonardo, Botticelli, Michelangelo, and Pico della Mirandola.[3]

In 1873, the "conventional decency in apologizing for reprints from periodicals", noted by Saintsbury in 1896, took a more inhibited form. Pater's book produces the transformation of "journalism" into "art" tacitly, without any explicit admission. The nature of the embarrassment in the journalistic origins of the aesthetic book may be gauged from its author's concern with the detail of the appearance of the book – the quality of the paper and the color and material of the binding – in the correspondence with Macmillan's. The book is meant to look and feel quite distinct from a journalistic and serialized commodity. That said, the two periodicals nurtured this young author, and in turn left their imprint on his work. Implicated in the intertextuality that the *Renaissance* and the two periodicals share are the occasional dimension of these essays, the dominant discourses of the periodicals, the different sequences in which the texts appear, and the different audiences they address. The juxtapositions and disjunctions of the 1873 *Renaissance* text, commented on by some reviews, are due in part to distinct forms of literary production and the inscriptions of the suppressed "voices" and texts of the *Westminster Review* and the *Fortnightly*.

The author in question was a young and new classics fellow at Brasenose College, Oxford, and something of a rarity insofar as he held a nonclerical fellowship; that is, unlike the great preponderance of his colleagues, he had not taken holy orders. This decided and outstanding secularism was to distinguish his periodical work in the 1860s and to be one of the bases of his contributions to the *Westminster* and the *Fortnightly*, renowned for their freedom from the yoke of theology and for their commitment to rationalism. None of the essays Pater published in the 1860s would have been welcome to editors or readers working within an Anglican framework. John Morley, editor of the *Fortnightly* at the time Pater published there, unashamedly reviewed the *Renaissance* in 1873, and he makes plain the *Fortnightly*'s stance on theology and on Pater:

But here is Mr. Pater courageously saying that the love of art for art's sake has most of the true wisdom that makes life full. The fact that such a saying is possible in the mouth of an able and shrewd-witted man of wide culture and knowledge, and that a serious writer should thus raise aesthetic interest to the throne lately filled by religion, only shows how void the old theologies have become.[4]

There is one other point about Pater's periodical writing in the 1860s. It appeared to have very little to do with his formal university work in classics, and the divergence is significant. In twentieth-century terms Pater had two careers in this early period, one in the university and one as a journalist, writer, and eventually "author." English literature was not yet a degree subject, nor was art history. While the world of contemporary writing, then as now, included a significant proportion of university staff, the divergence between topics of teaching and those of writing was often far greater than at present, as the syllabuses of the oldest universities were so restricted. But there is a covert link, one that was to be publicly alleged by censorious colleagues and critics in the aftermath of book publication.

I want to turn now to the *Westminster Review*, which in the early 1860s was in the position of appearing with a frequency (quarterly), in a format (the review), and at a price that were soon to be supplanted as the dominant periodical form by competition from the new, cheaper monthly magazines typified, after 1860, by the *Cornhill* and *Macmillan's*. However, John Chapman, unlike the editors of the other quarterlies, had brought new intellectual vigor to the quarterly in the 1850s in the wide range and nonpartisan scope of the *Westminster*'s reformist articles and in the emphasis it placed on both foreign and contemporary literature, which had its own sizeable section each quarter, written by erudite, if anonymous, contributors. Such was the value Chapman placed on this latter category that he paid two guineas more per sheet (twelve guineas rather than ten) to authors of this section. That was at the beginning, however. Chapman proved an atrocious businessman, quickly, and at least twice he had to sell off portions of the business and borrow money to keep afloat, before he had to sell out entirely. By 1866, when Pater began publishing there, Chapman was paying existing contributors only £5 per sheet and new contributors like J. A. Symonds (and Pater) nothing.

It could be argued, as James Sully does in his *Life*, that this omission of pay "gave more than one beginner a chance of publicity which might otherwise have been missed";[5] but there is good reason to believe that under these conditions Chapman had difficulty attracting new writers of renown to his journal. Given the anonymity of contributions, the dearth of copy from the famous might well be made up by unattributed material from neophytes such as Pater – willing, even grateful to be published without pay. So Pater, as an unpublished young writer, took the opening the *Westminster* afforded, but unsurprisingly, when the new *Fortnightly Review* was transformed by a change of editor and Pater's work became publishable there, he left the *Westminster* and never returned.

However, the work Pater published in the *Westminster* bears its inscription indelibly: the expansiveness and outspoken nature of "Winckelmann" and "Poems by William Morris" engendered by the discourse of the *Westminster* were to haunt Pater's subsequent career as a writer and university lecturer. These two essays are the earliest included in the *Renaissance* volume, and they represent a selection from the three pieces Pater published in the periodical between January 1866 and October 1868, all of which can be seen directly to address contemporary literature and culture. Of these, two treated modern, nineteenth-century work, the first in January 1866 – on "Coleridge's Writings,"[6] and the last in October 1868 – on "Poems by William Morris."[7] Coleridge had died only some thirty years before in 1834, and Morris was alive. The middle essay in January 1867 – on "Winckelmann,"[8] the eighteenth-century German classicist and writer on aesthetics, though apparently the most scholarly and antiquarian, is arguably the most committed, and as oriented to the contemporary reader as the Morris essay. These two characteristics – commitment and contemporaneity – which are so distinctive in all of Pater's *Westminster* pieces derive, I want to suggest, from the discourse of the periodical in which they appeared.

Although with the advent of John Chapman's reign as editor in 1851, all connections with the Philosophical Radicals and Benthamite origins of the *Westminster Review* were severed,[9] Chapman's support of freethinking and skepticism did not falter.[10] From the outset, the *Wellesley Index* claims,[11] Chapman's deployment of able and advanced thinkers made the *Westminster* as preeminent in the 1850s among its fellows as it had been under John Stuart Mill. Throughout the 1850s and 1860s Chapman published an array of bold, groundbreaking articles that attest to this, and Pater's pieces, on a number of counts, are among them.

For a new and young writer, the conditions of publication in the *Westminster* and its discourses were empowering in a number of ways. First of all, whatever Pater wrote, he was relatively (and certainly formally) safe under the system of anonymity that the *Westminster* offered as an older periodical, unlike many of its younger, cheaper competitors; in particular, the fledgling

Fortnightly (beginning in May 1865) was to make its name on the platform of signature, and to induce many others in the next decade to follow it. The safety of the anonymity afforded by the *Westminster* is shown by the denunciations in print and in the pulpit that greeted the *Westminster* portions of the *Renaissance* in and after 1873.[12]

Secondly, the reformist, freethinking, and radical posture of the *Westminster* offered a nonclerical fellow, interested in intellectual growth and self-exploration, friendly and open space. In the event, the *Westminster* allowed Pater to publish robustly expressed anti-Christian and profane notions with provocative juxtapositions between Christian and pagan in favor of the latter. Moreover, particularly but not only in "Winckelmann," he utilized the opportunity the periodical vouchsafed him to proselytize the philosophy of Greek love and (male) beauty and friendship, and to attempt and to polish a homosexual discourse. This element of Pater's *Westminster* essays may be compared with the numerous articles there in the 1860s in support of improvement of the position of women;[13] that is, the subject of gender and a gender discourse in connection with women were carried in this quarterly simultaneously with Pater's exploration of male culture and male discourse. I know of no other mainstream, nineteenth-century periodical of comparable profile at the time that carried such explicit material on gender across the board, unless it was to denounce it.[14]

Lastly, the *Westminster* countenanced a model of reform outside of the positions and power bases of the two dominant political parties, and repeatedly published exemplars of discourses that were both philosophical and proselytizing. Thus the endings of the essays on Winckelmann and Morris, which are at once formally discrete in their generality from what precedes them and so lengthy as to be unapologetically more than mere conclusions, are expansive (and dangerous) statements of conviction about the nature of life and art that come very near to instruction. In this they echo, for example, the endings of the two essays that precede and follow "Winckelmann."

These two essays are informative about the nature of the *Westminster* in the late 1860s in relation to their subject as well as their discourses. They are blatantly political and reformist. The sequence of articles[15] in the October 1868 number, in which the Morris essay appears, exemplifies these characteristics of Chapman's *Westminster* in the 1860s. It includes two articles on the position of women and three on sensitive political questions such as middle-class schools, civil-service reform, and land tenure. The article preceding "Winckelmann" in the January 1867 number that treats "The Ladies' Petition" (that petition of 1,500 signatures asking for voting rights for women property owners) includes in its final paragraphs: "But, in fact, as we have already pointed out, it is too late to be afraid of letting English women share in the life of Englishmen. We cannot shut up our women in harems, and devote them to the cultivation of their beauty and of their children."[16] The last paragraph of "Irish University Education," the piece following "Winckelmann," announces: "Here then we have a counter-proposition to the plan of the late Government – one the idea of which is eminently clear, logical, and complete, the operation of which would satisfy all just demands."[17] A *Westminster Review* article on "Church and State" that appeared in July 1868, the number before the Morris review was published, has an uncompromising initial paragraph[18] that Pater could well be echoing and reinforcing in his Morris essay in the following number. "Doubt is the parent of certainty, the precursor of knowledge," it reads in part:

Those who accept theories upon trust and as traditions, without doubting and testing and inquiring, can never attain to truth. And this is the case not only in physical science, but in morals, in politics, in religion. It is the most hopeful sign of our time that the sceptical and critical spirit, which has accomplished so much in the field of speculative labour, has begun to leaven the heavy inanimate irrational mass of political theory. We have worshipped constitutional fetishes too long; we are asked to give a reason for our faith; and so we are led first to doubt, then to test and examine, to prove, to reject, to modify, to recreate.

As part of such a series of articles, the exhortations in the conclusions of "Winckelmann" and "Poems by William Morris" to follow the model of "passionate coldness,"[19] for example, or to pursue joy or "an equivalent for the sense of freedom,"[20] appear unexceptionable, and no more *outré* in their contents than the enfranchising of women property owners or the brisk resolution of the unrest in Ireland.

The clear reformist element of these *Westminster* articles arises in part out of the close relation between readers and text that pertained in Victorian serial publication. Transferred to the pages of a bound and attributed book that is to be reviewed, these conclusions may well have proved inflammatory. Moreover, the hardy, seasoned, and habitual readers of the *Westminster Review* were predictably more likely to tolerate material of this nature than the readers and reviewers of *Studies in the History of the Renaissance*, who were ill-prepared for the contents of the book, which appeared from its title to be uncontentious and to pertain to history or art history. So despite the small readership of the first edition of the book – 1,250 copies of the *Renaissance* were printed in 1873[21] compared with the *Westminster*'s circulation of 4,000 in the 1860s[22] – transplantation of the *Westminster* essays to the *Renaissance* was bound to be risky due to the different if overlapping readership groups, and perhaps the high price of the book format.

There is one other factor that contributed to the extreme visibility that book publication conferred on the *Westminster* essays. These, the earliest writings in the collection, were grouped together at the end of the *Renaissance*, forming a double conclusion. The general (and extreme) statement treating the philosophy of life and art that appears at the end of the Morris essay in the *Westminster* reappears in the *Renaissance* as the conclusion to the entire book; truncated from its initial link with Morris's notion of an earthly paradise, the conclusion's valorization of heightened experience over all else[23] is very exposed. Likewise the "Winckelmann" essay, only tenuously linked with the Renaissance of the title through its neoclassicism, may be read in the book as primarily oriented to problems of modern life, in parallel with the "Conclusion" that follows. Its advocacy of male friendship and homosexual love, to say nothing of its approval of Winckelmann's conversion to Catholicism, a conversion of convenience, speak directly to nineteenth-century readers and the preoccupations of their period – which brings me to the review format of these *Westminster* essays.

When the essays were published in the periodical the titles of the books reviewed appeared as a headnote. Pater utilizes this convention differently in the Winckelmann and Morris essays. In the former, earlier essay he hardly defers to the biography he is ostensibly reviewing, or the translation of Winckelmann's work also listed. But the article carries a number of footnotes, from Goethe, Hegel, Quinet, Hermann, and Palgrave. These, and the format of biography, provide the author with an authority, a front, for the introduction of morally sensitive material, as do citations from Winckelmann's writings on Greek statuary. In the Morris review the successive books of poetry are more foregrounded and function similarly, as a blind to the authorial voice. This suppression of the authorial voice, its assumption into the form, except in the conclusion to each piece, is a technique that Pater was to develop assiduously. Pater's later capacity to absorb others' work seamlessly (and invisibly) into his own prose, and to inform quotations from others scholars with his own unacknowledged emendations or gloss, would worry later scholars, particularly those of our own period imbued with scholastic criteria of attribution and accuracy of quotation and allusion. These *Westminster* pieces, with their review format, permitted, even encouraged, fluid movement between the text "reviewed" and the new, review text.

I want to turn now to the *Fortnightly* and Pater's essays that appeared there and subsequently in the *Renaissance*. I think there were several reasons why Pater transferred his work from the *Westminster* to the *Fortnightly* in 1869. From its first number in May 1865, the *Fortnightly* appeared decidedly more literary than the contemporaneous *Westminster*. The *Fortnightly* included a serialized novel by Trollope, an article by George Eliot, a review of Swinburne's *Atalanta in Calydon*, a serialized manual on success in literature by the editor, and signed reviews by the art critic F. T. Palgrave and George Eliot, among others, while the April 1865 *Westminster* allocated only one of its six articles to literature, in a long piece on "Modern Novelists: Sir Edward Bulwer-Lytton," and reviewed no fiction in the contemporary literature section of that number. For Pater, however, there was a hitch: G. H. Lewes, the first editor, though an early defender of realism in literature and a frequent reviewer of fiction, seems to have shared George Eliot's distaste for aestheticism. Some features of Lewes's *Fortnightly* suggest a view of literature inimical to Pater's work, while others, such as the intensity of the literary and visual art coverage, might appear promising.

Although Swinburne's poems were not published by Lewes, two reviews of his work appeared, one of *Atalanta in Calydon* by J. Leicester Warren in the first number in May 1865,[24] and another of *Chastelard* by Swinburne's friend Lord Houghton in April 1866.[25] It is notable that Lewes inserted the phrase "minor poet" into Warren's review of *Atalanta*[26] and that Houghton's review is full of caveats (also stemming from the editor?) that dominate the onset of the review essay. Since the journal carried fiction, the following prominent and coded warnings seem addressed to the women who might be counted among the readership: "The public to which Mr. Swinburne appeals will consist exclusively of those readers who enjoy a work of art for its own sake, and who care more for the power of the representation than for any worth in what is represented; and these will always be few,"[27] and "a wilful complicity of intellectual artifice and sensuous desires repels and shocks beyond the real demerits of the artist."[28] Six months later, in October 1866, a similar early warning to women readers appeared in Moncure Conway's article on Whitman,[29] which begins with anecdotal allusions to attempts to read the poem aloud in mixed company and continues "The plainness of speech in 'Leaves of Grass' is indeed biblical; there is, too, a startling priapism running through it."[30]

Lewes's *Fortnightly* inscribes tensions of gender in the period; as the male editor of a new and "progressive" periodical carrying the gendered (and male) discourse of such a formation, he is forced to take women as well as male readers into some account. Having widened the remit of the new journal beyond that of the older serious (quarterly) periodicals to include fiction and to attract women readers, Lewes had to contend with them as readers of nonfiction as well. This he did, interestingly, not by excluding subjects deemed inappropriate to women (religion, philosophy, politics) as the *Cornhill* did beginning in 1860, but by inserting prominent warnings into articles on dangerous topics "unsuitable" for respectable women readers. The maleness of the dominant discourse in Lewes's *Fortnightly* was maintained and identified by these coded notices to women to "keep out."

Other features of Lewes's *Fortnightly* may have signaled to Pater the ambiguities of the periodical's position. On the plus side, in addition to the two review articles on Swinburne, whom Pater knew in this period, there were also full-length pieces on the poetry of Arnold, Morris, Clough, and Whitman, and two lengthy essays on theory. Moreover, Pater's friend Oscar Browning published an article in February 1866[31] in the same volume in which Houghton, Swinburne's friend, published his review of *Chastelard*. The periodical not only touched on Pater's immediate interests – theory, visual art, poetry, the poems of Morris, and the homosexual poetry of Whitman, but it also intersected Pater's literary circle – Swinburne, J. A. Symonds, Oscar Browning, Morris, and F. T. Palgrave.

On the negative side was Lewes's commitment to morality in art, a position that is aired, if not advocated, in both the articles on art theory that appear between May 1865 and December 1867, when Lewes relinquished the editorship. P. G. Hamerton's "The Artistic Spirit" in the first number[32] appears scientific by its division into nine topics that are rationally considered in turn, but it proves to be the effort of a professional artist but amateur critic who hedges his bets and proceeds with extreme caution: mildly defending art from the inroads of commercialism, religion, morality, and the bourgeois, military, and intellectual spirits, he contemplates the dangers of "the principle of art for art"[33] while embracing the artist's commitment to it:

A pernicious principle in one way, that it tends to deprive painting of much of its influence over the public by directing its efforts to aims in which the public cannot possibly take any interest, and yet a principle which has always had great weight with artists, which regulates the admission of pictures to exhibitions, and has more influence than any other consideration in determining the rank which an artist's name must ultimately hold in the catalogue of masters.[34]

If this empirical defence of art for art would not have satisfied Pater's philosophical mind, the limitations of Hamerton's theoretical position for Pater are explicit in Hamerton's intolerance of criticism and intellect: "The unfeigned contempt which almost all artists feel for critics – even for the best of them – is partly explicable by the fact that the artistic spirit can neither appreciate nor follow intellectual methods."[35] Hamerton published seven articles in Lewes's twenty-month reign, and only three after Morley took over, one (appearing in the February 1867 issue) almost certainly commissioned by Lewes.

The other arts theorist of Lewes's *Fortnightly* was Robert Buchanan, whose frequent appearances as poet, critic, and reviewer in the Lewes years identify him as an object of the editor's patronage. Buchanan, who vehemently attacked Swinburne, Rossetti, the Pre-Raphaelites, and the aesthetes in "The Fleshly School of Poetry" in the *Contemporary Review* in October 1871,[36] shows his early critical colors in one of his numerous contributions to the early *Fortnightly*, "Immorality in Authorship," which appeared in volume 4 in September 1866.[37] Increasingly intemperate ("It is fortunate that few females read Mrs. Behn; filth on a woman's lips shocks us infinitely more than filth on the lips of a man. No woman can utter a 'gaudriole' and keep her soul feminine. She becomes a raving and sexless Atys"[38]), this article moves from a position that links morality with sincerity and denies that morality is bigotry to the argument that immoral books must be winkled out of their willful obscurity and exposed: "It requires an occult judgment nowadays to find out immoral books . . . A shower of immoral books pours out yearly; many of them are read by religious societies and praised by Bishops, and by far the larger number of them find favour with Mr. Mudie."[39]

Published in September 1866 just before Morley's editorship, this was the last item Buchanan published in the *Fortnightly*, and Morley contested its assertion of the link between morality and literature at his first opportunity in the "Causeries"[40] he contributed to his first number as editor in January 1867. Using a critic from the *Pall Mall Gazette* as his apparent addressee, he denied the relevance of morality to art and displaced it with an aesthetic emphasis on the centrality of the Beautiful. In a series of categoric rebuttals of Buchanan's position, Morley signaled and prepared for the about-face of the *Fortnightly* from a journal antipathetic to aestheticism to one that was to foster it in its subsequent defense and publication of Swinburne and Pater. "Morality" he claimed, "is not the aim and goal of fine art, any more than it is an aim or measure of cobbling or the art of physic. Art has for its end the Beautiful, and the Beautiful only. Morality, so far from being of the essence of it, has nothing to do with it at all."[41] It seems clear from the intensification of this argument that he was attacking not only the critic on the *Pall Mall Gazette* and Buchanan in the *Fortnightly* in the preceding quotation but Hamerton in the following:

It would be a great improvement if we could all learn to enjoy the multiform Beauty which it is the business of the artist to reach and to represent, as an end in itself, without insisting on dwarfing it to the condition of being a mere motive to conduct. Why may I not enjoy Doré's[42] conception of Mr. Tennyson's landscape without feeling my moral pulse every moment, to see how my passions are faring? The moral hypochondriac is becoming a serious bore.[43]

Besides publishing a higher proportion of articles on art and literature than his predecessor, Morley defended a different aesthetic. In June 1868, at the time in which Pater may have been writing his review of Morris's poems, Morley himself published and wrote a favorable review of Morris's work in the *Fortnightly*.[44] Moreover, in the first numbers of Morley's *Fortnightly* Swinburne appears to have been the object of Morley's patronage,[45] as Buchanan was for Lewes. After Morley became editor in January 1867, numerous poems and articles by Swinburne were published, including Swinburne's review of Morris's *Jason* (July 1867),[46] Swinburne's poem dedicated to Baudelaire, "Ave Atque Vale" (January 1868),[47] and "Notes on Designs of the Old Masters at Florence" (July 1868).[48] Both the topics and the language of these pieces by Swinburne are echoed in Pater's subsequent writing.

It is a commonplace of criticism that Pater's early essays are heavily indebted to Swinburne's prose; even Swinburne remarked on it tartly at the time. But there are two points I want to make. Swinburne's contributions to the *Fortnightly*, which signaled that periodical's change of editor and its accompanying change of literary politics, may well have been a factor in attracting Pater to the *Fortnightly*, with its new conditions of publishing – which included signature. Secondly, Pater's indebtedness to Swinburne is shown by the *Fortnightly* interchanges to include the poems as well as the prose. For example, stanzas 7 and 17 of "Ave Atque Vale" seem to inform "Notes on Leonardo da Vinci,"[49] Pater's first contribution to the *Fortnightly*, and it seems apropos that Pater's essay in that November 1869 issue is immediately followed by Swinburne's poem "Intercession."[50] Nor is the dialogue one way; the February 1870 number carries Swinburne's poem "The Complaint of Monna Lisa,"[51] which alludes to the language of Pater's impressionist portrait of Leonardo's painting in the November issue. It begins:

> There is no woman living that draws breath
> So sad as I, though all things sadden her.
> There is not one upon life's weariest way
> Who is weary as I am weary of all but death.[52]

Another and final reason why Pater may have been drawn to the *Fortnightly* is that by this time, with the confidence of an author with a modicum of experience, he may well have sought payment, the recognition that signature offers, and freedom from the constraints of the review format.

In November 1869 Pater entered the monthly periodical form with "Notes on Leonardo da Vinci," a topic of his own choice, not dependent on the current publishing list.[53] The freedom that the

Fortnightly offered on this count may be seen in the coherence of the four articles on Leonardo, Botticelli, Pico, and Michelangelo that Pater published between November 1869 and November 1871. All treat Renaissance artists,[54] unlike the ragbag of the *Westminster* pieces on Coleridge's conversation and theology, Morris's poetry, and Winckelmann's life. It appears that once Pater had the freedom of choosing his own subject, the link between journalism and book publication was forged. While Pater was able to use, uneasily, two of the three *Westminster* essays in his first book, the *Renaissance* was conceived and born in the pages of the *Fortnightly*. That said, in the signed *Fortnightly* essays the author did not append conclusions to his essays in his own voice. The dramatized "biographies" of his Renaissance subjects are more distanced and "historical" in treatment than his *Westminster* subjects, and "descriptions" of the life and artistic work tend to carry the burden of the aesthetic ideology in the *Fortnightly* essays. While the distinctive and dominant note of the *Renaissance* is undoubtedly sounded and struck in the *Fortnightly* pieces, it is significantly the anonymous *Westminster* essays that made *Studies in the History of the Renaissance* controversial upon its publication in 1873, and its author notorious, as in book form "Winckelmann" and the "Conclusion" were scrutinized by the press that had spawned them, and widely denounced.

This instance of the character of the *Westminster Review*, which T. H. Huxley dubbed "wicked,"[55] suggests a category of Victorian periodical that is defined not through its party or class affiliations, but in writerly terms, through its freedom from censorship. It includes those periodicals, such as the *Westminster* under Chapman, the *Fortnightly* under John Morley and Frank Harris, and the *Nineteenth Century* under James Knowles, to which authors could resort to publish material toward which other editors and audiences were censorious and intolerant. The libertine character of the *Renaissance* in part derives from its periodical origins, and from the circumstances of the production of the periodical material that comprises it.

NOTES

1 For more on this point see my essay "'The Trepidation of the Spheres': the Serial and the Book in the Nineteenth Century," in *Serials and their Readers*, ed. Michael Harris and Robin Myers (Winchester: St. Paul's Bibliographies, 1993), 83–101.

2 George Saintsbury, *A History of Nineteenth Century Literature* (New York: Macmillan, 1896), 166.

3 See "Notes on Leonardo da Vinci," *Fortnightly Review* 6, n.s. (November 1869), 494–508; "A Fragment on Sandro Botticelli," *Fortnightly Review* 8, n.s. (August 1870), 155–60; "The Poetry of Michelangelo," *Fortnightly Review* 10, n.s. (November 1871), 559–70; and "Pico della Mirandola," *Fortnightly Review* 10, n.s. (October 1871), 377–86.

4 John Morley, "Mr. Pater's Essays," *Fortnightly Review* 13, n.s. (April 1873), 476.

5 James Sully, *My Life & Friends* (London: T. Fisher Unwin, 1918), 136.

6 [Walter Pater], "Coleridge's Writings," *Westminster Review* 29, n.s. (January 1866), 106–32.

7 [Walter Pater], "Poems by William Morris," *Westminster Review* 34, n.s. (October 1868), 300–12.

8 [Walter Pater], "Winckelmann," *Westminster Review* 31, n.s. (January 1867), 80–110.

9 "The Westminster Review, 1824–1900," *The Wellesley Index to Victorian Periodicals, 1824–1900,* ed. Walter E. Houghton, *et al.* (5 vols; Toronto: University of Toronto Press, 1966–89), vol. 3, 546.

10 *Ibid.*, 3:551.

11 *Ibid.*, 3:547.

12 Three sermons were preached in Oxford against the "message" of the "Conclusion" and "Winckelmann" by William Capes (Pater's undergraduate tutor), John Wordsworth (Pater's colleague and friend at Brasenose), and John Fielder Mackarness. The response to the volume was so hostile that Pater removed the "Conclusion" in the 1877 edition and took pains to explain his meaning in his next book, a two-volume novel published over a decade later. In 1894 obituaries of Pater were still objecting to this first volume.

13 See, for example [Helen Taylor], "The Ladies' Petition," *Westminster Review* 31, n.s. (January 1867), 63–79.

14 For example, *Punch.*

15 The sequence of articles in the October 1868 *Westminster* is as follows: "Landed Tenure in the Highlands"; "Poems by William Morris"; "Reform of Our Civil Procedure"; "Spielhagen's Novels"; "The Property of Married Women"; "China"; "The Suppressed Sex"; "Sea-Sickness" (this includes a review of the editor's book on the subject); and "Middle Class Schools."

16 [Helen Taylor], "The Ladies' Petition," 79.

17 [E. D. J. Wilson], "Irish University Education," *Westminster Review* 31, n.s. (January 1867), 132.

18 [Sheldon Amos?], "Church and State," *Westminster Review* 34, n.s. (July 1868), 151.

19 [Pater], "Winckelmann," 109.

20 [Pater], "Poems by William Morris," 312.
21 Samuel Wright, *A Bibliography of the Writings of Walter H. Pater* (New York: Garland, 1975), 60.
22 Alvar Ellegård, "The Readership of the Periodical Press in Mid-Victorian Britain," *Göteborgs Universitets Årsskrift* 63, 3 (1957), 27.
23 It was only by cutting the conclusion loose from the contemporary Morris material that Pater could accommodate it in his *Renaissance* volume. That its register was read in the volume as contemporary rather than historical is not surprising.
24 J. Leicester Warren [Baron de Tabley], "*Atalanta in Calydon*," *Fortnightly Review* 1 (15 May 1865), 75–80.
25 Houghton [R. M. Milnes], "Mr. Swinburne's *Chastelard*," *Fortnightly Review* 4 (15 April 1866), 533–43.
26 *The Wellesley Index to Victorian Periodicals*, vol. 2, 184.
27 Houghton, "Mr. Swinburne's *Chastelard*," 535.
28 *Ibid.*, 537.
29 Moncure Conway, "Walt Whitman," *Fortnightly Review* 6 (15 October 1866), 538–48.
30 *Ibid.*, 539.
31 Oscar Browning, "Trollope's *History of France*," *Fortnightly Review* 4 (15 February 1866), 70–86.
32 Philip G. Hamerton, "The Artistic Spirit," *Fortnightly Review* 1 (15 June 1865), 332–43.
33 *Ibid.*, 341.
34 *Ibid.*
35 *Ibid.*, 340.
36 Thomas Maitland [Robert Buchanan], "The Fleshly School of Poetry: Mr. D. G. Rossetti," *Contemporary Review* 18 (October 1871), 334–50.
37 Thomas Maitland [Robert Buchanan], "Immortality in Authorship," *Fortnightly Review* 6 (15 September 1866), 289–300.
38 *Ibid.*, 297.
39 *Ibid.*
40 Editor [John Morley], "Causeries," *Fortnightly Review* 1, n.s. (1 January 1867), 100–103.
41 *Ibid.*, 101.
42 P. G. Hamerton published "Gustave Doré's Bible," *Fortnightly Review* 4 (1 May 1866), 669–81.
43 [Morley], "Causeries," 102.
44 John Morley, "The Earthly Paradise. A Poem. By William Morris," *Fortnightly Review* 3, n.s. (June 1868), 713–15.
45 Two poems by Swinburne appeared in Morley's first volume in the new series, a Pre-Raphaelite ballad, "Child's Song in Winter," in the first number in January 1867, and "Of the Insurrection in Candia" two months later in March. In July and October of that year Morley published two review articles by Swinburne, one on Morris's poems

and one on Arnold's. See "Child's Song in Winter," *Fortnightly Review*
1, n.s. (January 1867), 19–26; "Of the Insurrection in Candia,"
Fortnightly Review 1, n.s. (March 1867), 284–89; A. C. Swinburne,
"Morris's *Life and Death of Jason*," *Fortnightly Review* 2, n.s. (July
1867), 19–28; "Mr. Arnold's *New Poems*," *Fortnightly Review* 2, n.s.
(October 1867), 414–45. It should be noted that Morley's patronage of
Swinburne is not visible in *Wellesley*, due to its policy of not including
poems in the itemized listings. The prominence and the existence
of Swinburne's long ballad as the second item in the January 1867
Fortnightly is only implicit in *Wellesley*, in the gap between the recorded
pagination of the first and third articles.
46 Swinburne, "Morris's *Jason*," 19–28.
47 A. C. Swinburne, "Ave Atque Vale," *Fortnightly Review* 3, n.s. (January
1868), 71–76.
48 A. C. Swinburne, "Notes on Designs of the Old Masters at Florence,"
Fortnightly Review 4, n.s. (July 1868), 16–40.
49 Walter Pater, "Notes on Leonardo da Vinci," *Fortnightly Review* 6, n.s.
(November 1869), 494–508.
50 A. C. Swinburne, "Intercession," *Fortnightly Review* 6, n.s. (November
1869), 509–10.
51 A. C. Swinburne, "The Complaint of Monna Lisa," *Fortnightly Review*
7, n.s. (February 1870), 176–79.
52 *Ibid.*, 176.
53 While the *Fortnightly* freed Pater from the constraints of the review
form, Pater drew on recent books for a number of his *Fortnightly*
essays.
54 While the *Fortnightly* covered contemporary art assiduously, Swinburne's article in July 1868, "Notes on Designs of the Old Masters at
Florence," was the first to treat Renaissance work; Pater's series began
in November of the next year, and initially follows Swinburne's model
of "Notes." Pater wrote "notes" on Leonardo in 1869, a "fragment"
on Botticelli in 1870, and "studies" in Renaissance history in 1873.
See "Notes on Leonardo da Vinci" (November 1869), 494–508; "A
Fragment on Sandro Botticelli," (August 1870), 155–60; and *Studies in
the History of the Renaissance* (London, 1873). Sidney Colvin adopted the
same genre: see Sidney Colvin, "Notes on Albert Dürer," *Fortnightly
Review* 7, n.s. (March 1870), 333–47.
55 Huxley Collection: 19.191, Imperial College, London.

CHAPTER 14

Serial fiction in Australian colonial newspapers

Elizabeth Morrison

With its beginnings traceable back into eighteenth-century England, the practice of issuing novels by installment was developed and popularized by Charles Dickens and his publishers in the second quarter of the nineteenth century.[1] With the appearance during the late 1850s of many new monthly fiction-carrying literary magazines, serialization became a standard initial mode of publication for novels, which were then issued shortly after in book form, usually as a three-volume set priced at thirty-one shillings and sixpence.[2] The cultural impact of the Victorian serial has now been addressed by Hughes and Lund, whose ground-breaking study claims that "the shaping influence of the installment text was often more important than has been recognized."[3] As textual scholars and critics are coming increasingly to acknowledge and study, "writing by numbers" was an integral part of the process of production and marketing for all sorts and conditions of Victorian novelists: it may be seen to effect in the work of William Thackeray and Thomas Hardy, for example, and was developed to a fine art by Anthony Trollope.[4]

The serial mode imposed particular demands on writer and publisher. Magazine editor and popular author George Manville Fenn was reported in 1885 to have said that the novelist writing for serial publication had to produce six to twenty "strong sensations," one for each installment, and that from a "commercial point of view" this was the most profitable way of publishing.[5] Letters from English-born colonial immigrant Ada Cambridge in 1874 to the editor of the *Australasian*, a newspaper coming out each week in antipodean Melbourne, also shed some light on specific features of writing for serialization.[6] Submitting the first two chapters for editorial inspection, Cambridge offers to provide a "tale" of about eight installments and promises to send "weekly portions as they are written." She wants a fixed rate for each number and with subtextual pressure indicates that in the event of a refusal she would "wish to slightly modify [the tale's] construction to suit an English magazine."

As Margaret Beetham has recently pointed out, magazine publishing worked within an economic system of rapid turnover and regular demand, with readers being stimulated in one number to purchase the next – and a "to be continued" novel was a key means to this end.[7] This was equally true of the newspaper press, with individual papers beginning to feature serial fiction regularly in the 1860s and the practice spreading the following decade when, as John Sutherland notes, "fiction [was] becoming the property of the newspaperman."[8] To understand the vast implications of serialization for the study of Victorian literary culture, one must see that the newspaper, by the late nineteenth century, was the dominant manifestation of the developing structures of print capitalism. When papers, adopting long-established conventions of magazine serialization, brought fiction to their readers, they were utilizing new technologies for mass production and distribution and thus creating a fiction readership of unprecedented size and scope.

If one aspect of the expanding Victorian publishing market was the appearance of novels in newspapers, yet another was the flourishing of this mode of publication in the farthest outposts of the British Empire. In an era of high imperialism, commodity texts procured from Great Britain and the United States together with those locally produced were consumed, in serially packaged form, by hundreds of thousands of readers in the Australian colonies.[9] Focusing on the Australian colonial phenomenon not only helps to round out the history of British publishing but also provides a privileged perspective for examining the international circulation of texts under conditions that emerged in the nineteenth century.

It is hardly surprising that, as many a traveler observed, Australian colonial society both mirrored the British from which it had been transplanted and seemed to display some American features. Trollope, visiting his son in outback New South Wales during 1871 and taking the opportunity to make an extensive Australian tour, saw that while the colonies were "rather a repetition of England than an imitation of America," yet when there was "any divergence from the old John Bull proclivities, it is towards the American side."[10] Similarly, Mark Twain, making a lecture tour in 1895, saw Englishness with "American trimmings."[11] Both elements were likewise often observed in relation to contemporary reading habits. Claiming "sensation" to be "the backbone of the bookseller's trade," an article entitled "What We Read" featured in the columns of the Melbourne daily *Age* of 3 August 1872 is typical: it cites Wilkie Collins, Edmund Yates, Miss Braddon, and "Ouida" as exponents of the "highest class" sensationalist writers and goes on to name many other stock British novelists of the day; it notes also that American literature is in "high favour," with Bret Hartes, Mark Twains, and many others emanating from the United States in cheap editions, and suggests that there must be "a remarkable sympathy" between Victorians (that is, inhabitants of the colony of Victoria) and Americans.

While titles that were best-sellers throughout the English-speaking world were indeed received in Australia through the medium of book and magazine imports, they were also channeled through local publishers – and these were, overwhelmingly, publishers of newspapers. For most of the nineteenth century there were few Australian book publishers and their output was small. And while there was a prolific and active local magazine press, for the most part circulations were tiny, finances precarious, and enterprises short-lived.[12] The newspaper press, by contrast, was large, vigorous, and thriving, partaking in the great expansion of the world press that began in the 1870s and also – as in other regions of recent European occupation – playing a vital role in the development of political, social, and cultural institutions.[13]

The 1892 edition of the *Australasian Newspaper Directory* records a total of 605 Australian newspapers in publication at the end of 1891, catering for some three million people resident in the six colonial capitals, in country towns, and in rural districts. Circulations ranged from the 100,000 boasted of by the Melbourne daily *Age* down to fewer than 100 for the newspapers of some tiny townships.[14] Price was no barrier to newspaper reading; there was a thriving penny press, threepence was the commonest price, and no paper cost more than sixpence. With compulsory, free education and a high literacy rate, inability to read was hardly a barrier either, at least for the white colonizers. At least one-third of these 600 or so papers carried one or two installments of serial fiction each week.[15] Crudely calculated, this amounts to a combined weekly issue of about 500,000 copies of newspapers publishing parts of novels.

The earliest group of Australian colonial newspapers to publish serial fiction (and the best-known among literary historians and bibliographers for so doing) were the weeklies published in capital cities as "companions" to individual metropolitan dailies: the *Sydney Mail*, which was associated with the oldest Australian daily, the *Sydney Morning Herald*; the *Australasian* with the conservative Melbourne *Argus*; the *Leader* with the liberal–reformist Melbourne *Age*; the *Adelaide Observer*, the Brisbane *Queenslander*, the Sydney *Town and Country Journal*, and many more, all with their daily counterparts. At a time when country areas were being assimilated, through the development of railway and telegraph networks and the activities of colonial parliaments, to capital-city dominance, these weekly papers were aimed particularly – though not exclusively – at country readers. Together with digests of the week's news taken from issues of the associated daily, their columns contained a host of feature articles on, for instance, sport, agriculture, churches, theater, and literature. The last usually included, under a banner such as "Novelist" or "Storyteller," installments of one or two novels. While there were a few isolated and atypical examples earlier, the practice can be seen as introduced in 1863 by the *Sydney Mail* and followed within a few years by the *Australasian* and others.

Numerous daily newspapers in the Australian colonial capitals also featured serial fiction in their Saturday issues and occasionally on Wednesdays as well. The Melbourne *Age* led the way in 1872, while most of the other dailies that featured serial fiction began to do so in the 1880s, when syndicating agencies with international reach facilitated the procurement of all kinds of copy – news, editorial comment, general reading, fiction, and increasingly, advertisements.

Outside the colonial capitals, some of the papers of provincial cities and regional towns – a few appearing daily, most twice or three times a week – were in the 1860s already providing general and literary reading to supplement the news columns. One such was the *Hamilton Spectator* in the wealthy pastoral heartland of Western Victoria, producing a weekly literary supplement that included some short fiction procured locally (most notably, items from the young Marcus Clarke, later to become one of Australia's esteemed novelists, who was then working on a property in the district). But these medium-sized country papers, like most of the smaller country and suburban weeklies, had neither the funds nor the contacts to procure long fiction for their exclusive printing, and those wishing to publish it turned increasingly to metropolitan-based agencies distributing preprinted sheets, the largest and most active being in Melbourne, the capital of Victoria. By the 1880s Melbourne, though barely fifty years old, as a result of the mid-century goldrushes was the wealthiest Australian capital city and, with some half million inhabitants, the most populous: though twice its age, Sydney was slightly smaller. George Augustus Sala, visiting in 1885, dubbed it "Marvellous Melbourne."[16] It was then also the leading Australian colonial center of journalism and newspaper publishing.

The featuring of serial fiction in newspapers has to be understood in the context of campaigns for mass readership; these, in turn, need to be seen as part of the deeply political purposes of Australian colonial newspapers. Mass readership entails mass production, and here there were problems. Throughout the world, the newspaper press had been expanding in the 1860s, utilizing the telegraph to spread news and the railways to spread papers. But there were technological constraints on this expansion until the development in Europe and the United States, late in the decade, of web-fed rotary presses able to exceed existing limits of printing 4,000 four-page sheets per hour.[17] David Syme of the Melbourne *Age* and *Leader* imported the new technology into Australia in 1872, the first newspaper proprietor to do so.[18]

In this *annus mirabilis* when Australia became connected by overland telegraph and submarine cable to the outside world and messages, albeit terse and expensive ones, could be sent between Australia and Europe in a matter of hours instead of the customary six to eight weeks for the steam-powered vessels that brought the English mails, Syme took delivery of two Victory presses manufactured by the Liverpool firm of Duncan and Wilson. With enhanced production capabilities, he proceeded to double the Saturday issue of the *Age* to eight pages, thus, as explained in the editorial for the issue of 13 April, accommodating more advertisements and introducing new general and light reading features, with the installment of a novel as a central attraction. The circulation of the paper, 16,000 copies in 1871, rose to 20,000 in 1873, in 1880 was 41,000, and increased steeply thereafter to reach 100,000 by the end of the decade. No other Australian paper came anywhere near.

In making the changes, the *Age* claimed it was following the practice of leading provincial papers in England and Scotland: the *Manchester Guardian*, the Manchester *Examiner and Times*, the *Leeds Mercury*, the *Scotsman*, and others. But clearly there was more than imitation at issue, for Syme was then embarking on a determined political campaign for the hearts and minds of Victoria's electorate. Wanting land, tariff, and constitutional reform, his campaign was carried out in fierce competition with the more conservative *Argus* and *Australasian* combination, which represented old money, property interests, and the "squattocracy."[19] Competition was even carried through to the procurement of serial fiction copy.

The *Age* serial fiction program was launched with the bestselling English author Mary Elizabeth Braddon's latest novel *To the Bitter End*, a protracted story of seduction and revenge that ran in thirty-seven weekly installments from Saturday 20 April 1872. Syme had purchased exclusive rights to republication in the Australian colonies, paying the sum of £125 to John Maxwell, then Braddon's publisher, literary representative, and companion, and later to be her husband.[20] This novel was not Syme's choice, and he believed, moreover, that the price had been too high. Working through his agents in London, with whom he communicated by letter and telegraph, he was attempting to secure works by those he considered the "best" authors, including Trollope and George Eliot.[21] To George Street he wrote on 27 March 1873: "We are anxious to get a new tale from you & you have my list of authors beyond which you need not go"; to George Levey he wrote on 13 August: "I enclose you a list – I forwarded to Street to choose from, & the names are arranged mainly in the order in which they stand in my estimation."

In seeking out works by certain authors he was competing with his politically opposed newspaper rivals. But it was unequal competition: his opponents, probably having more capable London representatives and London connections, had serialized Trollope in the *Australasian* since 1867, beginning with *Phineas Finn*, followed by *He Knew He Was Right*.[22] During 1872 and 1873 Syme missed out also on *The Eustace Diamonds* and George Eliot's *Middlemarch*, both of which appeared in the *Australasian*.[23] Instructing his agents that his standard price was £50 for a story in weekly installments for six months and £75 for one that would go for nine, he clearly put a high value on George Eliot, for he stated that he would be willing to "strain a point in the case of a tale from Mrs. Evans." It seems, however, that the opportunity to do this did not arise.[24]

Syme did not accept works from his chosen authors indiscriminately, for in a letter dated 15 July 1873 he rejected *Phineas Redux*, stating enigmatically that he hated Trollope. (Perhaps it was the politics of the novel that he disliked.) The antipathy was short-lived, however, for in August he was telegraphing acceptance of a Trollope tale by Christmas, and in October writing that he was glad to have got it and that it ought to be worth the money (though we do not know what he paid). In a brilliant coup, he had secured the Australian rights to Trollope's *Harry Heathcote of Gangoil*. Set in the Australian outback and drawing on the author's antipodean travels two years earlier, the short novel deals with the very topical clashing interests of squatter and free selector and the conciliation brought about by intermarriage between the "classes." Contrary to general belief, its first appearance was not in the London *Graphic* on 26 December 1873 but in the Melbourne *Age*, where it ran in weekly installments from 15 November 1873 until 3 January 1874.[25]

One may reasonably assume the source of supply was the *Graphic* and not Trollope himself.[26] Whether or not this illustrated weekly London newspaper, published from 1869, was a regular supplier of Australian newspapers throughout the 1870s and 1880s has not yet been established. Certainly it was active in 1891, selling to the *Sydney Mail* the Australian serial rights to the expurgated version of Thomas Hardy's *Tess of the d'Urbervilles*.[27] The *Graphic* supplied the Sydney paper with a set of unrevised proofs, as it did also to the English *Nottinghamshire Guardian*, possibly to other provincial papers, and certainly to an as yet unidentified Indian publication. The *Graphic* paid Hardy £50 for the Australian rights; what the *Sydney Mail* was required to pay is not known. Under the title *A Daughter of the D'Urbervilles*, Hardy's novel appeared in the Sydney paper from July to December 1891 simultaneously with its English serialization.

Hardy was a familiar and popular author in Australia, with his novels serialized in many papers throughout the 1880s: to name but a few, *A Laodicean* in the *Sydney Mail*, *Two on a Tower* and *The Mayor of Casterbridge* in the *Leader*, and the novella *Emmeline* in the Melbourne *Weekly Times*. One may be led, then, to assume that the serial *Tess* in the *Sydney Mail* had a wide and appreciative readership. While this assumption may add something to Victorian studies, this serial publication of an expurgated version of the Hardy novel can take on greater significance if examined following Norman Feltes's approach to the similar but not identical version in the London *Graphic*.[28] Feltes presents a reading of *Tess* in relation to its journalistic and pictorial context in the pages of the *Graphic*; his theories about editorial intervention and censorship in the interests of the "ideologies of 'class' journalism" might well be tested by reference to substantially the same text presented in a totally different context and to a totally different market. Moreover, as the editors of the 1983 Clarendon edition of *Tess* have demonstrated, the version in the Sydney paper is not identical in all respects with that in the *Graphic*, and it might be expected that as yet unlocated versions in other journals also supplied with proofs by the London paper would vary too – whether due to compositorial idiosyncrasies or editorial policy. There is certainly scope for further textual study to help reconstruct the texts of the now lost proofs and to gain further insights into what Feltes terms the "subtle and effective" control of commodity texts by magazine and newspaper publishers.[29]

David Syme's sources of fiction copy after *Harry Heathcote of Gangoil* and until 1880 are not yet clear. Works by Edmund Yates, Ann Thackeray, Wilkie Collins, Mary Braddon (again), and others were serialized, frequently with interruptions attributed to the nonarrival of "proofs" or "advance sheets" expected with the "Californian Mail."[30] While this may point to an American supplier, the source could equally or more probably have been in Britain, for English mail quite often came by the longer, alternative route across the Atlantic to New York, by railway to San Francisco, and then across the Pacific to Sydney.

There is little doubt, however, that when the *Age* serialized Braddon's *Just As I Am* beginning in March 1880 it was buying serial fiction from the fiction bureau of W. F. Tillotson & Son in Bolton, Lancashire.[31] As Michael Turner describes, the firm was set up in 1873, growing out of syndication arrangements for a group of provincial papers including the *Bolton Weekly Journal* at a time when the mass syndication of copy was becoming a dominant feature of newspaper production.[32] Within a few years Tillotson's was selling throughout the British Empire, in Europe, and the United States.

Meanwhile, in 1884 and across the Atlantic, Irish-born S. S. McClure, by his own account, "invented the newspaper syndicate service," aiming to sell to "country newspapers throughout the land to supply good reading matter for the country boys and girls."[33] His small, New York based business actually owed much to existing practice: Brooklyn journalist Irving Bacheller had started to sell serial fiction the previous year, and the New York *Sun* was selling to other papers short stories by William Dean Howells, Henry James, and Bret Harte.[34] With virtually no capital, McClure's was slow to take off – it was able to survive by supplying an author's copy free to one paper in return for sets of proofs to sell to others.

The enterprise apparently leaped ahead in 1887 after a meeting with Robert Louis Stevenson, and arrangements subsequently were made to republish *The Black Arrow*, which had been serialized in England years before.[35] Omitting the first five chapters and adding commissioned illustrations, McClure sold it in installments to his American newspaper customers as *The Outlaws of Tunstall Forest*, with fame and funds resulting. He also sold it to Tillotson's as part of a reciprocal agreement negotiated in late 1887 or early 1888, and it appeared in Australia soon after. Running *The Outlaws* beginning in May 1888, the Melbourne *Daily Telegraph* probably obtained copy from the English firm, for McClure's autobiography does not mention Australian dealings.

Becoming the largest fiction syndicates in Great Britain and the United States respectively, Tillotson's and McClure's were not without competitors. During November 1887 David Syme in Melbourne instructed a retainer in London to look into new syndicates because a "notice" for one was "going the rounds" in English papers and asked that the "lists" of new firms be forwarded.[36] In reminiscences composed around the turn of the century, Ada Cambridge implies that a London syndicate "took possession of the fiction columns" of Melbourne papers some time after 1888.[37] This is corroborated in the autobiography of roving journalist and aspiring novelist Randolph Bedford, referring to the same period: "big Australian dailies bought their serials from London, paying £10 or so for the rights of a serial running into sixty to one hundred thousand words."[38] Nonetheless, Tillotson's continued as supplier to many colonial papers in the 1890s (the firm bought serial rights to Hardy's *The Pursuit of the Well-Beloved*, which appeared in the Melbourne *Leader* beginning in October 1892 concurrently with its publication in the *Illustrated London News*, for instance) and indeed well into the twentieth century.

In presenting a fixed set of wares to the newspaper proprietors, the fiction syndicates brought down costs and facilitated acquisition, but they also dictated the range of titles. In tandem with newspaper interests and keeping pace with the growth and spread of newspapers, they were expanding the market for fiction to the profit of the authors and themselves and were also helping disseminate a common literary culture around the English-speaking world. More specifically, Tillotson's and similar agencies helped create best-sellers, for the novels in question were normally published as books after serialization had commenced – sometimes after it had concluded – and the very process of serial publication contributed to the overall success.

While the staple fare was the British best-seller, usually from the pen of an English or Scottish author, with an occasional work from the Continent or the United States, Australian newspapers did not entirely neglect local writing, buying a fraction of their serial fiction directly from local authors. On average, the proportion of local works was probably about one-fifth of the total number of titles serialized over the twenty-five or so years considered in this chapter. Some papers – notably the *Sydney Mail* and the Melbourne *Leader* – also gave encouragement in the form of prizes for tales about Australia. Although Australian colonial authors were up against tough competition from expanding Anglo-American publishing interests, the support from the newspaper press enabled some – and most notably Ada Cambridge – to develop their novel-writing skills and cultivate a large reading public. Australian newspapers provided the primary and often only outlet for Cambridge's fiction for some twenty years, from 1872 until she was taken up by William Heinemann and other London publishers in the 1890s.

Cambridge, long dismissed as an insignificant, genteel, Anglo-Australian "lady" novelist has, like the American writer Kate Chopin, been "rediscovered"; like Chopin, she expresses, with subtle and delicate irony, facets of female sexuality and domestic entrapment.[39] This is seen particularly well in the short novel *A Woman's Friendship*, which owes much to Cambridge's reading of George Eliot, George Meredith, Henry James, and William Dean Howells, not to mention Mary Wollstonecraft and John Stuart Mill, and which for its satirical analysis of class, sexuality, and power in 1880s Melbourne reads today as a small masterpiece. Serialized in the *Age* during 1889, *A Woman's Friendship* did not appear in book form until 1988 after being brought to light through a serial indexing project.[40]

Neither in the original newspaper version nor in the new edition is it as the author had wished it to appear, for Cambridge, like Chopin with *The Awakening*, was a victim of censorship.[41] In the Australian author's case this was through the blue pencil of the *Age* editor David Syme, who deliberately made some changes to the text, including the excision of one whole scene that, he said, he could only describe as indecent, that his subeditors "roared over," but that would have been "no laughing matter" had it appeared in print.[42] What was cut by editorial fiat remains a mystery.

The increasing commodification of fiction texts, which was marked by the advent of the new class of "middlemen" whom Robert Darnton wants put back into literary history, went a stage further in Australia with the appearance of the "literary supplement" available for purchase by small newspaper businesses – usually country and suburban papers with circulations below 1,000 copies.[43] In Australia, as elsewhere, agency supplements developed from the practice of syndicating partly printed sheets. In England, Cassells began printing syndicate pages for provincial papers in the 1850s, while a service was set up by the National Press Agency in 1873 that included leading articles, parliamentary and law reports, London letters and gossip, a weekly letter for "ladies," and "original tales."[44] In the United States A. N. Kellogg began to issue "patent insides" for his own paper during the Civil War and developed this into a syndicate service in 1865, while by 1880 more than 3,000 American weeklies (two-fifths of all such papers being published) were being supplied with "ready prints" by twenty-one companies.[45]

At least one influential Australian newspaperman regarded supplements with disdain. Frederick Haddon of the *Argus* and *Australasian* business visited provincial newspaper offices in England and Scotland during 1874.[46] In a detailed report to the firm he claimed that "leading newspapers" such as the *Scotsman*, the *Glasgow Herald*, the *Leeds Mercury*, the *Manchester Guardian*, the *Manchester Examiner*, and others considered supplements out-of-date and preferred simply to enlarge the size or number of sheets to supply additional reading matter. It is significant that Haddon cites a set of exemplary British newspapers, as did the *Age* in 1872, which suggests that large British provincial papers were the models for leading colonial capital city papers. However, out-of-date or not, supplements – overwhelmingly of the syndicated type – were the coming thing for all but the large metropolitan newspaper businesses in the Australian colonies.

Around 1871 Melbourne magazine printer and publisher W. H. Williams, with some twenty years' colonial experience in countless and mostly ephemeral publishing enterprises, moved into the issuing of part-printed sheets for sale to country newspapers in Victoria and other colonies.[47] Some six years later his concern was taken over by Donald Cameron, a former country journalist, would-be novelist, publisher, entrepreneur, and for a brief period a member of the colonial parliament.[48]

Setting up the firm of Cameron, Laing, & Co., he transformed Williams's supplement (as the part-printed news sheets had become) into one component of a many-faceted experiment in the promotion of Australian colonial fiction writing. Selling a weekly two-page "literary supplement" on which a purchasing newspaper publisher had only to print a masthead and the imprint required by law, he grafted serial fiction from local authors onto a melange of reprinted material, most of the latter extracted from overseas – chiefly American – magazines and newspapers, and possibly obtained as ready made selections from an American syndicate.

Beginning with his own *Silverwater Bend; or, Twenty-Five Years of Australian Life*, thirty-four novels were serialized over the next twelve years. In striking contrast to the proportions of imported to local fiction serialized generally in colonial newspapers, no fewer than twenty-four of the novels in the Cameron supplement were of local authorship – mostly by male journalists. Of these Australian works, only a handful were ever published in book form, and the rest are virtually unknown today – a circumstance that must be ascribed not to their quality but rather to the book-based conventions for transmitting literary information (publishers' catalogues, book reviews, national bibliographies, and so on) and to the onset of a literary nationalism that turned its back on much of the colonial culture out of which it had developed.[49]

Cameron, Laing, & Co. branched out into the issuing of products derived from the literary supplement. First there were annual short story collections that reprinted in book form the colonial Christmas tales and "bush yarns" customarily filling an outsize Christmas issue of the literary supplement. Next, in 1882, the firm began the issue, in Melbourne, of the *Melbourne Quarterly*, later renamed the *Melbourne Journal*, comprising the contents of the thirteen preceding weekly supplements for country newspapers and carrying, in addition, a substantial number of advertisements. Clearly, Cameron, Laing, & Co. was attempting to maintain a financially viable enterprise for publishing Australian literature in a market increasingly dominated by imported products, stating in the October 1882 issue of the *Melbourne Quarterly* that while "hitherto almost the sole outcome for Australian literary talent has been afforded by the local press," English novelists were now "supplying Australian newspapers with advance proofs of their works at a rate which defies local competition," and announcing also their issuing of a new "Shilling Series" of Australian works. The firm's approach is remarkably like that taken by the American S. S. McClure some twelve years later, launching *McClure's Magazine* in 1894 and afterward claiming that the "magazine and syndicate combined were the machinery I offered to get the young men [that is, his authors] in whom I believed to the people."[50]

The homegrown "literary supplement" lasted as a vehicle for fiction, chiefly of local origin, until about 1889 when it was virtually driven out of the market by a profusion of imported products – supplements sold from capital-city agencies to suburban and country papers. Unlike Cameron's, these supplements were vehicles for advertising as well as containers of serial fiction and snippets of general reading. This competition from overseas was signaled early in the 1880s when the representatives of the Melbourne printing trade complained, to no effect, to a government commission of inquiry into protective tariffs about the unregulated importation of stereotype plates, including "tales" from the *Glasgow Citizen*.[51]

The substantial damage was done in 1889, however, when a Melbourne suburban newspaper concern became connected with the importation of ready-printed supplements "shipped out in bales from England" and described at the time as "simply an advertising medium."[52] Evidence points to the importing business being connected with the dominating colonial advertising and news agency of Gordon & Gotch, which had its headquarters in Melbourne and branches in Sydney, Brisbane, and London – one example of the international transacting of business and movement of capital that developed in the 1880s.[53]

By 1895 the imported supplement dominated the market. A deputation from the printing trade and the Melbourne Typographical Society to the Tariff Board in Victoria wanted protection from imported "cheap and nasty literature" and the "wholesale importation of stereo plates from America and elsewhere"; a spokesman said they were in no doubt that a locally produced supplement for country papers could not compete with the general supplements made in large quantities for distribution in all English-speaking countries.[54]

The works serialized in the competing imported supplements were, for the most part, insipid romances by prolific but unremarkable English writers such as Annie Swan and Americans such as Bertha Clay writing in the same vein. The damage to local colonial literary endeavors by these ventures was more than offset, however, by the general decline, beginning in the early 1890s, in the importance of the newspaper as both a primary publisher of local fiction and a major source of overseas novels of quality.

Though many Australian newspapers continued to serialize fiction well into the twentieth century, the high point of the press as disseminator of best-selling novels from overseas and primary publisher of colonial works was reached in the boom decade of the 1880s; decline began in the mid-1890s. In part this was brought about by economic depression and associated shrinkage in the size of newspapers. But also, with the hegemony of the three-decker superseded by a plenitude of cheap imported books, with the development of Australian publishing houses, and with the maturing of a new Australian-born generation of writers and readers, this period saw fundamental changes in the modes of cultural production.[55] By 1901, when the six separate Australian colonies joined to form the Commonwealth of Australia, literary spokespeople referred to newspaper fiction as a thing of the past, buried in the archives.[56]

The foregoing outline of serial fiction in late-nineteenth-century Australian newspapers points to the interconnectedness of English literatures on both sides of the Atlantic and at the ends of the earth during the post-1870 period, and sketches some aspects of the fiction text as commodity in the world of newspapers and journalism generally. In particular, it touches on the power held and exercised by newspaper editors with scant regard for authorial integrity (not to mention the textual changes introduced in the conveyor-belt circumstances of newspaper production), the incorporation of texts into syndicating mechanisms with international reach, and the build up of mass readerships.

Until recently, nineteenth-century literary studies in Australia have been predominantly book-oriented. However, attention is turning to the literary content of the colonial magazine and newspaper presses, and new indexing projects are opening up these archives. This may help examination of cultural influences from overseas in the colonial period, particularly in relation to the ideological impact of the fiction brought to colonial readers through the plentiful and cheap supply of local newspapers. Conversely, Australian research into fiction serialization and syndication may provide a basis for transatlantic English literary projects to widen the parameters of Victorian publishing studies and take fuller account of the significance of the expanded markets in the geographically distant but culturally connected British colonies.

NOTES

1 J. Don Vann, *Victorian Novels in Serial* (New York: Modern Language Association, 1985); Robert L. Patten, *Charles Dickens & His Publishers* (1978; reprint, Santa Cruz: The Dickens Project, University of California, 1991).

2 Alvin Sullivan (ed.), *British Literary Magazines, Volume 3: The Victorian and Edwardian Age, 1837–1913* (Westport, Conn.: Greenwood Press, 1984), xvi; John A. Sutherland, *Victorian Novelists and Publishers* (London: Athlone; Chicago: University of Chicago Press, 1976).

3 Linda K. Hughes and Michael Lund, *The Victorian Serial* (Charlottesville: University Press of Virginia, 1991), 14.

4 Edgar F. Harden, *The Emergence of Thackeray's Serial Fiction* (Athens: University of Georgia Press, 1979); Simon Gatrell, *Hardy the Creator: A Textual Biography* (Oxford: Clarendon, 1988); Mary Hamer, *Writing by Numbers: Trollope's Serial Fiction* (Cambridge: Cambridge University Press, 1987).

5 Interview in London, reported in the Melbourne *Age*, 7 November 1885.

6 Letter dated 16 June 1874 (MS 11242, W. P. Evans Papers; La Trobe Collection: State Library of Victoria); letters dated 15 and 23 December (MS 169/1, W. P. Hurst Papers, La Trobe Collection).

7 Margaret Beetham, "Towards a Theory of the Periodical as a Publishing Genre," *Investigating Victorian Journalism*, ed. Laurel Brake, Aled Jones, and Lionel Madden (London: Macmillan, 1990), 21–24.

8 Sutherland, *Victorian Novelists*, 199.

9 Or, indeed, the Australasian colonies, if one were to include New Zealand (which is outside the scope of this chapter).

10 Anthony Trollope, *Australia*, ed. Peter D. Edwards and R. B. Joyce (St. Lucia: University of Queensland Press, 1967), 705. First published in *Australia and New Zealand* (1873).

11 Mark Twain, *Mark Twain in Australia and New Zealand* (Ringwood: Penguin Books Australia, 1973), 125. First published in *Following the Equator* (1897).

12 Lurline Stuart, "Nineteenth-Century English and American Literary Periodicals and their Australian Counterparts," *Bibliographical Society of Australia and New Zealand Bulletin* 4 (1980), 180–90.

13 Anthony Smith, *The Newspaper: An International History* (London: Thames & Hudson, 1979); George Boyce, James Curran, and Pauline Wingate (eds.), *Newspaper History from the Seventeenth Century to the Present Day* (London: Constable, 1978); Elizabeth Morrison, "Reading Victoria's Newspapers, 1838–1901," *Australian Cultural History* 11 (1992), 128–40.

14 *Australasian Newspaper Directory* (3rd edn.; Melbourne: Gordon & Gotch, 1892). The total of 605 includes 18 dailies and 51 weeklies serving the colonial capitals with circulations in the tens of thousands, 59 suburban weeklies chiefly from the Melbourne conurbation and with circulations of a few hundred at most, and hundreds of country papers of varying frequencies with circulations ranging from a few hundred to about eight thousand.

15 This estimate, based on the author's samplings and soundings of colonial papers from the mid-1860s to the early 1890s and on an examination of issues of all papers in publication in the colony of Victoria at the end of August 1889, is conservative, possibly underrating the incidence of serial fiction.

16 Quoted in Graeme Davison, *The Rise and Fall of Marvellous Melbourne* (Melbourne: Melbourne University Press, 1978), 229.

17 James Moran, *Printing Presses: History and Development from the Fifteenth Century to Modern Times* (London: Faber & Faber, 1973), 173–219.

18 Elizabeth Morrison, "Press Power and Popular Appeal: Serial Fiction and the Rise of the *Age*," *Media Information Australia* 49 (1988), 49–52.

19 Charles E. Sayers, *David Syme: A Life* (Melbourne: Cheshire, 1965); Stuart Macintyre, *A Colonial Liberalism: The Lost World of Three Victorian Visionaries* (Melbourne: Oxford University Press, 1991).

20 Editorial, *Age*, 13 April 1872; copy of letter from David Syme to his London agent George Street, dated 22 April 1872, in Syme's letterbook (MS 9751, Syme Family Papers; La Trobe Collection: State Library of Victoria).

21 Copies of letters to George Street from April 1872 to March 1873 and

to George Levey from July to October 1873 are to be found in the Syme Family Papers.

22 The *Australasian* serialized *Phineas Finn* from 23 November 1867 through 20 May 1869, and *He Knew He Was Right* from 2 January 1869 through 26 March 1870. A recurring theme in Syme's correspondence, rivalry is also expressed repeatedly by the other side in the "Historical Records and General Information" volume of *"The Argus" and "The Australasian," 1846–1923* (Melbourne, 1924).

23 *The Eustace Diamonds* appeared in the *Australasian* from 12 August 1871 to 18 January 1873, and *Middlemarch* from 3 February 1872 to 22 March 1873.

24 Copy of letter to George Levey, 13 August 1873, Syme Family Papers.

25 Peter D. Edwards's recent edition of *Harry Heathcote* in the Oxford World Classics series (Oxford: Oxford University Press, 1992) does, however, acknowledge the prior Australian serialization.

26 Trollope refers in his *Autobiography* (1883; London: Geoffrey Cumberledge, 1950) to "writing a little story about Australia" for the *Graphic* in 1873 (357).

27 General introduction, Thomas Hardy, *Tess of the d'Urbervilles*, ed. Juliet Grindle and Simon Gatrell (Oxford: Clarendon, 1983), 10.

28 Norman N. Feltes, *Modes of Production of Victorian Novels* (Chicago: University of Chicago Press, 1986), 57–75.

29 John T. Laird, *The Shaping of Tess of the D'Urbervilles* (Oxford: Clarendon, 1975); Feltes, *Modes of Production*, 63.

30 For example, *Age*, 6 June 1874, on the nonarrival of "advance sheets" of Yates's *The Impending Sword* (serialized from 21 February through 26 September 1874); 17 October 1874, on the receipt of proofs of Collins's new "tale" (*The Dreamwoman*, which ran in five installments from 24 October to 21 November 1874); and 10 July 1875, on nonarrival of an installment of Ann Thackeray's *Miss Angel* (serialized from 13 February to 7 August 1875).

31 The copy of a letter from David Syme to G. J. Bowes dated 13[?] November 1887, Syme Family Papers, refers to long-standing arrangements for procurement from Tillotson & Son. The Tillotson Notebooks A & B, in 1982 the possession of Michael Turner at the Bodleian Library, Oxford University, contain details of amounts paid for purchase of publishing rights for novels in serial form and for short stories. *Just As I Am* is the earliest recorded title to tally with an *Age* serialization. However, as Aled Jones, in "Tillotson's Fiction Bureau: The Manchester Manuscripts," *Victorian Periodicals Review* 17 (Spring and Summer 1984), 42–46, discusses, a substantial Tillotson archive has been located in the John Rylands Library in Manchester, providing a basis for further research.

32 Michael Turner, "Reading for the Masses," *Book Selling and Book*

Buying: Aspects of the Nineteenth-Century British and North American Book Trade, ed. Richard G. Landon (Chicago: American Library Association, 1978), 52–72; and "The Syndication of Fiction in Provincial Newspapers, 1870–1939," (B.Litt. dissertation; Oxford, 1968).

33 S. S. McClure, *My Autobiography* (1914; New York: Ungar, 1963), 164–65.

34 Frank Luther Mott, *American Journalism: A History of Newspapers in the United States Through 260 Years* (revised edn.; New York: Macmillan, 1950), 482.

35 McClure, 184–201.

36 Copy of letter dated 13[?] November 1887, Syme Family Papers.

37 Ada Cambridge, *Thirty Years in Australia* (1903; Kensington: New South Wales University Press, 1990), 155.

38 Randolph Bedford, *Naught to Thirty-Three* (1944; Carlton: Melbourne University Press, 1976), 122.

39 Born in England, Ada Cambridge (1844–1926) arrived in the colony of Victoria with her clergyman husband in 1870. Her published work, including 5 anthologies of poetry, 29 novels and much short fiction, 2 autobiographical volumes, and several essays, was admired in her lifetime but thereafter virtually ignored until the 1980s. Several works are now again in print, and two substantial biographies were published in 1990. Kate Chopin (1850–1904), with a smaller but nonetheless remarkable literary output, was passed over for the first half of the twentieth century. Sandra Gilbert, introducing the Penguin edition of Chopin's most striking and controversial work, *The Awakening* (1899), says of Chopin that behind her "exemplary facade as devout girl and devoted wife . . . there seems always to have been another Kate Chopin, a young woman of independence and irony . . . haunted . . . by vague ideas of spiritual liberation." *The Awakening and Selected Stories* (New York: Penguin, 1984), 11. Likewise, there seems to have been another Cambridge beneath the layers of reinforcing myth.

40 Ada Cambridge, *A Woman's Friendship* (Kensington: New South Wales University Press, 1988).

41 *The Awakening*, on publication, caused considerable stir in literary circles and was removed from the shelves of many American public libraries.

42 While no manuscript or setting copy has been found, correspondence in the Syme Family Papers between David Syme and his nephew and junior partner, Joseph, leaves no doubt of editorial interference (JCS to DS 10 and 16 September, DS to JCS 12 and 16 September 1889). It would appear that Joseph arranged to buy *A Woman's Friendship* and made an informal arrangement with Cambridge that it would not be altered; David, however, instructed that changes be made to the proofs.

43 Robert Darnton, *The Kiss of Lamourette: Reflections in Cultural History* (New York: Norton, 1990), 136–37.

44 Mott, 397; Lucy Brown, *Victorian News and Newspapers* (Oxford: Clarendon, 1985), 117–18.

45 Mott, 396–97, 479.

46 Memo of results of visits to provincial newspaper offices in England and Scotland, 26 February 1874 (Frederick William Haddon Papers, Box 352/6; La Trobe Collection: State Library of Victoria).

47 Williams advertised his service in the issues of the monthly *Australasian Typographical Journal* (Melbourne) throughout the 1870s.

48 Further discussed and referenced in Elizabeth Morrison, "'Distinctively Australian in Tone and Incident': Donald Cameron and the making of Australian Literature in 1880s Melbourne" (unpublished paper presented at the annual conference of the Association for the Study of Australian Literature (ASAL) in Brisbane, July 1990).

49 Geoffrey Serle, *From Deserts the Prophets Come: The Creative Spirit in Australia 1788–1972* (Melbourne: Heinemann, 1973), 60–88.

50 McClure, 224–35.

51 "Tariff: Report of the Royal Commission," Victoria, *Votes & Proceedings of the Legislative Assembly 1883* (2nd session), 4:1233.

52 *Australasian Typographical Journal*, July 1889.

53 Elizabeth Morrison, "The Contribution of the Country Press to the Making of Victoria, 1840–1890" (Ph.D. thesis, Monash University, 1991), 223–24.

54 *Australasian Typographical Journal*, May 1895.

55 Wallace Kirsop, "Bookselling and Publishing in the Nineteenth Century," in *The Book in Australia*, ed. Dietrich H. Borchardt and Wallace Kirsop (Melbourne: Australian Reference Publications, 1988), 42; Richard White, *Inventing Australia: Images and Identity 1688–1980* (Sydney: Allen & Unwin, 1981), 96–109.

56 For example, Clara Eyre Cheesman, "Colonials in Fiction," *New Zealand Illustrated* 7 (1903), 273–78, writes of the "dusty files" of newspapers that contain "stories of colonial life which have never struggled out of the papers into book form."

Index

This is an index to real, not fictional, persons, places, things, and concepts pertaining to the nineteenth century. Illustrations are italicized.

338INDEX